## Empire of Law

European legal integration is often justified with reference to the inherent unity of European legal traditions that extend to ancient Rome. This book explores the invention of this tradition, tracing it to a group of legal scholars divided by the onslaught of Nazi terror and totalitarianism in Europe. As exiles in Britain and the US, its formulators worked to build bridges between the Continental and the Atlantic legal traditions, incorporating ideas such as rule of law, liberty and equality to the European heritage. Others joined the Nazi revolution, which promoted its own idea of European unity. At the end of World War II, natural law and human rights were incorporated into the European project. The resulting narrative of Europe, one that outlined human rights, rule of law and equality, became consequently a unifying factor during the Cold War as the self-definition against the challenge of communism.

**Kaius Tuori** is Professor of European Intellectual History at the Centre for European Studies, Faculty of Social Sciences, University of Helsinki. He is a legal historian and author of three monographs and numerous articles spanning the topics of tradition, culture, identity, memory and the uses of the past.

## Cambridge Studies in European Law and Policy

This series aims to produce original works which contain a critical analysis of the state of the law in particular areas of European law and to set out different perspectives and suggestions for its future development. It also aims to encourage a range of work on law, legal institutions and legal phenomena in Europe, including 'law in context' approaches. The titles in the series will be of interest to academics; policymakers, especially those who are interested in European legal, commercial and political affairs; practising lawyers, including the judiciary; and advanced law students and researchers.

Books in the Series

*Empire of Law: Nazi Germany, Exile Scholars and the Battle for the Future of Europe*
Kaius Tuori

*In the Court We Trust: Cooperation, Coordination and Collaboration between the European Court of Justice and Supreme Administrative Courts*
Rob van Gestel and Jurgen de Poorter

*Beyond Minimum Harmonisation: Gold-Plating and Green-Plating of European Environmental Law*
Lorenzo Squintani

*The Politics of Justice in European Private Law: Social Justice, Access Justice, Societal Justice*
Hans Micklitz

*The Transformation of EU Treaty Making: The Rise of Parliaments, Referendums and Courts since 1950*
Dermot Hodson and Imelda Maher

*Redefining European Economic Integration*
Dariusz Adamski

*Human Rights in the Council of Europe and the European Union: Achievements, Trends and Challenges*
Steven Greer, Janneke Gerards and Rosie Slowe

*Core Socio-Economic Rights and the European Court of Human Rights*
Ingrid Leijten

*Green Trade and Fair Trade in and with the EU: Process-Based Measures within the EU Legal Order*
Laurens Ankersmit

*New Labour Laws in Old Member States: Trade Union Responses to European Enlargement*
Rebecca Zahn

*The Governance of EU Fundamental Rights*
Mark Dawson

*The International Responsibility of the European Union: From Competence to Normative Control*
Andrés Delgado Casteleiro

*Frontex and Non-Refoulement: The International Responsibility of the EU*
Roberta Mungianu

*Gendering European Working Time Regimes: The Working Time Directive and the Case of Poland*
Ania Zbyszewska

*EU Renewable Electricity Law and Policy: From National Targets to a Common Market*
Tim Maxian Rusche

*European Constitutionalism*
Kaarlo Tuori

*Brokering Europe: Euro-Lawyers and the Making of a Transnational Polity*
Antoine Vauchez

*Services Liberalization in the EU and the WTO: Concepts, Standards and Regulatory Approaches*
Marcus Klamert

*Referendums and the European Union: A Comparative Enquiry*
Fernando Mendez, Mario Mendez and Vasiliki Triga

*The Allocation of Regulatory Competence in the EU Emissions Trading Scheme*
Jospehine Van Zeben

*The Eurozone Crisis: A Constitutional Analysis*
Kaarlo Tuori and Klaus Tuori

*International Trade Disputes and EU Liability*
Anne Thies

*The Limits of Legal Reasoning and the European Court of Justice*
Gerard Conway

*New Governance and the Transformation of European Law: Coordinating EU Social Law and Policy*
Mark Dawson

*The Lisbon Treaty: A Legal and Political Analysis*
Jean-Claude Piris

*The European Union's Fight against Corruption: The Evolving Policy towards Member States and Candidate Countries*
Patrycja Szarek-Mason

*The Ethos of Europe: Values, Law and Justice in the EU*
Andrew Williams

*State and Market in European Union Law: The Public and Private Spheres of the Internal Market before the EU Courts*
Wolf Sauter and Harm Schepel

*The European Civil Code: The Way Forward*
Hugh Collins

*Ethical Dimensions of the Foreign Policy of the European Union: A Legal Appraisal*
Urfan Khaliq

*Implementing EU Pollution Control: Law and Integration*
Bettina Lange

*European Broadcasting Law and Policy*
Jackie Harrison and Lorna Woods

*The Transformation of Citizenship in the European Union: Electoral Rights and the Restructuring of Political Space*
Jo Shaw

*The Constitution for Europe: A Legal Analysis*
Jean-Claude Piris

*The European Convention on Human Rights: Achievements, Problems and Prospects*
Steven Greer

*Social Rights and Market Freedom in the European Constitution: A Labour Law Perspective*
Stefano Giubboni

*EU Enlargement and the Constitutions of Central and Eastern Europe*
Anneli Albi

# Empire of Law

*Nazi Germany, Exile Scholars and the Battle for the Future of Europe*

Kaius Tuori
*University of Helsinki*

CAMBRIDGE
UNIVERSITY PRESS

**CAMBRIDGE**
**UNIVERSITY PRESS**

University Printing House, Cambridge CB2 8BS, United Kingdom

One Liberty Plaza, 20th Floor, New York, NY 10006, USA

477 Williamstown Road, Port Melbourne, VIC 3207, Australia

314–321, 3rd Floor, Plot 3, Splendor Forum, Jasola District Centre, New Delhi - 110025, India

79 Anson Road, #06–04/06, Singapore 079906

Cambridge University Press is part of the University of Cambridge.

It furthers the University's mission by disseminating knowledge in the pursuit of education, learning, and research at the highest international levels of excellence.

www.cambridge.org
Information on this title: www.cambridge.org/9781108483636
DOI: 10.1017/9781108678582



First published 2020

*A catalogue record for this publication is available from the British Library.*

*Library of Congress Cataloging-in-Publication Data*
Names: Tuori, Kaius, author.
Title: Empire of law : Nazi Germany, exile scholars and the battle for the future of Europe / Kaius Tuori, University of Helsinki.
Description: Cambridge, United Kingdom ; New York, NY, USA Cambridge University Press, 2020. | Series: Cambridge studies in european law and policy | Includes bibliographical references and index.
Identifiers: LCCN 2019040382 (print) | LCCN 2019040383 (ebook) | ISBN 9781108483636 (hardback) | ISBN 9781108678582 (epub)
Subjects: LCSH: Jurisprudence – Europe – History – 20th century. | National socialism.
Classification: LCC KJC395 .T86 2020 (print) | LCC KJC395 (ebook) | DDC 342.4308/73–dc23
LC record available at https://lccn.loc.gov/2019040382
LC ebook record available at https://lccn.loc.gov/2019040383

ISBN 978-1-108-48363-6 Hardback

This book is dedicated (with love) to Taina.

# Contents

# Figures

# Preface

Many of the human sciences have extensively long histories but few have as intimate connection with their own pasts as law. What this has meant is that in legal debates references to ancient legal texts have continued to be used as authoritative examples and arguments about contemporary developments. Thus, medieval jurists would refer to Roman jurists, early modern lawyers to the Romans and the medieval, continuing a self-referential chain extending to the present. While it has become fairly rare, though not unheard of, to see references to ancient Roman juridical writings in modern court cases, in literature this effect continues to this day. As a lawyer and as a historian, I have found this to be a wonderful example of the historical continuities in scientific research, rivaled only by philosophy and perhaps theology.

However, the fact that there is a sense of continuity of more than two and a half millennia, as there is in law, requires not only a memory of the past but also a sense of tradition and identity to bind together the past and the present. Calling something a part of the European legal tradition or the Western legal tradition includes a process of both inclusion and exclusion. Why we are prone to include some and exclude others depends on how we define tradition. Why are the laws of Hammurabi or other laws of the ancient Near East remembered and celebrated, but not as part of a shared past, a common tradition, as the Roman jurists are? What counts as tradition and how we redefine tradition are the key themes of this book.

This book marks the final end point of a long and happy journey that began in 2012. Many people have helped me along the way and the book has been immensely improved as a result. First of all, I would like to thank the European Research Council for their funding, which enabled me to compose a research group that for five years has scoured the archives and discussed with me ideas of law, tradition and Europe.[1] I am very much in debt to the FoundLaw (Reinventing the Foundations of European Legal Culture 1934–1964) team members, Dr. Heta Björklund, Professor Magdalena Kmak, Dr. Tommaso Beggio, Dr. Ville Erkkilä and Professor Jacob Giltaij. During the project, we shared an extraordinary cooperation and I have been in the fortunate position of using them as a sounding board and as a test audience. As part of the project, we have also shared access to archival materials, enabling each member to read and use each other's archival notes and photographs (on the project, its other publications and source materials, see the website www.foundlaw.org or https://blogs.helsinki.fi/found-law). Alongside the project, we organized a series of workshops and conferences, where I have presented parts of my research and was enlightened by magnificent papers given by others. The organization of these workshops took place in collaboration with colleagues around the world, from Helsinki to Florence, New York, Rome and Stellenbosch. I would like to especially thank Professors Jacques Du Plessis (Stellenbosch), Bill Nelson (NYU) and Emanuele Conte (Rome).

I have been fortunate to have as my colleagues at the Faculty of Law the wonderful legal history people, many of whom participated in our conferences and workshops and gave important feedback. During the process of writing the book, I was hired by the then Network, now the Centre for European Studies at the University of Helsinki, a multidisciplinary research center where I was warmly welcomed by Professor Juhana Aunesluoma and Dr. Leena Malkki. During the final phases of the project, we put together with some of the project members and people from the network an ultimately successful application for an Academy of Finland Centre of Excellence, the "Centre of Excellence in Law, Identity and the European Narratives" (www.eurostorie.org). In the centers, this book has especially benefited from conversations with Drs. Timo Miettinen, Timo Pankakoski and Pedro Magalhães. A special thanks goes to Ville Suuronen and Adolfo Giuliani who read the entire manuscript and gave valuable comments.

The final stretch of the manuscript preparation was done at the Political Science Department of the University of California, Los Angeles, where I was a visiting associate professor for three months in

[1] This work has received funding from the European Research Council under the European Union's Seventh Framework Programme (FP7/2007–2013)/ERC grant agreement no. 313100 and from the Academy of Finland funded Centre of Excellence in Law, Identity and the European Narratives, funding decision number 312154.

2017–2018. I would like to thank Professor Anthony Pagden, my host, and all the wonderful colleagues, especially Mr. Mack Eason, for their hospitality and help in the process. The penultimate version of the manuscript was actually done with a laptop perched on top of a surfboard serving as a makeshift desk. For the final push, I am thankful for Professor Hans-Peter Haferkamp, who put the magnificent library of his institute, *Institut für Neuere Privatrechtsgeschichte, Deutsche und Rheinische Rechtsgeschichte*, at my disposal.

The Cambridge University Press was kind enough to accept the manuscript. My editor Tom Randall has moved the project forward from an idea to manuscript with unfailing precision. I would also like to thank the series editors of the *Cambridge Studies in European Law and Policy*, Laurence Gormley and Jo Shaw, for approving the book for their series.

Dr. Mark Shackleton has adeptly reviewed and corrected my text. The mistakes that remain are mine.

I have presented ideas and preliminary results in numerous conferences, including the annual conferences of the Société Internationale Fernand de Visscher pour l'Histoire des Droits de l'Antiquité, the American Society for Legal History, the Association of Ancient Historians annual conference and numerous larger and smaller meetings. Some of the research behind Chapter 3 has been published earlier.[2] I would like to extend my thanks to all who took the trouble to listen and comment, giving me feedback and helpful hints about where to look and what to search for.

[2] Kaius Tuori, "Hadrian's cosmopolitanism and Nazi legal policy," *Classical Receptions Journal*, 9 (2017), 470–486.

# Abbreviations

| | |
|---|---|
| BGB | Bürgerliches Gesetzbuch, the German civil code |
| DDP | Deutsche Demokratische Partei |
| *Dig.* | The Digest of Justinian |
| EEC | European Economic Community |
| GWBB | Gesetz zur Wiederherstellung des Berufsbeamtentums |
| MPI | Max Planck Institute |
| NCO | non-commissioned officer |
| NGO | non-governmental organization |
| NL | Nachlass |
| NSDAP | Nationalsozialistische Deutsche Arbeiterpartei |
| OECD | Organisation for Economic Co-operation and Development |
| OSS | Office of Strategic Services |
| OUP | Oxford University Press |
| POW | Prisoner of war |
| RGBl. | Reichsgesetzblatt |
| SA | Sturmabteilung |
| SDP | Sozialdemokratische Partei Deutschlands |
| SPSL | Society for the Protection of Science and Learning |
| SS | Schutzstaffel |
| WASP | White Anglo-Saxon Protestant |

# 1 Introduction

In a letter to Max Radin on April 2, 1933, Hermann Kantorowicz writes how the situation in Germany took a turn for the worse after the Nazis took power:

> What is happening there is even more terrible than American newspapers report and if our Nazis proclaim these reports a justification for their "reprisals," this is a mere pretext. Everything now going on is according to the Nazi party program of February 25, 1920, especially to article 4, only no one believed such barbarism possible, myself excepted as you probably remember. The letters now written by thousands of German Jews denying every atrocity are, of course, written under the threat of still worse treatment. My own family has been severely stricken. Dozens of my cousins, in great part well-known lawyers and doctors, have lost their jobs and every means of subsistence, my brother, Professor in Bonn, is hiding I don't know where; his daughter, a girl of 21 years, has been imprisoned as a hostage; the Nazi-police tried to compel my mother, 74 years old, to give away the address of my brother; my late wife's cousin, the director of a theater in Silesia, has been kidnapped by a Nazi auto during a rehearsal, conducted out of town, stripped naked, beaten and then forced to walk home in this state. One of my best friends in Kiel, the lawyer Spiegel, has been murdered and of course I myself cannot venture to show myself again in the present Germany.[1]

As this example shows, the Nazi revolution upended many of the things considered self-evident in Europe at the time: it appeared that the ideals of humanity, equality, rights and security were abandoned. Compounding the sense of crisis was the notion that truth and falsehood had lost their meanings, becoming dependent on the vagaries of the powers that be. A mere decade and a half

[1] Letter reprinted in Max Radin, *Cartas Romanisticas (1923–1950)* (Naples: Jovene, 2001), p. 89.

after the carnage of World War I had ended, a new barbarism had risen in Germany, the land that had previously been considered the center of European civilization. The Nazi repression was a direct attack on the European tradition of justice and the rule of law. A jurist like Kantorowicz felt this acutely because among the main targets of Nazi repression after the takeover of power were the forces of law and order, meaning the police, the judiciary and lawyers, in order to bring down the German *Rechtstaat.*

Before World War II (WWII), the concepts of Europe and Europeanism were often considered to be more or less utopian. They shared a similar position to that of human rights, in that enthusiasts of the idea of a European tradition were thought to be odd characters, often slightly suspicious Leftists or intellectuals. This relative marginalization makes the rise of Europe and the European legal heritage as a concept all the more remarkable. Like the concept of human rights, after 1945 Europe emerged as a transformational idea that would lead to a reconceptualization of much of the political and legal landscape. While the creation of the modern human rights regime may be seen as a reaction to the horrors of war and totalitarianism, the idea of European integration was a counterreaction to the ultranationalism touted by totalitarian regimes such as Nazi Germany or fascist Italy. Though the link between nation and its laws was one of the foundations of nationalist thought, there emerged in a few years a new theory which claimed that Europe shared a common legal heritage that could form a foundation for its future integration.

The purpose of this book is to explore the emergence of this idea of a shared European legal tradition as the dominant theory of understanding the past and the future of law in Europe during the postwar period. This entails tracing the role that was given to Roman law as the foundation of European law and the shared legacy it provided. Central figures in this transformation were scholars such as Franz Wieacker and Paul Koschaker, who would, based on very different positions, be instrumental in the coming resurgence of both the Roman law tradition and the idea of a shared European heritage in law.

The main research questions revolve around the genealogy of this theory of a common legal past:

1) How did the idea of the shared legal heritage of Europe emerge? What was the impact of totalitarianism and exile in this process?
2) How was the theory disseminated and how did it become dominant? What legal, political and cultural factors contributed to its success?

These two research questions are interlinked and shed light on the main issue: the reformulation and reinterpretation of a scientific tradition and the understanding of the past in the process of finding arguments for the present. Following from the use of the past arises the second problem in the analysis of foundational narratives, namely how the present influences a view of the past and how in historiography of the past is transformed to conform to the expectations of the present.[2] The analysis of these questions is vital because the whole concept of Europe as a cultural and legal community is changing rapidly, leading to questions of the relevance of a common theory on the past.

Behind this transformation was a group of innovators, a handful of scholars and law professors, who were forced to reinvent themselves and their science abroad, after being ousted from office and exiled by Nazi Germany. This reinvention meant that they had to first reconceptualize and rethink all that they had previously done and then address a new audience in a new language, beginning to write in English and to explain their views to their colleagues in Oxford, Princeton or New York. In the process, they tried to make sense of the disaster that had befallen both them and their country. They had to face the fact that not only had the hallowed *Rechtsstaat* collapsed but their colleagues and neighbors had also turned against them.[3] In response, these exiles began to formulate a theory of a common European legal culture, a culture that was founded on equality before the law. A reaction to the totalitarian regimes and their nationalistic ideologies, this reinterpretation of the past sought to show that a great European legal tradition based on liberty and justice did exist.

What emerged from the works of the exiles was a powerful new theory on the shared European legal past that laid the foundation for the idea of a common European legal culture. From this common foundation, ideals such as the rule of law, law as science and law independent from political power would have spread to form a liberal European legal culture. This theory was further developed by legal scholars and historians who had at some point collaborated with the regime. The uniting factor was that these were German-speaking legal

[2] William McNeill, "Mythistory, or truth, myth, history, and historians," 91 (1986) *The American Historical Review*, 3; Peter Burke, *The Fabrication of Louis XIV* (New Haven: Yale University Press, 1992).

[3] An important early contribution to the discussion on legal scholars in exile is Jack Beatson and Reinhard Zimmermann (eds.), *Jurists Uprooted: German-Speaking Émigré Lawyers in Twentieth-Century Britain* (Oxford: Oxford University Press, 2004).

scholars with some background in Roman law and legal history. Thus, the formulators can be divided into two distinct groups: 1) exiles and outcasts, those who were driven from their posts; and 2) the collaborators and bystanders, who either thrived in the new circumstances under the Nazis or managed to avoid controversies. Of the first group, I have selected three significant scholars, of which Fritz Schulz (1879–1957)[4] and Fritz Pringsheim (1882–1967)[5] were exiled[6] in Britain, while Paul Koschaker (1878–1951)[7] was sidelined and retreated to a provincial university. From the second group, I have selected two younger scholars, Franz Wieacker (1908–1994),[8] a pupil of Pringsheim, and Helmut Coing (1912–2000),[9] whose post-WWII careers cemented the position of the common past theory. Their works are contextualized by juxtaposition and comparison with contemporaries such as Hannah Arendt, Franz Neumann, Ernst Kantorowicz, F. A. Hayek, David Daube, Leo Strauss, Ernst Levy, Guido Kisch and Arnaldo Momigliano, who explored the formulation of the European legal tradition in exile. The scholars who were involved with the Nazi and fascist regimes, the narratives of those who stayed are juxtaposed with examples such as Salvatore Riccobono, Max Kaser, Emilio Betti, Karl August Eckhardt, Ernst Schönbauer, Pietro De Francisci and Carl Schmitt. They are naturally a small selection of the scholars involved, but through their works I seek to illustrate the change in a scholarly tradition.

The exiles wrote about the Europe of law as a hope and aspiration, arguing for the language of the rule of law, rights and reason against the language of blood and culture embraced by nationalistic and totalitarian regimes such as Nazi Germany. I argue that it was crucial for the

[4] Wolfgang Ernst, "Fritz Schulz," in Beatson and Zimmermann, *Jurists Uprooted*, pp. 106–204; Jacob Giltaij, *Reinventing the Principles of Roman Law* (April 24, 2019). Available at SSRN: https://ssrn.com/abstract=3377309 or http://dx.doi.org/10.2139/ssrn.3377309 (date accessed May 22, 2019). Full bibliographies of the main characters may be found in their respective chapters.

[5] Tony Honoré, "Fritz Pringsheim," in Beatson and Zimmermann, *Jurists Uprooted*, pp. 205–233.

[6] Other influential Roman law exiles in Britain were David Daube, Ernst Rabel and Franz Haymann.

[7] Tomasz Giaro, *Aktualisierung Europas, Gespräche mit Paul Koschaker* (Genoa: Name, 2000); Tommaso Beggio, *Paul Koschaker: Rediscovering the Roman Foundations of European Legal Tradition* (Heidelberg: Winter Verlag, 2018).

[8] Viktor Winkler, *Der Kampf gegen die Rechtswissenschaft. Franz Wieackers "Privatrechtsgeschichte der Neuzeit" und die deutsche Rechtswissenschaft des 20. Jahrhunderts* (Hamburg: Verlag Dr. Kovač, 2014); Ville Erkkilä, *The Conceptual Change of Conscience: Franz Wieacker and German Legal Historiography* (Tübingen: Mohr Siebeck, 2019).

[9] Beyond short notes and an autobiography, no major works exist on Coing.

development of the idea of a European legal heritage that the main figures were exiles who were immersed in a foreign culture. After initial difficulties, including being suspected of espionage and internment on the Isle of Man in June 1940, the change proved to be an impetus for rethinking and reinventing. The scientific innovation that followed would probably not have been possible without their horrendous removal from their homeland. Because they had expertise that was lacking in their adoptive countries, they eventually gathered students and a loyal following that was necessary to become successful. In the emerging sociological theories on academic tribes, the focus has traditionally been on indoctrination of the young.[10] In contrast, this study seeks to examine the implications of exile for the work of established scholars under extreme circumstances. It demonstrates how the exile process is much more complicated than previously thought but that in some instances the exiles form a kind of a bridge or conduit between cultures and traditions.[11] In this case, the result was the creation of a new kind of formulation and understanding of European legal culture that spanned both the continental and the Atlantic traditions.

It is quite common for political events to change the course of intellectual history. What this book seeks to offer is a twist from the usual story, in that the reinvention of the meaning of science and legal culture had a second, even more influential life after the war. Both the bystanders and the active participants in the Nazi regime in academia, such as Koschaker, Wieacker and Coing, were deeply affected by the events of 1933–1945 and were forced to reconsider the implications of totalitarianism in academia. What the anti-totalitarian narrative formed by the

[10] See, for example, Tony Becher and Paul Trowler, *Academic Tribes and Territories: Intellectual Enquiry and the Cultures of Disciplines* (Ballmoor: Society for Research into Higher Education & Open University Press, 2001).

[11] On an assessment of the development of exile studies beyond the acculturation hypothesis, see Renato Camurri, "The exile experience reconsidered: a comparative perspective in European cultural migration during the interwar period," *Transatlantica* 1 (2014), http://journals.openedition.org/transatlantica/6920. In the authoritative style of argument favored at the time, what was a statement of desire was turned into a statement of fact. As a method, this is comparable to the anthropological theories of literary cultures. As senior professors, the exiles had the clout to be believed because they possessed mastery over their sources and were hence convincing. On the challenges of bridging legal and political cultures, see Alfons Söllner, *Political Scholar: Zur Intellectuallengeschichte des 20. Jahrhunderts* (Hamburg: Europäische Verlagsanstalt, 2018), p. 88. As Seyla Benhabib has noted, the exiles leaving Germany were a very exceptional group, consisting of the best minds of a generation. Seyla Benhabib, *Exile, Statelessness, and Migration: Playing Chess with History from Hannah Arendt to Isaiah Berlin* (Princeton, NJ: Princeton University Press, 2018).

exiles offered was an explanation and a new self-understanding of law and legal science as a bulwark against dictatorship. It was crucial for the success of the new interpretation that it enabled them to respond to the challenge of communism and to criticize the suppression of the legal sphere by the political sphere. As has recently been demonstrated, this turn coincided with the emergence of human rights as a fundamental element in the European self-understanding in the post-WWII years.[12]

This book was born out of a sense of frustration about the simplistic way in which the notion of a shared past has been used as an argument for the future in European legal discourse. This frustration was then channeled into a large research project funded by the European Research Council, leading to a series of books on the matter.[13] The current volume represents a central part of that project. Studying correspondence, lecture notes and published materials, the project sought to follow how the idea of a common European legal past was formulated, discussed and disseminated. The starting point of the study, 1933, is the first academic reaction to the Nazi takeover and the expulsion of civil servants of Jewish ancestry, while the end point, 1964, includes the response to the erection of the Berlin Wall and the consolidation of the hostilities between free and communist Europe.

Through the histories of these scholars, the book traces the genealogy of the idea of a common European legal past based on ideas such as the rule of law. In doing so, it seeks to radically reevaluate the creation, influence and implications of this theory as an ideological project formulated between 1933 and 1964. Influenced by the failure of utopian theories of society, the formulators of the theory proceeded to first transform the past to create an air of inevitability to the developments and interpretations they proposed. This new, non-nationalized version of the past emerged at an opportune moment and gained political momentum in the bankruptcy of the nationalist movements at the end of World War II and the new division between

12 Marco Duranti, *The Conservative Human Rights Revolution: European Identity, Transnational Politics, and the Origins of the European Convention* (Oxford: Oxford University Press, 2017).

13 The ERC StG project "Reinventing the Foundations of European Legal Culture 1934–1964," project number 313100. The books are Kaius Tuori and Heta Björklund (eds.), *Roman Law and the Idea of Europe* (London: Bloomsbury, 2019); Beggio, *Paul Koschaker*; Erkkilä, *Conceptual Change of Conscience*, initially Ville Erkkilä, "The Conceptual Change of Conscience: Franz Wieacker and German Legal Historiography 1933–1968," PhD thesis, University of Helsinki (2017); Giltaij, *Reinventing the Principles of Roman Law*. For links to the publications, see www.foundlaw.org or https://blogs.helsinki.fi/found-law/publications-of-the-project.

the East and the West. In the creation of a mythical past, the drafters of the theory took heed of the lessons of the nineteenth-century debates on the use of the past in legal reform, using the language of culture and civilization and being careful not to tie themselves to specifics. This book will explore the different intellectual strands from the interwar years, from Catholic legal universalism to conservative cultural Europeanism and Anglo-American liberalism and the transatlantic debates over the rule of law. It will show how all these strands contributed to the formation of the European legal narrative.

Their opponents originally used a nationalistic (or *völkisch*) argument, referring to the people as a nationalistic ideal and as a source of tradition. What the founders did was to turn the criticism around, arguing that the long duration of historical tradition was proof of its legitimacy. This was a return to the arguments of the nineteenth-century Romanist-Germanist debates. I argue that this combination of the two arguments about legal tradition, the universalist legal science and the nationalist tradition, was central to the success of the shared past theory of the European legal tradition.

## How This Book Contributes to the Discussion

One of the reasons why there has been virtually no previous critical research in the common past theory is that the theory is in itself an interpretation of history. While historical interpretations are open to criticism in their own terms, the languages of history and law strive to accept introspection, not fundamental criticism. In this project historical writing that delineates the origins and foundations of a legal culture is associated with the concept of foundational narrative.[14] This constructivist concept emphasizes the degree to which historical lineage is a choice. However, the aim is decisively not to argue for a revealing criticism that would prove the narrative wrong. Though the self-understanding of modern law is often conceived as being based on rationality and science, it has been claimed that this position of modern law as value-free and positivist is in itself a construction

[14] John Waddell, *Foundation Myths: The Beginnings of Irish Archaeology* (Wicklow: Bray, Co., 2005); David Carr, "Narrative and the real world: an argument for continuity," in Brian Fay, Philip Pomper and Richard T. Vann (eds.), *History and Theory: Contemporary Readings* (Oxford: Wiley-Blackwell, 1998), p. 137: "Narrative is not merely a possibly successful way of describing events; its structure inheres in the events themselves."

that has narrative and mythical dimensions.[15] Foundational narratives, such as those provided by history, are to a large degree stories of belonging and self-definition. Through these histories, the community defines itself and its virtues.[16]

Through the construction of identity, history is an essential part of the foundations of most legal traditions.[17] European legal cultures are no different in this respect, as lineages and ancient pedigrees are presented to answer the existential question of origins. Even though conventionally the nineteenth century is thought of as the age of constructing national identity through history and myths and the twentieth century as the era of deconstruction of national identity, the project claims that parallel to the destruction of national myths a new European tradition arose with its own mythical elements that perpetuated nationalism in a new guise.[18]

The common past theory offers an argument of continuity from the past. Such arguments have since proliferated and had later incarnations in a number of theories, for example that of tracing the history of human rights from antiquity.[19] As we take the task of seeing how the narrative emerged, it becomes obvious that there are many things that are not what they seem.

The success of the common past theory is implied in the extent to which current scholarship is embedded into the teleological narrative of the common past theory. Opinions are presented both for and against the common future of European legal traditions, but not against the

[15] Peter Fitzpatrick, *The Mythology of Modern Law* (London and New York: Routledge, 1992).

[16] Benedict Anderson, *Imagined Communities: Reflections on the Origin and Spread of Nationalism* (London: Verso, 1991).

[17] Richard B. Bernstein, *The Founding Fathers Reconsidered* (Oxford: Oxford University Press, 2009).

[18] Thomas Hylland Eriksen, *Ethnicity and Nationalism* (London: Pluto Press, 1993); Pierre Nora and Lawrence D. Kritzma (eds.), *Realms of Memory. The Construction of the French Past* (New York: Columbia University Press, 1996); Jonathan C. D. Clark, "National identity, state formation and patriotism: the role of history in the public mind," *History Workshop Journal*, 29 (1990), 95–102. For the nationalist debate in general, cf. John Breuilly, "Historians and the nation," in Peter Burke (ed.), *History and Historians in the Twentieth Century* (Oxford: Oxford University Press, 2002), pp. 55–87; Marc Ferro, *The Use and Abuse of History or How the Past Is Taught* (London: Routledge, 1984), pp. vii–xi; Margaret MacMillan, *The Uses and Abuses of History* (London: Profile Books Ltd, 2009).

[19] Tony Honoré, *Ulpian: Pioneer of Human Rights* (Oxford: Oxford University Press, 2002); Jacob Giltaij, *Mensenrechten in het Romeinse Recht* (Nijmegen: Wolf Legal Publishers, 2011); Jacob Giltaij and Kaius Tuori, "Human rights in antiquity? Revisiting anachronism and roman law," in Pamela Slotte and Miia Halme-Tuomisaari (eds.), *Revisiting the Origins of Human Rights* (Cambridge and New York: Cambridge University Press, 2015), pp. 39–63.

common past. The common past theory defines the debate by claiming that European law can be united only by jurisprudence and that European legal studies should search for their common roots to find the key to a common future,[20] or that common European values derived from shared historical experiences are the precondition of all integration and European values have a legal significance as such.[21] Even critics follow the logic of the common past theory, saying that European cultural diversity makes the whole idea of common European law impossible.[22] However, despite the great enthusiasm from the 1990s onwards concerning the unification of European law, especially in contract law, concrete advances have thus far been less than promising and divergences in legal and moral frameworks have been cited as hindering factors.[23] This book seeks to contribute to this discussion by opening up the theoretical and historical underpinnings of the idea of the link between the past and the future in the making of European integration through an exploration of the early history of this idea.

Though the analysis of the emergence of the common European legal heritage and its intellectual history forms the core of the book, it also touches upon three important debates on the intellectual history of law: 1) the uses of the past in totalitarian regimes; 2) the impact of émigré scholars; and 3) the emergence of the European project.

The contemporary significance of the study of the past and the tracing of lineages to ancient cultures has been the subject of increasing scholarly attention.[24] The political importance of classics in the twentieth-century totalitarian regimes has been an important subfield, where researchers have discussed how totalitarian regimes, especially the fascists in Italy, used ancient Rome as a model and justification for

[20] Raoul C. van Caenegem, *European Law in the Past and the Future: Unity and Diversity over Two Millennia* (Cambridge: Cambridge University Press, 2002).

[21] Christian Calliess, "Europe as transnational law," *German Law Journal*, 10 (2009), 1367–1382. See also, Hans Joas and Klaus Wiegandt, *The Cultural Values of Europe* (Liverpool: Liverpool University Press, 2008).

[22] Pierre Legrand, "A diabolical idea," in Arthur S. Hartkamp et al. (eds.), *Towards a European Civil Code* (Nijmegen: Kluwer Law International, 2004, 3rd ed.), pp. 245–272; Pierre Legrand, "European legal systems are not converging," *International and Comparative Law Quarterly*, 45 (1996), 52–81.

[23] Reinhard Zimmermann, "The present state of European private law," *American Journal of Comparative Law*, 57 (2009), 479–511.

[24] See, for example, Dimitris Tziovas (ed.), *Re-imagining the Past: Antiquity and Modern Greek Culture* (Oxford: Oxford University Press, 2014); Margaret MacMillan, *Uses and Abuses of History*.

their policies of militarization and aggression.[25] For the study of the classical past, this meant that the object of their study was made to conform to the expectations of the present, sometimes in very confusing and contradictory ways, such as providing precursors to racial policies. Important studies have demonstrated how the position of Roman law varied from being under threat to being coopted to the regime[26] but a concerted study of the impact in the field is still lacking. In contrast, during the last decades important work has uncovered the extent to which legal history was influenced in various and unpredictable ways by association with the Nazi regime.[27] What the book demonstrates is how contested the issue of historical lineage was in that while the official Nazi policy sought to erase historical links, within the legal profession resistance continued throughout the regime based on the traditional idealization of the Roman legacy.

Scholarship on émigré intellectuals has undergone a rapid transformation. The first generation of works, such as Fermi's pioneering book, consisted mostly of purely biographical studies of émigrés, for example studies on some 20,000 intellectuals (among which some 2,000 professors, roughly a third of the total) who left Germany in the 1930s. The second generation of studies has explored the impact that this migration had in Britain and the US, where new areas of research were born and other were revitalized with the influx of new talent from Germany and Italy.[28] For legal scholars, the study has thus far

[25] Jan Nelis, "Constructing Fascist identity: Benito Mussolini and the myth of Romanità," *Classical World*, 100 (2007), 391–415. In Germany, the Nazi educational policies explicitly stated that teaching of classical languages should be focused on militarism and conquest. Johann Chapoutot, *Der Nationalsozialismus und die Antike* (Darmstadt: Philipp von Zabern, 2014), p. 148.

[26] Massimo Miglietta and Gianni Santucci (eds.), *Diritto romano e regimi totalitari nel '900 Europeo* (Trento: Università degli studi di Trento, 2009); Peter E. Pieler, "Das römische Recht im nationalsozialistischen Staat," in Ulrike Davy, Helmut Fuchs, Herbert Hofmeister, Judith Marte and Ilse Reiter (eds.), *Nationalsozialismus und Recht* (Vienna: Verlag A. Orac, 1990), pp. 427–444.

[27] Michael Stolleis and Dieter Simon (eds.), *Rechtsgeschichte im Nationalsozialismus. Beiträge zur Geschichte einer Disziplin* (Tübingen: Mohr Siebeck, 1989); Franz-Stefan Meissel, "Deutsche Rechtsgeschichte im nationalsozialistischen Staat," in Ulrike Davy, Helmut Fuchs, Herbert Hofmeister, Judith Marte and Ilse Reiter (eds.), *Nationalsozialismus und Recht* (Vienna: Verlag A. Orac, 1990), pp. 412–426.

[28] Laura Fermi, *Illustrious Immigrants: The Intellectual Migration from Europe 1930–1941* (Chicago: University of Chicago Press, 1968); Mitchell G. Ash and Alfons Söllner (eds.), *Forced Migration and Scientific Change: Émigré German-Speaking Scientists and Scholars after 1933* (Cambridge: Cambridge University Press, 1996); Felix Rösch, *Émigré Scholars and the Genesis of International Relations. A European Discipline in America?* (London: Palgrave Macmillan, 2014); Martin Jay, *Permanent Exiles: Essays on the Intellectual Migration from*

been concentrated on the biographical aspect, with works like *Jurists Uprooted* (2004) detailing lives of émigré legal scholars, including some Roman lawyers such as Fritz Schulz or David Daube. Beyond that, the impact of their work in Britain, the US or in Germany after the war is still mostly unexplored.[29] In this study, various ideas of influence and impact are reversed in that an attempt is made to bring forward the agency of the émigrés, not only in taking up various themes such as law, culture and humanity in the European past, but also in transforming the discussion for their own benefit both materially and intellectually.

Of the vast scholarship on the European integration or the idea of Europe, only some works have investigated the history of the turn to Europe in historical scholarship after World War II.[30] While the European project has always presented itself as a counterreaction to totalitarianism, critical studies such as *Darker Legacies of Law in Europe* (2003) have illustrated how Nazi legal thought contained many of the same ideas as European integration did.[31] With regard to the impact of Roman law in the European project, the more prominent works have dealt with the way Roman jurisprudence actually influenced different European legal cultures[32] rather than on how Roman law was used as

*Germany to America* (New York: Columbia University Press, 1985); David Kettler, *The Liquidation of Exile: Studies in the Intellectual Emigration of the 1930s* (London and New York: Anthem Press, 2011); Söllner, *Political Scholar*; Benhabib, Exile, Statelessness, and Migration; Daniel Bessner, *Democracy in Exile: Hans Speier and the Rise of the Defense Intellectual* (Ithaca and London: Cornell University Press, 2018).

29 Beatson and Zimmermann, *Jurists Uprooted*, see also Magdalena Kmak, "The impact of exile on law and legal science 1934–64," in Kaius Tuori and Heta Björklund (eds.), *Roman Law and the Idea of Europe* (London: Bloomsbury Academic, 2019), pp. 15–34; Kyle Graham, "The refugee jurist and American Law Schools, 1933–1941," *American Journal of Comparative Law*, 50 (2002), 777; Marcus Lutter, Ernst C. Stiefel and Michael H. Hoeflich (eds.), *Der Einfluß deutscher Emigranten auf die Rechtsentwicklung in den USA und in Deutschland. Vorträge und Referate des Bonner Symposions im September 1991* (Tübingen: Mohr Siebeck, 1993); Leonie Breunung and Manfred Walther, *Die Emigration deutscher Rechtswissenschaftler ab 1933*, vol. 1 (Göttingen: De Gruyter, 2012), second volume forthcoming.

30 Hartmut Kaelble, *Europäer über Europa: Die Entstehung des europäischen Selbstverständnisses im 19. und 20. Jahrhundert* (Frankfurt and New York: Campus Verlag, 2001); Hagen Schulz-Forberg and Bo Stråth, *The Political History of European Integration: The Hypocrisy of Democracy-Through-Market* (London: Routledge, 2010).

31 Christian Joerges and Navraj Singh Ghaleigh, *Darker Legacies of Law in Europe* (Oxford: Hart Publishing, 2003). Even more pointedly, John Laughland, *Tainted Source: The Undemocratic Origins of the European Idea* (London: Sphere, 1998).

32 Reinhard Zimmermann, *Roman Law, Contemporary Law, European Law: The Civilian Tradition Today* (Oxford: Oxford University Press, 2001); Peter Stein, *Roman Law in European History* (Cambridge and New York: Cambridge University Press, 1999); Franz Wieacker, *A History of Private Law in Europe with Particular Reference to Germany*

part of the European project. Another key influence that has only recently received attention was the way human rights became a central feature of the European project and were embraced by conservative thinkers such as Winston Churchill.[33] By taking up not only liberal narratives of Europe but also totalitarian and conservative Europeanism, this book shows the multiplicity of the interests and motives that drove emergent Europeanism between the 1930s and the 1950s.

In short, this book seeks to fill an important lacuna in the academic debate and develop an analysis of the issues of the use of the past and totalitarianism, knowledge transfer and emigration, and the birth of the European idea as a reaction to the totalitarianism of the 1930s. In this way it seeks to offer a critical and analytical exploration of the creation of the historical foundation of the European legal project.

In order to provide a fresh start in the inquiry and the aspects of ideas, concepts and intellectual change, the book will employ a number of different methodological tools, from theories of scientific transfer to conceptual legal history. Early studies on exiles were founded on acculturation theories and an understanding that émigrés functioned as receptacles of culture that they were immersed in. In contrast, the present study applies a more complex approach, one that attempts to study the mechanisms that prompted changes in scholarly understanding. Far from being passive recipients or vessels for ideas, appropriation and the use of new ideas were processes of reappropriation and necessity. Ideas were taken up and used because they were usable and necessary to the authors' needs.[34]

The narratives that our five authors and their colleagues write are in essence about redefining the foundations of what European tradition

(Oxford: Clarendon Press, 1995). Critical scholars have expressed doubts about the role of Roman law as a foundation for European legal culture, see Alain Wijffels, "Le ius commune européen: Mythe ou référentiel indifférencié des discours sur la formation d'un droit européen?," in Boris Bernabé and Olivier Camy (eds.), *Les mythes de fondation et l'Europe* (Dijon: Editions Universitaires de Dijon, 2013), pp. 87–101; Douglas Osler, "The myth of European legal history," *Rechtshistorisches Journal*, 16 (1997), 393–410.

33 Marco Duranti, *Conservative Human Rights Revolution*. On the conservative ideology of Europe, see more generally Armin Mohler, *Die Konservative Revolution in Deutschland 1918–1932: Ein Handbuch* (Darmstadt: Wissenschaftliche Buchgesellschaft, 1989). On the rise of conservative anti-totalitarianism, see James Chappel, "The Catholic origins of totalitarianism theory in interwar Europe," *Modern Intellectual History*, 8 (2011), 561–590.

34 Mitchell G. Ash and Alfons Söllner, "Introduction," in Ash and Söllner, *Forced Migration and Scientific Change*, p. 11 discusses the move from studies of assimilation to acculturation and the challenges of defining external and internal factors.

meant. As such they could be interpreted as foundational narratives, ones that outline the core principles of the field and the shared foundations they rely on.

It is often claimed in the rights and culture debate that certain rights are a reflection of a European culture and tradition and are thus not universal. This debate has been based on the assumption that culture is inherent and stable. It has been considered, for example, that Europe has certain legal traditions such as the rule of law, which are culturally based and thus exporting them as universal values is imperialistic and culturally insensitive. What this book demonstrates, however, is that even in Europe the rights tradition is a conscious construction by a group of legal scholars reacting to contemporary events. The tradition was actually produced in Europe as a reaction to a certain expediency.

This reactionary nature also makes it difficult to place this discourse into such preset categories as liberalism or conservativism. The emergence of totalitarian thinking, from fascism to socialism to Nazism, both separated and united, leading to a process of realignment in traditional political thought. In the face of the Nazi revolution, both liberal and conservative thought took a positionalist stance, seeking to defend what they saw as valuable in the existing tradition. The idea of returning to history and tradition as a way of legitimating positions was of course inherently conservative, even though these positions were traditionally liberal, such as the ideas of the rule of law or equality. Equally, the idea that a legal order existed above and beyond the nation-state, much like the idea that there was a supranational moral order, was inherently conservative, even though that order was one based on the European traditions of Roman law or human rights.[35]

The aim of the present inquiry is to question the utility and accuracy of the common past theory by studying it as a construct with aims and means in order to dispel the illusion of inevitability suggested by the supporters of the theory. Theories of the European discovery of rights and reason have been used as a universalistic model but it will be argued that this was not the original intent of the formulators. What was intended as a defense of liberty and justice in the face of totalitarianism was only later transformed into a false universalism, the universalism of Empire in which no alternative to European liberal democracy was

[35] See, for example, the definitions of conservativism used in Jerry Z. Muller, *Conservatism* (Princeton: Princeton University Press, 1997), pp. 3–31.

accepted.[36] Instead of simply presenting a deconstruction relying on the drama of exposure, this book aims to chart a way forward in order to promote alternative discussion on the idea of the common core of European legal traditions. Through a radical reevaluation of its roots, this book seeks to show the creation of a European legal identity and legal past as processes with intentions, motives, agendas and human interaction.

## The Narratives of Exile and Return

Within the story of the exiles and those who stayed, the historical narrative itself demonstrates how nonlinear and serendipitous the sequence of events was. For example, in order to tell the story of the European legal narrative during the postwar period, we must begin in the 1930s with the crisis of Roman law. Point 19 of the (immutable) NSDAP party program of February 24, 1920 read:

*Wir fordern Ersatz für das der materialistischen Weltordnung dienende römische Recht durch ein deutsches Gemein-Recht.*

We demand substitution of a German common law in place of the Roman Law serving a materialistic world-order.

Considering that there were only twenty-five points to the program, the abolition of Roman law may be considered to have been fairly high on the Nazi agenda.[37] What Roman law in this context meant is an interesting question. Rather than being purely an ancient legal system, it was code for not only a system of law but also a methodology and a value system that was both international and conservative by nature. The Roman law tradition was a historical curiosity that had been the intellectual foundation of European legal tradition for millennia but because it contained assumptions for instance about property rights it was heavily criticized by different revolutionary movements.

36 Anthony Pagden, "Introduction," in Anthony Pagden (ed.), *The Idea of Europe: From Antiquity to the European Union* (Cambridge: Cambridge University Press, 2002), p. 11.

37 The party program was a curious mixture of elements, many of the sections being lifted directly from the Socialist party program of 1919. See Johann Chapoutot, "The denaturalization of Nordic law: Germanic law and the reception of Roman law," in Tuori and Björklund, *Roman Law and the Idea of Europe*, pp. 113–126, and Richard Gamauf, "Die Kritik am römischen Recht im 19. und 20. Jahrhundert," *Orbis Iuris Romani*, 2 (1995), 33–61.

When discussed in the general legal historical context, the narrative of crisis and renewal conceals the horrendous events that prompted the reevaluation of the European legal tradition. The emphasis on the general level equally muddles the connections and relations between actors who were often on opposing sides. While Koschaker was writing about the crisis of Roman law, at the same time some Romanists were experiencing their own personal crisis on account of their ethnic heritage and their political opinions. Fritz Schulz, Koschaker's colleague in Berlin, was ousted from his *Lehrstuhl* and eventually sought refuge in Britain. Fritz Pringsheim was likewise forced into exile, like many others. They left at the last moment, in Schulz's case taking the last boat to Britain before the war started.[38]

For others, the expulsion of their Jewish colleagues at the beginning of the Nazi regime meant career opportunities. Franz Wieacker, a young scholar of Roman law and legal history, was taken up by a group of conservative academics and recruited to the *Kieler Schule*, where Nazi scholars sought to lay the groundwork for the reform of legal education. Wieacker participated eagerly in the training program, going to camps where outdoor activities were combined with intellectual pursuits. Helmut Coing was likewise recruited to the movement, though his scholarship never showed a similar tendency to incorporate Nazi ideals. Both of them were in the army and would see frontline service during the war.

While there was great enthusiasm over the possibilities for legal reform and the notion of concrete order among the Nazi legal academia, jurisprudence did not prove to be a lasting commitment for the Nazi movement and the regime. Instead, it saw the negation of law through the declaration of the state of exception and with it the removal of all forms and formalities as the preferred way. This contradiction between reform and the reversal of law continued to be a source of contention between the movement and the legal scholars who supported it.[39]

Legal historians and Roman law scholars, like many scholars in Germany and Italy, were affected by the war years in different ways. On the extreme ends of the spectrum were those who lost their lives either as part of the totalitarian repression or fighting on the front. There were also scholars who were driven into exile; those who lost

[38] Please see later chapters for exact references.

[39] The use of the Weimar constitution's article 48 of course predated the Nazi coup, but the *Reichstag* Fire Degree and the Enabling Act in practice circumvented the legal system.

their jobs and were sidelined in academia. Then there were those who reaped the fruits of being among the up and coming generation where new professors were recruited to replace those who left or were fired. These were not clear-cut categories, of course. Wieacker, for example, enjoyed the benefits, but was then sent to fight. Coing, who was on active service throughout the war, saw his reserve unit sent to Stalingrad, he himself being saved only by a last-minute transfer to another unit. For exiles like Schulz or Pringsheim, the experience was one of social and academic demotion and alienation. All had friends and relatives who had died during the war and those who survived counted themselves as lucky to be alive. For the exiles, death in the Holocaust would have been very likely had they stayed. Those who saw active service late in the war, such as Coing or Wieacker, were also fortunate to survive, taking into account that late in the war German casualty rates reached several hundred thousand each month, the result of a complete lack of consideration given to the lives of soldiers.

There were, of course, strange occurrences. Wieacker was sent to occupied Paris in 1941 to give a lecture with Carl Schmitt about the superiority of German culture.[40] At the same time, the Nazis had proven to be enthusiastic Europeanists, though strictly on their own terms. They saw Europe as a cultural and economic entity under the dominant influence of Germany, who, they felt, had both a civilizing and an economically energizing influence. Whether Schmitt's theories on *Grossraum* are a reflection of this is unclear but it shows the connection between the world of politics and science. What the Nazi theorists saw was Europe as a bulwark against and counterweight to the menace of communism and racial impurity in the East.[41]

The long years of war, death and destruction were not idly spent. Scholars published works that were supportive of the German war effort or stridently neutral with regard to politics. The exiles worked on their integration into the new academic culture. When war ended, they all faced a new situation.

[40] Wieacker's letter on November 30, 1941, in Reinhard Mehring, *Carl Schmitt: Aufstieg und Fall* (Munich: Beck, 2009), p. 406.

[41] See Chapters 4 and 5. Schmitt's notion of *Grossraum* is quite definitely a European doctrine, but it was not reducible to the Nazi ideas. On this see Günter Maschke, "Vorwort," in Carl Schmitt, *Staat, Grossraum, Nomos: Arbeiten aus den Jahren 1916–1969* (Berlin: Duncker & Humblot, 1995), pp. xix–xxvi, and Schmitt himself: Carl Schmitt, "Die Auflösung der europäischen Ordnung im 'International Law' (1890–1939)," *Deutsche Rechtswissenschaft*, 5 (1940), 267–278.

The war ended in Europe officially with the surrender of Germany on May 7, 1945. In Italy, Mussolini was executed on April 27. This did not mean the end of violence as civilians were subjected to killings, expulsions, rape and starvation. For much of 1945 and the following years, things were still unsettled and violence was widespread. Millions of ethnic Germans were forced to leave their homes in areas that were on the wrong side of the borders in Poland, the Soviet Union and Czechoslovakia, or they fled from the occupying Soviet Army. Europe was in ruins.[42]

The end of the war found Wieacker and Coing in a POW camp, giving lectures to fellow officers at camp universities. Exiles like Schulz and Pringsheim were in Britain. Only Koschaker was in Germany. Considering the circumstances, the fact that his magnum opus *Europa und das Römisches Recht* ("Europe and Roman law") would come out in 1947, a mere two years after the war had ended, was a small miracle.

Roman law and legal history scholars were equally faced with a new reckoning. For the persons who had joined the Nazi movement or benefited from it, such as Wieacker and Coing, the bankruptcy had been both political and moral. They were suspect persons and faced obstacles in their future employment. The exiles would, some of them, return,[43] but with many the disillusionment of the return of former Nazis to positions of power and influence was great. Some, like Pringsheim, would write letters of recommendation to his former student Wieacker, helping him to be rehabilitated. Wieacker, as he had participated actively in the Nazi intellectual program, would spend the rest of his life erasing his past, sometimes even literally by replacing incriminating pages of his books in libraries around Europe (particularly *Vom Römisches Recht*) and writing denazified second editions.[44] Many, like Coing, would turn to natural law. Things looked bleak.

For the future of Roman law and its position as a source of European legal tradition, several things had to happen. One must not underestimate the political connection between Europeanism and legal history that was necessary for Western Europe to portray itself as the

[42] Keith Lowe, *Savage Continent: Europe in the Aftermath of World War II* (London: Picador, 2013).

[43] The number of returning exiles was fairly small in the sciences; in many fields of science none of the exiles chose to return. Marita Krauss, *Heimkehr in ein fremdes Land. Geschichte der Remigration nach 1945* (Munich: C. H. Beck Verlag, 2001).

[44] Compare Franz Wieacker, *Vom römischen Recht. Wirklichkeit und Überlieferung* (Leipzig: Koehler & Ameland, 1944) and Franz Wieacker, *Vom römischen Recht: zehn Versuche* (Leipzig: K. F. Koehler, 1961).

enlightened successor of the best intellectual traditions of Europe. The second factor was pure tenacity, shown by Roman law and legal history scholars enlarging the idea of the great tradition of occidental jurisprudence and linking the European legal heritage to the past and to the idealization of Roman jurisprudence. The third factor was the natural tendency of the legal sources to support such an interpretation. The fact that some interpretation was convenient, does not make it any less true. The converse is equally true, that historically truer explanations are often conveniently forgotten.

The central role of Roman law in the formation of the new narrative was partially due to its oppositional role during the Nazi years. In contrast, the study of Germanic legal history had been strongly favored by the Nazi policies, leading to it falling out of favor in the afterwar years.[45] One of the reasons why scholars such as Wieacker were so successful was their ability to combine and to bring together the two sides of German legal history.

Immediately after the war, the political situation completely changed the position of law in society. Not only had the Nazi experience demonstrated the logical end point of the totalitarian state and its utter negation of individual freedom at the expense of the Nazi movement and the *Führer*, it also presented the dangers of the totalitarian state to the free nations. While the totalitarian Nazi state had lost and was being dismantled, it was becoming clear on the Allied side that the other totalitarian state, Soviet Russia, was no less dangerous. Not only was the scale of the Soviet military force overwhelming but also the power of the communist parties believed to be directed from Moscow was considerable; they were getting 20–30 percent of the votes in many of the Western democracies. One totalitarian state was defeated, another was a growing threat to the West. The war effort had also changed the Western democracies. A more centralized government with powers to garner resources and combat dissent had been set up and it was not dismantled after the war.[46]

Thus, when we come to the creation of the great tradition, we find some common denominators. These basic tenets were shared by

[45] On the development of Germanic legal history, see Johannes Liebrecht, *Junge Rechtsgeschichte. Kategorienwandel in der rechtshistorischen Germanistik der Zwischenkriegszeit* (Tübingen: Mohr Siebeck, 2018).

[46] On the transatlantic implications of these developments, see Anne M. Kornhauser, *Debating the American State: Liberal Anxieties and the New Leviathan, 1930–1970* (Philadelphia: University of Pennsylvania Press, 2015).

scholars like Koschaker and Wieacker, whose 1952 *Privatrechtsgeschichte der Neuzeit* ("History of Modern Private Law") cemented the popularity of the interpretation. The main points were:

1) The origins of the Western legal tradition and especially the European legal tradition are in the great Roman jurists of the classical era.
2) There is an uninterrupted tradition of legal scholarship that spans from the Roman jurists to the modern European jurists.
3) There is a fundamental unity within European legal traditions due to these shared roots.

Many scholars have criticized the content of this theory, calling it a fiction, an imperialistic concoction or worse. They have noted how the theory cherry-picks suitable parts of history but as far as Europe is concerned leaves enormous areas out of the picture. I myself have called it an invented tradition seeking to justify a certain position for law and for lawyers.[47]

Unquestionably, however, the theory was a tremendous success. Romanists and legal historians succeeded in creating a shared conviction that the lineages traced to ancient Rome and its jurists were a true sign of the European heritage. Scholars like Raoul van Caenegem and Peter Stein would, like Aldo Schiavone or Mario Bretone, and most recently Reinhard Zimmermann, continue the gospel of the great heritage.

Consequently, scholars throughout Europe would search for signs of that tradition and utilize the concept of a shared heritage and themselves as the keepers of that heritage as tools for keeping themselves in business. In Eastern Europe, the teaching of Roman law was resurrected after the fall of the Soviet bloc by the early 1990s by people who managed to convince others that Roman law was a marker for belonging in the West and a connection with Western tradition. Even in Eastern Europe, historical writing turned to the European narrative.

Current scholarship has for the main part understood the common past theory to be a neutral and largely accepted statement of fact, and the criticism it faces is mainly of a nationalistic nature. What this book argues is that there is a forgotten history in the transmission and

[47] Douglas Osler, "The fantasy men," *Rechtsgeschichte*, 10 (2007), 169–192; Kaius Tuori, *Ancient Roman Lawyers and Modern Legal Ideals: Studies on the Impact of Contemporary Concerns in the Interpretation of Ancient Roman Legal History* (Frankfurt am Main: Klostermann, 2007); Pier Giuseppe Monateri, Tomasz Giaro and Alessandro Somma (eds.), *Le radici comuni del diritto europeo* (Rome: Carocci editore, 2005).

development of ideas. It is a case of a successful scientific revolution in which the supply and the demand for a theory meet. The common past theory had appeal in a number of ways even outside Europe and an important part of this book is to track the transmission from a national to an international debate, a process in which elements such as exile, language and demand play a part.

## Exiles and Innovation

In this book, exile is approached as a complex process that begins sometimes long before the person leaves the country, beginning from the initial marginalization or repression. The exiles fleeing Germany constituted a massive transfer of scientific know-how at a terrible human cost. However, this book is founded on the question whether the process of exile is also a form of knowledge production in that the events leading to exile, the experiences before, during and after, and the encounters with new ideas and the implications of ideas, led to new ways of thinking.[48]

The issue of exiles and the transmission of learning naturally has a very long history, from scholars fleeing religious persecution to rulers stamping out dissent. Scholars of course bring new ideas with them[49] but the question I raise is whether they also learn and produce new theories and combine previously unrelated ideas as a result of or prompted by the exile experience?

At the beginning of Nazi persecutions, scholars would take up different defensive strategies. Meetings with students were carefully organized, public demonstrations of opposition were avoided because they would be met with hate campaigns. Many retreated into what has been described as inner emigration or inner exile, concentrating on scholarly work that was either purely apolitical or carefully hid its message. They began using methods of analogy or, in the case of historical work,

[48] On scholarly change, see Ash and Söllner, *Forced Migration and Scientific Change*. On the transmission of scholarly excellence in law, see Ugo Mattei, "Why the wind changed: intellectual leadership in Western law," *The American Journal of Comparative Law*, 42 (1994), 195–217. On humanities scholars in exile at Oxford, see Sally Crawford, Katharina Ulmschneider and Jas Elsner (eds.), *Ark of Civilization: Refugee Scholars and Oxford University, 1930–1945* (Oxford: Oxford University Press, 2017). Much attention has been devoted to a numerically small group of exiles such as Arendt or Benjamin. See, for example, Benhabib, *Exile, Statelessness, and Migration*; Jay, *Permanent Exiles*.

[49] Peter Burke, *Exiles and Expatriates in the History of Knowledge, 1500–2000* (Waltham, MA: Stanford University Press, 2017).

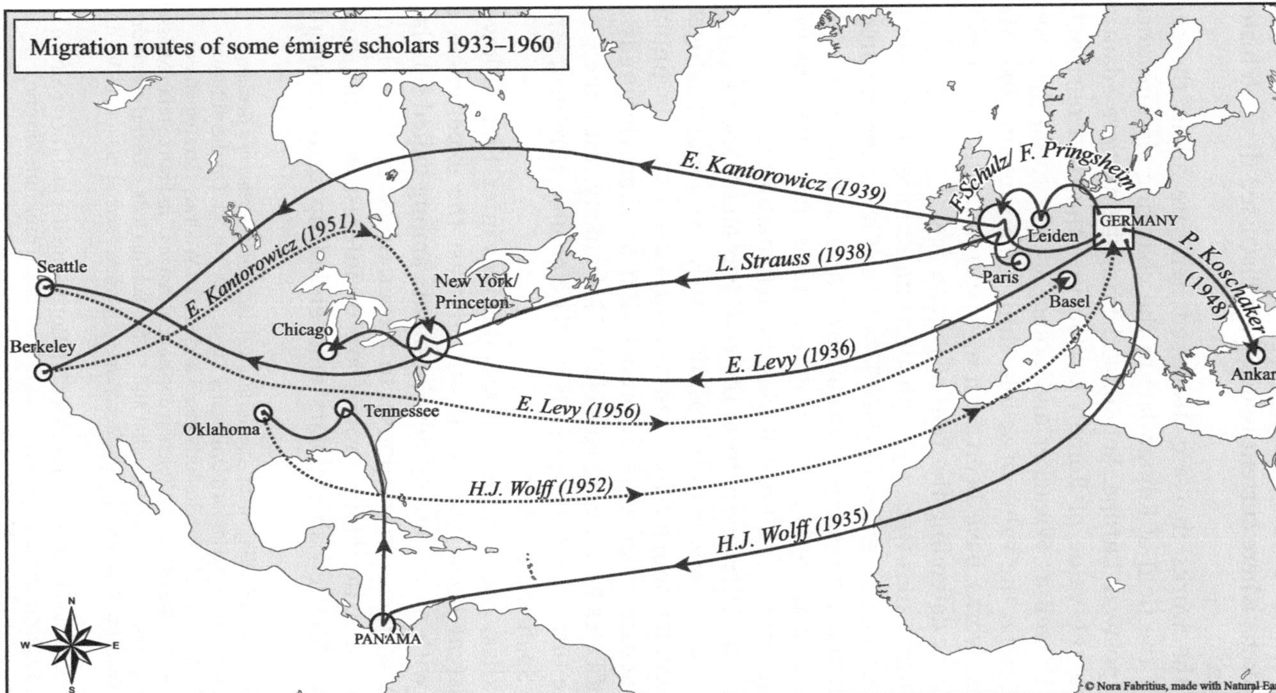


Figure 1.1 Routes taken by some exiled scholars. Nora Fabritius

a surrogate stage, where current issues were discussed through historical examples.[50]

Many of the works that are discussed here are about the self-definition of the field of Roman law in the changing circumstances of pre- and postwar Europe. Schulz and Pringsheim were adamant in defending the value of Roman law against the Nazi onslaught. Koschaker, as well as Wieacker and Coing, sought to do the same, namely to defend the value of scholarship. Even someone like Max Kaser, whose works have been seen as a surrender to Nazi ideals, may be seen as defending the role of Roman law.[51]

The scholarly exiles were not a phenomenon limited to Britain or the US. In Europe, the exiles of the 1930s joined innumerable predecessors, including exiles of the Russian Revolution or from the dissolution of empires and the founding of nation-states after 1918. The first exiles fleeing fascism and totalitarianism left Italy in the 1920s; in Spain the trickle of refugees from the civil war and Franco's purges became a flood in 1939. France, hosting nearly two million refugees from the aforementioned crises, had its own refugee crisis beginning with the evacuations of 1939 in preparation for war. Hundreds of thousands of Poles became refugees in 1939. In many cases, the seeking of refuge turned into a long exile with no chance of return, especially in the Spanish or Polish cases.[52]

Among exiles, there were innumerable destinies that followed a few consistent lines. This book will contrast the experiences of individuals with more general developments among exiled scholars to create new ideas in response to experiences in their home countries or in exile. Many groups are of interest, starting from the extremes like Jewish scholars who ended up in traditionally

[50] Steven P. Remy, *The Heidelberg Myth: The Nazification and Denazification of a German University* (New Haven, CT: Harvard University Press, 2003), p. 21. On the different coping mechanisms, see Franz-Stefan Meissel and Stefan Wedrac, "Strategien der Anpassung – Römisches Recht im Zeichen des Hakenkreuzes," in Franz-Stefan Meissel, Thomas Olechowski, Ilse Reiter-Zatloukal and Stefan Schima (eds.), *Vertriebenes Recht – Vertreibendes Recht. Die Wiener Rechts- und Staatswissenschaftliche Fakultät 1938–1945* (Vienna: MANZ Verlag, 2012), pp. 35–78.

[51] On Kaser, see Karl-Heinz Ziegler, "Max Kaser," in Horst Schröder and Dieter Simon (eds.), *Rechsgeschichtswissenschaft in Deutschland 1945 bis 1952* (Frankfurt: Vittorio Klostermann, 2001), pp. 77–98.

[52] Sharif Gemie, Laure Humbert and Fiona Reid, *Outcast Europe. Refugees and Relief Workers in an Era of Total War 1936–48* (London: Bloomsbury, 2012); Pierre Milza and Denis Peschanski (eds.), *Exils et migration. Italiens et Espagnols en France, 1938–1946* (Paris: L'Harmattan, 1994).

black colleges in the Jim Crow South or conversely exiles who became a central part of the US foreign policy machinery and the conservative establishment. In the first group, movement was from one place of violent racial oppression to another, where, in the words of one distraught scholar, the Jewish refugees "belonged not to the oppressed but to the oppressor." However, they were often able to revitalize whole departments with their energy and learning.[53] On the other end of the spectrum, émigrés who were recruited to the US state department and other foreign policy institution at the start of the Cold War were successful in carving out influential new careers and defining the US reaction toward communism.[54]

I maintain that the process of exile and innovation sometimes began long before the actual emigration. Even the ousting of professors and scholars was a long process that began in 1933 and continued until the beginning of the war. The process was closely followed abroad, with newspapers publishing lists of dismissed scholars.[55] In 1937 Edward Hartshorne attempted to calculate the exact number of dismissed scholars from full professors to assistants, coming to a grand total of 1,684 persons, of which 313 were full professors. This total number did not take into account the considerable variation between universities. In Berlin, for instance, 32 percent of the faculty had been dismissed within the first two years of Nazi rule, while in Tübingen the percentage had been only 1.6 percent.[56]

For institutions and NGOs abroad, the exiles were both an opportunity and a problem. Many institutes in the US were purely opportunistic, recruiting the best available talent. Alvin Johnson called them "Hitler's gift to American culture."[57] The Rockefeller Foundation was

[53] The recollection of Professor Ernst Manasse, reprinted in Gabrielle Simon Edgcomb, *From Swastika to Jim Crow: Refugee Scholars at Black Colleges* (Malabar, FL: Krieger Publishing Company, 1993), p. 67.

[54] Of these, the best recent work is Udi Greenberg, *The Weimar Century: German Émigrés and the Ideological Foundations of the Cold War* (Princeton, NJ: Princeton University Press, 2015).

[55] For example, *The Manchester Guardian Weekly*, May 19, 1933 contains a list of 194 professors dismissed between April and May 1933, among them celebrated legal scholars like Hans Kelsen, Kantorowicz, Walther Schücking, Guido Kisch and many others.

[56] Edward Y. Hartshorne, *German Universities and National Socialism* (Cambridge, MA: Harvard University Press, 1937), pp. 92–94. On the histories of law faculties during the Nazi era, see Eva Schumann, "Die juristische Fakultäten in der NS-Zeit," in Thilo Ramm and Stefan Saar (eds.), *Nationalsozialismus und Recht* (Baden-Baden: Nomos, 2014), pp. 39–154.

[57] Quoted in Ash and Söllner, "Introduction," p. 3.

one of the largest funders of exiles and even they were constantly worried that the supply of scholars was far outstripping demand. Even among the Jewish groups, there was concern regarding a backlash, especially the rise of anti-Semitism in the US both in the form of the Ku Klux Klan and emerging Nazi organizations in the US.[58]

There were numerous organizations that emerged to aid the refugee academics. The most important of them were the British Society for the Protection of Science and Learning, the Swiss Committee for Aid to Intellectuals and the US Emergency Committee in Aid of Displaced Foreign Scholars, while Alvin Johnson, the director of the New School for Social Research in New York, set up the University in Exile in 1933 to help refugee scholars to find meaningful work. Funding for these came in part from organizations such as the Rockefeller Foundation and the Oberlander Trust but also from donations from individuals and from the exiles themselves as voluntary contributions.[59]

However, despite the different organizations, the role of individual connections and aid from interlocutors was often crucial in helping exiles find positions in their new surroundings. Hermann Kantorowicz's introduction to his *Studies in the Glossators of the Roman Law* (1938) describes the situation well:

> When the country that I had long served to the best of my ability suddenly decided to relieve me of the burden of my official duties, it looked as if I should have to abandon my life-work as well. Then it was that, one after the other, great seats of learning, old and new, at New York, London, Oxford and Cambridge, stepped in and, with the no less generous help of the Rockefeller Foundation, enabled me to continue.[60]

Although Kantorowicz thanks only institutions, the fact that the book is dedicated to Francis de Zulueta and published in collaboration with

[58] Joseph H. Willits, from the Rockefeller Foundation's Social Science Division, wrote in June 3, 1940 that one should "take the initiative and shop for the best." Edgcomb, *From Swastika to Jim Crow*, p. 28; Ash and Söllner, "Introduction," p. 10; Erwin Panofsky, "Three decades of art history in the United States: impressions of a transplanted European," *College Art Journal*, 14(1) (1954), 7–27 describes how in art history American institutions actively recruited the best talent, some in jest remarking that "Mr Hitler is my best friend: he shakes the tree, I collect the apples." The same sentence, attributed by Panofsky to New York University's Walter Cook, is repeated in many of the recruitment stories.

[59] Horst Göppinger, *Juristen jüdischer Abstammung im "Dritten Reich": Entrechtung und Verfolgung* (Munich: Beck, 1990), pp. 215–217.

[60] Hermann Kantorowicz, *Studies in the Glossators of the Roman Law* (Cambridge: Cambridge University Press, 1938), p. vii.

William Buckland, both professors of Roman law and persons who had worked extensively to aid refugees, speaks volumes in itself.

Among the exiles there were countless experiences of life stories so multifarious that one would need to reach into the lives of émigrés from WWI and subsequent revolutions to find sufficient comparisons.[61] Professor Julius Lips, to take one example, was an anthropologist from Cologne, who after falsely being accused of plagiarism would end up in the US. He worked for a while at Columbia University, then took a job at Howard, a traditionally black university in the South. He was subsequently fired from there and finally ended up in communist East Germany as the first socialist rector of the University of Leipzig.[62]

The scholarship on exiles and totalitarianism, especially when discussing the early years of the Nazi threat, has adopted a very strong tendency to backshadow, namely projecting an anachronistic sense of impending disaster into their description of the past. This would take different forms, such as the Nazi leaders being presented as having a carefully thought out master plan for their misdeeds, and conversely the persecuted being represented as realizing too late the seriousness of the threat that we, later observers, always knew was there.[63] The contemporaries, of course, knew nothing of this future and could scarcely fathom the events taking place.

For most of the exiles in the UK and the US, the beginning of their time in exile was one of poverty and destitution. Edgcomb, a former exile herself, wrote how in the absence of scholarly jobs, most initially made do with menial jobs. Even then, it was often women who were able to find work doing household jobs and who were quicker in learning English.[64] Some were able to send children first, for instance Ernst Levy sent his daughter Brigitte and her husband Edgar Bodenheimer abroad to study at Columbia Law School in 1933, which helped his own exile tremendously because they already had good contacts within legal academia.[65]

[61] Dina Gusejnova, *European Elites and Ideas of Empire, 1917–1957* (Cambridge: Cambridge University Press, 2016).

[62] Edgcomb, *From Swastika to Jim Crow*, pp. 107–116.

[63] Noah Strote, *Lions and Lambs: Conflict in Weimar and the Creation of Post-Nazi Germany* (Yale University Press, 2017), p. 120.

[64] Edgcomb, *From Swastika to Jim Crow*, p. 23.

[65] Rosemarie Bodenheimer, *Edgar and Brigitte: A German Jewish Passage to America* (Tuscaloosa, AL: The University of Alabama Press, 2016), p. 62.

In this uncertainty and worry, like our exile examples, many other exiles were prompted to assess both the changes taking place in Germany and the nature of totalitarianism both there and in general, as well as rethink the foundations of law and society. One of the most influential émigré scholars was Franz Neumann who, along with Hannah Arendt and Leo Strauss, created a novel interpretation of totalitarian states, linking anti-Semitism with attacks on liberal democracy.[66]

One of the prime examples of personal experiences being channeled into the science of law was Hersch Zvi Lauterpacht. As a student in what was then Lemberg, currently Lviv, in the Austro-Hungarian Empire, he grew up in what was essentially a polyglot, multiethnic community. In high school, he joined local Zionist organizations and advocated pluralism and minority rights. However, the end of World War I led to conflict between Polish and Ukrainian movements seeking to reestablish their national states. This unfortunately meant that both Poles and Ukrainians considered Jews with suspicion. In November 1918, Polish troops took the city and with the help of local militias and civilians, began a three-day pogrom, killing, raping and looting as they went. 340 people were killed. Lauterpacht had attempted to organize Jewish defense squads but against the army they stood little chance. Even though the event caused an international outcry and an investigation, similar massacres continued throughout the war between Poles, Russians and Ukrainians for the following two years. Like most Jewish students at Polish universities, Lauterpacht was expelled. He continued his studies in Vienna under Hans Kelsen before taking the unusual step of doing another doctorate, this time at University College London, focusing on international law. This laid the groundwork for his meteoric rise to become the founder of modern international law that would safeguard both minority rights and human rights. Back in Lemberg, the fate of the Jewish community that Lauterpacht had sought to secure was tragic: horrendous pogroms by Ukrainians in 1941 were followed by German persecutions, leading to the death of nearly all of its Jewish inhabitants, including almost all of Lauterpacht's remaining relatives, including his parents and sister.[67] However, the connection between Lauterpacht's life experiences and his scientific career is based on

[66] For Neumann's influence, see Thomas Wheatland, "Franz L. Neumann: negotiating political exile," *Bulletin of the German Historical Institute*, 54, suppl. 10 (2014), 111–138.

[67] James Loeffler, *Rooted Cosmopolitans. Jews and Human Rights in the Twentieth Century* (New Haven, CT: Yale University Press, 2018), pp. 6–102.

guesswork because not once does he mention these events in his writing, his most famous work *Human Rights* containing the word Holocaust only in a quote in a footnote.[68]

It has been noted that in addition to Lauterpacht, there were at Nuremberg and in the fight for the post-totalitarian human rights regime a number of Jewish exile lawyers from Eastern Europe who had firsthand experience with the pogroms in the first decades of the twentieth century and whose families had been eradicated in the Holocaust. For long after the war, their personal lives were dominated by them often being the sole survivors of extended families, of whole towns or *shtetls* that had been wiped out to the last man, woman and child.[69] What this then meant for their work is a matter of personal tragedy in which individual differences are substantial. It was not without consequence that Eastern European Jewish communities had asked in vain for guarantees of their safety and dignity by appealing to the conceptions of justice and humanity.

For others, the scholarly change was prompted by the fact that the kind of scholarship they had pursued was of little or no interest in their adoptive homelands. For lawyers, this often meant a move to another field, such as comparative law or political science as was the case with Kelsen. It should be noted that the scholarly change discussed in this book was a marginal phenomenon in the field of scholarly exile or emigration research. Those who did such research were exceptional scholars who were willing to embrace new ideas and new ways of doing. To persons such as Schulz or Pringsheim, whose specialization was not in high demand in the Anglo-American world, this was the only way to succeed.

For the legal exiles, there was an added difficulty in that they were forced to change not only the language in which they wrote but also the

[68] Martti Koskenniemi, "Hersch Lauterpacht 1897–1960," in Beatson and Zimmermann, *Jurists Uprooted*, pp. 601–662, at p. 644.

[69] Michael R. Marrus, "Three Jewish Émigrés at Nuremberg: Jacob Robinson, Hersch Lauterpacht, and Raphael Lemkin," in Ezra Mendelsohn, Stefani Hoffman and Richard Cohen (eds.), *Against the Grain: Jewish Intellectuals in Hard Times* (New York: Berghahn Books, 2013), pp. 240–254. Lauterpacht himself would relate to the experience in exile when discussing Hugo Grotius and the right of resistance. He noted that Grotius was an exile in France, a victim of religious intolerance, an experience that may have shaped his views on natural rights. Hersch Lauterpacht, *International Law and Human Rights* (New York: Frederick A. Praeger, Inc., 1950), pp. 115–118.

legal culture they had been accustomed to.[70] Thus, for example, someone like Franz Neumann would have had difficulties in gaining employment as a German jurist specializing in labor law. As a consequence, many of the legal exiles would have to retrain and enter into fields such as comparative law or international law.

Future prospects also depended on where a scholar ended up. In America, there was still demand for specialists and most of the exiles would fairly soon be employed in positions sometimes more, sometimes less, suitable for their training. In contrast, in Britain the emphasis was on giving scholars grants, both to keep them occupied with scientific work and to discourage them from taking jobs from local scholars. This contrast was something that separated the settler societies and the European experience more generally. Due to the focus of this work, I deal primarily with exiles in Britain and the US. A very large number of researchers would go elsewhere, such as to Turkey, which had instituted a program to reform higher education and actively attracted German talent, but also to Spain and South America, which were popular among Southern European exiles.

There had been a rise in the level of German emigration to the US even before the war and among the very large German community a range of Nazi organizations also operated. While the exiles were often impressed by the American commitment to democracy and freedom, parts of the Nazi regime saw in the US, with its anti-miscegenation laws and racial segregation, a potential ally in the Aryan battle for world dominance.[71]

One notices in analyzing exile scholarship that while the number of scholars who consciously integrate their experience of exile into their writing is small, the number of exiles who came back to their homeland was also limited. Of the total number of roughly 500,000 German refugees, only a few returned. The highest number of returnees were

[70] Bernhard Großfeld and Peter Winship, "Der Rechtsgelehrte in der Fremde," in Lutter, Stiefel and Hoeflich, *Der Einfluß deutscher Emigranten auf die Rechtsentwicklung in den USA und in Deutschland*, pp. 183–200.

[71] There is a growing body of scholarship on Hitler's and the Nazi movement's fascination with America, its expansions and its racial policies. James Q. Whitman, *Hitler's American Model. The United States and the Making of Nazi Race Law* (Princeton, NJ: Princeton University Press, 2016); Timothy Snyder, *Black Earth: The Holocaust as History and Warning* (London: Vintage, 2015), pp. 12–16. On the organizational history of the Nazi movement in the US, see Sander A. Diamond, *The Nazi Movement in the United States, 1924–1941* (Ithaca: Cornell University Press, 1974). See also Arnie Bernstein, *Swastika Nation: Fritz Kuhn and the Rise and Fall of the German-American Bund* (New York: St. Martin's Press, 2013).

the non-Jewish "political" exiles, of which roughly half returned. Of the academics, only 12 percent returned. Of the Jewish refugees, only 4–5 percent returned.[72]

Regarding academic exiles, the rates of return varied very much based on discipline. In the hard sciences the rates were very low, in mathematics of 112 exiles only 8 returned, among biologists only 3 returned, all returning from Turkey. Of medical doctors, 5 percent returned. Regarding humanities, the numbers are somewhat larger. Of 134 historians, 21 came back in the early years, while of 122 philosophers, only 4 returned. However, these numbers do not tell the whole story as many did return to visiting positions and many of the older scholars had already retired. There were some particular cases, such as the return of the Frankfurt School, which had great symbolic value. This return also served as a demonstration of the investment that the university was willing to put into inviting exiles back to their posts and constructing a new building for the institute. Max Horkheimer even served as rector of Frankfurt University.[73]

One of the taboos relating to the return of the exiles was the constant anti-Semitism in Germany and in Europe even after the war. This was in opposition to official policies and manifested itself in both private and public interactions.[74]

If the scholarship on exiled scholars is only now beginning to reach beyond the purely biographical approach, research on scholars who stayed, accommodated and even joined the Nazis and fascists has been even more selective. For a very long time, a myth persisted that beyond a few examples to the contrary, German professors and scholars preserved their intellectual integrity during the Nazi years. This myth was created as early as 1945, when Gerhard Ritter published his influential text "Der Professor im 'Dritten Reich'" ("The Professor in the Third Reich"). In it, he maintained that scholarship had managed to maintain its autonomy from political interference and that professors were not interested in the Nazi ideology. Even when they joined the Nazi party or participated in its various administrative tasks, it was without personal conviction. The professors, he argued, sought to protect their careers

[72] Sean A. Forner, *German Intellectuals and the Challenge of Democratic Renewal Culture and Politics after 1945* (Cambridge: Cambridge University Press, 2014), p. 35; Krauss, Heimkehr in ein fremdes Land, pp. 9–10.

[73] Krauss, *Heimkehr in ein fremdes Land*, pp. 83–87.

[74] Krauss, *Heimkehr in ein fremdes Land*, p. 17.

and having a career without membership in the party was all but impossible.[75]

This line of argument became a standard and oft-repeated response. Helmut Coing, for example, uses it in his autobiography, claiming that he was explicitly told that in order to be promoted he would need to be a Nazi party member.[76] In Italy, the regime instituted an oath of allegiance, which was signed by all but twelve Italian professors.[77]

This myth was destroyed in 1946 by Max Weinreich's *Hitler's Professors.* Weinreich was an exiled linguist specializing in Yiddish, who came to New York in 1940. In his book, which was published in English, he demonstrates how the academic world eagerly took part in the creation of the intellectual foundation of Nazism and the persecutions in its midst. The transformation of anti-Semitism from a popular belief to a scientific worldview was a long process in which academics were active participants and used their scholarly credibility to further the aims of the regime. The book, however, was never translated into German, nor were its findings publicly discussed in Germany.[78]

Hence in Germany, the myth created by Ritter continued to give credence to the claims that professors were simply unenthusiastic about Nazism and the majority were not guilty of anything beyond not voicing their opposition due to the reign of terror. Those who had been active and visible participants, the likes of Schmitt or Heidegger, were singled out. The situation only really changed in the 1960s, when German students began to question the presence of former Nazis in academia. New studies began to demonstrate the extent to which academia had in fact participated in the regime, its ideology and its policies

[75] Gerhard Ritter, "Der deutsche Professor im Dritten Reich," *Die Gegenwart*, 1.1 (1945), 23–26; Remy, *Heidelberg Myth*, pp. 2–3.

[76] Helmut Coing, *Für Wissenschaften und Künste. Lebensbericht eines europäischen Rechtsgelehrten, hrsg., kommentiert und mit einem Nachwort von Michael F. Feldkamp* (Berlin: Duncker and Humblot, 2014), pp. 45–47, 56–57.

[77] On those who refused and those who did not, see the speech by Paolo Valabrega, *I dodici professori che non hanno giurato* (on May 6, 2014, at Politecnico di Torino), at https://www.swas.polito.it/services/poli_flash/foto/I%20dodici%20professori%20che%20non%20hanno%20giurato.pdf (accessed on April 1, 2019).

[78] Max Weinreich, *Hitler's Professors: The Part of Scholarship in Germany's Crimes against the Jewish People* (New York: Yiddish Scientific Institute, 1946). The book has only recently been translated into French (Max Weinreich, *Hitler et les professeurs. Le rôle des universitaires allemands dans les crimes commis contre le peuple juif* (Paris: Les Belles Lettres, 2014). While the intention of scholars in influencing the regime may have been considerable, Arendt noted in her review of Weinreich that they had little real say within the Nazi movement. Hannah Arendt and Jerome Kohn, *Essays in Understanding, 1930–1954: Formation, Exile, and Totalitarianism* (New York: Harcourt, Brace & Co., 1994), p. 201.

Despite these advances, the myth created by Ritter continued to be a widely shared conviction in Germany.[79] In the case of the legal profession itself, the myth of impartial lawyers being mostly unaffected by the Nazi regime was only destroyed only by the studies of Bernd Rüthers beginning in 1968.[80]

For the most part, the denazification of German universities was a short-lived proposition that encountered much hostility among university staff. While many exiles were recalled, those who had been appointed to fill their positions remained. This is, however, just a part of the image. After the war, although scholars who had been Nazi party members were removed from office, they still had an advantage when positions became vacant because they had had uninterrupted academic careers. Thus, for example, Koschaker would lament in 1947 that he was about to be replaced by one of two Nazis who were vying for his job.[81]

In conclusion, exile should be approached as a process in ways that encompass not only those who went abroad but also take into account phenomena such as inner exile. Psychological developments are still poorly understood as are the ways in which internal developments, trauma and people's motivations interact. What, moreover, are the issues at stake that contribute to creativity? In a similar manner, exile as a process does not begin with the boarding of a ship but also from the slow process of marginalization. Nor does exile simply end with a return, for the process of exile continues with the often very difficult adjustment of return and with reengagement with the former home country. Finally, it must be noted that exile was not simply an issue limited to the victims of Nazism, for as we will see Nazis could also represent themselves as exiles.

## Heritage and Europe

Although the idea of a shared past or common legal roots has been used as an argument for unity, as a common denominator, the question still

[79] Remy, *Heidelberg Myth*, pp. 2–3.

[80] Bernd Rüthers, *Die Unbegrenzte Auslegung. Zum Wandel der Privatrechtsordnung im Nationalsozialismus* (Tübingen: Mohr Siebeck, 2005).

[81] Koschaker to Kisch on November 27, 1947 (pp. 21–24), now in Guido Kisch (ed.), *Paul Koschaker, Gelehrter, Mensch, Freund. Briefe aus den Jahren 1940 bis 1951* (Basel: Helbing und Lichtenbahn, 1970). On the impact of totalitarianism in German legal history, see Hans-Peter Haferkamp, Jan Thiessen and Christian Waldhoff (eds.), *Deutsche Diktatorische Rechtsgeschichten? Perspektiven auf die Rechtsgeschichte der DDR. Gedächtnissymposium für Rainer Schröder (1947–2016)* (Tübingen: Mohr Siebeck, 2018).

remains what does a shared past actually mean? In discussions on history and cultural heritage, concepts such as legacy, heritage, tradition and lineage are often presented without definition or explanation. In this book I suggest that there are two aspects that should be separated: 1) the historical development where one issue is causally or culturally linked to another, for instance the reuse of ancient Roman legal sources in the later legal scholarship; and 2) the demonstration of a lineage between an esteemed earlier thing and a later phenomenon, for example to prove the value or legitimacy of the latter. What the theories of a shared European legal heritage contained was a mixture of the two, combining historical tradition with the processes of legitimating and justifying a particular choice.

The question of heritage is central to this volume, but in ways that are often contradictory. While German historical and legal thought had a strong culture of traditionalism, including the invocation of heritage and culture as legal foundations, these traditions were taken over by Nazi racial and legal theories. The crucial question is thus not the link between the theories of *Volksgeist* that were developed by Savigny and the Historical School and Nazi thought, but rather how Nazi ideology referred to the earlier tradition and sought to appeal to its supporters.

Even in early studies on the roots of Nazi ideology, scholars had established how the German revolution that Hitler sought to bring about was founded on what for example George Mosse describes as *völkish* thought. Mosse maintained that this thinking was not reducible to the past though there was a long history of the kind of popular nationalism that *völkish* thought represented. The link with nationalism and anti-Semitism was forged in the early nineteenth century in the first texts of the movement. At German universities, the influence of *völkish* thought came through two routes, one scholarly and one popular. The popular one was represented mostly by the students, who in the nineteenth century were actively hostile about the admission of Jewish students and Jews in general. Beginning at the turn of the century, incidents of student hostility toward Jewish teachers became increasingly common. In the case of the student organizations, such as the very nationalistic *Burschenschaften*, anti-Semitism had been prevalent in the nineteenth century. Thus, when the Nazi policies of official anti-Semitism were introduced, in 1934–1935 in Germany and in 1938 in Austria, the mental preparation was already in place and the ideology to a large degree accepted.[82] In addition to the mental preparation of nationalism and anti-Semitism, the influence of the ideological and practical racial practices established during the European colonial rule should not be forgotten.[83]

The move toward open racism in Germany was paradoxically one of the main factors that drove America and with it Britain to cement their commitment to ideas such as liberty, equality or the rule of law, especially after the pogroms of 1938. This was paradoxical because it was precisely the racist legal regime in the US, both the Jim Crow laws concerning political participation and the more widespread anti-miscegenation laws that served as the model for the Nazi Nuremberg laws in 1935. As James Whitman has recently noted, institutionalized racism in America was in fact too extreme and too harsh to be used against mostly assimilated German Jews in 1933–1935. For the Nazis, the US was considered to be one of the countries that had committed itself to maintaining the supremacy of the Nordic race. Against this background, the fact that Nazi policies were attacked both in the streets of New York and by Jewish magistrates and judges was met with fierce protests by the Nazi regime.[84] In a sense, while Germany was transforming from authoritarian tyranny into totalitarianism, the US underwent a move in the opposite direction, that of reinforcing its commitment to the tradition of liberty.

One of the ideas that connected early Europeanist thought and conservative ideology was the concept of *Abendland* (literally "Evening Land" or Occident, from Latin *occidens*), which signified the Western cultural sphere. Initially, the *Abendland* ideology was shared by Catholic conservative circles, who would use it to portray the values of Christian Europe. Much of the theory was a historical understanding of the classical and medieval heritage and its current relevance but politically it had a clear anti-socialist slant. Nazi propaganda would take over the conceptual basis of the *Abendland* ideology, utilizing it to broaden the basis of support

82 George L. Mosse, *The Crisis of German Ideology: Intellectual Origins of the Third Reich* (New York: H. Fertig, 1998 [1964]), pp. 191–203.

83 On this, the second part of Hannah Arendt, *The Origins of Totalitarianism* (London: Penguin, 2017) is still relevant.

84 Whitman, *Hitler's American Model*, pp. 18–21 raises the example of the *Bremen* incident of July 26, 1935 when thousands of protesters stormed the German ship *Bremen* and threw the Nazi flag into the Hudson River. Louis Brodsky, the presiding magistrate, had released the suspects and in his decision written that the swastika flag was similar to the pirate's flag in that it was antithetical to the American ideals of life, liberty and the pursuit of happiness.

for the movement. After the war, the same conservative thinkers who would see the connections between the aims of Christian conservatives and Nazism, would reinvent the ideology as a transatlantic one. In it, anti-communist thought would connect the US and European conservatives.[85]

When discussing how the European tradition was formed, a distinction needs to be made between historical events and their scholarly interpretation. The way that the same historical developments are discussed very much depends on how the author frames them. Authors who write for the European market, might well present the narrative as the history of European law,[86] while authors in the US might depict them as the Western legal heritage.[87]

All in all, one of the major issues of the conception of Europe that was utilized in early legal Europeanism was its concentration on Western Europe. The narrative focus was often on Germany and its tradition, interspersed by accounts of interactions with Italy, France and occasionally Britain. What remained invisible was the Northern and Eastern European experience.

Only quite recently has there been more debate on what the term European would mean in a legal context. Some, like Lupoi, have sought to question this narrative to negate the stigma it places on medieval scholarship and the era in general as a hiatus between two civilizations. He sought to criticize the idea of the birth of Europe as a unique event, proposing a more nuanced approach and a step back from the floral imagery of death and rebirth.[88]

The European legal narrative that our protagonists developed was hardly unique. Other contemporary authors would propose similarly grand narratives such as Kansas professor William Burdick, who in his 1938 *Principles of Roman Law and Their Relation to Modern Law* would present a global history of the reach of Roman law and its significance for common law. Other works were clearly inspired by the legal scholars

[85] Axel Schildt, *Zwischen Abendland und Amerika* (Oldenbourg: Wissenschaftsverlag, 1999), pp. 23, 27, 198. Here, there are also reflections on the contradiction between the deep German *Kultur* and more shallow European civilization that permeated German thought.

[86] Olivia F. Robinson, T. David Fergus and William M. Gordon, *European Legal History: Sources and Institutions* (London: Butterworths, 2000).

[87] Such as John E. Ecklund, *The Origins of Western Law from Athens to the Code Napoleon. 2 Vols* (Clark, NJ: The Lawbook Exchange, Ltd., 2014), which frequently cites Schulz.

[88] Maurizio Lupoi, *The Origins of the European Legal Order* (Cambridge: Cambridge University Press, 2000).

featured in this book. For example, Jolowicz's *Roman Foundations of Modern Law*, published posthumously in 1957 contains a very similar narrative and quotes Savigny frequently. Jolowicz also remarks upon the importance of Roman law in the development of European law, taking up the concept of Europe.[89]

The way in which Roman law and its role in European legal history operates is very much bound to the idea of jurists as a unified profession with its origins in ancient Rome.[90] This is a thread that connects the works of Schulz, Pringsheim, Koschaker, Wieacker and Coing.

In more recent scholarship, the narrative of Roman law that traces the development from ancient Roman jurists to German jurisprudence to modern private law is most aptly described by Reinhard Zimmermann, who has outlined the link in numerous works from the late 1990s to the present day. Zimmermann's thesis may be described as one that combines legal history and contemporary legal doctrine and thus reestablishes European legal culture.[91] For Zimmermann, law is a constitutive element and a characteristic trait of European culture.[92] This proposition was enthusiastically received in the 1990s and the early 2000s, producing a vast scholarship that sought to link Roman law doctrine and the emergence of modern European private law, a new *ius commune*. For this proposition, the crucial test was overcoming the boundary between the civil law and the common law systems, where the study of the various mixed jurisdictions became vital.[93]

Another crucial feature was the examination of jurisprudence and the long tradition stretching from the Romans to contemporary jurists. Here, instances such as legal transplants were of great interest as they could testify to the linkages between systems. In this context, critics have pointed out that the very idea of the contemporary applicability of the past runs counter to a deeper understanding of law as a historical tradition existing in its current form in a particular moment due to its

[89] William L. Burdick, *The Principles of Roman Law and Their Relation to Modern Law* (Rochester: The Lawyers Co-operative Publishing Co., 1938); Herbert F. Jolowicz, *Roman Foundations of Modern Law* (Oxford: Clarendon Press and Oxford University Press, 1957), p. 4.

[90] James Gordley, *The Jurists: A Critical History* (Oxford: Oxford University Press, 2013).

[91] Zimmermann, *Roman Law, Contemporary Law, European Law.*

[92] Reinhard Zimmermann, "Savignys Vermächtnis," in Pio Caroni and Gerhard Dilcher (eds.), *Norm und Tradition. Welche Geschichtlichkeit für die Rechtsgeschichte?* (Cologne, Weimar, Vienna: Böhlau Verlag, 1998), p. 293.

[93] On this debate, see Jan Smits, *The Making of European Private Law: Toward a Ius Commune. Europaeum as a Mixed Legal System* (Antwerp: Intersentia, 2002).

innate historical nature.[94] In a more direct form, due to the vast differences between ancient and modern social realities and relations of power, the efficacy of the guidance offered by Roman law is limited at best.[95]

Nearly all of this debate was about private law. However, much of the work on exiles focuses on rights and procedure, if not directly on public law or human rights. New work on the emergence of a European human rights regime has pointed to the centrality of human-rights language in shaping the agenda of European integration.[96]

The issue of the relationship between the present and the past, that of lineage and justification, has been central in all of these debates about Europe and its past and future. However, in most of the discussions that this book covers, it is taken as a given, with little thought about the theoretical implications beyond the debates on the nature of the reception of Roman law. In contemporary reception studies it has been noted that reception is an active process that takes place within a social and cultural context. Reception, moreover, has a purpose such as its use as an authority or as legitimation. Reception, appropriation and adaptation are all acts that are motivated by the present to interpret the past, where labels such as classical are bestowed not as descriptive but as normative labels that signify value.[97]

In the case of an extremely long historical continuum such as the idea of a European legal tradition that extends from the ancient Romans to the present day, the question is whether it is possible to say that there is a continuum and to what extent that continuum is merely a convenient vehicle for ideals. Historical epochs and stages are of course didactic tools, but they also contain value statements and normative notions of identity formation and belonging.

In spite of this, one must also remember the novelty of the turn toward Europe and the idea of a European tradition as the subject of history. From the nineteenth century onwards, historical writing became increasingly nationalized and the nation came to be seen

[94] Giuliano Crifò, "Pandettisti e storicisti nel diritto romano oggi," *Diritto romano attuale*, 1 (1999), pp. 24–27, pointing to the earlier debates about revitalizing or historicizing Roman law.

[95] Federico Spantigati, "La discontinuità nella continuità (commento a Leo Peppe)," *Diritto romano attuale*, 4 (2000), 89–94.

[96] Duranti, *Conservative Human Rights Revolution*.

[97] Lorna Hardwick, *Reception Studies* (Oxford: Published for the Classical Association by Oxford University Press, 2003), pp. 2–8.

as a natural category and thus as an actor in history.[98] It was perhaps the historical breadth of the tradition and the search for points of origin from ancient and medieval history which made it possible to circumvent nationalist instincts.

The concept of tradition as a historical concept is a curious thing. What scholars of history such as Jörn Rüsen have pointed out is that tradition is a tool of historical sense-generation in that it presents the world where despite changes there is an order that is maintained, an order which links the past and the future. Tradition presents a cultural orientation, a paradigm through which events and actions are presented with a certain reference to the past.[99] In all of the historical reinterpretations discussed in this book, what is at stake is the reinterpretation and redirection of tradition, changing what is held to be valuable and true, and what is representative of the tradition. Much like in parallel discussions about democracy,[100] historians craft a past that is suitable for the present and its needs. The past may truly be a foreign place where they do things differently but it can also be shaped to conform to the expectations of the present.

## The Outline of the Book

The book is divided into five main chapters, preceded by an introduction and followed by a conclusion. Each chapter focuses on one of the main chosen figures and sets out to explore first their narrative in its historical context and then to contextualize it and present parallel and contemporary thinkers.

Laying out the aims of the book, the introductory chapter sets out the research questions and how the book answers them. How did the idea that there was a shared European tradition of law based on liberty, legalism, the rule of law, rights and the independence of law emerge? It presents the collapse of the Weimar Republic and the rise of Nazi repression, the process of exile and the fates of my chosen scholars in exile and in Germany, setting the stage for the theoretical underpinnings of the book: the exile experience, the reformulation of the tradition of law and the reconfiguring of ideas about Europe.

[98] Breuilly, "Historians and the nation," p. 73.

[99] Jörn Rüsen, "Tradition: a principle of historical sense-generation and its logic and effect in historical culture," *History and Theory*, 51(4) (2012), 45–59.

[100] P. J. Rhodes, *Ancient Democracy and Modern Ideology* (London: Duckworth, 2003).

Chapter 2 starts with Fritz Schulz's famous principles of liberty and humanity as the foundation of Roman law and the Western legal tradition, outlining how he presents the ancient Roman legal tradition as a counterargument against Nazi legal theory.[101] From Schulz's idealization of Roman law against the Nazi politicization of law, the chapter expands on the central role of legal science in maintaining the autonomy and humanity of law. These themes are then compared with other exiled scholars such as Hannah Arendt, Franz Neumann and Arnaldo Momigliano and how they developed the idea of liberty and the influences they took from the Atlantic discourse.

Chapter 3 explores ideas of equality, cosmopolitanism and the rule of law as opposites to Nazi policies, using Pringsheim's article on Hadrian as an example of the uses of the past.[102] The chapter presents two comparisons with Pringsheim's experience, namely Franz Neumann's and his theory on the rule of law and the totalitarian state as well as Riccobono's on the fascist idealization of Roman law. By analyzing the idea of jurisprudence as a culture of shared values, the chapter builds on the roots of the ideas later presented by David Daube in postwar scholarship.

Chapter 4 starts with the themes of crisis and the discovery of the future for Roman law in Europe in the form of the common legal heritage in the seminal works of Paul Koschaker.[103] These build on the role of tradition in law and work to present a role for Roman law in the new order, first in the Nazi reign and second in the new postwar Europe. This chapter compares the conceptions of law and Europe between Nazi and fascists policies and their ideas for Roman law, the reorientation of legal education and the new role for Europe in the new order. These totalitarian visions of Europe are then compared with the ideas of other Europeanists such as the Catholic conservative Jacques Maritain or the liberals,

[101] Fritz Schulz, *Prinzipien des römischen Rechts* (Berlin: Duncker & Humblot, 1954 [1934]); Fritz Schulz, *Roman Legal Science* (Oxford: Oxford University Press, 1946).

[102] Fritz Pringsheim, "Legal policy and reforms of Hadrian," *Journal of Roman Studies*, 24 (1934), 141–153; Fritz Pringsheim, "Höhe und Ende der Römischen Jurisprudenz," in *Gesammelte Abhandlungen 1* (Heidelberg: Carl Winter & Universitätsverlag, 1961 [1930]), pp. 53–62.

[103] Paul Koschaker, "Die Krise des römischen Rechts und romanistische Rechtswissenschaft," *Schriften der Akademie für Deutsches Recht: Römisches Recht und fremde Rechte*, 1 (1938), 1–86; Paul Koschaker, *Europa und das römische Recht* (Munich and Berlin: Beck, 1966 [1947]).

socialists and communists behind the Ventotene Declaration in 1941.

Chapter 5 turns to the younger generation of scholars and the tortuous route by which they came to the idea of a European legal tradition. By looking at the opportunistic young Nazi scholars in the legal academia and their attempts at reform based on the racialized order, the stage is set for their conversion after the war. Through the works of Franz Wieacker,[104] the chapter analyzes the return to tradition and the discovery of Europe and Roman law within that tradition among German legal historians and the spread of these ideas in Europe. It discusses the role of denazification and the continuities of Nazi policies in the formation of the role of Europe in the legal culture of that time.

Chapter 6 investigates the reconfiguring of the legal tradition through the work of Helmut Coing and his idea of the tradition of rights as a jurisprudential construct.[105] This is contextualized through the rise of the rights tradition in human rights scholarship and the commitment of the new German state to democracy and rights. The chapter concludes with an analysis of the spread of the European narrative about the role of Roman law and its greatest proponents, such as Reinhard Zimmermann.[106]

104 Franz Wieacker, *Das römische Recht und das deutsche Rechtsbewußtsein* (Leipzig: Barth, 1944); Franz Wieacker, *Privatrechtsgeschichte der Neuzeit, unter besonderer Berücksichtigung der deutschen Entwicklung* (Göttingen: Vandenhoeck & Ruprecht, 1952 [1st ed.], 1967 [2nd ed.]).

105 Helmut Coing, "Zum Einfluss der Philosophie des Aristoteles auf die Entwicklung des römisches Rechts," *Zeitschrift der Savigny-Stiftung für Rechtsgeschichte: Romanistische Abteilung*, 69 (1952), 24–59; Helmut Coing, "Römisches Recht in Deutschland," *Ius Romanum Medii Aevi*, 5.6 (1964), 26–28; Helmut Coing, "Die ursprüngliche Einheit der europäischen Rechtswissenschaft," in *Gesammelte Aufsätze zu Rechtsgeschichte, Rechtsphilosophie und Zivilrecht: Band 2* (Frankfurt: Vittorio Klostermann, 1982), pp. 137–156.

106 Zimmermann, *Roman Law, Contemporary Law, European Law*.

# 2 Legal Refugees from Nazi Germany and the Idea of Liberty

## Abstract

This chapter starts out with Fritz Schulz's famous principles of liberty and humanity as the foundation of the Western legal tradition, outlining how he presents the Roman legal tradition as a counterargument against Nazi legal theory. From Schulz's idealization of Roman law against the Nazi politicization of law, the chapter expands on the central role of legal science in maintaining the autonomy and humanity of law. These themes are then compared with other exiled scholars, such as Hannah Arendt, Franz Neumann and Arnaldo Momigliano, showing how they developed the idea of liberty and what influences they took from the Atlantic discourse.

## Introduction

After the NSDAP took power in Germany in 1933, legal scholars of Jewish heritage faced ever-increasing repression, leading many to seek their fortunes abroad in exile. For most, this transfer was simply a matter of relocation, while for others the exile meant a change in the understanding of the scholarly tradition.[1]

The purpose of this chapter is to examine the emergence of the idea of liberty as a legal concept fundamental to the European tradition. To do this I will trace the scholarly change in ideas of Fritz Schulz (1879–1957),

[1] Fermi, *Illustrious Immigrants*; Ash and Söllner, *Forced Migration and Scientific Change*; Rösch, *Émigré Scholars and the Genesis of International Relations*. On exiled lawyers, see also Graham, "The refugee jurist and American Law Schools, 1933-1941"; Lutter, Stiefel, Hoeflich, *Der Einfluß deutscher Emigranten auf die Rechtsentwicklung in den USA und in Deutschland*; Breunung and Walther, *Die Emigration deutscher Rechtswissenschaftler ab 1933*, vol. 1 and vol. 2.

one of the most influential historians of Roman law and legal science, as he reacts to totalitarianism.[2] My focus is on the concepts of "liberty" and "authority" in Schulz's *Principles of Roman Law* (1936, German original *Prinzipien des römischen Rechts* 1934),[3] and the way that they delineate the relationship between legal and political order. This chapter addresses issues of individual liberties and individualism and the authorities of both the state and the private sphere. It is argued that Schulz's work should not be read only as a veiled criticism of the authoritarian Nazi state,[4] but that the discussion contains fundamental arguments of political philosophy and law. The underlying theme is the dilemma of liberty and the relationship between the individual and the state. What Schulz presents is a novel exploration of the foundations of the Western tradition of liberty in the Roman law tradition, making a connection between the German and the common law tradition of law. For Schulz, these issues were integrally connected with the role of law and lawyers. If the law was ultimately a mere expression of the will of the legislator, lawyers would be reduced to interpreters and

[2] The main biography is still Ernst, "Fritz Schulz"; other works: Giltaij, *Reinventing the Principles of Roman Law*; Werner Flume, *Fritz Schulz. Gedenkrede, gehalten bei einer von der Rechts- und Staatswissenschaftlichen Fakultät der Universität Bonn am 25.7.1958 veranstalteten Gedächtnisfeier* (Bonn: Hanstein, 1959). There is a section on Schulz in Breunung and Walther, *Die Emigration deutscher Rechtswissenschaftler ab 1933*, vol. 1, pp. 432–442. On his significance, see Gian Gualberto Archi, "Fritz Schulz," *Studia et Documenta Historiae Iuris*, 24 (1958), 451–459.

[3] Schulz, *Prinzipien des römischen Rechts*; Schulz, *Roman Legal Science*. On this book, see Giltaij, *Reinventing the Principles of Roman Law*; contemporary reviews: Heinrich Lange, "Deutsche Romanistik? Grundsätzliche Bemerkungen zu Fritz Schulz, 'Prinzipien des römischen Rechts,'" *Deutsche Juristen Zeitung*, (1934), 1493–1500; Matthias Gelzer, "Prinzipien des Römischen Rechts," *Gnomon*, 11 (1935), 1–6; Artur Steinwenter, "Prinzipien des römischen Rechts von Fritz Schulz," *Historische Zeitschrift*, 152 (1935), 115–116; Arthur Schiller, "Review of the *Principles* [et al.]," *American Bar Association Journal*, 24(12) (1938), 1015–1017; Mario Lauria, *Studia et Documenta Historiae Iuris*, 1 (1935), 219–226; A. H. Campbell in *The Times Literary Supplement* (February 6, 1937); W. L. Moll in *Virginia Law Review*, 5 (1937), 858; P. W. Duff, *The Classical Review*, 51(6) (1937), 238–239. There is also Buckland's review of both the German and the English edition in *The University of Toronto Law Journal*, 2(2) (1938), 392–393 and J. G. Lautner in *Internationalen Zeitschrift für Theorie des Rechts*, 9(2) (1938).

[4] Even the early reviewers noted the political implications of several principles. Gelzer, "Prinzipien des Römischen Rechts." On the formation and character of the German administrative system under the Nazi period, for a contemporary view, see Ernst Fraenkel, *The Dual State: A Contribution to the Theory of Dictatorship* (New York: Oxford University Press, 1940). On the Nazi law, see Michael Stolleis, *The Law under the Swastika: Studies on Legal History in Nazi Germany* (Chicago: University of Chicago Press, 1998); Carolyn Benson and Julian Fink, "New perspectives on Nazi law," *Jurisprudence*, 3(2) (2012), 341–346.

consolidators of that will. If, however, law was an expression of the legal culture, the authority of lawyers in forming law was paramount. Thus, at the heart of his argument was a fundamental concern with the authority and freedom of legal science.

The *Principles* may be seen as an example of the early influence of the exile process, where the author stands between the two traditions and attempts to make sense of the changes taking place. The book was developed through a phase of transition as the Nazis took power. In these early years of their rule it was still unclear how the new regime would transform the country, or what kind of future scholars like Schulz would face. The question is what did these turbulent and violent changes mean concerning ideas of law and justice? In order to analyze any such works written under a suppressive regime, one has to uncover the intended meaning hidden beneath the layers of subterfuge and allusions used to evade detection by the authorities.

Schulz's *Principles* has often been seen as a curious work with no real comparisons. As such, it has aroused little interest. The main scholarly contributions on it are the comprehensive biographical article by Ernst in the volume *Jurists Uprooted* (2004) and the works of Jacob Giltaij, who focuses on the reception of the *Principles* in Roman law scholarship. While most of the scholarship has recognized the *Principles* as a novel work with a strong political background, and as a statement against Nazi rule, there have also been opposing voices. For example, both Stolleis and Schermaier link Schulz's *Principles* to the literature that sought to reconcile Roman law with Nazi legal policies.[5]

This inquiry is aimed at a different aspect, namely the way that Schulz's *Principles* reflects and builds upon a fundamental legal, political and philosophical controversy of that time, the conflict between individual liberty and state authority. Through the *Principles*, Schulz

[5] Flume, *Fritz Schulz*, p. 21; Ernst, "Fritz Schulz," p. 123; Jacob Giltaij, "Fritz Schulz, refugee scholarship, and the Riccobono Seminar," *Roman Legal Tradition*, 12 (2016), 1–19; Giltaij, *Reinventing the Principles of Roman Law*; Michael Stolleis, "'Fortschritte der Rechtsgeschichte' in der Zeit des Nationalsozialismus?", in Stolleis and Simon, *Rechtsgeschichte im Nationalsozialismus*, p. 186; Martin Josef Schermaier, "'Fritz Schulz" *Prinzipien*. Das Ende einer deutschen Universitätslaufbahn im Berlin der Dreißigerjahre, in Stefan Grundmann, Michael Kloepfer and Christoph G. Paulus. (eds.) *Festschrift 200 Jahre Juristische Fakultät der Humboldt-Universität zu Berlin* (Berlin: Humboldt-Universität zu Berlin, 2010), pp. 683–700. Of the recent commentaries, Fara Nasti, "Pensiero giuridico romano e tradizione europea nei *Prinzipien* di Fritz Schulz," in Pierre Bonin, Nader Hakim, Fara Nasti and Aldo Schiavone (eds.), *Pensiero giuridico occidentale e giuristi romani. Eredità e genealogie* (Torino: Giappichelli, 2019), pp. 225–247 and Lucia Fanizza, "I Principi di Fritz Schulz," *Studia et Documenta Historiae et Iuris*, 72 (1996), 543–549 see it as a strong political act against Nazi policies.

processes the rapid changes in legal and social thought and the challenges these presented for legal academia. In the latter part of this chapter, this dilemma is contextualized through the exile experience and the ways in which it was reflected in the works of legal and history scholars. Like many other émigrés, Schulz did not leave an extant archive. Thus, much of the following is based on published works. There is, however, a selection of letters and other correspondence that pertains to Schulz.[6] Some of his correspondence has been found in the collections of their recipients.

The connecting thread through the chapter will be the ideas of freedom and authority and their implications for the relationship between law and politics. The experience of Schulz and the way in which he processed the changes facing the legal system and the science of law are juxtaposed with those of other exiles, such as the ancient historian Arnaldo Momigliano, political theorist Hannah Arendt, lawyer Franz Neumann and Roman law scholar Ernst Levy. They were all faced with the same dilemma of how to understand political freedom and liberty as a legal and a political problem after the utter destruction Nazism had left behind. In the case of Levy and Momigliano, they presented similar arguments to Schulz on the connection of freedom and republicanism and the lure of authoritarianism. For Neumann, as for Schulz, the challenge of factuality, the inclusion of real arguments into legal argumentation as done by legal scholars of the free law school of the late nineteenth century onwards to the legal realists was tied to the challenge presented by both Marxist and Nazi jurisprudence. In this debate, Schulz was an enthusiastic supporter of the independence of law from external circumstances such as political factors.

## Schulz from His *Prinzipien* to *Principles*

When the Nazis came to power and the overt persecution of Jews began on January 30, 1933, Schulz was at the height of his career. He had ascended the steps of German academia through chairs in Innsbruck (1910), Kiel (1912), Göttingen (1916) and Bonn (1923), before taking up the chair of Roman law in Berlin (1931), widely considered to be the pinnacle of an academic career. He was fifty-four years old, living

[6] This collection is currently held by Professor Wolfgang Ernst, Universität Zürich, who kindly gave the project researchers access to it.

Figure 2.1 Members of the SA parade advocate Dr. Michael Siegel through the streets of Munich in March 1933. Siegel went to the police after being attacked by Nazis, only to be taken by the SA, stripped barefoot and paraded with a sign saying "I will never again trouble the police." Siegel survived. Source: Wikimedia Commons. Bundesarchiv, Bild 183-R99542/CC-BY-SA 3.0

comfortably in Dahlem, his five children in good schools and his academic life more or less in order.[7]

Schulz's work or career up to that point had shown little signs of political involvement. He had been a member of the German Democratic Party (*Deutsche Demokratische Partei*) since 1918 but was not known for being politically active. The party was mainly progressive liberal and due to the high number of academics, such as Max Weber, among its members, it was derogatively known as the party of professors and Jews. As a student, Schulz had been taught by leading scholars of Roman law such as Jörs, Eisele and Seckel. The themes on which Schulz had published were to a large degree technical and focused on the post-classical sources of Roman law, including fragments of Sabinus and the epitome of Ulpian.[8]

[7] The biographical details have been gathered from Ernst, "Fritz Schulz"; Giltaij, *Reinventing the Principles of Roman Law*; Flume, *Fritz Schulz*.

[8] The main early works of Schulz are: *Sabinus-Fragmente in Ulpians Sabinus-Commentar* (Halle: M. Niemeyer, 1906); " System der Rechte auf den Eingriffserwerb," *Archiv für die*

The takeover of power by the Nazis meant enormous changes in the universities. Jewish teachers were harassed and threatened by Nazi mobs even at the universities, and Nazi student organizations organized lecture boycotts. The main threat to teachers was the so-called Law for the Restoration of the Professional Civil Service, enacted on April 7, 1933, which dictated the expulsion of Jewish civil servants, including university professors.[9] Schulz was a Protestant from an assimilated Jewish family from Silesia. Because his grandparents had been Jewish and his wife Martha was Jewish, he counted as Jewish according to the Nazi racial criteria that emphasized both blood relations and association in real life.

Instead of acquiescing to the pressure, during the spring semester of 1933 Schulz presented a course on the principles of Roman law, a lecture series that he soon published as a book with the prestigious publishing house Duncker & Humblot in Berlin. In a composition that otherwise appeared neutral, he presented Roman law as one of the greatest achievements of Western culture. Of the principles he outlined, many were purely technical, such as abstraction or simplicity relating to the technique of jurisprudence. Others had an intense political context that made them appear dangerously opposed to the current regime. The book was dedicated to his wife, in blatant disregard for official Nazi party policy.[10]

Public opposition like this was exceedingly rare and only very few professors would embark on this path. Even someone with full German nationalist credentials such as Ernst Kantorowicz would only manage to do this for a very short time, his famous second inaugural lecture series in 1933 being cut short by the intimidation of the Brownshirts. While Schulz spoke of principles, Kantorowicz lectured on ideals such as beauty as the true German calling. His national reawakening was a spiritual one, in opposition to the Nazis, who offered only "rabble, corpses, and vomit." For Kantorowicz, who had been a fighter not only in World War I but also in the right-wing paramilitaries during the

*civilistische Praxis*, 105 (1909), 1–488; *Einführung in das Studium der Digesten* (Tübingen: Verlag von J. C. B. Mohr, Paul Siebeck, 1916); *De claris iuris consultis by Thomas Diplovatatius*, edited by Hermann Kantorowicz (Berlin: W. de Gruyter, 1919); *Die epitome Ulpiani des Codex vaticanus reginæ 1128* (Bonn: A. Marcus und E. Weber, 1926).

[9] Law for the Restoration of the Professional Civil Service in April 7, 1933 (*Gesetz zur Wiederherstellung des Berufsbeamtentums*, GWBB, RGBl. I 175). This law was subsequently amended to include different categories such as notaries, and numerous ordinances were used to implement it.

[10] Schulz, *Prinzipien des römischen Rechts*, p. 1 readily admitted that the Romans themselves did not really talk about principles of law as their focus was different. But see Laurens C. Winkel, "The Role of General Principles in Roman Law," *Fundamina*, 2 (1996), 103–120.

Communist uprisings after the war, it was impossible to accept the rejection of the ideals of patriotism and the higher arts as a national calling that had been at the heart of the George circle.[11]

The real physical threat posed by the Nazi paramilitaries should not be underestimated. Beginning already in March 1933, capturing opponents in broad daylight, dragging them to a cellar or other SA or SS hideout to be tortured or simply beaten to death was a typical mode of operation for the Nazi gangs (see Figure 2.1). While law professors were not among the victims, several Jewish lawyers were murdered in such a way. The objective of this open violence was naturally to terrorize and to dissuade people from opposing the Nazis and their policies.[12] While these acts of street violence were common, they were not in fact encouraged by the Nazi leadership, which considered them "individual actions" comparable to the lynchings in the American South.[13]

Because of the threat of violence, it is not certain that the lectures upon which the *Principles* were based were actually held. Giltaij has noted that the lectures are not marked in the university lecture calendar, at least not under the title of *Principles*.[14] However, within academia, there was a more insidious threat, that of slow marginalization by scholars who saw academics of Jewish origin and their presence as threats to institutions. Thus, for instance, Hans Kreller wrote to Schulz in 1934 how the Savigny journal, the *Zeitschrift der Savigny-Stiftung*, should adapt to the principles of the new state and include more about the new generation.[15] The underlying message was that his participation was toxic to the future of the journal.

The politically relevant principles outlined in Schulz's work were isolation, tradition, nation, liberty, authority, humanity, fidelity and security. While the Nazi policy and jurisprudence maintained that law

[11] Robert E. Lerner, *Ernst Kantorowicz: A Life* (Princeton, NJ: Princeton University Press, 2017), pp. 159–171, quote from p. 159. That the circle would in the last years of George's life include many Nazis was also a source of distress for Kantorowicz. Lerner vehemently rejects the claims by Cantor that Kantorowicz would have in fact been a Nazi sympathizer.

[12] Göppinger, *Juristen jüdischer Abstammung im "Dritten Reich,"* p. 62.

[13] Whitman, *Hitler's American Model*, p. 82 argues that the Nazi leadership emphasized the need for an organized, centralized and properly supervised persecution.

[14] Archiv der Staatsbibliothek, Berlin, Prussian Cultural Property, AH 10100 (1932–1934), p. 18. Giltaij, *Reinventing the Principles of Roman Law*, p. 74. There are three lectures marked for Schulz in the *Vorlesungsverzeichnis*, a course on Roman legal history, exegesis of the *Digest of Justinian* and a seminar on Cervidius Scaevola.

[15] University of Zurich, Wolfgang Ernst Collection of Fritz Schulz Correspondence. 1931–1949.12: Letter to Schulz, from Hans Kreller on December 30, 1934.

was a tool for achieving political aims, Schulz stressed the indifference of Roman law to political or economic conditions (the principle of isolation). Law was an independent and self-referential science that shunned strategic thinking or political aims. While the Nazi principle was that the will of the Führer was the highest law and that law was a mere tool for advancing political purposes, Schulz stuck to the idea developed by German conceptual jurisprudence that law was an independent science.[16]

When Nazi legal theory sought to present new law as a way to achieve new ends and to brush away old structures, Schulz's Roman law was conservative and bound to tradition (the principle of tradition). Law and legal thought built upon the continuous tradition and gained its legitimacy from it. The Nazi policies of building a new state and law sought not only to remove Roman law from German legal experience, but equally to replace the BGB (the German Civil Code) with a new codification of the people's law (the *Volksgesetzbuch* project).[17]

In the case of nationality and citizenship (Schulz's principle of nation), the Nazis emphasized ethnic status, while the Romans were pointedly flexible, accepting aliens as Roman citizens on their merits. What was the most radical feature of Roman practice was the acceptance of people from the lowest ranks, namely manumitted slaves, into citizenship. This was in stark opposition to the Nazi idea of nation as a closed blood community that was determined by ethnicity or

[16] Schulz, *Prinzipien des römischen Rechts*, pp. 13–26. In addition to the works of Carl Schmitt, where this idea of law as political was repeatedly stated, it was expressed more bluntly by less refined lawyers such as Heinz Hildebrandt, *Rechtsfindung im neuen deutschen staate: ein Beitrag zur Rezeption und den Rechtsquellen, zur Auslegung und Ergaenzung des Gesetzes* (Berlin: W. de Gruyter, 1935) (tr. Benson and Fink, "New Perspectives on Nazi Law"), pp. 31–32:

> The initial point of national socialism is neither the individual nor humanity, but the entire German people; its aim is the securing and promotion of the German blood community. … The outcome of this are certain principles of law: first, the unconditional alignment of the correctness of the law with the general good and the future of the German blood community; second, the constant evaluative primacy of the correctness of law over legal security; and third, the increased acceptance of legal flexibility over legal constancy!

[17] Schulz, *Prinzipien des römischen Rechts*, pp. 57–73. The *Volksgesetzbuch* project was headed by Justus Wilhelm Hedemann, but beyond a few publications the initiative foundered during the war. In 1943 it was declared that it would need to wait until the end of the war. Justus Wilhelm Hedemann, *Das Volksgesetzbuch der Deutschen. Ein Bericht* (Munich: Beck, 1941); Hans Hattenhauer, "Das NS-Volksgesetzbuch," in Arno Buschmann, Gerhard Otte, Werner Schubert and Franz-Ludwig Knemeyer (eds.), *Festschrift für Rudolf Gmür* (Bielefeld: Gieseking Verlag, 1983), pp. 255–279.

lineage.[18] It is somewhat puzzling that these two chapters, on the principles of tradition and nation, are the ones that have prompted some to claim that Schulz had been accommodating to Nazi policies in his work and had attempted to combine the Roman legal tradition with them.[19]

In stressing the humanity of Roman law, Schulz presented a contrast with the dehumanization of non-Germans advocated by the Nazis (the principle of humanity). While, for example, the use of capital punishment was common in ancient Rome, Roman law moved continuously to restrict cruelty and inhuman punishments, emphasizing the punishment of only the guilty. The Nazi law and legal practice would, especially during the later years, be extraordinarily harsh, with capital punishment meted out for the smallest of offenses. However, this was nothing compared with the treatment of individuals who did not enjoy the protection of the law.[20] The operation of the legal machinery became increasingly perverted, and the fundamental protections of law and the principles of law were explicitly abandoned.[21]

Equally, the nonretroactivity of law was raised as opposed to the retroactive laws enacted by Nazis (the principle of fidelity). Here Schulz proposes that the rule encompasses two important tenets of the rule of law: First, that the magistrate is bound by the law, even to the rule he has himself set, and second, that law has no retroactive force. Nazi jurisprudence would oppose such formal rules, maintaining that officials should have free range of operation. However, fidelity even encompassed the binding nature of the social ties of friendship, a theme that had unfortunate importance in the ways that adherence to the new regime led to the abandonment of old friendships.[22]

The final principle was the security of the law, which was naturally a way of criticizing the terror of Nazi rule (the principle of security).

[18] Schulz, *Prinzipien des römischen Rechts*, pp. 74–94. The idea behind the law of the blood community was that the innate sense or feeling of law should be supreme.

[19] Schermaier, "'Fritz Schulz' *Prinzipien*."

[20] Schulz, *Prinzipien des römischen Rechts*, pp. 128–150; Franz Leopold Neumann, *Behemoth: The Structure and Practice of National Socialism, 1933–1944* (London: Rowman & Littlefield, 2009), pp. 452–458. On Roman law and humanity, see Luigi Garofalo, "L'humanitas tra diritto romano e totalitarismo hitleriano," *Teoria e storia di diritto privato*, 7 (2015).

[21] Robert D. Rachlin, "Roland Freisler and the *Volksgerichthof*," in A. E. Steinweis and R. D. Rachlin (eds.), *The Law in Nazi Germany: Ideology, Opportunism, and the Perversion of Justice* (New York: Berghahn Books, 2013), p. 80.

[22] Schulz, *Prinzipien des römischen Rechts*, pp. 151–161. The extreme threat of Nazi oppression meant that people would frequently abandon friends and relatives when they were singled out for persecution.

What this entailed was that law should be predictable, give adequate protection, and that the courts that applied it were knowledgeable and impartial. The Nazi law and legal practice would operate largely based on general principles, where individual acts were seen as violations of a principle and punishable simply on those grounds. The concept of security was equally valid as a reference to the freedom of opinion and the possibility of teachers and officials fulfilling their duties without being threatened or molested.[23]

One of the important features of the Nazi machinery of terror was the unofficial pressure that street fighters and storm troopers could put to bear (see Figure 2.1), ejecting judges and magistrates from their offices and preventing professors from holding lectures. Not only Nazi street fighters, for Nazi students were also a threat. Lecture boycotts were organized regularly against Jewish professors, and public signs of opposition from rectors and other university authorities led to dismissals. From April 1, 1933 onwards, the Nazi student organizations vowed to post guards to warn students from entering lecture halls where a Jew would be teaching.[24]

All of this is, of course, purely hypothetical. Schulz never alludes to the political circumstances of Nazi rule, nor does he make direct references beyond a reference to "recent political experience" in the conclusions of the book (1934, p. 172; 1936, p. 253). Even in the early days of Nazi rule, that would have been unwise and dangerous. Instead, what it presents is a veiled criticism, a fundamental condemnation of the Nazi legal policy in the guise of an analysis of Roman law. One should not on the other hand make the mistake of assuming that the book was not about Roman law but rather that it operated (at least) on two levels: on the level of ancient Roman law and level of the role of law in contemporary society. The references in the book are clear indications of the different ways in which Schulz addresses his diverse audiences: There are purely Romanistic references to research literature; there are references to Anglo-American legal literature, and a surprising number of references to social scientific works; there are even references to Nazi

[23] Schulz, *Prinzipien des römischen Rechts*, pp. 162–171. The Nazi sense of legal security was also based on the sense of law shared by the blood community, for example Hermann Göring, *Die Rechtssicherheit als Grundlage der Volksgemeinschaft* (Hamburg: Hanseatische Verlagsanstalt, 1935), wrote how law should not be founded on the letter of the law or even on law itself, but rather an innate sense of law; Neumann, *Behemoth*, pp. 440–450.

[24] Göppinger, *Juristen jüdischer Abstammung im "Dritten Reich,"* p. 193.

and Fascist authors. Thus, Schulz may refer to his colleague Carl Schmitt (both in Bonn and in Berlin), but equally to Max Weber or to Benjamin Cardozo. Whether Schulz writes in code, so to say, or what were his true intentions are to a large degree beyond our knowledge because he does not discuss the issue in his writings. However, what is beyond dispute is that contemporaries read the book as a defense of law in general and Roman law in particular against the political attacks of the time.[25]

In the following, I will focus on two particular principles, liberty and authority due to their centrality to the political and legal developments.

## Liberty and Authority in Their Two Contexts

The concepts of liberty and authority are fundamental to the European traditions of law and politics, as they have been since the Greek and especially Roman classical tradition. Liberty or freedom could mean the freedom of the individual from interference from either the state or other individuals, while authority could refer to public power wielded by the state and its magistrates, if necessary by coercing individuals and limiting their freedoms. Schulz presents the two as a pair, principles that are integrally joined in their understanding and execution. For him, the extreme individualism and liberalism of Roman law was possible only in conjunction with the unquestioned power of the *paterfamilias* and the magistrate.

The concept of liberty was used both constitutionally and in private law. Schulz begins his exploration with the Roman political concept of *libertas* as an overarching constitutional principle. According to Schulz, "the individual was not free when he was a slave, a whole nation was not free when at its head was an absolute monarch or when it was subject to a foreign yoke" (p. 140). The political idea of *libertas* was thus expressed through a negative, the lack of outside domination that would privilege both the *libera res publica* and the free Roman citizen. This freedom was not so much a factual one, but a legal definition, as it depended not on the economic dominance or participation of the citizens in government, but rather on the formal freedom possessed not only by the citizens, but equally the "free" cities and communities.

25 Oxford University Press Archives, Oxford, Schulz PB ED 010384, 28, letter of F. H. Lawson to K. Sisam on June 25, 1935: "professor Radbruch of Heidelberg told me that only a German could appreciate how acute and bold an answer the book is to popular attacks on Roman law."

What Schulz underlines is that Roman constitutionalism could appear hypocritical to outsiders.[26] For the Romans themselves, however, this freedom was fundamental.

In Roman private law, classical law placed little constraint on the individual: "The Roman principle of liberty led to extreme individualism in the domain of private law" (p. 146). The state did not intervene in areas such as marriage, where the freedom of partners was considerable, including the maintenance of separate properties. The Roman law of *societas*, including partnerships, communities and such, sought to limit joint obligations and to dissolve them if conflict arose. Similarly, Schulz writes how joint ownership was considered an abnormality. Ownership rights were as a rule unlimited, whereas duties and restrictions were minimal. Similar ideas governed the law of succession.[27]

In general, the rule that Schulz outlines is that the principle of liberty was observed both in the relationship between individuals as well as between the individual and the state. The principle of non-interference was applied not only in the private rights of individuals (such as ownership rights), but also in the way that freedom of religion, and freedom of expression and movement were respected. However, these freedoms were not really guaranteed constitutionally, but rather realized through restraint (pp. 159–163).

While Schulz does not mention either fascism or Nazism, the implications were obvious. What he does mention is the radical nature of Roman liberty even in the earlier European context. He states that the Roman lack of limitations to ownership rights is in stark contrast to the way that land ownership was limited in Germany, Austria and France up to the agrarian laws enacted at the end of the eighteenth century (pp. 154–155). This was in fact one of the reasons why supporters of Germanic law opposed Roman law. However, even later on Roman liberalism was unparalleled. In a curious construction in referring to authority, he quotes Max Weber quoting Theodor Mommsen *c.*1848. Mommsen, who was active in the liberal revolution of 1848, wrote then that the liberty accorded by Roman law and its refusal of solidarity is so great that its application in modern-day Europe would be equivalent to a revolution.[28] In another name dropping of note, he quotes

[26] Fritz Schulz, *Principles of Roman Law* (Oxford: Oxford University Press, 1936), pp. 141–146 relates this to the debates over the position of the emperor since Augustus, and the conscious avoidance of the terminology of dominance.

[27] Schulz, *Principles of Roman Law*, pp. 146–157.

[28] Schulz, *Principles of Roman Law*, pp. 157–158, referring to Max Weber, *Wirtschaftsgeschichte* (Berlin: Duncker & Humblot, 1924), p. 292. Weber was, of

Burckhardt a few pages later on the general tendency of "the men of our race" to demand "an undisturbed home and an independent domain of thoughts."[29] This was an almost British statement of the unassailable right to privacy and the individual sphere of freedom.

What the principle of liberty meant in the Nazi context was another thing entirely. Nazi legal thought was in principle opposed to the individual freedoms in both private and public law, approaching them through the state. Individualism and liberalism were both antithetical, and political freedoms were subjected to the state. Nazi and Fascist thought urged the state to interfere in social issues, in marriages and in relations between individuals. Though it often framed its opposition to freedoms and rights as an opposition toward the ideas of the Enlightenment, there was a second, realist trait to the equation. This was the quasi-Marxist idea of false equality and freedom in the capitalist state that influenced especially earlier fascist and Nazi thought. Instead of freedom, the promise of Nazi policies was to ensure the dignity of the German people and to secure the position of workers (see Figure 2.2).[30] Thus, it was logical that Carl Schmitt would praise the Nuremberg laws as being the constitution of freedom, a law that would return "German blood and German honor" to the center of the legal order instead of the false equality of German and alien.[31] The

course, intimately aware of the agrarian history and the work of Mommsen, who was one of his supervisors and a friend of the family. On Mommsen, Weber and the classics, see Luigi Capogrossi Colognesi, *Le radici della modernità, Max Weber 1891–1909* (Rome: La Sapienza Editrice: 1997, 2nd ed.); Marianne Weber, *Max Weber, ein Lebensbild* (Heidelberg: Verlag Lambert Schneider, 1950).

29 Schulz, *Principles of Roman Law*, p. 160, quoting from Jacob Burckhardt, *Griechische Kulturgeschichte I* (Berlin: Spemann, 1898, 4th ed.), p. 81.

30 James Q. Whitman, "On *Nazi Honor* and the New European Dignity," in Joerges and Ghaleigh, *Darker Legacies of Law in Europe*, pp. 243–266; George L. Mosse, *The Fascist Revolution: Toward a General Theory of Fascism* (New York: H. Fertik, 1999).

31 Carl Schmitt, "Die Verfassung der Freiheit," *Deutsche Juristen-Zeitung*, 40 (1935), 1134:

> For centuries, instead of freedom the German people had only liberties or liberalism. The liberties of the German constitution of the seventeenth and eighteenth centuries guaranteed the national disunity of our people to beneficiaries of this sad state in domestic and foreign politics. The liberal freedoms of the constitutions of the nineteenth century were used by the international powers to elevate the religious and class disruptions of the German people to a basic right. Thus constitutional freedom became a weapon and motto for all Germany's enemies and parasites. But we have seen through this deception. We have realized that liberal constitutions become typical camouflages for foreign domination. A people can have the most liberal constitution in the world and still be but a herd of rent and wage slaves. And a constitution can, as is our experience today, be notorious and ridiculed as medieval by all of international liberalism and Marxism, and in that very way give evidence that a people has found its own way and freed itself from foreign spiritual domination.

Figure 2.2 “Paragraphs against freedom fighters” and “Justice is ours, yours is the law.” Published in the Nazi paper *Der Angriff* (The Attack) in 1928. Picture by the author.

language of freedom and honor dominated the official Nazi ideas of the foundation of the nation but the circle of the beneficiaries of these ideals was limited to the members of the community.[32] Ernst Forsthoff wrote in his famous *Der Totale Staat* (1933) that the whole point was to negate the focus on the individual and the ideas of liberalism and the rights of the individual.[33]

Translation from Arthur J. Jacobson and Bernhard Schlink, *Weimar: A Jurisprudence of Crisis* (Berkeley: University of California Press, 2000), p. 324.

32 See, for example, the statement of Hermann Göring, January 30, 1933, quoted in Strote, *Lions and Lambs*, p. 119.

33 Ernst Forsthoff, *Der Totale Staat* (Hamburg: Hanseatische Verlagsanstalt, 1933). It has been noted that Schmitt’s influence in Forsthoff’s theories was considerable.

Regarding the principle of authority, Schulz maintains that the almost extreme freedom granted to the Romans in private law and constitutional law was balanced by the almost equally extreme authority that was given to both the *paterfamilias* and the Roman magistrate.

Schulz begins with the authority of the state to develop rules and enforce them. The state was "so liberal in granting and protecting the freedom of the individual, never omitted to uphold the principle of authority; and truly, individual freedom is impossible in the long run without authority" (p. 165). The *auctoritas* of the political system was guaranteed through the internalized discipline embodied in the *mos maiorum*.[34] For many of the scholars attempting to reconcile Nazi ideology and the Roman political and legal system, this type of militaristic authoritarianism was a very tempting basis for making parallels between the Roman and German cultures.[35]

The Roman *paterfamilias* enjoyed a similar unquestioned position of authority but the nature of that arrangement was that this authority was used with utmost restraint: "The very nature of authoritative government demands that its boundaries shall be as wide as possible, that wide space shall be accorded to the discretion of the person in authority, and that judicial control of its exercise shall be excluded or restricted. Roman law carried out this principle with ruthless exactitude" (pp. 165–166). This, naturally, refers to the *ius vitae necisque*, the power of the *paterfamilias* over the life and death of the members of the *familia*. Of course, in the Roman setting the autonomy of the *familia* meant that the jurisdiction of the state was until quite recently restricted to matters between the families.[36]

What limits there were to the use of that authority were primarily procedural. While the *paterfamilias* could in theory put to death a person

Florian Meinel, *Der Jurist in der industriellen Gesellschaft: Ernst Forsthoff und seine Zeit* (Berlin: Akademie Verlag, 2011).

34 On the *mos maiorum* as a legal term, see Jochen Bleicken, *Lex publica: Gesetz und Recht in der römischen Republik* (Berlin and New York: de Gruyter, 1975). On how *mos maiorum* constantly changed, see Andrew Wallace-Hadrill, "*Mutatio morum*: The Idea of a Cultural Revolution," in T. Habinek and A. Schiesaro (eds.), *The Roman Cultural Revolution* (Cambridge: Cambridge University Press, 1997), pp. 3–22.

35 There were numerous cases where authors sought to present Roman law and history as compatible with Nazi ideology. See, for example, Max Kaser, *Römisches Recht als Gemeinschaftsordnung* (Tübingen: Mohr Siebeck, 1939).

36 On the private jurisdiction, see Matthew Perry, "The *Paterfamilias* and the Family Council in Roman Public Law," in Kaius Tuori and Laura Nissin (eds.), *Public and Private in the Roman House and Society* (Portsmouth, RI: Journal of Roman Archaeology Supplement Series, 2015), pp. 77–86.

under his power, the decision needed to be made with the judicious use of council. The *consilium* had no power but their authority and they could not prevent a decision.[37]

According to Schulz, the relationship between the citizen and the state and its magistrates followed the same principle. Since the magistrates were from the ranks of the elite, they had at the outset the *auctoritas* and social standing of their background, and through the *cursus honorum* they gained further authority. The central role of the magistrate was reinforced by the way that procedure took place in the assemblies, where the only one allowed to speak was the magistrate. The magistrates had an equally wide individual jurisdiction, which was only partially limited by the theoretical possibility of appeal.[38]

From the limited position of the authority of the magistrate, the authority of the Senate was different as it was both long lasting and overarching. Similarly, the authority of the law and the jurist were both dependent on recognition by the public. These shared a trait that they were not so much providing an ability to command but rather the shared conviction that these were people whose opinions should be listened to.[39]

However, the authority of the *princeps* was qualitatively different, one that Schulz describes as charismatic authority as defined by Weber. Though this authority began as the personal charisma of Augustus, it was later transformed into an institutional charisma.[40] The main reference in the later discussions over *auctoritas* was the use of the concept in Augustus' *Res Gestae* and how *auctoritas* formed the basis for the overarching authority of the emperor in the Roman world.[41]

Schulz's main point about authority and freedom is that they existed in a mutually reinforcing relationship. For Schulz, this "original yet simple system" (p. 187) was the cornerstone of the Roman state, one that was peculiarly Roman and beyond the grasp of outside observers.

[37] Schulz, *Principles of Roman Law*, p. 168.

[38] Schulz, *Principles of Roman Law*, pp. 172–179. Schulz had an ambivalent relationship with the disputed right of *provocatio*, especially Theodor Mommsen's interpretation. On the modern interpretations, see Judy E. Gaughan, *Murder Was Not a Crime: Homicide and Power in the Roman Republic* (Austin: University of Texas Press, 2010), pp. 56–59.

[39] Schulz, *Principles of Roman Law*, pp. 180–187.

[40] Schulz, *Principles of Roman Law*, pp. 181–182.

[41] Res Gestae 34.3. Post id tempus auctoritate omnibus praestiti, potestatis autem nihilo amplius habui quam ceteri, qui mihi quoque in magistratu conlegae fuerunt. On the interpretations, see Edwin S. Ramage, *The Nature and Purpose of Augustus' "Res Gestae"* (Wiesbaden: Franz Steiner Verlag, 1987), pp. 43–54; Lucia Fanizza, *Autorità e diritto. L'esempio di Augusto* (Rome: L'Erma di Bretschneider, 2004), pp. 51–56.

The Roman citizen recognized and accepted authority as belonging naturally to the arrangement of the political community.

What makes Schulz's analysis interesting is not the way that different authorities were described as they do not deviate excessively from the standard scholarship of the day. What is unusual is the references that Schulz makes. Not only does he refer to people like Goethe or Max Weber but he also notes Carl Schmitt's *Verfassungslehre* as well as Biondo Biondi's *Romanità e Fascismo* (p. 164). When discussing state authority, he refers to both Savenkouls' study of the English cabinet system and Ziegler's *Autoritärer oder totaler Staat* (p. 168). While Schmitt and Biondi were key players in the Nazi and fascist academic worlds, Ziegler was an exile from the Nazis, who fled first to Prague and then to Britain.[42]

What the complicated background hides is the interesting composition of the way in which political and legal authority would be joined. This combination of sources from the opposing sides of the political spectrum was very typical of Schulz's approach in the *Principles*. Carl Schmitt was not only the self-proclaimed intellectual leader of the Nazi legal academia, he was also Schulz's colleague both in Bonn and in Berlin and they were in contact.[43] This tendency of using sources from different sides of the political spectrum would lead to his audience becoming more diverse and, one may assume, his criticism being lost on some. For example, showing how even a Nazi might be oblivious to the criticism. For example, J. W. Hedemann wrote two laudatory letters to Schulz about the *Prinzipien* after receiving a copy from the author, something that he may not have done if he would have expected the work to contain criticism of the Nazi movement and its ideals.[44] Schmitt's intent was of course the dismantling of the liberal state that had descended into the stale formalism of the *Rechtstaat* while pretending at the same time to protect individual liberties. Of these examples, Biondo Biondi's 1928 inaugural lecture is more interesting as Biondi takes up a fairly similar notion of the relationship between liberty and authority as Schulz. According to Biondi, in Rome the freedom of the

[42] In Britain, Heinz Otto Ziegler (not to be confused with the German general of the same name) would join the RAF and die on a combat mission late in the war.

[43] Mehring, *Carl Schmitt*, pp. 141, 332, 356.

[44] Hedemann's letters to Schulz on July 13, 1934 and on August 27, 1934, University of Zurich, Wolfgang Ernst Collection of Fritz Schulz Correspondence. Giltaij, *Reinventing the Principles of Roman Law*, writes how many of the Nazi sympathizers did not seem to detect the aspect of criticism (pp. 50–53).

individual is not curtailed by some general public will, but rather the very precise forms of a magistrate's authority. Thus only with the fulfillment of authority is true freedom possible. This explained why in their long history Romans would never rise in revolution to demand liberty.[45]

The principles of authority and liberty operated in two quite different contexts, the ancient Roman and the modern European. How Schulz weaves the combination of the two is both skillful and cunning, framing the Roman discourse of liberty and its radical nature as a diametrical opposite to the Nazi ideas of liberty as the freedom of the nation and not that of the individual. For Schulz, Roman individualism is tempered by the authority of the state, the Senate and the magistrate but their relationship was one of mutual reinforcement. In the linkage to modern European discourse, Schulz employs the tenets of classical liberalism and the British tradition, forming the connection between liberty and law that would become central in postwar discussions on the European legal heritage. In a curious way, Schulz presents a conservative defense of the liberal tradition.

## Liberal Theory and the European Heritage?

The way Schulz presents the dualism of liberty and authority can be translated not only into a criticism of the Nazi legal policy, but also into a more nuanced argument over issues related to individualism and sovereignty. The question of liberty and authority may be considered the fundamental question of Republicanism. Thinkers like Machiavelli considered liberty to be an innate quality of a community, one that once imbued could not be dispelled. This theory of liberty was about the liberty of the community against tyranny, just as the Roman state was liberated from kingship and was free to elect magistrates to govern itself. Others, like Hobbes, considered liberty to be an individual's prerogative, and, as Quentin Skinner notes, for Hobbes "where law ends, liberty begins" and "Liberty is the silence of the law." What all of these notions have in common is that the issue of liberty vs. authority consists of a relationship between the individual and the state and the capacity of the individual to enjoy civil rights. Of course, both of the traditions, the freedom of the state or the freedom of the individual, had a Roman

[45] Biondo Biondi, "Romanità e Fascismo," *Annuario della R. Università degli Studi di Catania*, 7 (1929, repr. 2001), pp. 760, 762.

foundation. What was not Roman (or even Machiavellian) was the conception of individual rights against the state.[46]

The traditional political thought that Hobbes represents can be seen as presenting a negative concept of freedom, one that is defined by a lack of constraints or domination. That is, naturally, a view that Roman law might be construed to support. The Roman concept of liberty was at its foundation Republican, one based on the idea of nondomination. As Schulz underlines, being free was being free of the domination of others, such as the domination of a slave by his master. Of course, Hobbes developed this idea of liberty as noninterference through the introduction of the natural and civil rights that limit the individual without oppressing him or depriving him of his liberty.[47]

The modern theories of liberty continued to examine the way that liberty and authority were balanced. John Stuart Mill would in *On Liberty* famously raise the rights of citizens as well as constitutional checks as vital limits to the authority or tyranny of government. Mill's work would exert an enduring fascination on exiles in the years to come. Arnaldo Momigliano, a fellow exile, would speak about liberty in the ancient world in Oxford and when he was interned on the Isle of Man when Italy joined the war, among his possessions was this very book.[48]

Mill's work continued the notion of individual liberties being the foundation of the modern conception of freedom. Benjamin Constant, in his famous speech, "The Liberty of Ancients Compared with that of the Moderns" (1819), distinguished ancient and modern types of liberties, comparing the ancient Greek and Roman political community with modern society. According to Constant, the prime difference was that ancient liberty was the liberty of the community, whereas modern liberty was the liberty of the individual. In the first, the individual would have the freedom and expectation to participate in political life, whereas

[46] Thomas Hobbes, *Leviathan* (Oxford: Oxford University Press, 1996), chapter 21, p. 152; Quentin Skinner, *Liberty before Liberalism* (Cambridge: Cambridge University Press, 1998), pp. 5, 9, 17–18, 45; John G. A. Pocock, *The Machiavellian Moment* (Princeton, NJ: Princeton University Press, 1975); Philip Pettit, *Republicanism: A Theory of Freedom and Government* (Oxford: Oxford University Press, 1997).

[47] Hobbes, *Leviathan*, chapter 21, p. 153; Quentin Skinner, *Visions of Politics III* (Cambridge: Cambridge University Press, 2002), p. 221.

[48] Oswyn Murray, "Arnaldo Momigliano on Peace and Liberty," in Crawford, Ulmschneider and Elsner, *Ark of Civilization*, p. 204, tells the story that when Momigliano reported to the police station at Oxford, he was asked to empty his pockets and out came a copy of Mill's *On Liberty*.

modern freedom would leave the individual the choice of retreating into private life, protected by constitutional guarantees and the rule of law.[49]

Schulz's vision of authority and freedom was one of conservative ideas, that of the permanence of order and the space it allowed for the individual. He had little appreciation for the radical visions of human rights that still reflected the understanding of revolutionary Enlightenment ideals. It could be even said that Schulz depicted, consciously or unconsciously, a reflection of the British liberal tradition, one of continuity and tranquility. Schulz's style was idiosyncratic and his way of presenting his argument carried multiple layers. Though in German philosophy from Kant and Hegel to Schelling there was a very strong tradition of discussing liberty, very little of that influence is notable in Schulz. In the legal philosophical tradition, he placed himself and the *Principles* in a continuum reaching back to Jhering and Savigny. However, in the chapter on liberty there is no reference to Savigny, nor does the focus on principles compare with the more conceptually inclined Historical School of their followers.[50]

There is a clear connection between Schulz's and Jhering's discussion of liberty.[51] Jhering's *Spirit of Roman Law* (*Geist des römischen Rechts*, 2 vols., 1852–1865) discussed at length the principle of liberty as a balancing act between individual freedom and the collective purpose.[52] However,

[49] Benjamin Constant, "The Liberty of Ancients Compared with that of the Moderns," the original *De la Liberté des Anciens Comparée à celle des Modernes* was a speech held in 1819 in Paris. Translation in Benjamin Constant, *Political Writings*, translated and edited by Biancamaria Fontana (Cambridge and New York: Cambridge University Press, 1988).

[50] On the influences of Schulz, see Giltaij, *Reinventing the Principles of Roman Law*. The idea of freedom was central in the works of Savigny, where the sphere of individual freedoms is demarcated by where they do not infringe on the freedoms of others. See Friedrich Carl von Savigny, *System des heutigen römischen Rechts*, vol 1 (Berlin: Bei Veit und Comp., 1840), pp. 331–334. Schulz's inherent conservatism was noted already by Antonio Mantello, "La giurisprudenza romana fra Nazismo e Fascismo," *Quaderni di Storia*, 13(25) (1987), 23–71.

[51] Giltaij, *Reinventing the Principles of Roman Law*, pp. 23–25. Schulz also mentions the inspiration of Jhering in the introduction. Schulz, *Prinzipien des römischen Rechts*, p. 1.

[52] Rudolf von Jhering, *Geist des römischen Rechts auf den verschiedenen Stufen seiner Entwicklung. Teil 1–2* (Aalen: Scientia, 1993), vol. 2, p. 24. The connection with Jhering was significant also because there was a recurring interest in Jhering among Nazi and fascist authors, who sought to trace their own lineage to him. See Antonio Mantello, "L'immagine di Jhering fra nazionalsocialismo e fascismo: analisi d'una vicenda ideologica," *Index: quaderni camerti di studi romanistici = international survey of Roman law*, 23 (1995), 215–250, especially pp. 234–236 on Jhering's concept of freedom.

even more noteworthy is the way that Jhering's discussion on juristic freedom and independence is picked up in Schulz.

What was clear was the way that Schulz's ideas would reflect the entanglement of the European tradition in the roots of the Roman tradition of liberty. Both the tradition of the free state and the tradition of the freedom of the individual were based on Roman sources, the first on the reading of Livy's account on Roman constitutionalism, the second on the emphasis in Roman law on individual freedom. Hobbes would write that ancient texts were like the poison in the bite of a mad dog, whose readings could launch revolutions by corrupting contemporary thought.[53]

Schulz's *Principles* were clearly written to multiple audiences, not only the German or European Roman law community, but equally to the general legal community. It makes clear references to both the liberal tradition and to totalitarianism as its negation, juxtaposing Nazi ideals with the tradition of Roman law. The reception of the *Principles* was mixed, receiving much praise from sometimes unexpected directions, even Nazi scholars writing positive responses. Giltaj, in his analysis of the letters that Schulz received after the publication, notes that the book was read widely even beyond the narrow circle of Roman law scholars.[54]

The relationship between Schulz and liberal theory and its different strands of definitions of liberty is difficult to define because the multi-layered argument that he presents does not really belong to a particular school of thought but rather combines elements that come from various directions. The clear foundation was formed by the classical conception of liberty as expressed through the negative; liberty was nondomination. However, the idea of liberty was equally seen as that of a community, namely liberty from foreign domination. In this sense, Schulz's liberty drew not only from the background of Roman constitutionalism but equally from the classical liberalism of the nineteenth century.[55]

[53] Hobbes, *Leviathan*, chapter 29: "Venime" comparable "to the biting of a mad Dogge." It should be noted that he was specifically discussing the influence of Aristotle.

[54] Giltaij, *Reinventing the Principles of Roman Law*, pp. 39–59. There were in total 56 letters from some of the most distinguished scholars in the field.

[55] The conception of liberty and the ancient world was part of a larger dispute that is still ongoing. See, for instance, Peter Astbury Brunt, "Libertas in the Republic," in Peter Astbury Brunt, *The Fall of the Roman Republic and Related Essays* (Oxford: Clarendon Press, 1988), pp. 281–350, who criticized Schulz's views, though the position was recently defended by Valentina Arena, *Libertas and the Practice of Politics in the Late Roman Republic*

It is not surprising that Momigliano and Fritz Schulz would write about liberty and peace when they were both in short supply. Momigliano's text was only later published in his collected works but it shows a deep engagement with the British intellectual tradition of liberty. In these lectures, held during the first months of 1940, during the so-called phoney war, but published only in 2012, Momigliano outlined the Greek idea as the foundation of the Western conception of liberty: "Liberty is the eternal force of human activity. Where we find moral life, we may safely presuppose liberty" (p. 53). However, according to Momigliano, Greek liberty was lost on the Romans, who had no conception of how to combine the idea of freedom with peace. Momigliano knew he was presenting a minority position like Edward Gibbon before him when he maintained that Christianity was the ruin of the ideal Roman empire of peace. According to Momigliano, "Roman peace was authoritarian, it suppressed freedom" (p. 53). He ventures into the fields of political freedoms and human dignity, but finds even more important the "human duty to give peace to one's own soul by obeying a rational and universal order" (p. 55). In conclusion, the modern concept of liberty comes from the unification of these two elements.[56] In essence, Momigliano's liberty was pluralistic but his turn away from political order is a move guided by Christian authors and prejudiced against the earthly community.

Freedom and liberty were fundamental concepts not only on the texts of philosophy and politics in the US and Britain but equally in the political discourse at that time. Affinity to the concept of liberty had been an American trait that manifested itself in all the major documents of the republic. From the Preamble to the Declaration of Independence, where the "unalienable Rights" included "Life, Liberty and the pursuit of Happiness" to the Gettysburg Address's "new nation, conceived in liberty," the idea of liberty has been a mainstay of political rhetoric in the US.

In Nazi Germany the stated intellectual stance was opposition to the ideals of the Enlightenment such as freedom and equality. This is

(Cambridge and New York: Cambridge University Press, 2012). The division between the negative and positive concepts of liberty was later popularized by Berlin in Isaiah Berlin, *Two Concepts of Liberty: An Inaugural Lecture Delivered before the University of Oxford, on 31 October 1958* (Oxford: Clarendon Press, 1958).

56 Armando Momigliano, "Peace and liberty in the Ancient World," in Riccardo Di Donato, *Decimo contributo alla storia degli studi classici e del mondo antico* (Rome: Edizioni di Storia e Letteratura, 2012), p. 9; Murray, "Arnaldo Momigliano on Peace and Liberty," pp. 204–205.

outlined separately by both Hitler himself as well as intellectuals such as Carl Schmitt. In the US, the attitude toward the concept of human equality was almost as reverent as the concept of liberty. In the Preamble to the Declaration of Independence it is boldly stated that "all men are created equal," which is echoed in the Gettysburg Address's "proposition that all men are created equal." That equality was not really compatible with the fact that segregation was still the law of the land in much of the country even after WWI, but even more so during the drafting of the documents.

The issue of freedom became of course a pressing concern for exiled political theorists such as Strauss or Arendt not only due to the failure of the liberal state in Germany but also on account of the problems of the modern liberal state in general. While the stereotypical American thought had been to view Nazi Germany as an aberration in the march toward liberty and civil rights, émigrés like Arendt claimed that through structures such as the rule of law and the negative concept of freedom, the liberal state subjects the individual to the state and disguises the ultimately political foundation of the system.[57] Thus, in the *Origins of Totalitarianism*, Arendt writes how the ultimate aim of totalitarian repression was to destroy not only freedom but also the will to freedom, to destroy all human spontaneity as such.[58] While the Frankfurt School exiles had been critical of the consumerism and mass culture in America, not to mention its unbridled capitalism, they had ultimately a positive view about the American culture of democracy and freedom. Even Theodor Adorno, who had spent his exile first in Britain, then from 1938 onward in New York and three years later in Los Angeles, wrote how gratifying it was to experience the ways in which democratic forms had penetrated the whole of life in the US, while in Germany, by contrast, they continued to be mere rules of the game.[59] Arendt writes in amazement to Jaspers in 1946 how in

[57] Liisi Keedus, *The Crisis of German Historicism. The Early Political Thought of Hannah Arendt and Leo Strauss* (Cambridge: Cambridge University Press, 2015), pp. 152–153.

[58] Arendt, *Origins of Totalitarianism*, p. 622.

[59] Theodor W. Adorno, "Scientific Experiences of a European Scholar in America," in Bernard Bailyn and Donald Fleming (eds.), *The Intellectual Migration: Europe and America, 1930–1960* (Cambridge, MA: Belknap Press of Harvard University Press, 1969), p. 367. Adorno continued to praise the "inherent impulse in American life toward peaceableness, good-naturedness and generosity, in the sharpest contrast to the dammed-up malice and envy that exploded in Germany between 1933 and 1945" (pp. 367–378).

America the feeling of freedom is so strong that many people consider that one cannot live without freedom.[60]

The cause of liberty and the fight for liberty was a long-standing US foreign policy objective, being once again evoked during the World War I. According to Neumann, during WWI, Germany had two ideological enemies, Bolshevism and Woodrow Wilson's New Freedom.[61] That fight led to the victory of the principle of self-determination and the breaking up of empires. In World War II, liberty and freedom took an even more prominent place, from Roosevelt's Four Freedoms speech in 1941 to the war propaganda. A propaganda poster published during the war was decorated with the Statue of Liberty and the flags of the twenty-six allied nations with the caption: "The United Nations Fight for Freedom." Never mind that the flag of Stalin's Soviet Union was there as well. After the war, the defense and expansion of freedom became a staple of Cold War rhetoric with Kennedy's 1961 phrase "The great battlefield for the defense and expansion of freedom today is the whole Southern half of the globe – Asia, Latin America, Africa, and the Middle East."[62]

The notion of liberty outlined by Schulz was a multifaceted interpretation of the European tradition of liberalism that presented a continuum from the Roman concept of freedom as nondomination, a typically negative conception of liberty and the classical liberal tradition that focused on the individual. While the Nazi notion of liberty had been the liberty of the nation, Schulz presented the tradition of liberty in the Anglo-American sense, linking it with the Roman law tradition.

## Autonomy and Humanity

Schulz's escape from Germany was made in slow motion. He was increasingly marginalized at the university but the position of professor protected him for a long time. Though Schulz was himself not Jewish but Evangelical Protestant, the fact that he was of Jewish origins, i.e., his grandparents were members of the Jewish religious community and his wife was Jewish, was the deciding factor in Nazi policies. The first round of mass firings of university professors took place during the spring of 1933 and they gained wide international attention. In May 1933, for

[60] Letter of Arendt to Jaspers January 29, 1946, in Lotte Köhler and Hans Saner (eds.), *Hannah Arendt/Karl Jaspers: Correspondence, 1926–1969* (Munich: Piper, 1993), p. 66.

[61] Neumann, *Behemoth*, p. xix.

[62] President John F. Kennedy speaking to Congress on May 25, 1961.

example, *The Manchester Guardian* published a list of nearly two hundred professors who had been dismissed in April and May.[63]

During 1935, several questionnaires were circulated at the University of Berlin with the intention of singling out not only Jews but also opponents of the regime. The aim was fairly obvious as the short questionnaire first requested the membership number to the Nazi party. If not a member, one had to answer whether one had any grandparents who had been members of the Jewish religious community. During all this bureaucratic nightmare, what is notable is the impersonal way that the administration executed its tasks, mentioning the relevant laws simply by their number. Schulz himself was not fired but was instead first denied the right to teach, depriving him of the income it brought and then forcibly moved to the University of Frankfurt. Finally, he was forced to take early retirement. The narrowing of space that was left for Schulz is evident in the personnel files at Berlin University, where one sees the Schulz family first being forced out of their home in leafy Dahlem and then taking up residence in progressively worse neighborhoods as more and more areas were taken over by the new Nazi elite and declared off limits to Jews. The five children were one by one sent to schools abroad and Schulz's wife Martha began to search for a way out of their nightmare. Schulz himself sank into depression.[64]

Leading the effort to evict Schulz and others was a fellow legal historian, Karl August Eckhardt. He was a young professor who had, like many others, made a spectacular career for himself under the Nazi regime. He organized a purge in the ministry responsible for education and would later in 1936 be hired by the law faculty in Berlin. This was part of the general tendency to appoint active supporters of the Nazi regime to the most important university in the Reich's capital. Another active Nazi supporter was Carl Schmitt, who was appointed (without request from the Berlin faculty) as professor in October 1933.[65]

[63] "Nazi purge at universities - long list of dismissals," *The Manchester Guardian Weekly*, May 19, 1933.

[64] This development is visible in stark detail in Schulz's file in the university archives. Universitätsarchiv, Humboldt-Universität, Berlin, UK Personalia Sch 303, Personal-Akten des Prof Dr Schulz. On the administrative details of Schulz's ouster, see Ernst, "Fritz Schulz," pp. 14–25.

[65] Reinhard Zimmermann, "'Was Heimat hieß, nun heißt es Hölle.' The Emigration of Lawyers from Hitler's Germany: Political Background, Legal Framework, and Cultural Context," in Beatson and Zimmermann, *Jurists Uprooted*, pp. 1–72, at 33–34. On Eckhardt, see Ralf Frassek, "Eckhardt, Karl August," in A. Cordes et al. (eds.), *Handwörterbuch zur deutschen Rechtsgeschichte*, vol 2, Band I (Berlin: Erich Schmidt Verlag, 2008), pp. 1179–1180; Hermann Nehlsen, "In memoriam: Karl August Eckhardt,"

Schulz was still allowed to travel and foreign scholars were allowed to visit him. The limits of his freedom, however, were growing tighter and manifested themselves in seemingly strange ways. One was that he was given a new first name, with the requirement that he should use it in all correspondence. Thus all who received a letter from a Fritz Israel Schulz would know that the sender was a Jew.[66] His library privileges were revoked, perhaps the most striking insult to an academic. This process of marginalization and the transformation of German universities was recorded by an American scholar named Edward Hartshorne. Hartshorne was a houseguest with the Schulz family in Berlin and sections of the book on the persecution of individual scholars are mostly about them.[67] Hartshorne was also active in 1938 in the ultimately unsuccessful effort to hire Schulz at Harvard.[68]

Early in 1936, Schulz made a contract with Oxford University Press on the publication of a translation of *Principles* that would be expanded and amended for a British readership. The translation was quickly carried out by Marguerite Wolff, the sister of Roman law scholar Herbert Jolowicz, and the work was published in October.[69]

Schulz began to search for a new position abroad, but with little success. In early 1936, Schulz gave a lecture tour in the US, speaking at Harvard, the Riccobono Seminar at the Catholic University of America in Washington D.C. and in Louisiana.[70] It is notable that in 1936 Hans Kelsen too was touring the country, looking for a job.

The tour did not result in a job offer and other attempts came to nothing. Finally, he managed to secure a temporary position in the Netherlands, allowing him to escape from Germany in April 1939 with the help of the Dutch Academic Relief Fund (*Academisch Steunfonds*) and

*Zeitschrift der Savigny-Stiftung für Rechtsgeschichte: Germanistische Abteilung*, 104 (1987), 497–536; Martin Niemann, "Karl August Eckhardt," in Mathias Schmoeckel (ed.), *Die Juristen der Universität Bonn in "Dritten Reich"* (Cologne: Böhlau, 2004), pp. 160–184. On Schmitt's cooperation with the Nazi movement, see Mehring, *Carl Schmitt*, pp. 304–380.

66 This was in accordance with the ordinance of the application of the law on the use of family names and first names (*Zweite Verordnung zur Durchführung des Gesetzes über die Änderung von Familiennamen und Vornamen vom 17. August 1938*) (RGBl I, 1044). The law stated that Jewish men must add Israel as a first name and women Sara.

67 Hartshorne, *German Universities and National Socialism.*

68 Schumpeter to Fay (January 4, 1939). Harvard University Archives, Pusey Library, Cambridge, MA, HUGFP 4.8, Papers of Joseph Alois Schumpeter, Carbons of JAS's correspondence.

69 The translation was suggested by one of Schulz's pupil, Alexander Gurwitsch. Giltaij, *Reinventing the Principles of Roman Law*; Ernst, "Fritz Schulz," pp. 130–132.

70 Ernst, "Fritz Schulz," pp. 139–140.

his Dutch colleagues. He stayed in Leiden, preparing for what he thought would be a longer visit. By coincidence, three major exiled Roman law scholars, Schulz, Pringsheim and Edoardo Volterra, were in Leiden at the same time during the summer of 1939. After four months, the Schulzes left on the last ship for Britain before the war started on August 26, 1939. He then arrived at Oxford in October 1939. In this effort, Schulz was aided by Kenneth Sisam, his loyal editor at OUP, F. A. Mann, a former student and fellow refugee, and Francis de Zulueta, a Spanish professor at Oxford, not to mention Eduard Fraenkel, a refugee classicist from Freiburg. There were a number of different organizations helping refugees, from Christian charities to various informal committees such as the Oxford Refugee Committee. Sisam is another link between Momigliano and Schulz as Sisam was also Momigliano's editor and helped both to gain stipends. These stipends were not money from OUP, but from the Rockefeller Foundation, which organized this support through the Society for the Protection of Science and Learning (SPSL). Sisam had a very particular idea of how refugees should be helped, mainly involving getting them funding to do research rather than finding them academic positions. While the ostensible aim was to minimize the animosity that the flood of refugees might have caused should they start competing with locals for the few jobs available, it also meant that many were left with little local contact.[71] This may also explain why many of the refugees in Britain like Schulz were employed on short temporary contracts whereas in the US they would, if successful, enter into permanent positions.

It was usual for the future exiles to hold on to their positions in Germany as long as they could. For example, after his lectures were canceled, Ernst Kantorowicz went to Oxford in January 1934 on research

[71] Rockefeller Foundation Archives, R.G. 1.1, series 401R Oxford University Press – Refugees, Schulz, box 63, series 401, RG 1.1 RAC, folder 830.4; April 2, 1941: letter of Sisam to O'Brien (of the Rockefeller Foundation) with proposal attached with a list of refugees and advisors. The care shown by Sisam is evident in his letters during the war. Oxford University Press Archives, Oxford, Schulz CP GE 000344, 1-31, contains 31 letters where Sisam works different angles to get yet another grant for Schulz, sometimes for unexpected circumstances such as his son's illness. Schulz's escape and its circumstances are discussed at length in Ernst, "Fritz Schulz," pp. 148–168. On the Schulzes' stay in Leiden, see Pierangelo Buongiorno, "'Ricordi di anni lontani e difficili.' Romanisti a Leiden nella lunga estate del 1939," *Index: quaderni camerti di studi romanistici = international survey of Roman law*, 44 (2016), 479–490. Volterra had been fired in 1938 due to the fascist racial laws. He went to initially to Egypt and France but returned to Italy during the war, fighting among the partisans, being arrested and set free with the fall of fascism. He was one of the founding members of the Partito D'Azione.

leave but then returned to Germany. His salary was tied to being in Germany and his family was there. He was also protected by not only his status as a fighter on the front in World War I, but also by highly placed friends like Albrecht Graf von Bernstorff. This relative comfort ended in 1938 when he was deprived of his passport. With the help of his friends in Oxford and the US and funding by NGOs like the Emergency Committee, he began to prepare for a job search by taking on a lecture tour. After numerous difficulties with visas and funding, culminating in spending *Kristallnacht* and the days after it hidden in Bernstorff's apartment, Kantorowicz escaped to Oxford and soon to the US.[72]

When war broke out on the Western front, Schulz was, along with numerous other refugees, interned at the Isle of Man as enemy citizens in July 5, 1940. Schulz was interned in one of the German camps while Momigliano was detained in the Italian camp. With Schulz, there was also Fritz Pringsheim and David Daube. For most of the detainees, especially the older ones, the time spent there was fairly short and they returned to their families after some months, Schulz on October 13, 1940.[73] The incident was traumatic to many and left a lasting impression of the precariousness of their position. For Schulz, his internment also meant that the OUP funding for his family would stop. This did not mean that the press's opinion on Schulz would have changed; they were in fact quite explicit on their stand. A personnel card in the OUP archives on Schulz states that he is "A good scholar, very hard working. A leading Democrat in Berlin, and first forbidden to lecture on that ground."[74]

One of the main reasons why Schulz ended up in Oxford was the planned "Oxford History of Legal Science" where Schulz was commissioned to write a chapter on Roman law. Work on this chapter occupied Schulz for much of the run up to the war and was the ostensible reason why Schulz was kept at Oxford and he was given continued subsidies by the publisher. The editors of the work (whether the work was originally conceived as a single or multiple

72 Lerner, *Ernst Kantorowicz*, pp. 187–213.

73 Ernst, "Fritz Schulz," pp. 158–160. Internees were classified according to the level of danger they posed with exiles from Nazi persecution classified as the least dangerous.

74 Oxford University Press Archives, Oxford, Schulz CP GE 000344, 26, 31. The evaluation also demonstrates how there was a particular model by which refugees were compared, which included industriousness, gratitude, but also frugality: "An economical household, and all show the best spirit." OUP was assisting at that time between ten and eighteen exiled professors and scholars working on various book projects between 1941 and 1944, among them Schulz, Pringsheim and Momigliano.

volume is unclear) were Hermann Kantorowicz and Francis de Zulueta. Kantorowicz was a famous jurist and legal historian of German origins but who had gained a sizable reputation both in the US and in Britain, and de Zulueta was the Regius Professor of Civil (Roman) Law at Oxford.[75] Like many commissioned introductory works, this volume too began to expand and Schulz's chapter was finally cut down to a size suitable to be published as a separate book. That book was his *Roman Legal Science* (1946).[76]

The link between Hermann Kantorowicz and Schulz was formed in Germany. They had collaborated on the publication of an edition of Thomas Diplovatatius (1468–1541) *De claris iuris consultis*, a collection of jurists' biographies. Kantorowicz was also an exile but he had even earlier worked in the US and when he returned to New York as part of the University in Exile, he was quick to take part in the debates in the US.[77] If one considers the context of the proposed work, it fits fairly well into the general theme of Kantorowicz's work, that of the professionalization of legal expertise and the creation of legal science. Though he has been depicted as a proponent of the free law movement, Kantorowicz's work is to a large degree that of the criticism and reinterpretation of the legacy of the Historical School and the central role it gave to jurisprudence.[78] The role of de Zulueta in this project was, in addition to his substantial input, to be a link with the establishment at Oxford. The fact that Schulz even came to Oxford was largely due to the work of de Zulueta, who helped both Schulz and Pringsheim in their journey to England and to settle there.[79]

[75] See Lorena Atzeri, "Francis de Zulueta (1878–1958): An Oxford Roman lawyer between totalitarianisms," in Tuori and Björklund, *Roman Law and the Idea of Europe*, pp. 53–71.

[76] It was not published in German translation until 1961 under the title *Geschichte der römischen Rechtswissenschaft* (Weimar: H. Böhlaus Nachfolger, 1961).

[77] On the connections between American and European realism, see Hermann Kantorowicz, "Some Rationalism about Realism," *Yale Law Journal*, 43 (1934), 1240–1253; Katharina Isabel Schmidt, "Law, modernity, crisis: German free lawyers, American legal realists, and the transatlantic turn to 'life,' 1903–1933," *German Studies Review*, 39 (2016), 121–140; Heikki Pihlajamäki, "Against metaphysics in law: the historical background of American and Scandinavian legal realism compared," *The American Journal of Comparative Law*, 52 (2004), 469–487.

[78] Especially Hermann Kantorowicz, *Was ist uns Savigny?* (Berlin: C. Heymanns Verlag, 1912); Hermann Kantorowicz, "Savigny and the Historical School of Law," *Law Quarterly Review*, 209 (1937), 326–343. On the Historical School, see Hans-Peter Haferkamp, *Die historische Rechtschule* (Frankfurt: Klostermann, 2018).

[79] The project was abandoned after Kantorowicz's death in 1940. Oxford University Press Archives, Oxford, Schulz CP ED 000129, 17, De Zulueta to Sisam (on February 18, 1940) on the state of affairs after Kantorowicz´s death: "we should have to replace Jolowicz for

Though the issue of jurisprudence and its relationship to political power was a matter of importance in scholarship throughout history, Schulz's contribution was fundamental. He had touched on the issue in the *Principles* but the themes of authority and science and the equilibrium between the two runs through the whole of *Roman Legal Science*.[80]

In the *Principles*, Schulz had written on the principle of isolation (*Isolierung*), which he understood as the autonomy of law in relation to political power, to economic considerations and so forth. He maintained that "Law must be distinguished from all that is not law, the territory of the law must be delimited and an independent legal system developed" (p. 20). This separation and isolation were not purely or even primarily a matter of politics, they were founded on the idea that all matters of custom and religion should be excluded. From this ancient Roman conviction, Schulz carries the discussion to the influence of the principle of isolation in nineteenth-century Germany. There, he enlists not only Puchta but also Jhering as the supporters of the idea of isolation. Even Laband, in the field of public law, is drawn in to support the cause. The opposition and main threat to splendid isolation was found in the inclusion of facts and reality by the likes of Ehrlich (p. 38). The point of Schulz's principled stand against the realm of factuality was that once that barrier is removed, legal consideration ceases to be legal and the argument begins to take a different logic.[81]

The issue of facts and factuality and their relation to law were central in the debates over legal realism. What this signified was that the legal realism movement that was very strong in the US at the time found common ground with the Nazi legal ideology that likewise emphasized the dominance of facts over norms.[82] Schulz responds to the idea of

the Greek chapter and it was very hard to think of a substitute, unless we turned the first vol. into a cabinet of exiled Jews." Oxford University Press Archives, Oxford, Schulz CP ED 000129, 9, De Zulueta to Sisam and Berger (on July 10, 1942): projected *History of Legal Science* definitively abandoned.

80 Here, Schulz created the so-called theory of the *Werktypen* that has influenced both German and Italian studies of Roman law.

81 The political relevance of this principle is demonstrated by the review of Steinwenter, "Prinzipien des römischen Rechts von Fritz Schulz," p. 116, where he notes that the ideal of isolation is mostly restricted to small, conservative Roman law circles.

82 In the US, legal realism was championed by Pound (Roscoe Pound, "The Call for a Realist Jurisprudence," *Harvard Law Review*, 44 [1930–1931], 697–711) and Llewellyn but the movement took different forms and approaches in their relationship between law and

legal realism, that law should not be blind to real arguments, with a dual argument: the isolation of law is vital to the very functioning of legal reasoning but equally legal science as a scholarly inquiry should be very conscious about the social, political and intellectual context of law. For example, in a letter to OUP about the translation of *Roman Legal Science*, he outlines that "The idea of this book is to relieve the History of Roman Jurisprudence from the barren juristic isolation and to understand and to write this history as a part of Antiquity."[83]

The Nazi jurists appreciated legal realism for its anti-formalistic qualities. Nazi jurisprudence had, even before the emphasis on ideas such as the concrete order, raised issues such as general principles and the feelings of right above strict law. This was naturally a paradoxical element in the transatlantic exchange of ideas: lawyers such as Roland Freisler, notorious as the head of the People's Court, the supreme Nazi court, praised American common law for its freedom from formalities and the independence of its judges to drive policies forward.[84]

The outline of *Roman Legal Science* was at the outset a very ambitious presentation of the history of Roman jurisprudence and its development. The chief point Schulz wished to make was the scientific nature of law and its difficult relationship with scientific roots in other fields, especially in Greek philosophy. Beyond that narrative, Schulz presented another important narrative of isolation, that of the distinction between law and political power.

*Roman Legal Science* was a historical work but behind the historical template there was a message and an agenda. For Schulz, the lasting value of Roman law was its practical scholarly method of resolving issues and building on the works of previous jurists. This ensured that the law was flexible and adaptable but nevertheless did not deviate from the principles laid out earlier. Law was seen as cumulative and purely the work of jurists. If there were anathemas, they were the rash political influences that entered into law and the codification of law that would petrify it. The message was one of conservatism and elitism. However, it was equally a message about the pure practicality of law, about law laid out by jurists to ensure the smooth resolution of legal disputes. As such,

the factual. See John Henry Schlegel, *American Legal Realism and Empirical Social Science* (Chapel Hill, NC: University of North Carolina Press, 1995); Laura Kalman, *Legal Realism at Yale 1927–1960* (Chapel Hill, NC: University of North Carolina Press, 1986).

83 Schulz to Sisam (February 11, 1945), p. 1. Oxford University Press Archives, Oxford, Schulz PB ED 010383, no. 13.

84 Whitman, *Hitler's American Model*, pp. 150–151.

it was antithetical to the conception of law as social engineering set out to fulfill policy goals.

The freedom of legal science and the separation of law from politics was a trait that connects Schulz to the German nineteenth-century tradition of law. What this had meant for the jurists of the nineteenth century was the rejection of codification and the commanding role that lawyers should have in shaping law. For the works that Schulz had produced, the same principle carried a deeper meaning, namely the preservation of justice itself from capricious and violent political systems. Like many of his peers, Schulz was deeply distrustful of the very idea of natural law. As the system of legal positivism that had been debated with gusto in the early twentieth century was little better, the only viable alternative was tradition. Legal tradition was the only check on political power and the changes it wished to introduce. This formulation proved to be extremely important in the debates over natural law and the reconstitution of law after the war, but equally in the 1990s debates over the foundations of European legal unity.

## Exiles and Scholarly Change

Schulz and others were part of the so-called great exodus of scholars escaping totalitarianism. It is estimated that some 20,000 intellectuals were among the roughly half a million people leaving Germany. This included roughly one-third to one-fourth of the total number of university professors. The numbers varied slightly from field to field. Of the 496 higher education teachers in law, in total 131 were fired or removed from office after 1933. Of those, 89 were removed due to their Jewish heritage and 42 on ideological or political grounds. In total 69 would emigrate, while 24 would die or be murdered before 1945.[85] These numbers each represent an individual disaster, a life interrupted and a career derailed. However, in the following, we will explore the changes in the ideas of law, freedom and justice in the works of Franz

[85] Breunung and Walther, *Die Emigration deutscher Rechtswissenschaftler ab 1933*, vol 1, pp. 6–7; Zimmermann, "'Was Heimat hieß, nun heißt es Hölle.' The Emigration of Lawyers from Hitler's Germany," pp. 45–54. The biographies collected in Göppinger, *Juristen jüdischer Abstammung im "Dritten Reich,"* looking at the total deaths within the legal profession illustrate how in addition to those murdered either in Germany or in concentration camps, there is a very large number of people who would in desperation commit suicide before being deported to the East.

Neumann, Ernst Levy and Arnaldo Momigliano as examples of the transformative power of exile.

Exile is a powerful intellectual phenomenon. A person is taken from his physical and intellectual surroundings, one's colleagues and friends, and plunged into a new and sometimes hostile environment. Because the process of exile often involves violence and separation from one's loved ones, it can be traumatic in the extreme. This experience of trauma and rejection produces reactions that are highly individual and hard to predict. Extreme circumstances lead some to seek religious consolation, while others descend into depression and anxiety.[86]

For scholars, as with authors and artists, the process of exile and its repercussions provide an even wider field to demonstrate their effects. However, the problem is whether it is possible to verify a causal link. Of course, one may easily argue that the works of scholars such as Hannah Arendt or even Ayn Rand are reactions to the experience of totalitarianism and exile. Arnaldo Momigliano wrote that biography has either a conscious or an unconscious effect on scholarship, meaning that even though many seek to hide the effect of things like exile, traces are obvious for those who know where to look.[87] However, the effect of external circumstances and the experiences an author has may be processed through the work itself and the work forms a statement regarding the ordeal, or the experience of exile is more subtly incorporated into a more neutral outline. As a whole, the impact of exile in science is difficult to evaluate, either among scholars themselves or in the scientific community at large.[88]

Of the first group, Hannah Arendt produced a sizable production in exile in which she explored not only the creation of totalitarianism and fascism, but also her own experience in exile. Her *Origins of Totalitarianism* traced authoritarianism and anti-Semitism, leading up to the understanding of totalitarian states

[86] Burke, *Exiles and Expatriates in the History of Knowledge, 1500–2000*.

[87] Armando Momigliano, "Ancient biography and the study of religion," in Armando Momigliano (ed.), *Ottavo contributo alla storia degli studi classici e del mondo antico* (Rome: Edizioni di Storia e Letteratura, 1987), p. 199. For Momigliano, the classical example was Rostovtzeff, an exile from Russia. See also Glen W. Bowersock and T. J. Cornell, *A. D. Momigliano: Studies on Modern Scholarship* (Berkeley: University of California Press, 1994), pp. ix–x.

[88] There are some bibliometric studies, though their results have been more a demonstration of the limits of bibliometrics than of real analytic value. Fabian Waldinger, "Peer effects in science: evidence from the dismissal of scientists in Nazi Germany," *The Review of Economic Studies*, 79 (2012), 838–861.

as completely novel entities. In her other writings, she would discuss at length the role of the exile and the refugee as a perpetual outsider.[89] Arendt's work on exile can be seen as a kind of primal scream against totalitarianism. Her work was equally marked by an encounter with American political and legal tradition, especially that of American Republican thought, but equally to the institutionalized racism.[90]

Of the second group, Franz Neumann is one of the most famous examples where the experience of totalitarianism, exile and law was sublimated in the work on those themes, into the scholarship that drew upon but did not rest upon the exile process. Neumann had been a social democratic activist and labor lawyer who was forced into exile early on. Neumann left Germany in 1933, first studying at the London School of Economics under Harold Laski, and then in 1936 going to the Institute for Social Research in New York. He was an exile who felt continuously ill at ease in his adopted country. He was associated with the Frankfurt School but was occupied mainly with administrative and practical legal work. During the war, Neumann worked with the Office of Strategic Services (the OSS, the predecessor of the CIA) alongside fellow members from the Frankfurt School, Herbert Marcuse and Otto Kirchheimer, to produce reports on Nazi Germany.[91] These led to *Behemoth* (1944), where he traced the collapse of the Weimar Republic and the emergence of the Nazi state and law. In *Behemoth*, Neumann describes how the Nazis used institutionalized racism in the form of anti-Semitism to consolidate their power. While Nazi racism was certainly used to justify unequal rights, it gradually formed the philosophical foundation of Nazi ideology. In this, they relied on the long tradition of German anti-Semitism, one that was present even in liberal theories. What the Nazi theory of liberty was, if such a thing can be construed,

[89] Hannah Arendt, "Exiles, enemies, or emigrants," reprinted in M. Anderson (ed.), *Hitler's Exiles: Personal Stories of the Flight from Nazi Germany to America* (New York: The New Press, 1998), pp. 253–262; Hannah Arendt, "We refugees," *Menorah Journal*, 31 (1943), 69–77. On Arendt's experience and her influences in America, see Richard H. King, *Arendt and America* (Chicago: The University of Chicago Press, 2015).

[90] King, *Arendt and America*, pp. 148–155. It should be noted, like King does, that Arendt did not subscribe to a dichotomy of totalitarianism and liberalism where liberalism, even in America, was seen as purely positive. Her admiration was more reserved for the Republican tradition. See also Margaret Canovan, *Hannah Arendt: A Reinterpretation of Her Political Thought* (Cambridge: Cambridge University Press, 1992).

[91] Reproduced in Raffaele Laudani (ed.), *Secret Reports from Nazi Germany* (Princeton: Princeton University Press, 2013).

was the idea of the freedom of the nation from internal and external enemies. According to Neumann, the Jew became an essential part of this theory. Hence, in Carl Schmitt's theory of politics as struggle, the extermination of the enemy is the precondition of unification and freedom.[92]

Neumann's case shows the contradictions that exiles were continuously exposed to and the demands that were placed upon them. As a socialist, Neumann abhorred the Nazi state, but the process that he went through in exile was neither simple nor reducible to a singular ideological trait, nor can its impact be easily defined. Even before the war, he was a staunch advocate of the rule of law and the ideas of equality before the law but this conviction extended beyond the Nazi state. He was equally critical of the US and after the war condemned the centralization of power and policies of racial segregation. A more controversial issue was his connections with communism and the Soviet intelligence services. Neumann became friends with classical scholar Moses Finley (originally Finkelstein), who worked at Columbia University. Finley was a socialist and a member of the Communist Party who became one of the leading scholars in ancient history, integrating Marxist theories into the field. In this process, Neumann served as a crucial influence. Whether Finley was Neumann's connection with the Soviets remains unclear. Though Neumann had worked with the OSS, this did not preclude him from providing information to the Russians up until 1944.[93] Thus, Neumann could be both an antitotalitarian working with the OSS against Nazi Germany and at the same time work with Soviet intelligence. He could write about the rule of law and liberty, while simultaneously approaching critically the problems of liberalism and capitalism and promoting the use of Marxist theory in the humanities and social sciences.

Neumann's conception of totalitarianism and liberty was not only about an appreciation of the American political culture, it also opposed

[92] Neumann, *Behemoth*, pp. 99, 109, 125: "Carl Schmitt has maintained that politics is a struggle a foe who must be exterminated." This notion of extermination is not supported by the writings of Schmitt himself, who does not mention the term *Vernichtung* in this context. On Neumann as an archetypical political exile scholar, see Kettler, *The Liquidation of Exile*, pp. 43–82; Söllner, *Political Scholar*, pp. 87–128. Neumann was later appointed professor at Columbia in 1948 but continued to travel between New York and Berlin.

[93] Daniel P. Tompkins, "The making of Moses Finley," in Daniel Jew, Robin Osborne and Michael Scott (eds.), *M. I. Finley: An Ancient Historian and His Impact* (Cambridge: Cambridge University Press, 2016), pp. 13–30.

the forces of totalitarianism that used anti-Semitism as "a kind of dress rehearsal" for their attack on the middle classes.[94]

Is it possible to evaluate scholarly change in writers who do not discuss it explicitly? Even the assessment of what the process of exile meant for social science scholars who did process the experience openly is fraught with difficulties. Is it thus possible to evaluate the impact of exile in the works of scholars of Roman history and especially Roman law such as Schulz?

Schulz's case is, on the surface, a fairly straightforward example of scholarly change in that his early work was almost without fail technical in character, concerned as it was with the legal analysis of texts and their provenience. But starting from the *Principles*, Schulz's works begin to have both covert and open political themes that delve into the fundamentals of the legal system in ways that can be construed to be prompted by the Nazi takeover of power and the way in which it influenced the legal system. As a result, his work shows what can be described as a textbook case of the exile process. Or does it? Many of his works are still very much bound to the German and Italian style of academic scholarship, more in tune with the extreme self-consciousness of the Roman law tradition, where the historiographical parts of an analysis were primarily concerned with one's allegiances.[95]

For scholarly exiles, the exile experience was in many ways similar to that of people in general but there were also marked differences. There was, for example, an elaborate network of NGOs and government agencies helping exiles, from the British Society for the Protection of Science and Learning to the University in Exile.[96] For scholars, the challenge was whether they could continue their careers in some form abroad. With the flood of desperate people coming in, as seen now in Europe, exiles encountered both lack of resources and hostility. Like Kenneth Sisam, Schulz's contact at OUP, many worried that the scholarly exiles would be seen as competition to home-grown academics.[97]

94 Wheatland, "Franz L. Neumann: negotiating political exile," p. 129.

95 Within scholarship on Schulz, the notion of whether Schulz was writing in code is highly debated. Schermaier suggested that Schulz was in fact accommodating Nazi ideas, while Ernst and Giltaij are more pronounced in their support of Schulz's loyalty to his principles. Whether writing in code was intentional or not is of course beyond our knowledge because Schulz remained silent on the matter.

96 The history of the organizations involved in the helping of exiles has yet to be written. For a list of organizations active in the US, see Edgcomb, *From Swastika to Jim Crow*, p. 22.

97 In his correspondence, Sisam reveals at times his lack of patience with the refugees and their complaints. Sisam to C. H. S. Fifoot (October 17, 1939). Oxford University Press

For many, the process of exile also meant changing one's research focus. For historians, this was a minor concern[98] but for legal scholars the change was considerable. Many law professors such as Hans Kelsen, Otto Kirchheimer or Hans Morgenthau who acquired positions in the US ended up in political science departments. Some took up new research topics that were more in tune with the traditions of their adopted countries, turning for example toward empiricism, which was favored in the US. For the younger scholars, the possibility of reeducation opened up new connections and thus employment opportunities. For Franz Neumann, this was a crucial factor in his career, having Laski, one of the most famous social scientists of his generation, as his teacher. David Daube, despite having completed a doctorate in Germany, wrote another one in Britain with influential Roman law scholar and historian, William Buckland.

Fritz Schulz was one of the more senior of the scholarly exiles and as such the avenues open to him were not promising. On the positive side, he had learned English early on and was thus not isolated on that account like many of his peers. He had the connections and authority that would be useful in the search for a new position. However, he was already fairly old and the prospects available to him might have appeared bland and unexciting after the exalted status he once enjoyed in Berlin. A good example of local prejudice that Schulz faced was the search for a professor of Roman law in Edinburgh. The list of candidates was excellent, some of the leading Roman law scholars of their generation were in the race, including Schulz and Pringsheim. However, instead of choosing one of them, Edinburgh selected a local barrister for the job.[99]

In Britain, Roman law scholars and Roman historians faced somewhat unequal opportunities that had much to do with the undeveloped state of British law schools. While the fields of ancient history and classics were studied in an almost cosmopolitan manner and scientific excellence was seen as essential in producing first-rate scholars, the law schools were more practical in orientation. The British law school

Archives, Oxford, Schulz PB ED 010382, no. 47: "I cannot stand the refugees who are always grumbling about their lot at a time when most of us have something hard to think about; but a few of them, and Schulz is one, are of a different class, and recognize that they are lucky to be here."

98 This becomes apparent in the works collected in Crawford, Ulmschneider and Elsner, *Ark of Civilization*.

99 Honoré, "Fritz Pringsheim," pp. 140–141. It should be noted that the chair was under the patronage of the Faculty of Advocates and thus not a free choice of the university.

focused on producing practical lawyers for the bench and the bar, not scholars or researchers. Even the idea of a science of law may have been alien to many law schools in the interwar period.[100]

However, the practice of Roman law had its supporters, not least in Scotland, where the Roman-Dutch legal tradition had a strong influence. In the major universities, there were chairs in civil law, which included Roman law, and thus the background was there for the integration of refugees. This meant that the younger generation of refugees such as David Daube had a comparatively easier task in applying for jobs and getting them. While the older generation remained in precarious positions, Daube would rise to the top of British legal academia with ultimately a Regius professorship.

In the US, the situation was harder. Roman law scholarship was almost nonexistent at the time. For legal scholars in general the transfer was difficult, and even a luminary like Kelsen was only hired by the political science department at Berkeley. In the correspondence received by one of the few US Roman law scholars of that time, A. Arthur Schiller at Columbia, the desperation comes through. Again and again letters come in from his contacts in Europe, asking whether he would be able to find a position for this or that talented young scholar of Roman law.[101] The desperate situation was compounded by the fact that many more would join the exile later as the war spread. Thus Professor H. R. Hoetink, who had helped exiles to secure a position in the Netherlands, was himself dismissed from his post in 1942 as a Jew. He was arrested and sent to a concentration camp. He was momentarily released but had to spend the rest of the war hiding with his family in constantly changing safe houses.[102]

It is hard to say precisely why Schulz's search for a position in the US was unsuccessful but his age may have been a contributing factor. He was fifty-six at the time, fifty-nine when he arrived in Britain. The translation of the *Principles* had not yet appeared and little of his work was published in English. By 1936 the supply of exiled scholars had

[100] On this, see for example William Rodolph Cornish and Geoffrey de N. Clark, *Law and Society in England: 1750–1950* (London: Sweet & Maxwell, 1989), pp. 45–120.

[101] Rare Book and Manuscript Archive, Columbia University, New York, Arthur Schiller Papers, Boxes 1–6, MS#1125. Among those writing to Schiller asking for help were Adolf Berger, Edoardo Volterra, Egon Weiss and Walter Ullman. Michael H. Hoeflich, "Legacy," in Lutter, Stiefel and Hoeflich, *Der Einfluß deutscher Emigranten auf die Rechtsentwicklung in den USA und in Deutschland*, pp. 15–17 rightly urges us to remember not only the successful applicants, but also the less fortunate ones.

[102] Hoeflich, *Legacy*, p. 17.

already rapidly outpaced demand, especially in fields as marginal as Roman law in the US. Kelsen, who was fifty-eight at this time, was appointed at the German University in Prague, but had to leave when Czechoslovakia was occupied by Germany. His return to the US in 1939 was similarly full of desperation, with his friends seeking to help him get a job but his applications were repeatedly rejected in favor of younger competitors. In the end, Kelsen received a temporary position at the University in Exile, and his friend Roscoe Pound managed to offer him a lecturership in Harvard for two years. From there, he moved to Berkeley, but again only to a temporary position.[103]

But perhaps age was not the sole determining factor, as Ernst Levy (1881–1968), who was roughly the same age as Schulz, managed to gain a professorship in the US. Levy came to the US after being forcibly retired from his chair in Heidelberg in 1935 as well as from the editorship of the *Zeitschrift der Savigny-Stiftung für Rechtsgeschichte*. He was hired in 1937 as Professor of European History and Roman Law at Washington University in Seattle, where he remained for fifteen years.[104] Despite this, he had considered his exile to be temporary and hoped to be recalled to Heidelberg as soon as the war ended. In the case of Levy, his situation was helped by the fact that his daughter Brigitte was married to Edgar Bodenheimer, a fellow legal exile. With the help of Karl Llewellyn, Professor of Law at Columbia, both Levy and Bodenheimer would go to Seattle, where Bodenheimer studied American law. At the end of the war, Bodenheimer worked with the American government's team in preparation for the Nuremberg trials and traveled back to Germany. While Levy wished to return, his family sought to dissuade him. In the end, no

[103] Thomas Olechowski, "Hans Kelsen, the Second World War and the US Government," in J. Telman (ed.), *Hans Kelsen in America – Selective Affinities and the Mysteries of Academic Influence* (Berlin: Springer Verlag, 2016), pp. 102–103; Horst Dreier, "Hans Kelsen (1881–1973). 'Jurist des Jahrhunderts'?", in Helmut Heinrichs, Hans-Harald Franzki, Klaus Schmalz and Michael Stolleis (eds.), *Deutsche Juristen Jüdischer Herkunft* (Munich: Beck, 1993), pp. 705–732. Pound lamented to Guido Kisch that he felt that he had not been as lucky as he had earlier been in helping people in gaining employment. Guido Kisch, *Die Lebensweg eines Rechtshistorikers* (Sigmaringen: Thorbecke, 1975), p. 141.

[104] Wolfgang Kunkel, "Ernst Levy zum Gedächtnis," *Zeitschrift der Savigny-Stiftung für Rechtsgeschichte: Romanistische Abteilung*, 86 (1969), xiii–xxxii; Dieter Simon, "Levy, Ernst," *Neue Deutsche Biographie*, 14 (1985) 403–404; Dieter Simon, "Ernst Levy," in B. Diestelkamp and M. Stolleis (eds.), *Juristen an der Universität Frankfurt am Main* (Baden-Baden: Nomos, 1989), p. 94; Ernst C. Stiefel and Frank Mecklenburg, *Deutsche Juristen im amerikanischen Exil (1933–1950)* (Tübingen: Mohr Siebeck, 1991), pp. 51–52; Catherine Epstein, *A Past Renewed: A Catalog of German-Speaking Refugee Historians in the United States after 1933* (Cambridge: Cambridge University Press, 1993), pp. 190–195.

invitation and call to his old chair was issued and Levy remained with some reluctance in Seattle until his retirement.[105] Levy would stay in constant contact with his student, Wolfgang Kunkel, who joined the SS. In their correspondence, politics is mentioned only obliquely with regard to colleagues who were fired from their positions due to their faith or conviction. Levy would constantly pester Kunkel about different jobs he should apply for, including his own vacated chair. Ironically, in one letter where he announces that he has fled to the US, he also inquires whether Kunkel has been made lieutenant yet.[106]

How, then, did exile figure in Levy's work, beyond the fact that he would write a two-part book, the first part in English and the second in German? In his main work on West Roman vulgar law, no major indications are given of his exile background and, unless we consider that the theme of the book, which is about the slow degradation of a legal system, reflects Levy's own feelings. However, Levy would in 1948 write about natural law and Roman law, positing natural law as a polar opposite to totalitarianism. Roman law was produced in a time of relative peace, where even the wrongs committed by emperors like Caligula, Nero, Domitian or Commodus were relatively minor: "their regimes never aimed at a systematic interference with civic rights as they then were understood. Mass extermination, deportation or expropriation of citizens was something not even imagined as a potentiality." Levy contrasts this with a situation where "mankind in general or some country in particular faces a cataclysm threatening to destroy or distort the fundamental liberties." In these cases, a resort to laws and courts are of no avail and only war or revolution is possible. In these instances lawyers turn to the "ultimate groundwork of justice," namely natural law.[107]

[105] Bodenheimer, *Edgar and Brigitte*. Karl Llewellyn appeared to be extremely helpful to some but not to others. For example, Guido Kisch mentions that while his teacher Paul Koschaker had recommended him to Llewellyn (who had been his guest in Leipzig), he proved to be not at all interested. Kisch, *Die Lebensweg eines Rechtshistorikers*, p. 121.

[106] Dorothee Mussgnug (ed.), *Ernst Levy und Wolfgang Kunkel. Briefwechsel 1922–1968* (Heidelberg: Universitätsverlag Winter, 2005), letter no. 50 from Levy to Kunkel on February 22, 1937. Kunkel was a curious example of a student who would join the different Nazi organizations but never showed any affinity to the ideology behind it. On Kunkel, see Marc Foerster, "Wolfgang Kunkel," in Mathias Schmoeckel (ed.), *Die Juristen der Universität Bonn in "Dritten Reich"* (Cologne: Böhlau, 2004), pp. 456–519. Kunkel wrote a curious autobiographical piece about the Nazi era, Wolfgang Kunkel, "Der Professor im Dritten Reich," in Helmut Kuhn (ed.), *Die Deutsche Universität im Dritten Reich* (Munich: Piper, 1966), pp. 103–133.

[107] Ernst Levy, "Natural law in the Roman period," in A. L. Scanlan (ed.), *University of Notre Dame Natural Law Institute Proceedings 2* (Notre Dame: Notre Dame Law School, 1949), 19.

For less-known Roman law scholars, the situation could be even more dire and the opportunities for scholarly employment even rarer. The example of Hans Julius Wolff illustrates this in many ways. Wolff (1902–1983) was among the younger generation of exiles and thus had at least the advantage of youth on his side. In 1935, he left for Panama via one of the NGOs, the *Notgemeinschaft deutscher Wissenschaftler im Ausland*, and became Professor of Roman and Civil Law at the University of Panama. He then moved to the US in 1939, studying at Tennessee and Michigan. From there, he started working in different mid-Western universities, ending up in 1952 as a law librarian at the University of Oklahoma City. Considering that Wolff had worked among other things for the prestigious *Thesaurus Linguae Latinae* project, his career trajectory abroad was hardly in line with what his position had been in Germany. Wolff's work in the US did not leave a great impact, although he did publish a fairly successful textbook on Roman law in 1951. Only on his return to Germany would Wolff make an impressive career by refocusing on Greek law. In general, Wolff's scholarship reveals fairly little about the exile experience. In the preface of one of his books in exile published in 1939, he remarks that it was written in Panama with no adequate public library in which to conduct research. This makes it all the more remarkable that he thanks Vienna Professor Ernst Schönbauer, one of the most fervent Nazis in the Roman law community, for his help.[108]

For all of the Roman law exiles, one of the main factors whether they were able to secure a permanent position or not was the support given by established colleagues. In this, the help provided by different intermediaries such as de Zulueta or A. Arthur Schiller was crucial. Among these intermediaries were a number of recent immigrants, some of whom were very successful in their endeavors in helping refugees. One example of such a helper is Columbia Professor of Jewish History, Salo W. Baron, who emigrated to New York from Vienna in 1927. He assisted Guido Kisch, a legal historian from Halle who had been dismissed in 1933, in coming to America and finding a position in New York. Baron met him in the harbor, arranged for a hotel room and pushed him to learn English. He was also contacted by Hannah Arendt, whom he recruited as the

[108] Hans Julius Wolff, *Written and Unwritten Marriages in Hellenistic and Postclassical Roman Law* (Haverford: American Philological Association, 1939). The textbook was Hans Julius Wolff, *Roman Law: An Historical Introduction* (Norman, OK: University of Oklahoma Press, 1951).

executive secretary of the Jewish Cultural Reconstruction, Inc., an organization seeking to redistribute ownerless Jewish cultural artifacts mainly to communities in the US, and Hans Kelsen, who was seeking a place after Geneva.[109]

But even though help might be offered, numerous exiles experienced trust issues and loss of faith. The British internment of enemy aliens in 1940 would strengthen this distrust. Fritz Schulz, Fritz Pringsheim, Arnaldo Momigliano and David Daube all ended up in British internment camps on the Isle of Man. David Daube would later darkly comment that being bundled up in one place on the island, the Germans would have had no trouble in getting their hands on them if Britain had fallen in 1940.[110]

For the refugees, talk about the cause of liberty may sometimes have appeared naïve and simplistic and many were quick to shed any illusions about the way in which the ideals of liberty and equality were implemented in the US. Especially on the East Coast, traditional research universities were still using quotas to exclude Jews and in the big New York law firms and businesses only those with a WASP background were likely to be hired. During the 1930s and 1940s, segregation was still mostly unchallenged and the civil rights movement had not yet taken root. But for many exiles, liberty and equality, although somewhat tarnished concepts, was still the most important distinction between a society based on the rule of law and totalitarianism. Whether this distinction would be expanded beyond Nazi and fascist states and directed toward the Soviet Union was a crucial question that was faced at the start of the Cold War.

A further challenge to individual freedoms and the very concept of liberty was the rise of the executive branch, and the emergence of the administrative state. During wartime regulations, executive privilege was reinforced by different emergency powers and to an exceptional degree even for the US. It is ironic to note that in his Four Freedoms speech, Roosevelt maintained that during war the

[109] The extent of this aid is evident in Baron's correspondence. See Special Collections & University Archives, Stanford University Libraries, M0580 Salo W. Baron Papers, Series 1: Correspondence, Box 6, folder 4 Guido Kisch, containing twenty letters between 1933 and 1934. On Kisch's exile, see his autobiography Kisch, *Die Lebensweg eines Rechtshistorikers*, pp. 97–166.

[110] Ernst, "Fritz Schulz," pp. 158–160; Honoré, "Fritz Pringsheim," pp. 221–223; Calum Carmichael, *Ideas and the Man: Remembering David Daube* (Frankfurt: Vittorio Klostermann Verlag, 2004), p. 63.

country should be able to defend itself by all possible means, including limitations to basic freedoms. Even within these developments in the US, German refugees were vital in raising awareness of the challenges that executive privilege brings with it, especially those of discretionary powers wielded by the executive to curtail constitutional protections.[111]

Despite the difficulties that exiles faced in their adopted countries, the question of return was not easy. Many had been away for more than a decade after the war ended and return to a destroyed land where former Nazis were still in positions of authority was not tempting. In a letter to Salvatore Riccobono, Schulz writes that despite his difficult financial situation, he has no wish for returning to Germany because it would the end of his scientific work.[112] Schulz became a British citizen in 1947, again with the help of Sisam and others. In the previous year, he had written to Sisam that "Actually I have already decided – in spite of the precarious state of my finances – never to return to Germany for good."[113] This was a stance that was not uncommon among refugees: even a German nationalist like Ernst Kantorowicz would decide against a return, having received US citizenship and a permanent position in Berkeley, but even more importantly feeling that beside the few friends left, the Germany that he loved had vanished by embracing the "monstrous obscenity" of Nazism.[114] For exiles, many things spoke against return, such as the resurgence of anti-Semitism in Germany, the fact that almost all Jewish families had lost numerous members in the Holocaust and that they had by now started a new life. In many cases they had fought against Nazism by joining the Allied armies,

[111] Kornhauser, *Debating the American State*, pp. 49, 79.

[112] Letter from Schulz to Salvatore Riccobono, July 21, 1946, Collection of correspondence by Professor Salvatore Riccobono, currently at the disposal of Professor Mario Varvaro, at the Faculty of Law of the University of Palermo.

[113] Schulz to Sisam (September 5, 1946). Oxford University Press Archives, Oxford, Schulz PB ED 010382, no 36. Reacting to the reparations and recalls offered by German universities, Schulz wrote to the Rector of the University of Berlin in 1946 but the response was not positive as he was too old to teach in Germany and the bankruptcy of the German state meant that he was not going to receive the back pay owed to him. University of Zurich, Wolfgang Ernst Collection of Fritz Schulz Correspondence. 1931–1949.39: from Rektor Uni-Berlin, to Schulz (May 29, 1946 and April 23, 1946). Schulz did receive both an honorary professorship in Bonn in 1951 and pension, see Universitätsarchiv, Friedrich-Wilhelms-Universität Bonn, Personalakte Schulz, Fritz 9234.1-12.

[114] Lerner, *Ernst Kantorowicz*, p. 285.

and by gaining a new citizenship. This meant that they were often considered to be traitors in their native land by joining the enemies of Germany.[115]

The changes in scholarly thought that took place in exile or as a consequence of the exile process are complex and hard to classify. Söllner, in his famous account of exiled political scientists in the US, remarks that a tremendous scholarly effort was made to analyze Nazi policies and the reasons behind the revolution. The clear objective of these works was to fight against Nazism and often for democracy (or socialism).[116] Due to the nature of totalitarian society and the repression it entailed, the idea of liberty was a clear element in these works. In contrast, with scholars like Schulz, such changes were not as straightforward or easy to categorize. There was a crucial and clear reorientation of his scholarship from purely technical or discipline-internal debates to political argumentation. Instead of the ideas of democracy or political activity, Schulz began to rephrase the European tradition of liberty through a new reading of the classical tradition. His objective was plain: he wished to make a clear and evident opposition between the European tradition of liberty and Nazi policies. The fact that the ideas of liberty and equality became such central themes in the war effort and in US foreign policy became an incidental merging with the wider significance of these discussions in the antitotalitarian narrative. What for Schulz was an understated early discussion, became with Momigliano and Neumann a fully actualized political discourse about the opposition to totalitarianism and the implications of the idea of liberty in that opposition.

## Conclusions

Schulz writes that "Recent political experience has shown us the Roman Empire and its law in a new and clearer light."[117] What he does not do is clarify what he meant by this statement. When

[115] On the difficulties of reemigration, see Krauss, *Heimkehr in ein fremdes Land*. Many exiles did serve in the Allied forces. For example, of Schulz's children a son served in the First American Army and a daughter in the British Army. Oxford University Press Archives, Oxford, Schulz CP GE 000345, 11, letter Schulz to Sisam on January 8, 1945.

[116] Ash and Söllner, *Forced Migration and Scientific Change*, pp. 263–265.

[117] Schulz, *Principles of Roman Law*, p. 253.

addressing the ways in which Schulz discusses the principles of Roman law, it is soon fairly obvious that Roman law, or more precisely the principles and values embedded in the Roman legal and political system, becomes a counterpoint to the emerging Nazi legal order.

The idea of liberty is one of the great legacies of the Western liberal tradition. The notion it entailed was that protecting individual freedom should be the foundation of the relationship between the state and the individual. However, tracing modern freedom back to the ancient political tradition or even to the Roman law tradition was unusual, to say the least. In "The Liberty of Ancients Compared with that of the Moderns," Constant came to the conclusion that it was precisely the focus on the individual and his or her liberties which separate the modern conception of liberty from the ancient. Thus, ideas such as individual rights would be limited to the modern world.[118]

During the interwar period, the notion of liberty as a shared legacy came under heavy criticism from different directions, from authoritarians to revolutionaries and nationalists of various kinds. Economic crises, value crises and political crises appeared to show the impotence of the liberal state and the false promise of equality it held. Schulz, in his idiosyncratic fashion, seeks to present a novel understanding of liberty and justice based on Roman, German and British traditions, combining classical liberalism with the Roman legal tradition.

The concepts of freedom and order that are at the heart of this chapter became central in the reconception of German culture after the war. In attempting to make sense of the essence of German culture and being after the Nazi years, there was a widescale return among intellectuals to the classics, where the debates over culture, spirit and *Bildung* were central. In the postwar discussions about democracy, the issues of freedom and order were concerned with the self-definition of (West) Germany, using the concepts of individual freedom and democratic institutions as key definitions.[119] The attack of Nazi jurisprudence against the independence of law and its openly political conception of law demanded a counterpoint, one that was based not only on ideas of

[118] The relationship of both Constant and Schulz to the so-called neo-Roman tradition of liberty is a fascinating notion of historical reinterpretation. On this, see Luca Fezzi, *Il rimpianto di Roma. Res publica, libertà "neoromane" e Benjamin Constant, agli inizi del terzo millenio* (Milan: Mondadori Education, 2012).

[119] Forner, *German Intellectuals*, pp. 77–78.

freedom and democracy but also the notion that within law there was a long tradition of institutions that sought to secure individual liberties and rights.

The purpose of this chapter was to explore how this change in the understanding of the ideals of freedom and equality was understood and processed as a transatlantic discourse on law. The works of Schulz are part of a continuum with other émigré scholars, who in their writings sought to make sense of the Nazi attack on liberty but were also concerned with the future of the legal tradition. Other émigré scholars such as Franz Neumann sought to work through the meaning of totalitarianism and its implications based on their own experience. They did that through three main contexts: 1) the German and more generally European legal heritage; 2) the experience of repression in Nazi Germany; and 3) their contact with the British and American tradition of liberty and equality. In doing this, they both sought to provide a historical understanding and sought reference from the classical tradition.

The example of Schulz's *Principles* is an atypical work in this respect. It is an early response to Nazi persecution and the eradication of the tradition of law that had guaranteed ideas such as equality, liberty and the rule of law. It was, in a sense, a swansong to the tradition founded on Roman law that united European legal science. Its German version came out at the last moment, just before the ban on Jewish scholarly publications. It was, it should be added, a very strange book, one that combined hidden messages and an exploration of the roots of the European legal tradition in Roman law. As such, it was both historical and anachronistic. Its principles, the purported principles of Roman law, presented to all a clear counterpoint to Nazi policies. It lauded the freedom of law from politics instead of law as politics; citizenship based not on ethnicity but belonging; the continuity of law and legal tradition rather than revolution; the humanity of law and punishment against cruelty and inhumanity; the rule of law and security against terror and fear.

Within the theme of liberty, Schulz juxtaposes ancient and modern conceptions but presents the Roman tradition of freedom as nondominance, an idea later defined as a negative conception of freedom. This meant that freedom was served through the restraint of the state in the face of individual freedoms and the private sphere. It served as a fundamental criticism of Nazi ideology, which focused on the state and the negation of the individual as an actor. But in contrast to some notions of freedom, Schulz's freedom was paired with the concept of authority.

For a German author, Schulz's theory of liberty was founded on two unlikely sources: the legal scholarship of Jhering and the classical tradition of liberalism. There were no references to Kant or Hegel, not even to Savigny. The concept of liberty was not only a political or a legal one, for it combined both constitutional and private law approaches.

After publishing the *Principles,* Schulz was progressively marginalized, subject to the purge of the faculty by his fellow professors. His search for a position abroad confirmed the difficulties that his fellow exiles had noted, that more senior professors in fields with little interest abroad were least likely to find a new position that would have been in any way comparable to what they had left behind.

While Arendt, Neumann and others openly analyzed the Nazi state, observing a change in authors such as Schulz is much more difficult. In comparison with other scholars of ancient law who emigrated, it is possible to note similar changes of focus and discussions of themes of totalitarianism and repression, along with the value of civilization and tradition. Schulz's *Principles* can thus be juxtaposed with authors such as Momigliano, who had in their exile been engaged with both the experience of repression and flight, as well as a sense of tradition which they tried to recapture.

# 3 Redefining the Rule of Law, Jurisprudence and the Totalitarian State


## Abstract

This chapter explores the ideas of equality, cosmopolitanism and the rule of law as opposites to Nazi policies. Beginning with Fritz Pringsheim's article on Hadrian as an example, it analyzes how historical cases can be used to present the past as a covert argument against totalitarianism in the present. It juxtaposes Pringsheim's experience with two contemporaries, Franz Neumann and his theory on the rule of law and the totalitarian state, and Salvatore Riccobono on the fascist idealization of Roman law. By exploring the idea of jurisprudence as a culture of shared values, the chapter investigates the roots of the ideas presented later by David Daube in postwar scholarship and the origins of the concept of a European legal culture.


## Introduction

The past can be used in various ways for contemporary purposes. Nazi and fascist states harnessed the past to legitimize their policies, while Schulz, for example, founded his counternarrative on a novel usage of Roman material. The purpose of this chapter is to examine one example of the use of the past. German scholar of ancient Roman and Greek legal history, Fritz Pringsheim (1882–1967), before being exiled in Britain, sought to reinterpret the history of Roman law and seek a starting point for the cosmopolitan idea of legal equality in the Roman Empire. For this, he used the earlier tradition glorifying Hadrian's Rome to present an alternative to the racist authoritarian state that was being constructed by the Nazi regime. What this chapter demonstrates is that the understanding of a historical tradition is essentially situational and malleable, and can be reconfigured to suit new expediencies. Drawing from theories of narrativism, I claim that exiled scholars sought not only to gain recognition in their new environments but also to formulate a narrative to explain their personal experiences. The use of classical works and ancient history to express not only personal experience but also to debate political issues has a rich history. Pringsheim was just one among many scholars to take Roman emperors as a kind of surrogate stage, a means to deal with contemporary issues of power and leadership. Volkmann's 1935 book on Augustan jurisdiction was a parallel narrative to Hitler's emerging authoritarianism, while Pietro De Francisci, Mussolini's Minister of Justice, would write in a similar way about Augustus' powers in 1941. In England, Syme's famous 1939 work on Augustus presented a mirror to fascism and totalitarianism.[1]

I argue that one of the main reasons why Pringsheim's historical narrative was so effective is that it tapped into a long historical continuum and the intellectual authority of esteemed predecessors. In this case, the ancient Greek rhetorician Aelius Aristides started a tradition of idealizing Hadrianic Rome that resurfaced with Gibbon and later in nineteenth-century historical scholarship. This idealization extended to the glorification of Hadrian's legal policies in the Roman law tradition. Later, the historical tradition around Hadrian was utilized for contemporary purposes. It is this narrative tradition that Pringsheim explored in his important articles on Hadrian and the ideal of the rule of law.[2]

Much like Schulz, Pringsheim's early career gave little indication of this turn. He was, for all intents and purposes, a scholar of Roman law whose main works had until the Nazi takeover focused on fairly technical legal issues such as contracts of sale. A student of Ludwig Mitteis, Pringsheim was not, however, a typical Romanist working on classical Roman law, for he concentrated on the law of the Eastern part of the empire, known mostly from papyri. Instead of the idealized constructions of pure Roman law, Pringsheim's field was the law in practice, where different legal traditions mixed. Another formative experience

[1] Hans Volkmann, *Zur Rechtsprechung im Prinzipat des Augustus. Historische Beiträge* (Munich: Beck, 1935); Pietro De Francisci, *Genesi e struttura del principato Augusteo* (Rome: Reale Accademia d'Italia, 1941); Ronald Syme, *The Roman Revolution* (Oxford: Oxford University Press, 1939).

[2] Pringsheim, "Legal policy and reforms of Hadrian"; Pringsheim, "Höhe und Ende der Römischen Jurisprudenz."

was World War I, where he served as a junior officer in the front lines for five years, earning several medals for bravery. Considering the casualty rates of junior officers, he was lucky to be alive. This military service strengthened his already robust patriotic sense as a member of the educated middle class, the *Bildungsbürgertum*. The loss of his friends, such as Hans Peters, in the war left a lasting imprint.[3]

The ideals that Pringsheim raised as the core of Roman law, namely equality and the rule of law, were not as anachronistic as one might assume. In fact, the way Pringsheim approaches the question can be seen as historically accurate though his conclusions are fairly modern. However, for the contemporary reader of that time, their foremost relevance was how they addressed the threat of inequality and arbitrariness that the rise of totalitarianism had made so brutally pertinent. Pringsheim was far from alone in linking Roman law and the legal heritage it was associated with to the emergence of the ideals of equality and rule of law in European tradition. A similar process of reinterpretation of the European tradition of the rule of law and legalism and its value was embraced by a number of other exiles. In addition to Franz Neumann, we shall be looking at scholars like Leo Strauss and F. A. Hayek, who were central in defining the rule of law as a concept in opposition to totalitarianism.

The earlier literature on Pringsheim is scant, limited to a few obituaries. Of his experience in exile, the only more extended piece is Honoré's 2004 chapter.[4] It would appear that Pringsheim made an impact in two respects. First, as a teacher, where his influence was fundamental. Second, his scientific works, where his impact was less dramatic, due to his tendency to focus on minor issues. It is no doubt for this reason that his contribution to the emergence of the European historical narrative has been neglected.

## Pringsheim and the Nazi Takeover

Fritz Pringsheim's role as a fundamental figure in the creation of the narrative of the European legal tradition may appear surprising, all the more so because his main field was rather different. He was a leading

[3] Elmar Bund, "Fritz Pringsheim (1882–1967). Ein Großer der Romanistik," in Helmut Heinrichs, Hans-Harald Franzki, Klaus Schmalz and Michael Stolleis (eds.), *Deutsche Juristen Jüdischer Herkunft* (Munich: Beck, 1993), pp. 736–738.

[4] Honoré, "Fritz Pringsheim"; Breunung and Walther, *Die Emigration deutscher Rechtswissenschaftler ab 1933*, vol. 1, pp. 406–431; Bund, "Fritz Pringsheim."

scholar in the very specialized field of the Egyptian law of the papyri and especially the Greek law of sale.[5] However, Pringsheim had another field of interest, namely Roman legal scholarship and tradition, upon which he wrote numerous important articles.[6] In them, he strongly favored and idealized Classical Roman legal thought as opposed to the postclassical.

As with many scholars discussed in this book, Pringsheim's academic work gained a political edge as a result of Nazi policies targeting Jewish professors. Pringsheim's marginalization was a slow process and reflected his strong position within the academic community in Freiburg. Though Pringsheim was a World War I war hero and a Christian, he was nevertheless persecuted by the Nazis, dismissed from his chair in Freiburg in 1935 on account of his Jewish heritage and became an exile in Britain in 1939. Freiburg was at the time one of the leading academic centers in Germany and the Pringsheim family had a respected position among academic social circles. The family was not only wealthy, it also contained a large number of esteemed academics. While both Schulz and Pringsheim had been members of the DDP, their political outlook was quite different. Schulz was liberal, Pringsheim was a nationalist. This made little difference after the enactment of the Law for the Restoration of the Professional Civil Service in April 7, 1933 (GWBB, RGBl. I 175) that dictated the expulsion of Jewish civil servants, including university professors. In this early phase, Pringsheim himself was excluded from the scope of the law as he was protected by both his status as a soldier at the front in World War I (*Frontkämpfer*) and his long employment at the university. The purge of Jewish scholars in Freiburg was carried out under the leadership of the Rector, philosopher Martin Heidegger, who oversaw the implementation of the decree that ousted even his own predecessor Edmund Husserl. Pringsheim helped some of his students, such as David Daube, to gain a position in Britain. Another colleague, Eduard Fraenkel, escaped to Oxford in 1934. In Freiburg, Pringsheim was supported by his current and former students but that could not last, even though the official pressure was not as high as that faced by Schulz in Berlin. During the *Reichskristallnacht* on November 9, 1938, Pringsheim was arrested and put into a concentration camp at Sachsenhausen as

[5] Honoré, "Fritz Pringsheim"; Fritz Pringsheim, *The Greek Law of Sale* (Weimar: H. Böhlaus Nachfolger Pringsheim, 1950).

[6] Pringsheim's main works are collected in *Gesammelte Abhandlungen*, showing his combative and assertive style of scholarly debate.

the Nazis wanted to keep hostages in case of a reaction from abroad. He was released after three weeks due to pressure from friends and pupils but his mother had died during his imprisonment. For Pringsheim, this was the last straw that removed all illusions of his status and security. To his friends in Oxford, who had managed to secure him a five-year grant at Merton College, this meant that preparations for getting him out of the country became much more urgent.[7]

While his exile started only in 1939, the actual process of academic marginalization began in 1933. It manifested itself in small and gradually larger ways until the true impact of the regime became visible. The

Figure 3.1 Captured Jewish men being led to a concentration camp in Baden-Baden. Some 30,000 men, including Fritz Pringsheim, were imprisoned after *Kristallnacht* (November 8–9, 1938). Source: Wikimedia Commons. Bundesarchiv, Bild 183-86686-0008/CC-BY-SA 3.0, CC BY-SA 3.0 de

[7] Honoré, "Fritz Pringsheim," p. 220. Bodleian Library, Oxford, Archives of the Society for the Protection of Science and Learning, MS. SPSL. 438.4, 560: General Secretary of SPSL David Thomson to Under Secretary of State Cooper, November 14, 1938: "We have to-day heard that Professor Pringsheim is in a concentration camp as a result of the events of the last few days in Germany." SPSL requests that the Home Office allow him to come to Britain.

most visible forms of exclusion were difficulties with regard to teaching and publishing. As far as teaching was concerned, Pringsheim was protected by his status and was suspended only in 1935, being officially fired the following year. In contrast to many of his colleagues, his lectures were not disturbed by Nazi student organizations and he continued to teach until the spring of 1936. Pringsheim did not keep his dislike for the new regime secret and openly criticized its policies, even with Nazi brown and black shirts present. This was possibly due to the smaller social circles of Freiburg that restricted Nazi attacks to a certain extent.[8] Regarding publishing, his last published work in Germany is from 1934. Some of his students like Franz Wieacker, later one of the most influential legal historians in Germany, moved toward Nazism, allying themselves with academics sympathetic to the regime such as Carl Schmitt or Heidegger.

Pringsheim's esteemed position and his subsequent fall resembled in many ways that of Ernst Kantorowicz, who like Pringsheim had been a WWI frontline veteran and a conservative nationalist who moved in higher social circles. Kantorowicz could openly challenge the Nazis and argue against his treatment, having allies and friends who to a degree could protect him from harm. His calls for the preservation of human dignity and honor came from a position of privilege but did not ultimately protect him from losing his job. Even when leaving for exile, his travel permits were secured with the help of highly placed friends.[9]

Pringsheim's exile experience was not easy. At Oxford, Pringsheim secured a position of sorts at Merton College with the help of Francis de Zulueta, his former colleague Fraenkel, his former student Harry Lawson and others. One of the major issues was the size of his family, Pringsheim had six sons whose upkeep would demand considerable resources. He was, however, not an easy fit in Oxford. Not only did he have an air of superiority about him, the whole family was musical in a very loud and very German way. Following complaints from neighbors and an incident regarding a radio, which prompted suspicions of espionage, he was arrested on May 27, 1940 and interned with his sons on the Isle of Man even before the general internment of enemy aliens in June 1940. He was later only grudgingly released on December 19, 1940, months after his peers. During his years in exile, Pringsheim focused on research, living a quiet life at Merton College. While his

[8] Bund, "Fritz Pringsheim," p. 741.
[9] Lerner, *Ernst Kantorowicz* pp. 158–239.

sons took to the British way of life, Pringsheim never lost his connection with the German tradition and his sense of belonging. This is not to say that he would not have appreciated the British ideals of fairness, trustworthiness and self-control. After the war, he taught both at Oxford and after 1947 at Freiburg. The impact of Pringsheim's scholarship is reinforced by the fact that Tony Honoré, one of the main historians of Roman law in Britain after the war, was a pupil of Pringsheim.[10]

The issue of classical receptions often revolves around the questions of reuse and repurposing of themes, ideas and texts to serve new purposes. As in all questions concerning the influence of context in the works of an author, the central difficulty is that of intent. We shall in this chapter take one example of the glaring difference between Pringsheim's ideas and those of official Nazi ideology to see how Pringsheim utilized the classical heritage as well as the later scholarly tradition to present a contrast to Nazi theories and to practices of segregation and repression. However, it is impossible to say whether Pringsheim intended his work to be a criticism of anything contemporary. In the end, it is of secondary importance here, as the work presents such a contrast despite or beyond the intention of its author. Even in his lectures, Pringsheim was highly critical of Nazi policies and especially their legal reforms and the Nazi opposition to Roman law.[11] Scholars like Leo Strauss have maintained that writing under persecution operates under a different technique, where "writing between the lines" becomes the way in which crucial things are expressed in a shared understanding between the author and readers knowledgeable enough to recognize the intended meanings.[12] There was perhaps more to this phenomenon than meets the eye. Volkmann, De Francisci and Syme were all safe and respected within their own contexts but nevertheless their references to contemporary ideas and events are

[10] Bund, "Fritz Pringsheim," pp. 742–743; Archives of the Society for the Protection of Science and Learning, Bodleian Library, Oxford, MS. SPSL. 272.1, 30, letter of the General Secretary of AAC (= Adams) to Jolowicz (November 18, 1936), "Because of the responsibility of his six sons he is really in need." There are over 200 letters in the SPSL archives (MS. SPSL. 272.1) that document the negotiations around Pringsheim's transfer to Britain, his internment, negotiations for release and work in Oxford between 1935 and 1951.

[11] Fritz Pringsheim, "Die Haltung der Freiburger Studenten in den Jahren 1933–1935," *Die Sammlung*, 15 (1960), 534–535.

[12] Leo Strauss, *Persecution and the Art of Writing* (Chicago and London: University of Chicago Press, 1988), pp. 24–25.

concealed in their academic prose. In fact, Strauss was one of the few who would present the juxtapositions between ancient and modern phenomena in an explicit fashion but did so only later, after the war.[13] Pringsheim's choice of using concealed references was thus consistent with the academic style employed by his peers but was also used in the earlier nineteenth-century debates on the utility of Roman law.[14]

The story of Pringsheim illustrates how ideological battles take place in the interpretation of history as a demonstration of the values and ideas that define a community. While the struggle between Nazi ideology and the ideals of liberalism such as the rule of law and equality have very little to do with a Roman emperor like Hadrian, in the highly specialized literary culture of Roman law it became a surrogate stage for a more fundamental debate. More importantly, the cases of Pringsheim and Hadrian show how the clear-cut categories of liberal and conservative, friend and ally, disintegrate in the long span of human interaction and the links that bind scholars together.

## The Cosmopolitan Idea of Empire

To describe an ideal state, the Rome of the time of Hadrian has been a popular model ever since the Greek orator Aelius Aristides lauded Roman peace and justice at the time.[15]

Thus it was fitting that Pringsheim in 1934, the year of the beginning of the onslaught of Nazi terror and repression, would use Hadrian's Rome as a model for the cosmopolitan empire. This article, entitled "Legal policy and reforms of Hadrian," published in the *Journal for Roman Studies* in 1934, depicted Hadrian's Rome as an empire of peace, prosperity and law. An empire where the emperor would personally ensure that justice was served even to the lowliest of people and where a highly professional class of legal officials would bring about a rule of law.[16]

[13] Leo Strauss, *On Tyranny* (Chicago: University of Chicago Press, 2000, originally 1948). Another was David Daube (for example David Daube, *Appeasement or Resistance* [Berkeley and Los Angeles: University of California Press, 1987]), a pupil of Pringsheim. Strauss was related to Daube.

[14] E.g., James Q. Whitman, *The Legacy of Roman Law in the German Romantic Era* (Princeton, NJ: Princeton University Press, 1990).

[15] On this idealization, see Aldo Schiavone, *The End of the Past: Ancient Rome and the Modern West* (London and Cambridge, MA: Harvard University Press, 2000), pp. 3–19.

[16] The same themes come up in both Pringsheim, "Höhe und Ende der Römischen Jurisprudenz" and Pringsheim, "Legal policy and reforms of Hadrian" but the

Not only was the Nazi ideology strictly against cosmopolitanism, it was also against Roman law itself, as mentioned earlier. As noted earlier, the Party Program of the NSDAP (1920) called for the abolition of Roman law and its replacement with national German law.[17] They sought to abolish Roman law from the law curriculum and to eradicate it from German law books through the ultimately failed *Volksgesetzbuch* codification program. Roman law scholars who sought to reconcile Roman law with Nazi ideology usually focused on earlier periods, such as archaic Rome. The themes they emphasized were martial, underlining military prowess, virtues and loyalty to the state. The Roman virtue of *fides* was translated as *Treue*, loyalty, and interpreted according to Nazi ideology. While a number of German Roman law scholars became eager Nazi supporters, many others began to explore themes relevant to the Nazi movement, such as Max Kaser, who wrote about Roman law as social ordering, or Franz Wieacker, Pringsheim's student, who extolled the militaristic virtues of early Roman law. However, these attempts to reconcile Roman law with Nazism were defensive works seeking to alleviate the hostility of the regime to Roman law. This was in stark contrast with the Italian side of the fascist alliance, where the glory of Rome, Roman law and Romanness were an integral part of the self-understanding and identity of the Italian fascist state.[18]

While German scholars close to the Nazi regime were eager to present early Romans as some sort of quasi-Germanic warriors,[19] Pringsheim idealized the cosmopolitanism, the rule of law, bureaucratization and

conclusions drawn and the explicitness with which they are presented are markedly different, the German text being much more technical and understated.

[17] Point 19 of the NSDAP party program from February 24, 1920: "We demand that Roman Law, which serves a materialistic world order, be replaced by a German common law."

[18] Kaser, *Römisches Recht als Gemeinschaftsordnung*, pp. 8–9: "Das stolze Bild das Schönbauer hier von echtem Römertum entworfen hat, erinnert in manchen Zügen stark an die ältere deutsche Rechtsgeschichte, sind es doch die gleiche Tugenden, 'männliche Selbszucht, nationaler Instinkt, starkes Sendungsbewußtsein, Größe im Unglück und Opferbereitschaft für das Gemeinwesen,' die den Character beider Völker bestimmen." ("The proud image that Schönbauer provides us of genuine Romans, resembles in many ways strongly the older German legal history. The same virtues, 'manly self-discipline, national instinct, strong sense of mission, greatness in misfortune and willingness for sacrifice for the common good,' define the character of both peoples.") Wieacker, *Vom römischen Recht*, pp. 38–85. Pieler, "Das römische Recht im nationalsozialistischen Staat," p. 440 on the choice of words such as *Bodenrecht*, *Blut* and *Rasse* as code for belonging to the new order. On the totalitarian approaches to Roman law, see Miglietta and Santucci, *Diritto romano e regimi totalitari nel '900 Europeo* and Nelis, "Constructing fascist identity."

[19] See, for instance, Hans Frank, "Die Zeit des Rechts," *Deutsches Recht*, 6 (1936), 1–3.

the professionalization of legal administration. Needless to say, these were things that the Nazis disliked on many levels.

Pringsheim's article for the *Journal of Roman Studies* presented Emperor Hadrian as an ideal sovereign, a cosmopolitan ruler who wanted to "bring order and peace to the land." Hadrian considered himself to be a Stoic "first servant of the state, whose primary duty was to protect his subjects, the poor as well as the rich." This policy was prompted by the aggressive wars of expansion waged by his predecessor Trajan, which had overstrained the resources of the empire and had led to the disappearance of small peasant farmers, who were the backbone of Roman culture and prosperity.[20] From this background, Pringsheim builds up to a crescendo of praise for Hadrian:

> His aim was to maintain eternal peace in his eternal and world-wide Empire, and to secure the happiness of his people by the wisdom of their omnipresent ruler. A statesman had succeeded a soldier, and stress was laid rather on practical wisdom than military virtues.[21]

Pringsheim continues for a while about the virtues of Hadrian but ultimately argues that the greatest achievement of the emperor was the reform of the administration of justice.

According to Pringsheim, Hadrian was the first emperor to defend the poor against the rich, helping those in distress by hearing their cases and offering legal recourse. He took the Stoic philosophical doctrine of the general rights of man and put it into practice in administration and legislation.[22] The Roman emperor was at this point a central figure in the administration of justice, being at the same time the highest judge and the chief legislator.[23]

[20] Pringsheim, "Legal policy and reforms of Hadrian," p. 141. The demise of peasant farmers was one of the main explanations for the fall of the Roman Empire.

[21] Pringsheim,"Legal policy and reforms of Hadrian," pp. 141–142.

[22] Pringsheim, "Legal Policy and Reforms of Hadrian," p. 143. How much Hadrian was actually influenced by Stoicism is hard to estimate, as opposed to his successors such as Marcus Aurelius.

[23] On the emperor's legal capabilities, see Jochen Bleicken, *Senatsgericht und Kaisergericht: Eine Studie zur Entwicklung des Prozessrechtes im frühen Prinzipat* (Göttingen: Vandenhoeck & Ruprecht, 1964); Fergus Millar, *The Emperor in the Roman World 31 BC–AD 337* (London: Duckworth, 1977); Tony Honoré, *Emperors and Lawyers: With a Palingenesia of Third-Century Imperial Rescripts 193–305 AD* (Oxford: Clarendon Press, 1994); Michael Peachin, *Iudex vice Caesaris: Deputy Emperors and the Administration of Justice during the Principate* (Stuttgart: Franz Steiner, 1996); Simon Corcoran, *The Empire of the Tetrarchs: Imperial Pronouncements and Government AD 284–324* (Oxford: Clarendon Press, 2000); Kaius Tuori, *Emperor of Law: The Emergence of Roman Imperial Adjudication* (New York and Oxford: Oxford University Press, 2016).

Pringsheim repeats the oft-told anecdote (without mentioning the source) about the old lady who stopped Hadrian on the street to present him with a petition. When Hadrian says that he is in a hurry and does not have time to listen to her grievance, she retorts that he should stop being emperor then. Chastened, Hadrian stops and listens to her case.[24] The story is one of the great narratives of kingship in the ancient world. Variations are known not only from Hadrian, but the same story is repeated by Plutarch with near identical wording about both King Philip II of Macedonia and King Demetrius Poliorcetes.[25] The story is an apt reference to the times in a number of ways because it brought to the fore a principle of leadership that was startlingly similar to that embraced by authoritarian regimes. According to such principles, the leader is ultimately responsible and should be capable of bringing about justice and advancing good causes.[26]

Pringsheim presents the enlightened way in which Hadrian advanced law through the theme of equality and leniency. Punishments are measured against the intent of the perpetrator; the misuse of the father's power over his family is prevented; and the use of torture is restricted. He would unify the law by consolidating the praetor's edict, one of the main sources of Roman law. In order to ensure that the law was applied with consistency, Hadrian set up a solid administrative structure where trained civil officials worked. His own legal service was equally strengthened with the addition of trained lawyers to his council.[27] He continues about the ways in which lawyers would then be integrated into the civil service and ends this paean with a final word of praise about the deliberate care that is evident in Hadrian's reforms:

> No hasty acts, no violent reforms born of the moment deface this picture. Everywhere appears the careful guiding hand which weighs all the consequences and acts at many points with the same aim – the cautious hand of the true statesman. The collection of all the available forces for the well-being of the Empire, discipline instead of confusion, order and clearness – those were his aims for the army and for the defenders of the frontiers as well as for the administration of justice, the amendment of the edict and the furtherance of legal science.[28]

[24] The source of the story is the epitome of Dio's *Roman history* (69.6); Pringsheim, "Legal policy and reforms of Hadrian," p. 143.

[25] The references in Plutarch are *Mor.* 179 C–D, *Demetr.* 42.11. For the spread of the story in other ancient literature, see Millar, *The Emperor in the Roman World*, pp. 3–4.

[26] See also Jas Elsner, "Paideia: ancient concept and modern reception," *International Journal of the Classical Reception*, 20 (2013), 136–152.

[27] Pringsheim, "Legal policy and reforms of Hadrian," p. 143.

[28] Pringsheim, "Legal policy and reforms of Hadrian," pp. 152–153.

Pringsheim's vision of the Rome of Hadrian was of a golden age, of an empire at peace with itself. But while there had been a number of ancient authors who praised Hadrianic Rome, none had the gusto and intensity of Aelius Aristides.

Aristides was a second-century Greek rhetorician from Mysia in Asia Minor. He is best known for his so-called speech to Rome, in which he lauded the Roman Empire and its government.[29] He praised it for bringing about an era of peace and prosperity, a golden age much like one presented by Pringsheim later. Like Pringsheim, Aristides would see the administration of justice as a central part of the appeal. A clearly fascinated Aristides writes about appealing to the emperor:

Cases under judicial review, like an appeal from one's demesmen to the courts, take place with no less fear in regard to the verdict on the part of those who institute the appeals, so that one would say that people are now governed by

[29] The speech is conventionally titled Oration 26. On Aristides and the speech on Rome, see Ulrich von Wilamowitz-Möllendorf, "Der Rhetor Aristeides," *Sitzungsberichte der preussischen Akademie der Wissenschaften*, 28 (1925), 333–353; James H. Oliver, "The ruling power: a study of the Roman Empire in the second century after Christ through the Roman oration of Aelius Aristides," *Transactions of the American Philosophical Society*, 43 (1953), 871–1003; Glen W. Bowersock, *Greek Sophists in the Roman Empire* (Oxford: Oxford University Press, 1969); Peter Astbury Brunt, "Laus imperii," in Peter D. A. Garnsey and C. R. Whittaker (eds.), *Imperialism in the Ancient World* (Cambridge: Cambridge University Press, 1978), pp. 159–191; Vivian Nutton, "The beneficial ideology," in Peter D. A. Garnsey and C. R. Whittaker (eds.), *Imperialism in the Ancient World* (Cambridge: Cambridge University Press, 1978), pp. 209–223; Richard A. Klein, "Zur Datierung der Romrede des Aelius Aristides," *Historia*, 30 (1981), 337–350; Richard A. Klein, *Die Romrede des Aelius Aristides* (Darmstadt: Wissenschaftliche Buchgesellschaft, 1981); Richard A. Klein, "Zum Kultur- und Geschichtsverständnis in der Romrede des Aelius Aristides," in B. Kühnert, V. Riedel and R. Gordesiani (eds.), *Prinzipat und Kultur im 1. und 2. Jahrhundert* (Bonn: R. Habelt, 1995), pp. 283–292; Jean-Marie André, "La conception de l'État et de l'Empire dans la pensée gréco-romaine des deux premiers siècles de notre ère," *Aufstieg und Niedergang der römischen Welt*, 2.30.1 (1982), 3–73; Stephen A. Stertz, "Aelius Aristides' political ideas," *Aufstieg und Niedergang der römischen Welt*, 2.34.2 (1994), 1248–1270; Chiara Carsana, *La teoria della costituzione mista nell'età imperiale romana* (Como: Edizioni New Press, 1990); Charles A. Behr, "Studies on the biography of Aelius Aristides," *Aufstieg und Niedergang der römischen Welt*, 2.34.2 (1994), 1140–1233; P. Volpe, "Armonia e taxis nell'Encomio a Roma di Elio Aristide," in F. Giordano (ed.), *L'idea di Roma nella cultura antica, Atti del Convegno di Studi (Salerno 14–16 ottobre 1996)* (Naples: Edizioni scientifiche italiane, 2001), pp. 305–312; Tim Whitmarsh, *Greek Literature and the Roman Empire: The Politics of Imitation* (Oxford: Oxford University Press, 2001); Tim Whitmarsh, *The Second Sophistic* (Oxford: Oxford University Press, 2005); Jaap-Jan Flinterman, "Sophists and emperors: a reconnaissance of sophistic attitudes," in B. E. Borg (ed.), *Paideia: The World of the Second Sophistic* (Berlin and New York: De Gruyter, 2004), pp. 359–376; William V. Harris and Brooke Holmes (eds.), *Aelius Aristides between Greece, Rome, and the Gods* (Leiden and Boston: Brill, 2008).

those sent out to them in so far as it pleases them. How is this form of government not beyond every democracy? There it is not possible after the verdict is given in the city to go elsewhere or to other judges, but one must be satisfied with the decision, unless it is some small city which needs outside judges. But among you, now a convicted defendant or even a prosecutor, who has not won his case, can take exception to the verdict and the undeserved loss. Another great judge remains, who no aspect of justice ever escapes. And here there is a great and fair equality between weak and powerful, obscure and famous, poor and rich and noble. And Hesiod's words come to pass: "For easily he makes one strong and easily he crushes the strong," this great judge and governor, however justice guides him, like a breeze blowing on a ship, which does not, indeed, favor and escort the rich man more and the poor man less, but equally assists him to whomever it may come.[30]

It should be noted that Pringsheim does not quote Aristides in his text, even though it is hard to imagine that he would be unaware of it or of the poignant similarities that the two texts have. As a lawyer, Pringsheim does refer to a number of legal cases from Hadrian in the *Digest of Justinian*, in which the emperor is clearly writing in the first person and advancing enlightened legal policies. In these, Hadrian curbs the abuse of a father's power, emphasizing compassion, not cruelty (*Dig.* 48.9.5.). He likewise punished a woman for horribly abusing a slave girl, likewise demonstrating his outrage at the injustice (*Dig.* 1.6.2.) Finally, he quotes sources on how Hadrian had the best jurists of the land as his advisors.[31]

Aristides' speech was presented to an audience of notables from high society in Rome itself in the year 143 or 144. The venue was most likely the Athenaeum of Hadrian in the Roman Forum, a monument to the

30 Aristid. *Or.* 26.37–39: "(37) ὥστε ὑποχωρεῖ μὲν ἄρχων ἄρχοντι, ὅταν αὐτοῦ ὁ χρόνος ἐξήκῃ, καὶ οὐδ᾽ ἂν ἀπαντήσειε ῥᾳδίως: τοσοῦτον ἀπέχει τοῦ διενεχθῆναι ἄγαν, ὡς αὐτοῦ τῆς χώρας οὔσης. ἔκκλητοι δὲ ὥσπερ ἔφεσις ἐκ δημοτῶν εἰς δικαστήριον σὺν οὐκ ἐλάττονι τῶν δεξαμένων φόβῳ περὶ τῆς κρίσεως ἢ τῶν ποιουμένων γίγνονται. ὥστε φαίη τις ἂν τοσαῦτα ἄρχεσθαι τοὺς νῦν ὑπὸ τῶν πεμπομένων, ὁπόσα ἂν αὐτοῖς ἀρέσκῃ. (38) πῶς οὖν ταῦτα οὐκ ἐν τοῖς ἐπέκεινα πάσης δημοκρατίας; οὔκουν ἐκεῖ ἔξεστι μετὰ τὴν ἐν τῇ πόλει ψῆφον ἐνεχθεῖσαν ἐλθεῖν ἄλλοσε οὐδ᾽ ἐπ᾽ ἄλλους δικαστὰς, ἀλλὰ στέργειν ἀνάγκη τοῖς ἐγνωσμένοις, εἰ μή τις ἐστὶ μικρὰ πόλις, ὥστε προσδεῖσθαι δικαστῶν ὑπερορίων παρὰ τὴν ἀξίαν, ἢ καὶ διώκοντα μὴ κρατήσαντα, μηδὲ τῷ νενικῆσθαι: ἀλλὰ μένει δικαστὴς ἕτερος μέγας, ὃν οὔποτε οὐδὲν ἐκφεύγει τῶν δικαίων: (39) κἀνταῦθα δὴ πολλὴ καὶ εὐσχήμων ἰσότης μικροῦ πρὸς μέγαν καὶ ἀδόξου πρὸς ἔνδοξον καὶ πένητος δὴ πρὸς πλούσιον καὶ γενναῖον ἀγεννοῦς, καὶ τὸ τοῦ Ἡσιόδου συμβαίνει, 'ῥεῖα μὲν γὰρ βριάει, ῥέα δὲ βριάοντα χαλέπτει' οὗτος ὁ δικαστής τε καὶ ἡγεμὼν, ὅπως ἂν τὸ δίκαιον ἄγῃ, ὥσπερ πνεῦμα ἐν νηὶ, οὐ δή που πλουσίῳ μὲν μᾶλλον, πένητι δὲ ἧττον χαριζόμενόν τε καὶ παραπέμπον, ἀλλ᾽ ὅτῳ γένοιτο ἀεὶ, τοῦτον ὁμοίως ὠφελοῦν." Translation by Charles A. Behr (ed.), *P. Aelius Aristides: The Complete Works*, vols. 1–2 (Leiden: Brill, 1981–1986).

31 SHA *Hadr.* 18.1, 22.11–12; Cass. Dio 69.7.1–2.

learning and civilization of Hadrian and the link he wanted to make between Rome and the Greeks.[32] Pringsheim's audience was the Faculty of Law at the University of Cambridge. There is a reason why the audience matters. For Aristides, the chance of performing in Rome at the age of twenty-six was an opportunity, a chance to make a name for himself. As has been shown in studies on Roman provincial elites, they were the staunchest supporters of the empire and not coincidentally its greatest beneficiaries.[33] By making a good impression, Aristides had a chance of gaining imperial patronage and with it a position as the emperor's adviser. If he played his cards right, he would soon be rich and powerful. For Pringsheim, the setting was similar. He was talking to an audience of British academics, and like Aristides he was presenting his own learning and culture. But while Aristides sought to present the advantages of Rome in the language of Greek philosophy and kingship theory, Pringsheim had the more upsetting subtext of the rise of the Nazi regime and the distress it brought to Jewish scholars and Roman law. Both had a clear agenda, namely to establish a new beginning and open up new possibilities.

## Reinterpretations of a Historical Tradition

Pringsheim's Rome or his ideal of Rome was not born in a vacuum. On one hand, there was the lawlessness of the Nazi repressions that influenced him, on the other, the far-reaching idealizing tradition.

At first sight, Pringsheim's presentation demonstrated the advances made by Hadrian and Rome in the administration of law, a fairly typical outline of facts. What made it different was the context of the speech and the weight that he put on the almost liberal virtues of Rome. Simply put, the exemplarity of Rome highlighted what was wrong in Germany since the Nazi takeover.

The paper was presented at Cambridge on October 27, 1933 and published the following year in an expanded form. After a tumultuous period, Adolf Hitler was appointed *Reichskanzler* of Germany on January 30, 1933. After the fire in the Reichstag building, the President's Decree on the Protection of the State and the People on February 28, 1933 gave the chancellor unprecedented powers, which

[32] Schiavone, *End of the Past*, p. 3; Laurent Pernot, "Aelius Aristides and Rome," in Harris and Holmes, *Aelius Aristides between Greece, Rome, and the Gods*, pp. 175–201, at 178. The date of the speech is contested.

[33] Flinterman, "Sophists and emperors," pp. 362–365.

were further strengthened on March 24 with the Enabling Act (*Ermächtigungsgesetz* or *Gesetz zur Behebung der Not von Volk und Reich*). This law gave Hitler the power to enact laws without the approval of parliament. All parties except the NSDAP were soon banned and on July 14 it was the only permitted party. In the elections held on November 12, 1933, the voters were given just one option, to confirm the NSDAP takeover.[34]

Behind these bare facts was a nation gripped by confrontation and paralysis. The fear of communists staging a coup, until recently a very real danger, had subsided, but realization of the Nazi seizure of power had not quite sunk in. What lawyers like Pringsheim would comprehend was that the emergency decrees enabled Hitler to act without legal constraint. A pliant legislature had already accepted the firing of Jewish officials even though war veterans such as Pringsheim were initially excluded. How much he considered that to be a lasting exemption is impossible to say but the writing was already on the wall. It was clear from early on that constitutional guarantees of civil rights were no longer to be trusted and the replacement of civil servants with supporters of the new regime meant that laws were to be applied according to the aims of the state. One of the main results was that the limits placed by the forces of order on the power of the SS and the SA to terrorize opponents disappeared (see Figure 2.1). Even earlier, few of the culprits were punished. Now, Nazi gangs would forcibly remove civil servants, judges and professors, beat them up and throw them into the street without restraint.[35]

Pringsheim's account of the reforms of Hadrian forms a counterpoint to these alarming developments. Like so much of the art and scholarship that addresses sensitive issues during a time of crisis and repression, this too operates with an elegant ease that avoids making any reference to current circumstances. It is also entirely possible that Pringsheim never intended it as an overt criticism of Nazi policies. However, there are earlier examples where Pringsheim writes about the dangers of politically motivated influences to the legal order. In his

[34] The process has been dealt with extensively in the literature. See, for example, Martin Broszat, *Die Machtergreifung. Der Aufstieg der NSDAP und die Zerstörung der Weimarer Republik* (Munich: Deutscher Taschenbuch-Verlag, 1984); Richard J. Evans, *The Coming of the Third Reich* (London: Allen Lane, 2003).

[35] Claudia Koontz, *The Nazi Conscience* (London and Cambridge, MA: The Belknap Press, 2003). On the legal process of gradual exclusion, see Stolleis, *Law under the Swastika*; Michael Stolleis, *Geschichte des öffentlichen Rechts in Deutschland. 3. Band, Staats- und Verwaltungsrechtswissenschaft in Republik und Diktatur 1914–1945* (Munich: Beck, 1999).

German writings in the 1920s and early 1930s, he warned of the departure from the letter of the law, and of using general concepts to derive solutions that were only nominally within the law. In these debates, he had framed the contradiction between Byzantine and Roman law, where the Byzantine way had been to use general concepts like equity to form new law. The danger of such a practice is that it enables judges to use this flexibility to advance political aims. By resorting to general principles, an unscrupulous judge could bring about tyranny by using them to override legal protections. Far from being alarmist, this proved to be prescient, as this was precisely what Nazi judges would often do in their judgments. In these contributions, Pringsheim makes similar disguised references to totalitarianism while others made direct links to Soviet Russia.[36] It is somewhat ironic that one of the few scholars who would also recognize the danger of the frequent use of general principles to subvert law was Hedemann, who would become one of the main architects of Nazi legal reform.[37]

Though the way Pringsheim discussed the impact of the loosening of legal standards and the criteria of law were by and large oblique and visible only to specialists, he did not shy away from controversy. On November 20, 1933, a month after his lecture in Cambridge, he sent an open letter to Carl Schmitt asserting the enduring value of Roman law and contradicting the party program calling for its suppression. Schmitt was at that point at the height of his power during his time in the Nazi regime. A professor in Berlin and holder of the title *Staatsrat*, he would be central in legitimating the elimination of Jewish scholars and ideological opponents from German legal academia. Pringsheim would press the issue in his notes to a very reluctant Schmitt, asserting that the heritage of Roman law was an essential part of German legal tradition, sweeping aside imaginary Germanic frameworks and ethnic categories favored by the Nazis.[38] This shows how strong Pringsheim felt his

[36] Fritz Pringsheim, "Aequitas und bona fides," in *Gesammelte Abhandlungen* 1 (Heidelberg: Carl Winter & Universitätsverlag, repr. 1961, orig. 1930), 160–162; Hans-Peter Haferkamp, "'Byzantium!' – *bona fides* between Rome and 20th century Germany," in Tuori and Björklund, *Roman Law and the Idea of Europe*, pp. 145–157.

[37] Justus Wilhelm Hedemann, *Die Flucht in die Generalklauseln: eine Gefahr für Recht und Staat* (Tübingen: Mohr Siebeck, 1933).

[38] The debate between Pringsheim and Schmitt is now reproduced in Pringsheim, "Die Haltung der Freiburger Studenten in den Jahren 1933–1935," pp. 532–538. On Schmitt's position, see Mehring, *Carl Schmitt*; Gopal Balakrishnan, *The Enemy: An Intellectual Portrait of Carl Schmitt* (London: Verso, 2000); Andreas Koenen, *Der Fall Carl Schmitt* (Darmstatt: Wissenschafliche Buchhandlung, 1995). On Schmitt's ambivalence to Roman law, see Luigi Garofalo, "Carl Schmitt e la 'Wissenschaft des römischen Rechts.' Saggio su un

position was, not to mention his personal courage, to take on publicly the intellectual leader of the Nazi legal academia.[39]

The use of Hadrianic Rome as an idealized counterpoint to the emerging totalitarian state was a novel idea but it did have a number of precedents. Ever since the works of Gibbon, the idealizing tradition of Hadrianic Rome has been strong. Gibbon himself famously presented the Rome of the four good emperors as the happiest state of mankind. Gibbon writes:

> In the second century of the Christian era, the Empire of Rome comprehended the fairest part of the earth, and the most civilised portion of mankind. The frontiers of that extensive monarchy were guarded by ancient renown and disciplined valor. The gentle but powerful influence of laws and manners had gradually cemented the union of the provinces. Their peaceful inhabitants enjoyed and abused the advantages of wealth and luxury. The image of a free constitution was preserved with decent reverence: the Roman senate appeared to possess the sovereign authority, and devolved on the emperors all the executive powers of government. During a happy period (AD 98–180) of more than fourscore years, the public administration was conducted by the virtue and abilities of Nerva, Trajan, Hadrian, and the two Antonines.[40]

Gibbon would in his influential chapter 44 present Roman law as the foundation of this remarkable social peace.[41] Similar points were raised in the literature of the nineteenth century, where the peace and happiness of the empire was combined with it reaching its largest extent geographically. Gregorovius and others painted Hadrian in admiring terms as a truly enlightened sovereign, their works somewhat obviously building up the general theme of the admiration of all things imperial prevalent in the era.[42]

cantore della scienza giuridica europea," *Anuario da Facultade de Dereito da Universidade da Coruña*, 11 (2007), 299–323.

39 This incident is discussed in passing in Mehring, *Carl Schmitt*, p. 317.

40 Edward Gibbon, *The Decline and Fall of the Roman Empire*, vol. 1 (New York: International Book Company, 1845), p. 27.

41 Edward Gibbon, *The Decline and Fall of the Roman Empire*, vol. 3 (New York: International Book Company, 1845), pp. 209–258. The contemporary relevance of Gibbon's work and the possibility of seeing it as a parable for the decline of the British Empire would be worthy of a whole new study.

42 Ferdinand Gregorovius, *Geschichte des römischen Kaisers Hadrian und seiner Zeit* (Königsberg: Bonn, 1851); Bernard W. Henderson, *The Life and Principate of the Emperor Hadrian* (London: Methuen, 1923); Anthony R. Birley, *Hadrian: The Restless Emperor* (London: Routledge, 1997). On the idealization of empires, see Ines Stahlmann, "Vom Despoten zum Kaiser. Zum deutschen Augustusbild im 19. Jahrhundert," in K. Christ and Arnaldo Momigliano (eds.), *L' Antichita nell'Ottocento in Italia e Germania* (Bologna: Società editrice il Mulino, 1988), 303–319.

What Pringsheim did was to use this earlier tradition to prove his point. He presented Rome as a cosmopolitan empire that embraced as citizens people of different ethnicities and backgrounds. It protected even the lowliest of people, such as slaves, against abuses. It guaranteed the independence of the law and the legal profession, even though the legal administration was centralized and professionalized. All of these were issues that made a strong contrast with the state of law after the Nazi takeover. For the Nazis, law was a continuation of political will. Thus, rights were not something that were guaranteed to all citizens. Rather, they were determined by racial and ethnic factors. Carl Schmitt himself had denied the existence of human equality, universal human rights or even universal human value, by stating that not every being with a human face should have human dignity.[43] As was discussed in Chapter 2, Nazi legal ideology was strongly against the whole conception of equality against the law, arguing that law should grant different, preferential treatment to the members of the German blood community. The rule of law defined by strict legalism and the observance of the law by officials was equally to be replaced by adherence to the spirit of the law and the flexible use of the principles behind the law (see Figure 2.2). This idea, the unification of the legal order and the ideological or political order, was described with the idea of "concrete order" (*konkrete Ordnung*), a concept popularized by Schmitt.[44]

The very conception of the rule of law or *Rechtsstaat* was criticized by the very people who had helped create it. For example, Walter Jellinek, the son of Georg Jellinek, one of the founders of the German *Rechtsstaat*, maintained that the strict actions of the state were necessary to create unity and things like forced sterilizations were necessary for the well-being of the people. For him, the crucial part of the justification was that the Nazi effort was an antiliberal national revolution that suppressed

[43] Oliver Lepsius, "The problem of perceptions of National Socialist Law or: was there a constitutional theory of National Socialism?", in Joerges and Ghaleigh, *Darker Legacies of Law in Europe*, pp. 19–41; Koontz, *Nazi Conscience*. Quotation reproduced by Koontz, *Nazi Conscience*, p. 2; the original was published in "Das gute Recht der deutschen Revolution," *Westdeutscher Beobachter*, 9(108), May 12, 1933. Schmitt's original words were a criticism of Fichte's phrase "Gleichheit alles dessen, was Menschenantlitz trägt," but it became a general Nazi way of implying the worthlessness of lesser races. Schmitt was, of course, in favor of the equality of the members of the German people.

[44] See Bernd Rüthers, *Entartetes Recht* (Munich: Beck, 1989), p. 62 and passim on the evolution and implications of this concept.

the individual. The individual is nothing without the state. Human dignity itself is preconditioned by subordination to the state.[45]

The ideas outlined by Pringsheim were not necessarily liberal in themselves and he was certainly not a liberal himself. Pringsheim was a member of the conservative academic classes that formed the backbone of the civil service and legal academia in Germany. He had served as an officer in World War I and was clearly a proud German nationalist.[46] His embrace of the cosmopolitan ideal was thus not self-evident and it is worth looking at the way he outlined it. The vision he presents is in fact a conservative one, where the learned and professional civil service and legal administration were central in fulfilling the ideals of Hadrian's empire. There was very little in the way of popular engagement, not to mention democracy. The egalitarianism that Pringsheim praised was in essence the theoretical legal equality of the same rules being applied to all.

One interesting feature was that Pringsheim's pupils such as Franz Wieacker would continue to develop this idea. What makes this remarkable is that Wieacker joined the Nazi Party and wrote extensively about how to combine Nazi ideas with legal historical scholarship and the study of Roman law. Despite this inherent controversy, Wieacker's article on the reforms of Hadrian was published the following year (1935) and made a number of similar points about the value of the legal elite and the professionalization of the law.[47] Missing from Wieacker's presentation, however, were any references to cosmopolitanism. Wieacker became one of the Nazi "young lions" in legal academia and would only return to this theme after the war and after, with Pringsheim's help, his rehabilitation. This shows how the links between pupil and teacher overcame such political and racial divisions as those between the Nazis and their opponents.

## Narrative and Exile

The repression of academic scholarship and scholars has often been seen as a simple process in which scholars facing repressive measures

[45] Walter Jellinek, "Le droit public en l'Allemagne en 1933," *Annuaire de L'Institut International de Droit Public*, (1934), 52–53.

[46] Honoré,"Fritz Pringsheim," p. 212; Jacob Giltaij and Ville Erkkilä, "An interview with Tony Honoré," *Forum Historiae Iuris* (February 26, 2015).

[47] Franz Wieacker, "Studien zur Hadrianischen Justizpolitik," *Romanistische Studien: Freiburger Rechtsgeschichtliche Abhandlungen*, 5 (1935), 43–81.

either flee into exile or are imprisoned or marginalized. What this overlooks is the fact that the formation of totalitarianism is a gradual process and thus repression should also be approached as a process. The scientists exiled by Nazi Germany represent just a small, albeit visible, part of the phenomenon of exile scholarship. However, exiles like Pringsheim were for a long time conduits between two worlds and were able to present new ideas both before and after exile. What I am suggesting is that there is a moment during which criticism of the regime is still possible and the texts written during this time can be read as having a double meaning, one at the surface level and the other a deeper, concealed political meaning.

What was this political meaning? Pringsheim's article for the *Journal of Roman Studies* and its similarity to those of Aelius Aristides and Gibbon are concerned with praise of ancient Roman law and its legal administration, hardly at the outset a politically volatile topic. However, the position of Roman law was at the heart of the planned Nazi reconfiguration of the German legal system. According to Nazi ideology, the idea of the abolition of Roman law was that the law should reflect the German national spirit, the feeling of justice as imagined by the Nazis. As such, the onus of the law should be the people and the community not the elite structure of the legal profession. Roman law was not only materialistic, to many it also represented a Semitic influence. This meant that classical Roman law would have been influenced by jurists from the Middle East like Ulpian, who the Nazis suggested had Semitic roots.[48] The Nazi conception of the people and the idea of the blood community was not purely ethnic but rather a mixture of misguided eugenics and old German mysticism.[49]

Not surprisingly, scholars of Jewish heritage like Pringsheim and Fritz Schulz lauded the autonomy of Roman law and its scientific nature as

[48] This Semitic theory can be traced to the nineteenth century but it spread to a wider audience through the works of Spengler. The theory was heavily criticized and never spread to Italy. On the literature, see Beggio, *Paul Koschaker*, p. 60; Gamauf, "Die Kritik am römischen Recht im 19. und 20. Jahrhundert." The Nazi theories of Germanic law had its roots in the German law scholarship or *Germanisten*, who opposed the continuing influence of Roman law.

[49] Much has been written about the nationalist elite groups like the Stefan George circle and their role in the intellectual foundation of Nazism as a combination of nationalism, elitism and mysticism but the intellectual lineage is much too confused to offer any explanations. See, for example, Ernst Osterkamp, "The legacy of the George circle," in D. Kettler and G. Lauer (eds.), *Exile, Science and Bildung: The Contested Legacies of German Emigre Intellectuals* (Berlin: Springer, 2005), pp. 19–26 showing how the émigrés that had belonged to the George circle took very different routes in exile.

a contrast to the oppression and lawlessness of the Nazi regime. This is also the moment when they were able to do that, because after 1935 the journals and publishers had effectively stopped publishing texts from scholars that were either Jewish or of Jewish heritage.[50] Even in 1933–1934, open criticism was dangerous as the universities were a target of purges from student organizations who were critical of the slowness with which the universities performed the process of Aryanizing.

Historical writing on the origins and foundations of a legal culture can be seen as much more than a way of presenting factual history. Such historical writing operates as a foundational narrative, emphasizing not only the origins, but also the fundamental nature of a tradition.[51] As such, historical lineages are a choice. When analyzing the way Pringsheim presents the origins of the themes of cosmopolitan law and the ideas of equality and legality, this approach opens ways to discuss the text beyond the purely historical level. The issue of origins has near mythical connotations, despite the insistence of modern law on being rational and scientific.[52] Stories of origins are foundational narratives, stories of belonging that reveal the essential nature of the legal culture. By doing so, they define not only the past but seek to demarcate the potential for the future as the birth of nationalist ideologies so clearly demonstrates.

Pringsheim, like Schulz, wanted to show a different kind of past, a tradition of law and legal scholarship that also reflected a vision for the future, perhaps unknowingly. Thus, a historical narrative is not only an attempt at depicting reality, it is a normative reformation of tradition. A vision of a golden age, like Pringsheim's, is a way to project onto the past the ideals of the present.

For Pringsheim, to present these to a new audience in Britain was an opportunity to develop new themes and to continue old ones. He would continue the narrative of legal scholarship as a self-

[50] A study by Thomas Finkenauer and Andreas Herrmann, "Die Romanistische Abteilung der Savigny-Zeitschrift im Nationalsozialismus," *Zeitschrift der Savigny-Stiftung für Rechtsgeschichte. Romanistische Abteilung*, 134 (2017), 1–48, examines statistically how the principle of self-censorship led to the gradual elimination of references to Jewish scholars and how this was reflected in the scientific journals of legal history and Roman law. This policy was already outlined in *Das Judentum in der Rechtswissenschaft* (1935), the publication of the Nazi seminar on removing Jewish influence in law led by Hans Frank, the Minister of Justice for Bavaria, and Carl Schmitt.

[51] Tuori, *Ancient Roman Lawyers and Modern Legal Ideals.*

[52] On this illusion of rationality, see Fitzpatrick, *Mythology of Modern Law.*

referential pursuit that ought to set the standard for law, even though it was in conjunction with state power. That particular narrative was less familiar to the British audience than it was to the German, making it important that the underlying theme of the glorification of Hadrian was so well established in Britain by Gibbon's *Decline and Fall.*

Pringsheim would appeal to tradition, and to continuity and heritage as a criticism toward the present and the policies that it entailed. The glorifying narrative that he creates is not only a vision of an imaginary golden age, it is also an alternative to the policies of reform, the *Gleichschaltung* (roughly translatable as falling in line or subordination to the party) of the state around the principles of the Nazi racial hierarchies.

Fundamentally, Pringsheim's article told the story of the role of law and the legal profession in society. He, among many others, including many former Nazis (including his own pupil Franz Wieacker), would later present the narrative of the long tradition of legal scholarship, the primacy of law and legal learning as a shared European heritage.

## Equality, the Rule of Law and European Tradition

Raising the principles of equality and the rule of law as foundations of European tradition dating back to ancient Rome and its legal heritage was in many ways problematic. Not only was Roman law itself prepared to categorize people in a multitude of ranks that received different treatment and had different rights but also the conception of the rule of law was historically an illusion. The political and legal idea of equality and legalism in ancient Rome was, however, a deeply held conviction among the Romans themselves from Cicero to Ulpian and beyond. Never mind the fact that who was included in this sphere of equals was a matter of dispute.[53]

What was not a matter of dispute, however, was how these ideals had infiltrated legal discourse and influenced the whole European conception of law. It was seen as a system that was universal within its bounds, and if no exceptions were stated, all were equal under the law. Because the German legal tradition had been a prime mover in the solidification

[53] On this illusionarity of the republic and its constitution, see Louise Hodgson, *Res Publica and the Roman Republic: "Without Body or Form"* (Oxford: Oxford University Press, 2017).

of the legalistic tradition, culminating in the conception of the *Rechtsstaat*, the dissolution of this system under Nazi rule prompted numerous counterreactions among exiles. In this section, we will explore how this challenge of legalism was seen by contemporaries such as Neumann and F. A. Hayek. They represent two opposing traditions about Nazism and the ideal of the rule of law that emerged among the exiles. In the conception of Neumann, the collapse of the rule of law was possible because the Nazis used the framework of jurisprudence and that of monopolitistic capitalism to their advantage. Hayek presented a completely opposing view, where he ties together socialism, Nazism and progressivism as inimical to the rule of law and freedom.

One of the crucial traits of the exile process was its ties with the transatlantic transfer of ideas. Intellectual and institutional connections between Germany, France, Britain and the US, not to mention other European countries, spread ideas and practices on an unprecedented scale. The legal, social and political changes brought about by the rise of industrialization and urbanization led to a need for new solutions, and in matters like social policy progressive thought spread as different models were sought. While in the nineteenth century, such developments had largely spread from Europe to North America, the success of the American experiment led to a corresponding scholarly interest. Conversely, the early authoritarianism and its apparent success in solving economic, political and social issues led to a new interest in authoritarian progressivism as a solution to the crisis of democracy.[54]

In the field of law and politics, the interest in the American experiment had since de Tocqueville ranged from ideas of liberal democracy and freedom, but now since the early years of the twentieth century exciting new ideas of legal realism were coming from the States. With the stark realities of Nazism emerging during *Kristallnacht* and the increasingly harsh repression and lawlessness of the regime becoming clearer, a clear shift was apparent in American public opinion. While the Nazi ideology had been appealing, especially to the German immigrant population in the US, whose organizations were heavily influenced by Nazism, the highly public rampages against innocent civilians had an inoculation effect. Some have even maintained that

[54] Daniel T. Rodgers, *Atlantic Crossings: Social Politics in a Progressive Age* (Cambridge, MA: Harvard University Press, 2000), pp. 411–412.

the negative US reaction to the Nazis was one of the reasons why the strict interpretation of constitutional protections and individual rights became the defining traits of American legal culture. Tolerance of minorities, the curbing of the rights of the police to infringe on individual privacy and generally religious, ethnic and value pluralism were both commonly espoused and enshrined in law and judicial practice. Equality and freedom became not only the leading principles of the judiciary, where judges conceived themselves to be the protectors of equality and freedom but increasingly a matter of American self-definition.[55]

Neumann's 1942 *Behemoth* is an attempt to comprehend the Nazi regime, its ideology and practices, but it can be also read as an analysis of the demise of the rule of law in Germany. It clearly shows Neumann's legal background, containing a large section on the Nazi legal system and its logic. Neumann, in ways that make apparent both his function as a trade union lawyer and his legal theoretical understanding, seeks to lay out the foundations of the Western democratic legal system and the ways that the Nazis systematically sought to undermine them.

According to Neumann, what National Socialism did was to destroy the generality of the law, the independence of the judiciary and the prohibition of retroactivity. However, Neumann sees behind these events the developments in legal doctrine and in monopolistic capitalism that preceded them. In order to describe the Nazi legal system, Neumann begins with the basic conceptions of law from natural law theories to positivism: "The formal structure of the law became decisive" (p. 441). Modern law rests on the propositions of the rule of law, the denial of natural law, including morality, and the subordination of the judge to the law. For Neumann, the central developments revolve around the concepts of freedom and equality before the law, which are embedded in the deep structure of the European legal tradition. National Socialism took advantage of the inherent weakness of these ideas, claiming, like Marxist critics before them, that freedom and equality are mere shams behind which real exploitation is hidden. Instead of equal rights, the Nazis offered equal duties.[56] In fact, much of the criticism of liberalism and law, the formalism and the irrelevance of the real iniquities, is common to both Neumann and Schmitt.

[55] William E. Nelson, *The Legalist Reformation: Law, Politics, and Ideology in New York, 1920–1980* (Chapel Hill, NC: University of North Carolina Press, 2001), p. 130.

[56] Neumann, *Behemoth*, pp. 440–452.

What Nazi legal practice amounts to is law only if one reduces law to the command of the leader. But to Neumann, Nazi "law" was not rational in either form or content. In Nazi Germany the existing system of law was gradually turned into an administrative process that in criminal cases served to instill deterrence through terror, and civil law served the interests of monopolistic businesses. This is in contrast to the professed legal ideology, and here Carl Schmitt is Neumann's main source. The prevailing Nazi legal ideology was institutionalistic, using concepts such as "concrete order" that rejected legal personhood in favor of an organic conception of the state as a community that is built of communities. The role of the individual is thus reduced to his or her status in society or the community. As such, the generality of the law is no longer possible as each case must be resolved individually, taking into account the intuition of the judge and the aims of the movement.[57] The flexibility of the law was thus a threat that made it vulnerable to the whim of the judge. Within concrete order, there is no equality before the law.

The impact of exile in the US is very clearly present in the works of Neumann, where he shows the background of a Germanic understanding of the legal system and seeks to convey its implications to a new readership. More specifically, he outlines the conceptions of the rule of law and *Rechtsstaat*, a comparison between the Continental and Anglo-American concepts and their relationship. There are two overriding themes in this presentation: first, the issue of what went wrong in the *Rechtsstaat* that enabled the Nazi system to be created; and second, the implications raised for the American audience. In the first instance, Neumann lays the blame not only on the Weimar Constitution and its practice but also on the free law movement and its casually iconoclastic mentality. There are some quite specific references to the German discussions such as the debates over general clauses and their interpretation and implications concerning the possibility of tyranny.

In his 1944 *The Road to Serfdom*, F. A. Hayek (1899–1992) lays out his opposition to the interventions of the state, while supporting the rule of law as a principle of market economy and competition. What Hayek and Neumann shared was support for the ideas of freedom, equality and the rule of law. Hayek was an Austrian economist but he had worked at the London School of Economics (LSE) since 1931. After the *Anschluss*, the

[57] Neumann, *Behemoth*, pp. 448–458.

annexation of Austria in March 1938, he was unable to return and stayed in Britain, gaining citizenship in 1938.

Hayek's idea of freedom in *The Road to Serfdom* was a very fundamental concept for the role of the state in society. According to Hayek, the same characteristics of central planning and statism were evident in both Nazism and socialism, not to mention progressive policies in democracies. Hayek presents them all as forms of socialism that are without doubt a threat to freedom. Thus for Hayek, Western democracies had abandoned the ideas of nineteenth-century liberalism and had embraced the ideas of totalitarianism. Even before the rise of totalitarianism in Europe, the West "had progressively been moving away from the basic ideas on which Western civilization had been built" (p. 12). This meant abandoning not only the values of modern civilization but also breaking with the "whole evolution of Western civilization," the "salient characteristics of Western civilization as it has grown from the foundations laid by Christianity and the Greeks and Romans." He continues that this means that:

> Not merely nineteenth- and eighteenth-century liberalism, but the basic individualism inherited by us from Erasmus and Montaigne, from Cicero and Tacitus, Pericles and Thucydides, is progressively relinquished.[58]

It was not only a dispute over the rule of law or liberty, it was a fundamental battle over the whole tradition of Western civilization. The freedom and liberty of the West was no idle concept but the very foundation of the commercial success that enabled the growth and unprecedented development of societies in Western Europe. The key for Hayek was that there was no despotic political power to stifle this development.[59]

The crucial continuum where Hayek ties in with many of the other exiles is the reference to European tradition. While for the legal positivists or for Nazi legal theorists tradition had no value in and by itself, here tradition is posited as a foundational concept of the West. Hayek's tradition, such as that of Schulz and Pringsheim, was a long continuum where culture and learning accumulated over centuries are central.

Hayek's idea was that nineteenth-century liberalism as outlined by de Tocqueville and others was based on the idea of freedom as a concept

[58] Friedrich Hayek, *The Road to Serfdom* (Chicago: University of Chicago Press, 1944), p. 13.
[59] Hayek, *Road to Serfdom*, pp. 14–15.

that included not only freedom of thought and political freedom but also economic freedom. A planned society, be it of the progressive or socialist variety (Hayek does not really differentiate between the two), was fundamentally antithetical to freedom in all its manifestations. For them, economic freedom meant the freedom from want, a reference to social and economic rights, which were far more important than, for example, political freedom and thus curbing other freedoms was a suitable means to achieve this objective.[60]

With all his emphasis on freedoms, Hayek's main point was the rule of law as the cornerstone of a free society. For Hayek, the rule of law meant that the government was bound by "rules fixed and announced beforehand" (p. 72), allowing individuals to plan their actions accordingly and preventing the government from "stultifying individual efforts" (p. 73). The planned economy and the planned government relies on just that, the ad hoc control over how individuals operate and what kind of decisions they make. Here, Hayek was referring not only to the Soviet planned economy or the Nazi and fascist states that relied on planned corporativism but also to the progressivist ideas in the UK and the US. To Hayek, economic planning was far from being an innocent activity, it was instead the key to building a totalitarian state. In this, Hayek was naturally not simply presenting a neutral argument but an ideological statement.

Kornhauser argued that the émigrés from Nazi Germany were central in bringing the ideal of the rule of law to America. The crucial distinction was that while they were critical of pure positivism as the strict separation of law and politics, they still held on to legalism. What is important is that when that legalism and the rejection of things like natural law met US legal culture, at that time dominated by legal realism (and formalism, though Kornhauser does not mention it), they were in new territory as the issues of law and the state were not thus far on the agenda. What the Germans contributed was an understanding of the ethical dimension of formalism as an adherence to freedom and equality.[61] Earlier, John Langbein noted that for German émigrés, the important features that they noted in the US had been the focus on civil liberties and political toleration, things that had been lacking in Germany. They were considerably less interested in taking up such

[60] Hayek, *Road to Serfdom*, pp. 24–25.
[61] Kornhauser, *Debating the American State*, pp. 95–97.

issues as strict formalism or the *Rechtsstaat* that had contributed to the failure of the liberal state in Germany.[62]

Similarly, Leo Strauss wrote extensively about totalitarianism, making parallels between Nazism and communism. Strauss had left Germany in 1932 to study in France, but the Nazi coup transformed a research stay into an indefinite exile. He left for Britain in 1934 and continued to the US in 1938. For Strauss, communism was ideologically the more dangerous enemy due to the promise of radical freedom and equality that masked the reality of tyranny. Only America could provide an answer to this philosophical and political challenge and expose the deceit of communism. According to Strauss, the premise of Marx, Lenin and the Soviet leaders was the destruction of Western civilization. As such, the prospect of communism was even worse than Nazism. With the Soviet Union, the only possibility was victory by any means possible.[63]

Strauss's anticommunism took root during the Weimar years and became a major theme after his emigration. As many other scholars show, even texts that were nominally about Greek philosophy could be read as reflections of the present. This is made obvious by references to current events such as the Hungarian Uprising of 1956 when discussing ancient Greece.[64] This conviction of the moral imperative led Strauss to condemn positivism and the moral relativism inherent in theories such as Hans Kelsen's legal positivism. This moral blindness leads Kelsen to the kinds of indefensible positions like those he took in *Allgemeine Staatslehre* in 1925, where Kelsen maintains that even a despotic rule could be a legal order. While others would claim that the arbitrary actions of a despot are not legal, Kelsen sees it as a legal order because the despot sets the norms. For Kelsen, mixing a normative and a moral judgment would be to confuse the separation between Is and Ought. Even though Kelsen appears to offer an internally logical explanation, Strauss would point to an inherent nihilism in Kelsen's argument.[65]

62 John H. Langbein, "The influence of the German émigrés on American law: the curious case of civil and criminal practice," in Lutter, Stiefel and Hoeflich, *Der Einfluß deutscher Emigranten auf die Rechtsentwicklung in den USA und in Deutschland*, p. 330.

63 Adi Armon, "Leo Strauss reading Karl Marx during the Cold War," in Ezra Mendelsohn et al. (eds.) *Against the Grain: Jewish Intellectuals in Hard Times* (New York: Berghahn, 2014), pp. 40–41.

64 Armon, "Strauss," pp. 43–45.

65 Hans Kelsen, *Allgemeine Staatslehre* (Berlin: J. Springer, 1925), quoted in Leo Strauss, *Natural Right and History* (Chicago: University of Chicago Press, repr. 1963 [orig. 1953]), p. 4; Elisabeth Lefort, "Arriving at justice by a process of elimination: Hans Kelsen and

At this point, Kelsen was already in America and would soon publish his own treatise on liberty and democracy, a long article titled "Foundations of Democracy." In it, he engaged in a long and critical discussion on the nature of liberty and the fundamentals of the Soviet and the Nazi states. The remarkable thing about this essay was its argumentation. Like Strauss and many other exiles, Kelsen founded his argument on a very broad discussion of the European political tradition, seeking to demonstrate its founding tenets as a historical succession in a way that to some extent resembles Schulz's *Principles*.[66]

According to Armon, Strauss saw liberalism and communism as erstwhile allies against authoritarism, both aiming to fulfill the liberal ideal. What liberals failed to see, however, was that communism was not an ally with similar aims but rather an enemy seeking to construct a violent tyranny.[67] Thus, at one and the same time, Strauss could be a critic of the liberal state philosophically but a staunch defender of the Western version of liberalism against communism politically.

Strauss's views on tyranny and totalitarianism were founded on both personal experience and philosophical inquiry and a mixing of the two. For example, in his extensive analysis of Xenophon's *Hiero* (originally 1948) and in the debates that followed, Strauss and his commentators ended up having a very curiously classical debate on whether it is possible for a philosopher to be a virtuous adviser to a tyrant and thus improve him or whether this simply debases the philosopher and turns him into an accomplice. While Kojève, a leftist apologist of the Communist regimes, thought improvement possible, Strauss held a firmly negative view. As he wrote in his analysis, political scientists had failed even to recognize tyranny when they saw it.[68] This was a clear reminder of the unwillingness of leftist intellectuals to see communist regimes as tyrannies. For Strauss, the benefit of the classical examples was that it enabled one to understand the true nature of tyranny: "This basic stratum of modern tyranny remains, for all practical purposes, unintelligible to us if we do not have recourse to the political science of the classics."[69]

Leo Strauss," in J. Telman (ed.), *Hans Kelsen in America – Selective Affinities and the Mysteries of Academic Influence* (Berlin: Springer Verlag, 2016), pp. 116–122.

66 Hans Kelsen, "Foundations of democracy," *Ethics*, 66(1:2) (1955), 1–101.

67 Armon, "Strauss," p. 43.

68 Strauss, *On Tyranny*, p. 23; Victor Gourevitch and Michael S. Roth, "Introduction" to Strauss, *On Tyranny*, pp. xxi–xxii.

69 Strauss, *On Tyranny*, p. 23.

To Strauss, the unstated message of *Hiero* was that benevolent and enlightened tyranny was still tyranny. By its very definition, tyranny is the polar opposite of equality and the rule of law since there was no equal to the tyrant and he was bound by no law: "the tyrant is necessarily 'lawless'."[70]

The aim of tyranny, thought Strauss, was to keep subjects away from public affairs and to focus them on private, contractual relations among themselves. The conception of freedom as a counterpart to sovereignty was very dangerous to tyranny. Instead of public virtues, bravery and justice, befitting the ideals of freedom, subjects are expected to obey the laws and see justice in them.[71]

Some of the exiles, such as Ernst Kantorowicz, turned to politics mainly when the outside world encroached upon the intellectual realm of the university. Kantorowicz had done so in his second inaugural lecture (November 14, 1933), where he spoke of the "Secret Germany" in maintaining the duty of the professor to speak the truth. In his ultimately unnecessary resignation letter he attacked the "privation of his basic civil honor and rights" without the possibility of redress. Kantorowicz would return to the same theme when he was at Berkeley. There, at the height of the "Red scare," the university had instituted an oath of loyalty, which the faculty opposed. Kantorowicz would eagerly join the fight, arguing vehemently against the oath as a totalitarian first step to control the professors. Again, the fundamental issue for Kantorowicz was the freedom of judgment, human dignity and the responsible sovereignty of scholars.[72]

The conception of the rule of law was a modern concept that was only with difficulty used to describe premodern societies. In the case of Roman law and the Roman law tradition, such discussions were supplanted with ideas of the independence of law and the legal tradition from political interference. This was also the tradition that Schulz used in his works on jurisprudence. The topic of political justice was equally shared by many of the Frankfurt School exiles. Otto Kirchheimer, for instance, wrote in his *Political Justice* how each regime creates its own enemies. As a former student and friend of Schmitt who had escaped to the US, he was painfully aware of this fact.[73]

[70] Strauss, *On Tyranny*, p. 119.
[71] Strauss, *On Tyranny*, pp. 70–71.
[72] Lerner, *Ernst Kantorowicz*, pp. 161, 314.
[73] Donna E. Arzt, "Otto Kirchheimer: critic of the administration of justice," in Lutter, Stiefel and Hoeflich, *Der Einfluß deutscher Emigranten auf die Rechtsentwicklung in den USA und in Deutschland*, p. 38.

Hayek and Neumann would continue to work on the topic of the rule of law and were instrumental in bringing the debate to the fore. While many of the exiles became politicized in exile, in the case of Pringsheim the effect was somewhat unexpectedly the opposite. In Oxford, Pringsheim would continue work on the manuscript of *The Greek Law of Sale*, a book which was conspicuously free from all contemporary implications. This was a project supported by SPSL and OUP but the finished manuscript was in the end published in East Germany in 1950.[74] Even during the war, Pringsheim's attitude toward the college and his helpers in Britain caused exasperation and some even called him ungrateful.[75] However, he was naturalized as a British citizen in 1947 and later wrote to the SPSL to express his gratitude.[76]

Though his scholarly work became depoliticized, the end of the war meant growing activity in the practical political sense. While other exiles would wait and see how the situation developed, Pringsheim took a very different approach, returning to his homeland and getting involved in the local level as soon as possible. Pringsheim returned to Freiburg for the first time in the summer of 1946, and more permanently the following year, although he held on to the apartment in Oxford. He taught at Oxford during the winter and at Freiburg in the summer. He became very active in reinvigorating the Freiburg Law Faculty after the war and his influence, felt also through his allies, was dominant up to the sixties.[77] In practice, this was an effective strategy because it allowed him to consolidate his influence as long as

[74] Rockefeller Foundation Archives, Rockefeller Archive Center, Sleepy Hollow, NY, Pringsheim box 63, series 401, RG 1.1 RAC, folder 832: report of Sisam to O'Brien (June 5, 1944), mentioning Pringsheim and *The Greek Law of Sale* as one of the recipients of the Rockefeller grant.

[75] Warden of Merton College to Sisam (January 13, 1944) about Pringsheim, who has "prickly sensitiveness about his own resultant position." He states that "I think the College has treated him very handsomely, and am surprised that he shouldn't recognize it," concluding that he is a "very difficult case." Oxford University Press Archives, Oxford, Schulz CP GE 000345, no. 23.

[76] Archives of the Society for the Protection of Science and Learning, Bodleian Library, Oxford, MS. SPSL. 272.1, 233, Pringsheim to Ursell (May 13, 1951).

[77] Archives of the Society for the Protection of Science and Learning, Bodleian Library, Oxford, MS. SPSL. 272.1, 233 on his schedule; 190, Pringsheim to Ursell (April 3, 1946), on his intent to go to Freiburg in need of certificate of identity from the HO and a return visa; MS. SPSL. 272.1, 191 Skemp to Under Secretary of State (April 5, 1946), application for traveling papers for Pringsheim, who is willing to assist in the educational reconstruction of Germany, short-term, children remain in Britain. Letters 192–206 about the arrangements of travel to Germany show how difficult movement was at the time.

those compromised by their actions during the Nazi years were out of the game.

This reintegrating approach was one shared by fellow émigré Ernst Fraenkel. In Weimar Germany, Fraenkel had been a Jewish labor lawyer, sharing a legal practice with Franz Neumann. While Neumann fled early on, Fraenkel stayed on though ending his open political activity, coining the phrase inner emigration. Fraenkel would write pieces for underground publications arguing for resistance, pressing for the provocations that would force the Nazi regime to reveal the extent of its refusal to follow the rule of law and freedoms.[78] During the Weimar years, Fraenkel had been one of the few advocates for the idea of *Rechtsstaat* in the German Left, taking up Heller's idea of social *Rechtsstaat.* Even for the workers, the stability and predictability, not to mention legal recourse, offered by the rule of law was a vital tool for protecting and advancing their interests. It only needed to be supported by a system of collective democracy to ensure equal participation.[79] Fraenkel, too, fled after Jewish lawyers had been definitely disbarred, ending up in Britain in September 1938. From there, he went to New York in 1939, hoping to join Neumann at the New School. Unable to find a suitable position, Fraenkel enrolled to study law again in Chicago. At the same time, he worked on an important book on the Nazi state titled *The Double State,* published in 1941, which began his new career as a political scientist. Fraenkel's most important contribution was his work on his return to Germany after the war, when he would be central in the building of the new political science faculties in Germany. However, he had initially judged a return to Germany impossible, changing his mind only after five years spent in Korea. A reluctance to return was not unusual, and returning émigrés faced much resistance from those who had stayed. Söllner claims that in these conflicts and the fight to break university resistance to new approaches, émigrés played a crucial role though they were hardly the only ones who developed new disciplines.[80]

[78] Douglas Morris, "Discrimination, degradation, defiance: Jewish lawyers under Nazism," in A. E. Steinweis and R. D. Rachlin (eds.), *The Law in Nazi Germany: Ideology, Opportunism, and the Perversion of Justice* (New York: Berghahn Books, 2013), pp. 124–128; Jens Meierhenrich, *The Remnants of the Rechtsstaat. An Ethnography of Nazi Law* (Oxford and New York: Oxford University Press, 2018).

[79] Greenberg, *Weimar Century*, 81–87.

[80] Ash and Söllner, *Forced Migration and Scientific Change*, p. 268; Alfons Söllner, "Ernst Fraenkel under die Verwetlichung der politischen Kultur in der Bundesrepublic Deutschland," in *Fluchtpunkte, Studien zur politischen Ideengeschichte des 20. Jahrhunderts*

In the report Pringsheim produced from his first visit to Freiburg in the summer of 1946, he returns to the issues of democracy, rationalism and anti-totalitarianism. He describes how he gave a paper on English democracy to a large group of eager Freiburg students, being asked to give a repeat performance the same night. He began to make arrangements for the return of orderly conditions to university life. He offers a description of the harsh living conditions in the French zone of occupation, where food shortage, seizure of homes by the French and the destruction caused by the war were evident. He maintains that "By far the best way of educating students politically is to begin by teaching them scientific thinking." In order that the ideas of democracy could take root, one must get rid of the idea of collective guilt and recognize the resistance against the Nazis among students and faculty. Thus, what Pringsheim recommends is showing, not telling what freedom and democracy means, by increasing connections between German and foreign students and visits to democratic countries to dispel the lies and untruths that had pervaded the political culture for over a decade: "The only way of teaching them democracy is to demonstrate its spirit by realizing it in person." Pringsheim then returns to the idea of the human community and connections between people as the way to foster and promote the values of humanity and freedom:

> The sooner the terrible isolation ends the better. The task is extremely urgent. Once the utter hopelessness begins to lift, and a community of European nations appears possible, then the dormant and faint trust in liberation and in a new life, thus set free for action, will show surprising results.[81]

The urgency that Pringsheim shows is clearly linked with the idea of the human community or cosmopolis, the free exchange of ideas and self-governed intellectual life. If the Nazi conception of the community and its law had been one of concrete order, the link between the political, ethnic, intellectual and legal orders, what Pringsheim advocates is the intellectual cosmopolis, the scientific and learned community.

It would appear that Pringsheim was tolerant of colleagues who had jumped on the Nazi bandwagon. He continued to collaborate with former students such as Wieacker. The only one he continued to disapprove

(Baden-Baden: Nomos Verlag, 2006), pp. 223–223. On Fraenkel in exile, see Greenberg, *Weimar Century*, pp. 76–119.

[81] Report of Pringsheim to Ursell October 19, 1946 on his recent visit to Germany. Archives of the Society for the Protection of Science and Learning, Bodleian Library, Oxford, MS. SPSL. 272.1, 213–219.

of was Schönbauer, whose conduct he judged to be dishonorable.[82] The extent that Pringsheim took to the rearrangement of academic life in Freiburg is evident in his extensive correspondence, which deals with academic minutiae and engagement with students.[83] His continuing influence shows in the run-up to the celebrations in Freiburg for his eightieth birthday, where former students arranged for full academic honors to be bestowed upon him. There, his public refusal in 1933–1934 to accept the reasoning of Carl Schmitt was seen in a completely different light now that Schmitt had been formally excluded from academic life.[84]

The conscious eradication of the principles of equality and the rule of law in Nazi Germany led many exiles to take not only a theoretical but also a political stance. Across the political spectrum, exiles such as Neumann, Hayek, Fraenkel and Strauss emphasized the importance of these principles not only in law but in political life that had a considerable impact in American discourse. While Pringsheim's own scholarship did not return to political themes, in his practical work in returning to Germany he continued to strive toward democracy, freedom and anti-totalitarianism. In a letter in 1958, Pringsheim compares the work of Radbruch to a lighthouse in dark times, a beacon that shows the true image of humanity. This should be the foundation of the legal conscience (*Rechtsgewissen*) of the nation, just as in England one sees the strong feeling of justice forming the basis of the law.[85]

## Conclusions

The idealization of Hadrianic Rome was a theme with a long heritage from the writings of contemporaries such as Aelius Aristides to the works of Gibbon and the nineteenth-century enthusiasm for imperial

[82] This is evident from his correspondence. Rare Book and Manuscript Archive, Columbia University, New York, Arthur Schiller Papers, Uncatalogued correspondence, Box 5, Pringsheim to Schiller (December 20, 1955): "I was not in Vienna because Schoenbauer dared to invite me, in spite of his hot and disrespectable antisemitism under Hitler, and his personal and very insincere attack against A. B. Schwarz (katagraphe) who could not defend himself at this time. In other case I am tolerant, but this was too much and revealed his bad character."

[83] Universitätsarchiv Albert-Ludwigs-Universität Freiburg, Nachlass Erik Wolf, Bestand C130 sig. 146.

[84] In the arrangements Thieme, Wieacker and Felgentraeger were all involved. Universitätsarchiv, Albert-Ludwigs-Universität, Freiburg im Breisgau, NL Hans Thieme, bestand C46, signum 124.

[85] Universitätsarchiv Albert-Ludwigs-Universität Freiburg, Nachlass Erik Wolf, Bestand C130 sig. 146. Letter of Pringsheim to Erik Wolf on July 26, 1958.

sovereignty. An important part of that idealization was the realization that the enlightened rule under which peace and prosperity reigned coincided with the enlightened tradition of law, where principles like the protection of weaker parties or equality before the law became prominent. As Hadrian himself was the author of numerous legal opinions and resolutions where he emphasized the ideas of humanity and justice, the historical theme of Hadrian as the wise emperor judge had both a sound footing in historical sources and a solid following among scholars.

Faced with the beginning of the repression of Nazi Germany, Fritz Pringsheim began an intellectual exodus toward safety and freedom. Part of the beginning of his process of exile was, in addition to his marginalization in Germany, to lay the groundwork for the move to Britain by traveling there and giving talks at British universities. In one such talk, given at the Faculty of Law at Cambridge and later published in the *Journal of Roman Studies*, Pringsheim reformulated the idea of Hadrian as a good king to Hadrian as the enlightened Stoic philosopher and cosmopolitan ruler. His Hadrian was a judge and legislator but equally an administrator that created a virtually modern professional legal administration.

The way Pringsheim took the historical figure of Hadrian and presented him in a new light may be considered a reaction toward the coming Nazi repression and the violations of the constitution, the law and the legal tradition it entailed. Like most writers under threat by repressive regimes, Pringsheim does not mention the threat, nor does he specify the Nazi regime. However, the context of the text and his other contemporary writings make the reference clear.

The rule of law was one of the cornerstones of constitutional order and one of the first foundations that the Nazi regime would destroy. In arguments about the rule of law, Nazi criticism sought to use those who criticized legal formalism and present a case for the common good of the nation, *Volk*, as higher than the letter of the law. While Pringsheim would argue for the Roman law tradition and values and principles such as the rule of law within it, other exiles would present the rule of law in a modern context. Franz Neumann, a social democrat and a labor lawyer, was highly conscious of the social criticism of the rule of law as a false premise in which apparent equality masked the very real exploitation along class lines. Nevertheless, he wrote how the concrete order thinking did not resolve anything, indeed, quite the opposite. What Nazi theory and even more Nazi practice did was to remove the small guarantees of justice that existed in capitalist societies and in their legal systems. In his contact with the US system and the conceptions of law, Neumann's thinking became even more critical of totalitarianism and the spread of policies that would enable totalitarian policies, even though he never let go of the criticism of capitalism.

Like Neumann, Hayek grounded his criticism of totalitarianism on the concept of the rule of law but took a different view that espoused a more directly conservative agenda. For Hayek, the rule of law was a formative concept in society, going as far as describing it as the foundation of the Western free society. As an economist, Hayek considered a free society to be one where free enterprise and government intervention were polar opposites. The rule of law, where the rules of economic activity were known beforehand and were not subject to the whim of the rulers, was fundamental to economic prosperity. Societies where there was a long-standing tradition in which the rule of law was paramount represented a defining feature of Western cultural tradition and one that guaranteed other freedoms. For Hayek, the intrusion of flexible rules and leeways based on social considerations was a threat that was not only limited to totalitarianism but was also creeping into Western democracies in the form of progressive policies.

In the US, the emphasis on freedom and the rule of law became a mainstay of postwar policies and this direction was enthusiastically supported by many German exiles. Strauss, for example, would emphasize how the contradiction between true freedom and the radical freedom offered by communism lay in the approaches to rules and law. The formal equality of liberal democracy was not a false pretence of liberty but rather the fixity of its rules that separated it from the lawless tyranny of communism.

While the German exiles in the US would either continue their opposition to totalitarianism by refocusing on communism after the fall of Nazism, many of the exiles who returned to Germany would reattach themselves to the postwar society there. Rather than continuing to write about the dangers of totalitarianism, Pringsheim went back to attempting to reform the university and to preventing a resurgence of Nazism.

The changes in the legal understanding of freedom and repression, equality and inequality, are good indicators of the fundamental shifts that were taking place. The exploration of the creation of an understanding of a shared European legal heritage and the role of Roman law within that heritage, demonstrates how the shifts in the foundations of law led to a new engagement with the fundamental ideas of European legal tradition. The rise of the Nazi regime had exposed the critical faults of the German *Rechtsstaat* and its reliance on formal positivism. With the principled rejection of natural law, the search was now for some solid foundation for law that would not be vulnerable to the assault of unscrupulous political aims like Nazism. What the Roman law scholars argued was that this solid foundation was history, the heritage of Roman law that was embedded into the legal culture and beyond the reach of a simple command. Neumann advocated the rule of law as an ethical principle. Strauss, struggling with the ideas of value crisis and religion, advocated militant liberalism and anti-totalitarianism.

# 4 The Long Legal Tradition and the European Heritage in Nazi Germany


## Abstract

The chapter starts with the themes of crisis and the discovery of the future for Roman law in Europe in the form of the common legal heritage in the seminal works of Paul Koschaker. These build on the role of tradition in law and work to present a role for Roman law in the new order: first in the Nazi reign and second in the new postwar Europe. The chapter compares the conceptions of law and Europe between the Nazi and fascists policies and their ideas on Roman law, the reorientation of legal education and the new role for Europe in the new order. These totalitarian and conservative visions of Europe by authors such as Salvatore Riccobono are then juxtaposed with the ideas of other Europeanists such as the Catholic thinker Jacques Maritain or liberals, socialists and communists, such as Altiero Spinelli, behind the Ventotene declaration.


## Introduction

Viewed from the outside, it appears that the study of Roman law has a peculiar affinity to the idea of crisis. While the subject had by its own definition lurched from crisis to crisis since the days of Justinian, the crisis of the 1930s was by far the most peculiar.[1] This crisis can be understood as a reflection of a more general sense of crisis not only in

[1] Ernst Schönbauer, "Zur 'Krise des römischen Rechts'," in *Festschrift Paul Koschaker mit Unterstützung der Rechts- und Staatswissenschaftlichen Fakultät der Friedrich-Wilhelms-Universität Berlin und der Leipziger Juristenfakultät zum 60. Geburtstagüberreicht von seinen Fachgenossen*, II (Weimar: Verlag Hermann Böhlaus, 1939), pp. 364–365 mocks the continuous talk of the crisis of Roman law that comes up regularly.

the sciences but also in higher education in general. The reasons for this pessimism were twofold. First, the practical applicability of Roman law had ceased in Germany with the advent of the BGB in 1900. For scholars of Roman law, this meant that the justification of the teaching of Roman law became tenuous. Even many researchers within Roman law saw its future in legal history, not in legal dogmatics. In consequence, the hours that were devoted to Roman law in the German legal curriculum were cut, and the professors would need to find new sources of income as pay was often tied to teaching. Second, the takeover of power by the Nazis in 1933 would mean that political power was held by a party that disliked Roman law so much that they even took the trouble of making it part of their party program. Third, the interwar years were defined by a constant mentality of crisis. While there was clearly a real political and economic crisis, the sense of crisis was amplified by a continuing discussion of the crisis of values, civilization and morality on top of the economic and political crises.[2]

While one would struggle to understand the mentality of crisis in Roman law from a modern perspective, the concept of crisis and discussion around it marked scholarship during the whole interwar period. The study of Roman law was at a high level in Germany and Italy, and many scholars worked on the subject under the notion that legal scholarship could be a scientific pursuit rather than a purely pragmatic work of explaining and harmonizing legal rules. But despite this, a deep pessimism reigned about the future of the subject.

The purpose of this chapter is to examine one of the most influential responses to the crisis, that by Paul Koschaker (1879–1951),[3] which

[2] Emilio Betti, "La crisi odierna della scienza romanistica in Germania," *Rivista di Diritto commerciale*, 37 (1939), 120–128 interpreted the crisis as a cultural one.

[3] A number of obituaries and articles have been published on Koschaker. See Pietro De Francisci, "Paul Koschaker (1879–1951)," *Studia et Documenta Historiae et Iuris*, 17 (1951), 384–388; Karl-Heinz Below and Adam Falkenstein, "Paul Koschaker," *Zeitschrift der Savigny-Stiftung für Rechtsgeschichte: Romanistische Abteilung*, 68 (1951), ix–xix; Karl-Heinz Below, "Paul Koschaker," *Zeitschrift der Deutschen Morgenländischen Gesellschaft*, 104 (1954), 1–44; Gunter Wesener, *Römisches Recht und Naturrecht* (Graz: Universität Graz, 1978), pp. 112–115; Gunter Wesener, "Paul Koschaker," in Rafael Domingo (ed.), *Juristas universales, III. Juristas del siglo XIX. Da Savigny a Kelsen* (Madrid and Barcelona: Marcial Pons, 2004), pp. 971–974; Gunter Wesener, "Paul Koschaker (1879–1951), Begründer der altorientalischen Rechtsgeschichte und juristischen Keilschriftforschung," in Karl Acham (ed.), *Rechts-, Sozial- und Wirtschaftswissenschaftlichen aus Graz* (Vienna: Böhlau Verlag, 2011), pp. 273–285; Gerhard Ries, "Paul Koschaker," *Neue Deutsche Biographie*, 12 (1980), 608–609; Manfred Müller, "Paul Koschaker (1879–1951). Zum 100. Geburtstag des Begründers der Keilschriftrechtsgeschichte," *Altorientalische Forschungen*, 9 (1982), 271–284; Michael P. Streck and Gero Dolezalek, "Paul Koschaker: Zum 125. Geburtstag am 19. April 2004," in

reoriented the discussion toward the European narrative. Though two of Koschaker's texts, a comprehensive prewar article on the crisis of Roman law and a postwar book on Roman law, are well known, what has received less attention are the continuities between the two. Koschaker's ideas on Europe and law are juxtaposed with studies of other contemporary writers, from his conservative allies such as Salvatore Riccobono to fascist and Nazi scholars such as Pietro De Francisci and Ernst Schönbauer.

The aim is to demonstrate how relatively unchanging Koschaker's vision concerning the relevance of Roman law was and to examine the roots of Koschaker's turn toward Europe. While both epitomized the *Zeitgeist* and laid out a response to a different challenge, that response was not radically different. What I argue is that Koschaker's main claim to fame was his extraordinary sense of timing that enabled him both in 1938 and in 1947 to present an idea that responded both to the internal debates of Roman law scholarship as well as to the changing political and legal circumstances. He would present Roman law as a central part of the European tradition, a part that would function as almost a kind of "relative natural law."[4] This meant that Roman law would operate in the same way as natural law would but in the European context and without the speculative element. Koschaker's Roman law would thus be universal but in a somewhat illogical particular way it was part of a universal European tradition.

What makes Koschaker fascinating is not simply his influence as a scholar but rather the fact that he prepared not just one but two different responses to the crisis of Roman law. The first of these responses was his 1938 *Krisenschrift*: "Die Krise des römischen Rechts

*Jubiläen 2004. Personen-Ereignisse* (Leipzig: Universität Leipzig, 2004), pp. 31–34; Georg Neumann, "Paul Koschaker in Tübingen (1941–1946)," *Zeitschrift für altorientalische und biblische Rechtgeschichte*, 18 (2012), 23–36; Tommaso Beggio, "Paul Koschaker and the Path to 'Europa und das römische Recht' (1936–1947)," *Legal Roots*, 6 (2017), 291–326. There is just one monograph on Koschaker: Beggio, *Paul Koschaker*. On a different note, see Giaro, *Aktualisierung Europas*, a fictional discussion with Koschaker. Giaro has also published more conventional estimates on Koschaker's influence, for example "Der Troubadour des Abendlandes," in Horst Schröder and Dieter Simon (eds.), *Rechtsgeschichtswissenschaft in Deutschland 1945 bis 1952* (Frankfurt: Klostermann, 2001), pp. 31–76. From Koschaker himself there is a short autobiography that describes his career: Paul Koschaker, "Selbstdarstellung," in Nikolaus Grass (ed.), *Österreichische Geschichtswissenschaft der Gegenwart in Selbstdarstellungen*, II (Innsbruck: Wagner, 1951), pp. 105–125. A collection of letters between Guido Kisch and Koschaker were published by Kisch in 1970 with an introduction, see Kisch, *Paul Koschaker*.

4 Koschaker, *Europa und das römische Recht*, (1966), p. 346.

und die romanistische Rechtswissenschaft" (the crisis of Roman law and Roman law scholarship). Koschaker was then a fifty-nine-year-old professor of Roman law in Berlin whose main research interest was cuneiform law. The second response was his magnum opus, *Europa und das Römisches Recht*, which came out in 1947 two years after the war had ended. There was just nine years between the two but of those years six had been taken by the most destructive war that Europe had ever seen.

Paul Koschaker is not a natural fit for this role as a reformist advocating the continued relevance of Roman law in the European legal tradition. Born and educated in Austria, he became a student of Ludwig Mitteis, one of the most famous scholars of ancient legal history and legal papyrology. Koschaker would become a leading student of cuneiform laws, for example the Laws of Hammurabi, but remained dedicated to the dogmatic study of law. The study of cuneiform law gained unprecedented prominence with the discovery of the *Codex Hammurabi* in 1901–1902 and the publication of key texts continued during the first half of the twentieth century. What connected most of the scholars linked with the school of ancient legal history in the style of Mitteis was a strong sense of empiricism and a focus on discovered texts such as papyri or inscriptions. This was in opposition to more dogmatically oriented Roman law, which focused on the legal rules formulated by lawyers and their development. By the time he was invited to give the talk that led to the *Krise*, Koschaker had just moved from Leipzig to Berlin and was now the holder of one of the most prestigious chairs in the country as well as the founder director of a research center on the laws of the ancient Near East. For him, the transition from Leipzig to Berlin was not easy and later he considered the years in Leipzig (1915–1936) as the happiest of his life. The move to Berlin from a relatively laid-back Leipzig brought him into full contact with Nazi policies on science and universities along with what he later considered intensive Nazification. The Nazi ban on Jewish academics made it impossible for some of his close associates such as Assyriologist Benno Landsberger (1890–1967) to work at the university, leading to the destruction of what he had accomplished in Leipzig. Despite the promises he was given, the situation did not improve in Berlin and Koschaker accepted a position in Tübingen after only five years.[5] Landsberger would go into exile,

[5] Koschaker, "Selbstdarstellung," pp. 115–118; Koschaker to Kisch on November 27, 1947 (pp. 22–24), now in Kisch, *Paul Koschaker*. Koschaker would go as far as to write to the minister about the lack of support and resources for the new institute. Letter from

accepting first a position in Ankara and later moving to Chicago. The turn of events and the disappointment in the failure of his attempt in building a strong research center for the study of law in the ancient Near East became an impetus for his critical work on the European tradition.[6]

By comparing Koschaker's texts to contemporary scholarship, this chapter will explore the foundations of the turn toward Europe. It will examine both the inspirations behind it as well as the continuity of topics that grew into the European theme in his works. Comparisons between Koschaker and other scholars on Europe and the rise of Europeanism allow us to situate his writings among the numerous, often contradictory, theories on Europe. Europe became a catchword for a kind of quasi-universalism, a theme that was shared by conservative and liberal authors alike from Nazis and fascists to radical socialists.[7] For example, Italian Roman law scholar Pietro Bonfante wrote about the unification of Europe in similar terms, speaking about linguistic and cultural unity.[8] Koschaker's theories relied on the idea of tradition as a continuity, a shared notion that is sustained through time. His concept of tradition is thus similar to the idea of natural law as a shared set of values and norms. As a result, Koschaker's reputation has an odd duality. On the one hand he has been hailed as a principled anti-Nazi who was forced out of his job in Berlin, while in recent years he has been described by Giaro and Somma as an unwitting Nazi collaborator.[9] Beggio's recent book has

Koschaker to the *Reichsminister für Wissenschaft, Erziehung und Volksbildung* on April 19, 1940 (Universitätsarchiv, Humboldt-Universität, Berlin, UK Personalia K 274, Bd. II, Bl. 11–12).

6 This development has been newly researched by Beggio, *Paul Koschaker*. Koschaker's view of the situation was not shared by the university leadership in the correspondence that followed Koschaker's letter, Universitätsarchiv, Humboldt-Universität, Berlin, UK Personalia K 274, Bd. II, Bl. 6–12.

7 Mark Hewitson and Matthew D'Auria (eds.), *Europe in Crisis: Intellectuals and the European Idea, 1917–1957* (Oxford: Berghahn Books, 2012).

8 Pietro Bonfante, "Verso la Confederazione Europea," *Scientia*, 18 (1915), 326–342, now in Pietro Bonfante, *Scritti giuridici vari, Studi generali IV* (Rome: Sanpaolesi, 1925), p. 418; Valerio Marotta, "'Mazziniano in politica estera e prussiano in interna.' Note brevi sulle idee politiche di Pietro Bonfante," in *Giuristi e il fascino del regime* (Rome: Roma Tre-Press, 2015), pp. 267–288.

9 The original term was "un fiancheggiatore del Nazismo *malgré soi*" (Tomasz Giaro, "Paul Koschaker sotto il Nazismo: un fiancheggiatore 'malgré soi'," in *Iuris Vincula. Studi in onore di M. Talamanca*, IV (Naples: Jovene, 2001), pp. 159–187) portraying him as a kind of useful idiot. This negative evaluation has been repeated in Alessandro Somma, *I giuristi e l'Asse culturale Roma-Berlino: Economia e politica nel diritto fascista e nazionalsocialista* (Frankfurt: Klostermann, 2005), p. 282, and Alessandro Somma, "L'uso del diritto romano e della romanistica tra Fascismo e Antifascismo," in Miglietta and Santucci, *Diritto romano e regimi totalitari nel '900 europeo*, pp. 113–114, where the crux of the criticism was Koschaker's support of German intellectual primacy in Europe.

sought to define a more nuanced understanding of Koschaker's motivations through a meticulous study of archival sources.[10] Through an analysis of the implication of the different Europeanist strands of thought and the role of jurisprudence in them, this chapter seeks to situate Koschaker's work in its European context.

It is noteworthy that Koschaker grew up in the nineteenth-century tradition of Pandectism, the contemporary use of Roman law. Although this makes him an unlikely innovator, it does illustrate how the renewal of the old becomes a central preoccupation in his works. In a number of issues, the debates that Koschaker engaged in were rooted in the moment and the internal disputes of the role of Roman law and history. One example we will follow is the debate between supporters of ancient legal history (*Antike Rechtsgeschichte*) and those who supported the dogmatic study of Roman law. These two groups represented diametrically opposed views on the value of Roman law to contemporary law.

The Europeanism at the different ends of the political spectrum was founded on utopianism of various kinds, but these perspectives underwent a profound change during the war. The main streams in the German discussions during the interwar period were the idea of the *Abendland*, supported especially by advocates of spreading the influence of Catholicism; the concept of *Mitteleuropa*, which meant a Pan-German hegemony within Central Europe; or *Paneuropa*, the pro-European movement led by Count Coudenhoven-Kalergi, advocating the unification of Europe. Nazi Europeanism combined two separate discussions: first the idea of *Mitteleuropa* as a unified area dominated by German-speaking nations and an area of inherent unity. The second was the threat from the east, which jointly merged the danger of communism and the racial threat of Slavic and other eastern peoples. With these were mixed ideas of the Germanic *Drang nach Osten* (eastward expansion) as a historical mission as well as the concept of the *Neuordnung Europas* (the New Order of Europe) as the fundamental Nazi reorganization of political, racial and commercial relations in Europe.[11] In this chapter

[10] Beggio, *Paul Koschaker*.

[11] On the different conceptions of Europeanism, see Peter M. R. Stirk, *European Unity in Context: The Interwar Period* (London: Bloomsbury, 1989). Karen Schönwälder, *Historiker und Politik. Geschichtswissenschaft im Nationalsozialismus* (Frankfurt and New York: Campus Verlag, 1992), p. 91. In addition, there were different religious and spiritual movements advocating unity, for instance Rudolf Pannwitz's elitist idea of a Europe led by a cabal of *Übermenschen*, the foremost of them being Pannwitz himself. Jan Vermeiren, "Imperium Europaeum: Rudolf Pannwitz and the German Idea of Europe," in Hewitson and D'Auria, *Europe in Crisis*, p. 136. On the Nazi ideas of Neue Europa, see Carl Wege, "*Das*

we will see what Koschaker's role was between these different and partially opposing traditions and what was the origin of his particular type of Europeanism.

The reason why Koschaker's work and its convoluted background is so important even today is that after the war it became the foundation of an altogether new line of scholarship on Europe and Roman law. It inspired scholars around Europe, leading to an unprecedented renaissance in the field. Of particular importance was Francesco Calasso, who published an Italian translation of *Europa* and was instrumental in spreading the idea of Europe in postwar European legal history.[12] Equally, Helmut Coing and recently Reinhard Zimmermann have seen Koschaker as an important forerunner of the Europeanist tradition and European law.

## The Crisis of Roman Law

The *Krise* was presented originally to an audience of Nazi scholars at the Nazi academy of science (*Akademie für deutsches Rechts*) led by Hans Frank, the minister of justice (*Reichskommissar für die Gleichschaltung der Justiz*).[13] On the international scientific front, the *Krise* spread the idea of the crisis of Roman law. As the European scholarly world was in general gripped by a sense of crisis with journals filled with accounts of the crisis of science, the prime example being Husserl's theory of the crisis

*Neue Europa" 1933–1945: German Thought Patterns about Europe* (Stuttgart: Edition Axel Menges, 2016). On the essential incompatibility of European internationalism and Hitler's worldview, see Snyder, *Black Earth*.

12 Francesco Calasso, "Introduzione," in Paul Koschaker, *L'Europa e il diritto romano* (Florence: Sansoni, 1962) (translated by Arnaldo Biscardi), continued in Francesco Calasso, *L'unità giuridica dell'Europa* (Soveria Mannelli: Rubbettino Editore, 1985). On the response to Koschaker, see Adolfo Plachy, "Il diritto romano come valore culturale nella storia dell'Europa," in *L'Europa e il diritto romano. Studi in memoria di Paolo Koschaker*, I (Milan: Giuffrè, 1954), pp. 477–491; Dieter Simon, "Die deutsche Wissenschaft vom römischen Recht nach 1933," in Stolleis and Simon, *Rechtsgeschichte im Nationalsozialismus*, p. 171; Pieler, "Das römische Recht im nationalsozialistischen Staat."

13 On Hans Frank, see Christoph Kleßmann, "Der Generalgouverneur Hans Frank," *Vierteljahrshefte für Zeitgeschichte*, 19 (1971), 245–260; Dietmar Willoweit, "Deutsche Rechtsgeschichte und 'nationalsozialistische Weltanschauung'," in Stolleis and Simon, *Rechtsgeschichte im Nationalsozialismus*, pp. 25–42; Christian Schudnagies, *Hans Frank. Aufstieg und Fall des NS-Juristen und Generalgoverneurs* (Frankfurt: Peter Lang, 1989), pp. 21–28; Lothar Gruchmann, *Justiz im Dritten Reich 1933–1940: Anpassung und Unterwerfung in der Ära Gürtner* (Munich: De Gruyter, 2001) (3rd ed.), pp. 86–92, 637–645 on Frank's role in the machinery of terror, 746–930 on the legal reform plans and Frank's position in the various attempts.

of European science, this was not really much of a surprise. The literature on European crises was diverse, beginning with Spengler's *Untergang* and continuing with explanations of the moral, economic and social crises gripping the West. Within scholarly crisis literature, Koschaker's *Krise* was by and large grouped with other tracts of a similar kind.[14] Koschaker, however, was not the first to discuss the crisis, as Valentin Georgescu had published a book (in Romanian) on the topic in 1937, which Koschaker had promptly reviewed at the *Zeitschrift der Savigny-Stiftung für Rechtsgeschichte*. In his review, Koschaker notes that the connection between Roman law and materialism, a link already made by Spengler, himself a Nazi opponent, continues to haunt the subject in its crisis.[15] The issue of the crisis had also been discussed by Betti and Genzmer in their earlier articles, discussing it through its relationship with history but only Koschaker would put the crisis of Roman law center stage.[16]

[14] Around the same time, there were numerous other tracts about crisis in law, for instance Max Boehm, "Die Krise des Nationalitätenrechts," in *Festschrift für Rudolf Hübner* (Jena: Friedrich-Schiller-Universität Jena, 1935), pp. 172–189. The *Krise* received much critical attention, both of the damning and praising kind: Ernst Levy, "Review of *Die Krise des römischen Rechts und die romanistische Rechtswissenschaft* by Paul Koschaker," *The Classical Weekly*, 33 (1939), 91–92; Odoardo Carrelli, "A proposito di crisi del diritto romano," *Studia et Documenta Historiae et Iuris*, 9 (1943), 1–20; Betti, "La crisi odierna"; Schönbauer, "Zur 'Krise des römischen Rechts'"; Giuseppe Grosso, "Rec. di Koschaker, *Die Krise des römischen Rechts und die romanistische Rechtswissenschaft*, München/Berlin 1938," *Studia et Documenta Historiae et Iuris*, 5 (1939), 505–520 (now in Giuseppe Grosso, *Scritti storico giuridici*, IV (Torino: Giappichelli, 2001), pp. 101–116); Adolfo Plachy, "Rec. di Koschaker, *Die Krise des römischen Rechts und die romanistische Rechtswissenschaft* (1938)," *Rivista di Storia del Diritto Italiano*, 12 (1939), 388–394; Giovanni Pugliese, "Diritto romano e scienza del diritto," *Annali dell'Università di Macerata*, 15 (1941), 5–48 (now in Giovanni Pugliese, *Scritti giuridici scelti*, III (Naples: Jovene, 1985), pp. 159–204); Pierre Noailles, "La crise du droit romain," in *Mémorial des études latines offert à J. Marouzeau* (Paris: Belles Lettres, 1943), pp. 387–415. The discussion was continued later by Antonio Guarino, "Cinquant'anni dalla 'Krise'," *Labeo*, 34 (1988), 43–56, now in Antonio Guarino, *Pagine di Diritto romano*, I (Naples: Jovene, 1993), pp. 276–291.

[15] Valentin Georgescu, *Exista o crisä a studilor de Drept Roman?* (Czernowitz: Institutul de arte grafice si editura Glasul Bucovinei, 1937); Paul Koschaker, "Review of Georgescu, Exista o crisä a studilor de Drept Roman? (Gibt es eine Krise des Studiums des römischen Rechts?), Czernowitz 1937," *Zeitschrift der Savigny-Stiftung für Rechtsgeschichte: Romanistische Abteilung*, 58 (1938), 425–427.

[16] Emilio Betti, "Methode und Wert des heutigen Studiums des römischen Rechts," *Tijdschrift voor Rechtsgeschiedenis/Legal History Review*, 15(2) (1937), 137–174; Erich Genzmer, "Was heißt und zu welchem Ende studiert man antike Rechtsgeschichte?" *Zeitschrift der Akademie für Deutsches Recht*, 3 (1936), 403–408. In Italy, the whole conception of crisis was different. Although it was related to Koschaker's work, it was prompted more by the relationship between Roman law and positive law. Gianni Santucci, "'Decifrando scritti che non hanno nessun potere'. La crisi della romanistica

Koschaker's *Krise* was born out of a sense of gradual decay that was compounded by a fresh crisis. The prestige of Roman law professors had already diminished under the BGB. The new German 1935 *Reichsstudienordnung* had replaced lectures on Roman law with "ancient legal history." This removed the privileged position enjoyed by Roman law for centuries and made possible its reduction in the curriculum. Koschaker gave the talk in December 1937 and it was published in the following year with some alterations. He returned to the theme in a number of other writings published within a few years, once even in the notoriously Nazi oriented journal *Deutsche Rechtswissenschaft*.[17] The talk of a crisis was also a reflection of his experience in teaching in Berlin, where visiting students from Italy marveled that they witnessed this famous professor lecturing to an almost empty hall.[18]

In the *Krise*, Koschaker warned against two of the main themes of Romanistic scholarship at the time, the interpolationist and the historical directions, and laid the groundwork for the idea of the actualization of the past as a dogmatic analysis of legal sources. However, what the text brought to the discussion was a strong European slant. Koschaker spoke of the historical consciousness as the "*Grundlage der europäische Kultur*," the foundation of European culture. In particular, he discussed "*Romidee*," the idea of Rome (pp. 10–11), a political and cultural idea of the enduring character of the Roman Empire and its *renovatio* or renewal.

Even in the foreword, Koschaker takes up his own position with a sense of sarcasm and daring. He writes how he is not fighting for his subject, even though it would be understandable for an egocentric professor to do so, nor even that there should be professors of Roman law. Instead, his aim is to point out how Roman law has for the last two and a half millennia been an important factor in European culture and continues to be so as long as it is not replaced. Thus, while it was necessary to thank Hans Frank, the *Reichskommissar* (who was later executed as a war criminal after the Nuremberg trials) for the invitation, he added that the views he was presenting were solely

fra le due guerre," in Italo Birocchi and Massimo Brutti (eds.), *Storia del diritto e identità disciplinari: tradizioni e prospettive* (Torino: Giappichelli, 2016), p. 71.

[17] For example, Paul Koschaker, "Probleme der heutigen romanistischen Rechtswissenschaft," *Deutsche Rechtswissenschaft*, 5 (1940), 110–136.

[18] Tommaso Beggio, "Un commento alla proposta di riforma degli studi romanistici di Paul Koschaker in un documento inedito di Ulrich von Lübtow," *Index: quaderni camerti di studi romanistici = international survey of Roman law*, 46 (2018), p. 601.

his own. Koschaker explains that though his text is the inaugural publication in the new series for the *Akademie für deutsches Recht*, this is somewhat unusual as his text supports Roman law. The *Akademie*, under the direction of Frank, is tasked with the renewal of German law and renewal involves a conflict between Roman and national law (pp. iii–iv). Koschaker later described the experience in military terms. His maneuver was to attack the rear because a frontal attack would have been suicidal. He had been invited by the head of the Nazi legal machinery to talk to an exclusively Nazi audience and therefore to criticize directly the immutable the Nazi party program would have been not only pointless but even potentially dangerous. The only solution was to praise the greatness of Roman law as a cultural phenomenon and extol the German contribution. The result was, according to Koschaker, rousing applause and continued respect from the Nazis.[19]

The text of Koschaker's *Krise* is a fascinating read and there is little reason to doubt that the audience would have enjoyed it. How much they would have agreed with its content is another matter. What Koschaker does is to present a history of the universalization of Western culture from the basis of ancient civilization, resulting in a cultural layer that goes far beyond the boundaries of national states.[20]

What separates Koschaker from many of his peers is that he does not merely present a German view, for he also cites examples from British authors and scholarship. His Europe was not simply central or middle Europe, it encompassed the whole European continent.

However, if Koschaker's story has a hero, that would be F. C. von Savigny, the founder of the Historical School of jurisprudence. Koschaker's view of the Historical School and its relationship with contemporary romanticism was not without its contradictions and he writes in a strong combative tone in relation to Kantorowicz and other contemporaries. He is quick to note how many of the principled stands of Savigny's Historical School are actually fairly

[19] Koschaker, "Selbstdarstellung," p. 123. Despite his focus on the laws of the ancient Near East, Koschaker continued to study and teach Roman law, even writing an introductory textbook for student use. (A copy of this work from 1933, titled *System des römischen Privatrechts* is now at the Bibliothek des Max-Planck-Instituts für europäische Rechtsgeschichte, Frankfurt [signature: Manuscr. 155 Q R].)

[20] Paul Koschaker, *Die Krise des römischen Rechts und die romanistische Rechtswissenschaft* (Munich and Berlin: Beck, 1938), p. 10.

unimportant, but the main problem with Savigny's successors was not too little history but quite the opposite (pp. 20–28). The Historical School had become too historical.

Koschaker's criticism of the Historical School mirrored that of many of his peers and contemporaries, who felt that the Historical School's attention to minute textual debate missed the point. What really mattered was the notion of legal development.[21]

The problem was the influence of the Historical School allowed positivism to take hold, reducing Roman law to a historical anecdote. For Koschaker, the jurisprudence inspired by Roman law was creative. Jurisprudence, like common law, was reliant on a spirit of law that manifested itself in the creative power of jurists working in unison (p. 28). Thus it was not historical studies but the Pandectist jurisprudence of Savigny and Windscheid that had gained worldwide fame (p. 30). Savigny, Jhering and Windscheid were European jurists with international reputations. Neither before nor since had German lawyers gained such international influence (p. 33).[22]

Much of the text deals with the exalted history of Roman law in Germany and its influence. Koschaker goes as far as to maintain that Pandectism united Germany and its law before political developments did. However, the influence of the BGB led to the downfall of Pandectism and this reverberated on the standing of Roman law in Europe. However, an even greater threat was the rise of interpolationism. Like the textual criticism that had clumsily historicized Homer, the Bible and the *Nibelungenlied*, interpolationism sought to historicize the content of the *Corpus Iuris*. But what it did instead was destroy the authority of the text by establishing doubts concerning its accuracy. Justinian's compilation had relied on the idea of conveying the wisdom of the ancient classical jurists and thus the idea of the Roman Empire. Interpolationism claimed that this was all false because the texts were not genuine. Interpolationism was by that time beginning to be recognized as an extreme movement that was gradually losing steam due to the controversies that surrounded its results. Rather than neohumanism, it had become involved in fairly arbitrary removals of texts from the legal corpus based on the criteria of authenticity. While many

[21] Hans-Peter Haferkamp, *Georg Friedrich Puchta und die "Begriffsjurisprudenz"* (Frankfurt: Klostermann, 2004).

[22] On this, see Martin Avenarius, "Bernhard Windscheid (1817–1892). Der Spätpandektist und seine Wirkung auf das Rechtsdenken des europäischen Auslands," *Zeitschrift für Europäisches Privatrecht*, 25 (2017), 396–418.

established authors like Fritz Schulz, Gerhard Beseler or Siro Solazzi were supporters, the great project of the index of interpolations was much criticized.[23]

In addition to interpolationism, Koschaker's second bête noire was the historical study of Roman law. Especially at fault were Ludwig Mitteis, his own teacher, and Leopold Wenger, who had promoted ancient legal history (*Antike Rechtsgeschichte*). The result had been the joining of Roman law as part of the universal history of antiquity with other ancient laws; Roman law was merely seen as part of history and not as part of a great legal tradition.[24] In Italy there had been a counter-reaction by Bonfante, Scialoja and Riccobono, who had sought to preserve the connection between Roman law and modern law, in part due to the political importance that the Roman heritage had in the Italian state (pp. 42–49). However, even Riccobono was quick to note that there were historical layers in the *Digest of Justinian* and it should be seen more as a product of jurisprudence, and not as immutable law.[25] This turn against the excesses of philology and history was a continuation of the feelings that Koschaker had already had when studying with Mitteis.[26]

23 Koschaker, *Krise*, pp. 34–40. On Koschaker's relation to interpolationism, see Tommaso Beggio, "Paul Koschaker und die Reform des romanistischen Rechtsstudiums in Deutschland. Ein unveröffentlichtes Dokument," *Zeitschrift der Savigny-Stiftung für Rechtsgeschichte: Romanistische Abteilung*, 135 (2018), 645–680; Tommaso Beggio, "La 'Interpolationenforschung' agli occhi di Paul Koschaker: la critica a Gradenwitz e alla cosiddetta 'neuhumanistische Richtung' e lo sguardo rivolto all'esempio di Salvatore Riccobono," in Martin Avenarius, Christian Baldus, Francesca Lamberti and Mario Varvaro (eds.), *Gradenwitz, Riccobono und die Entwicklung der Interpolationenkritik* (Tübingen: Mohr Siebeck, 2018), pp. 121–155.

24 Wenger stated this clearly in *Der heutige Stand der römischen Rechtswissenschaft* (Munich: C. H. Beck'sche Verlagsbuchhandlung, 1927), p. 1 where he maintained that Roman law must become the legal history of the ancient world. On Mitteis and Wenger, see Evelyn Höbenreich, "À propos 'Antike Rechtsgeschichte': Einige Bemerkungen zur Polemik zwischen Ludwig Mitteis und Leopold Wenger," *Zeitschrift der Savigny-Stiftung für Rechtsgeschichte: Romanistische Abteilung*, 109 (2013), 547–562.

25 This tendency was continued with Bonfante's student, Emilio Albertario, who debated the issues with Riccobono. The debates also reflected the inner development of interpolationism itself. However, the opposition between dogmatism and interpolationism and historicism was not absolute; Riccobono, for instance, was a student of Grandenwitz, one of the pioneers of legal papyrology. See Mario Varvaro, "Circolazione e sviluppo di un modello metologico," in Martin Avenarius, Christian Baldus, Francesca Lamberti and Mario Varvaro (eds.), *Gradenwitz, Riccobono und die Entwicklung der Interpolationenkritik* (Tübingen: Mohr Siebeck, 2018), p. 74; Santucci, "Decifrando scritti," pp. 88–92.

26 The attack on Mitteis was in a way surprising, but in his autobiography Koschaker does dwell on his feelings of inadequacy when faced with *Wunderkinder* like Partsch. Koschaker, "Selbstdarstellung," p. 109.

According to Koschaker, Italy was an exception in the link between the national project and Rome. For most European states, the meaning of Rome was the *imperium Romanum*, the idea of the supranational (*Übernationales*), a cornerstone of the European house. In the purely historical inquiry, this significance was simply lost. Not only did law lose its autonomy, it lost its claim to a larger cultural heritage.[27] In the Italian discussion, this claim was met with resistance, Pugliese, for example, claiming that Koschaker had simply been wrong in his accusations against historical study. For Pugliese, the purely normative study of continuities was useless, whereas historical study that strove for an understanding of law in its changing contexts was fundamental.[28]

Koschaker then proceeds in the *Krise* to examine the role of Roman law in Italy, France and England, outlining how even the English have grasped the true meaning of Roman law as the lingua franca of European jurisprudence. What Koschaker does is use this survey to present opinions favorable to his own theses, the value of classical Roman law in the education of European lawyers and the future of law. In the English-language literature at that time, there were numerous examples of the value of Roman law for jurisprudence, such as Burdick's 1938 *Principles of Roman Law and Their Relation to Modern Law.*[29]

What then should the role of Roman law in German legal education be? The Nazi *Justizausbildungsordnung* (the legal education degree) of July 22, 1934 stated the possibility of including Roman law as the foundation of current law but studying Roman law was no longer mandatory. Some faculties had made the radical decision of making Roman law optional even in the doctoral examination. In the January 18, 1935 guidelines for the new *Reichstudienordnung* (national study regulation) the position of Roman law was relatively favorable, even though the new element of *Privatrechtsgeschichte der Neuzeit* had been instituted to include elements of legal history after the reception of Roman law. The author of the reform was K. A. Eckhardt, who was, in addition to being a professor of law in Berlin and leading the purge of his Jewish colleagues such as Schulz from the faculty, one of the leading lawyers in the SS with the

[27] Koschaker, *Krise*, pp. 49–52.

[28] Pugliese, "Diritto romano e scienza del diritto," pp. 8–11. Pugliese admits that criticism such as that already presented by Betti against interpolationism was partly accurate but this did not diminish the truth of the original claim.

[29] Koschaker, *Krise*, pp. 61, 65–66; Burdick, *Principles of Roman Law and Their Relation to Modern Law.*

rank of *SS-Sturmbannführer*. Eckhardt was nevertheless an accomplished legal historian of the Germanist variety. In the 1935 guidelines for the study of law (*Richtlinien für das Studium der Rechtswissenschaft*) he wrote that "German legal science still lives in the ways of the Roman law and *ius commune* . . . the foundations of law are still defined by the Pandectist system. Our battle is against this system."[30] When the Nazi regime had defined as its aim the Nazification of legal education, the issue that was still unresolved was how should one teach Roman law and the new forms of ancient legal history? This was one of the crucial issues that Koschaker sought to answer in the *Krise* (pp. 70–72).

On top of all this came point 19 of the party program, which declared Roman law to be the enemy of national law. This rejected the idea of Roman law as the foundation of European civil law and the uniter of nations. The result, according to Koschaker, had been growing opposition from students, who had taken advantage of the less strict regulations and had abandoned Roman law completely. As a consequence, Roman law professors had lost both their influence on future generations of lawyers and their position as Europeanists (pp. 73–74).

How then to fight this crisis? Koschaker rejects the negative conclusions of a permanent decline, opting more for the long perspective of the ebb and flow of alternating renaissances and declines. His main suggestion is to underline the role of Roman law as the representative of European cultural unity (*Kulturgemeinschaft*, p. 75), but how best to do that? A reorientation of scholarship, of course, from the destructive historicization. But should one reinstate the compulsory exams, which might be very unpopular with students? What he suggests is

[30] *Richtlinien für das Studium der Rechtswissenschaft*, January 18, 1935: "Noch immer lebt die deutsche Rechtswissenschaft in den Gedankengängen des römisch-gemeinen Rechts (. . .), die geistige Grundhaltung wird heute noch durch das Pandektensystem bestimmt. Diesem System gilt unser Kampf." On the reform and the underlying battles between Frank and his supporters and the *Kieler Schule*, see Stolleis, "'Fortschritte der Rechtsgeschichte' in der Zeit des Nationalsozialismus?"; Ralf Frassek, "Steter Tropfen höhlt den Stein – Juristenausbildung im Nationalsozialismus und danach," *Zeitschrift der Savigny-Stiftung für Rechtsgeschichte: Germanistische Abteilung*, 117 (2000), 294–361; Ralf Frassek, "Wege zur nationalsozialistischen 'Rechtserneuerung' – Wissenschaft zwischen 'Gleichschaltung' und Konkurrenzkampf," in Hans-Georg Hermann, Thomas Gutmann, Joachim Rückert, Mathias Schmoeckel and Harald Siems (eds.), *Von den "leges barbarorum" bis zum "ius barbarum" des Nationalsozialismus* (Cologne: Böhlau Verlag, 2008), pp. 351–377; Dorothee Mussgnug, "Die juristische Fakultät," in Wolfgang Uwe Eckart, Volker Sellin and Eike Wolgast (eds.), *Die Universität Heidelberg im Nationalsozialismus* (Heidelberg: Springer, 2006), pp. 301–302; Finkenauer and Herrmann, "Die Romanistische Abteilung der Savigny-Zeitschrift im Nationalsozialismus."

the actualization (*Aktualisierung*) of Roman law lectures so that they aimed at the present and the future (p. 76). Thus, Roman law would be not a historical curiosity studied by philologists and historians together with Assyrian laws but a living part of the contemporary legal tradition. This return to Savigny, the legal historical education of all jurists, would not only be a good and beautiful idea it would also be a *German* idea (p. 84). Koschaker's vision of Europe was thus very much a national vision, perhaps due to the myopia of a researcher in developing ideas that are international in character or, more likely, due to the text's audience.

Even later, Koschaker maintained that Romanists had alienated students with historicization. If one did not teach law students law and legal thinking, they would not be interested since most of them were going to practice law. Then again, a law student would learn anything if the exam required it, even the anatomy of an elephant.[31] The cultural interpretation was ultimately secondary to the practicalities of the reforms of law schools and the way that the legal education and ultimately legal scholarship should be developed. This was not easy for his critics to understand. In a letter to Salvatore Riccobono in 1940, he laments that he is being simplified as wanting to bring back the methods of Pandectism and as being the enemy of legal history (*Feind der Rechtsgeschichte*). The historical method has a clear value in the study of law.[32] What is paradoxical is that while Koschaker talks a great deal about dogmatic continuity and actualization, the dogmatic side of Koschaker is almost completely missing from the *Krise* and from other of his more famous writings.

The *Krise* was a bold gesture in a very difficult situation. Koschaker was at the time arguably at the height of his career. He was a professor in Berlin, a member of prestigious academies, the editor of the most important journal in the field, the *Zeitschrift der Savigny-Stiftung für Rechtsgeschichte* (*Romanistische Abteilung*). In the *Krise*, he attacks not only the Nazi party line but also his own teachers. For the Nazis, he demonstrated how the nationalistic legal policy was a failure. To his teachers (and by extension himself) he presented the previous decades of scholarly work as the main reason for the decline of Roman law. In their place, he presented a vision of a supranational legal tradition and its revitalization. He ends the *Krise* with a statement that demonstrates his

[31] Koschaker, "Selbstdarstellung," p. 121.

[32] Letter from Koschaker to Riccobono on January 20, 1940. Collection of correspondence by Professor Salvatore Riccobono, currently at the disposal of Professor Mario Varvaro, at the Faculty of Law of the University of Palermo.

idea of culture as a value: "We live today in a time of reevaluation of values. But if I am right, the European cultural community is a value that still has support today."[33]

## Conservatives and Extremists in Academia

The crisis that prompted Koschaker was both an internal and external crisis that shook the foundations of the conservative legal academia. The way that political movements such as Nazism, fascism and communism wanted to reform and ultimately destroy the social and legal order to refashion society also prompted others to resist change. That was hardly surprising, because legal academia was characteristically filled with traditionalists who favored conservatism, legalism and stability. In 1937, Koschaker at the age of fifty-eight was already one of the old guard, an established professor with deeply held convictions about the central role that law, rule of law and justice were to have. Like many of his peers, he chose to adopt a reactionary stance to the revolutionary tendencies of the Nazi movement. However, this resistance to the Nazis did not prevent him from accepting the position at the board of the *Zeitschrift der Savigny-Stiftung für Rechtsgeschichte* vacated by Ernst Levy, who had been forced to resign due to his Jewish heritage. Koschaker's opposition to the Nazi movement was not so severe as to have awakened the attention of the authorities. In fact, the political report prepared on Koschaker notes somewhat equivocally that there were no known signs of political untrustworthiness.[34]

There were many other signs that legal traditions were under threat. In Italy, the fascists had already established a program of legal reform that sought to bring new social policies into force. As with other radical movements, they maintained that law was ultimately a tool for exercising the political will. For the conservative legal academia, this was not acceptable but as in Germany they lacked the power to stop the reforms.[35]

33 Koschaker, *Krise*, p. 86: "Wir leben heute in einer Zeit der Umwertung der Werte. Aber wenn ich recht sehe, so gehört zu den Werten, die heute noch Bestand haben, die europäische Kulturgemeinschaft." Whether or not Koschaker meant this as a reference to the Nietzschean idea of "Umwertung aller Werte" is not certain.

34 Universitätsarchiv, Humboldt-Universität, Berlin, UK Personalia K 274, Bd. I, Bl. 26. On the situation in 1937 and the motives behind Koschaker's move to Tübingen, see Beggio, *Paul Koschaker*, pp. 104–117.

35 On shared traits in Italy and Germany, see Somma, *I giuristi e l'Asse culturale Roma-Berlino.*

Though they are currently thought of as extreme right-wing movements, both Nazism and fascism had a deep revolutionary agenda that combined elements from socialism and far-right nationalism. As a consequence, for conservatives of nearly every denomination, many of their ideas and policies were disconcerting. While anti-Semitism had been deeply rooted in Europe for centuries, the fact that Jewish colleagues as well as students and former students were persecuted for no fault of their own would no doubt have been considered unjust.

Koschaker was by no means the only legal scholar who would extol the role of cultural heritage and the lineages from antiquity to the present in the field of law. In Italy, one of the principal voices was Salvatore Riccobono (1864–1958), a professor of Roman law in Palermo.[36] Riccobono was a very international scholar who had studied in Germany with some of the most influential professors of the era, such as Otto Lenel and Otto Gradenwitz. A particular influence was Bernhard Windscheid (1817–1892), one of the key figures behind the BGB. Windscheid had overseen the transformation of the Roman law tradition into the foundation of the German civil code, presenting what would be a tenuous though lasting solution for the problem of how to combine Roman law and the need for legal reform. Riccobono traveled extensively and had a crucial influence in the US, initially in the Catholic universities and later in the field of law in general. Riccobono's conservatism was in many ways similar to that of Koschaker and it comes as no surprise that they became friends during their debates. Christianity and Christian values, the central role of ancient civilization and the learned tradition were Riccobono's main themes. Unlike Schulz and Pringsheim, Riccobono rejected Greek philosophical or scientific influences and even maintained that the Justinianic compilation was purely Roman in character. Thus, though

[36] On Riccobono, see Rosanna Ortu, "Salvatore Riccobono nell'Università di Sassari," *Diritto@Storia*, 3 (2004). His continuing influence may be seen in the way that he continues to be written about. See Cesare Sanfilippo, "In Memoriam. Salvatore Riccobono," *Iura*, 9 (1958), 123–133; Riccardo Orestano, "L'animus' di Salvatore Riccobono," *Iura*, 29 (1978), 1–8; Matteo Marrone, "Romanisti professori a Palermo," *Index*, 25 (1997), 587–616; Antonio Mantello, "Salvatore Riccobono," in Paola Luigia Carucci and Loredana Di Pinto (eds.), *"Romanisti lateranensi nel Novecento," Studia et Documenta Historiae et Iuris*, 68 (2002), pp. xvi–xxi; Mario Varvaro, "Riccobono, Salvatore sr.," in Italo Birocchi, Ennio Cortese, Antonello Mattone and Marco Nicola Miletti (eds.), *Dizionario biografico dei giuristi italiani (sec. XII–XX), II* (Bologna: Il Mulino, 2013), pp. 1685–1688; Ugo Bartocci, *Salvatore Riccobono, il Diritto Romano e il valore politico degli Studia Humanitatis* (Torino: G. Giappichelli Editore, 2012).

Riccobono had accepted the premise of interpolationist research, he was minimalist in his approaches, believing that alterations could be detected, as opposed to Schulz and Pringsheim, who were more in the maximalist tradition, believing that one could restore the original text. However, both shared the notion that there had been a continuous tradition through which the texts had developed, rather than an original classical text that had only been changed by compilators.[37]

The way Riccobono understood the connections between the European tradition and Roman law was quite similar to Koschaker:

> The Italian commentators down to Alciato (1550), who performed the task left by Justinian, showed the real character of the Compilation, and really established the foundations of modern law, which gradually spread throughout Europe.[38]

The point was that the formation of the tradition was an integral process where the Roman tradition was simply the starting point and the developmental arc where law was constantly adapted and adopted to new circumstances. This was a further connection with Koschaker, who wrote to Riccobono in 1939 that even though some had interpreted the *Krise* to mean that he would be proposing a return to the law of the Pandects, the nineteenth-century German way of studying Roman law as current law, nothing could be further from the truth. The law of the past, the Pandectist Roman law, was dead and buried and should not to be resurrected. Instead, a new *mos italicus* should be built where the results of contemporary legal history would be combined with the law in force.[39] What Riccobono insisted was that while it was undoubtedly true that historical development was taking place, Roman law presented a unitary tradition that extended from ancient Rome to the modern era.[40]

[37] Salvatore Riccobono, "Outlines of the evolution of Roman law," *University of Pennsylvania Law Review*, 74 (1925), 1–19. Riccobono would write on the theme at length in Italian journals. See, for example, Salvatore Riccobono, "Dal diritto romano classico al diritto moderno," *Annali del Seminario Giuridico della R. Università di Palermo*, 3–4 (1917), 165–729.

[38] Riccobono, "Outlines of the evolution of Roman law," p. 12.

[39] Letter from Koschaker to Riccobono on December 31, 1939. Collection of correspondence by Professor Salvatore Riccobono, currently at the disposal of Professor Mario Varvaro, at the Faculty of Law of the University of Palermo. Koschaker admired the Italian tradition of Roman law and Riccobono, whom he described as a "New Bartolus." Paul Koschaker, "Contributo alla storia ed alla dottrina della convalida nel diritto romano," *Iura*, 4 (1953), 1–89.

[40] See Varvaro, "Circolazione e sviluppo," 88–89 on the debate between Riccobono and Albertario.

To Riccobono, the idea of Roman law was not simply that of law or even jurisprudence: in Rome, jurisprudence was the master of all science, both doctrinally sound and nourished by the practical experience of life. It was this fact that made its contribution so vital:

> The essential contents of modern law, both considering the substance of its norms or its doctrines, is of Roman formation.[41]

These were also the main points that Riccobono would be presenting in his lectures abroad. In his lectures in London and Oxford in 1924, for example, he outlined that his message concerned Roman law and modern law, in particular the role of law in the making of modern science. It is noteworthy that his host in Britain was the same De Zulueta who would later help Schulz and Pringsheim in their escape to Britain.

Riccobono's involvement in the fascist movement began early on. In 1924 Mussolini visited Sicily and Riccobono was among the intellectuals recruited to take part in the meetings that were organized. It would perhaps be wrong to say that Riccobono wholeheartedly adopted the fascist ideology, and more accurate to say that his ideas were often in line with those of the fascists. The most important links were the belief in the long-term historical connections between ancient Rome and modern civilization and the talk of the legacy of antiquity, not to mention the very terminology of the empire. While admiration for authoritarism and the ideology of Romanness were quite typical of the era, perhaps the greatest sign of the ideological differences between Riccobono and fascism were his writings, which touched upon race. Observers like Cascione have noted that while Riccobono would write about ancestry (*stirpe*) and heritage, his writings almost always preserved the cultural binary of tradition and development and did not use the coded language of race and blood. Isolated examples to the contrary, such as a mention in a propagandist text of the dangers of slave manumissions that could lead to a "bastardization of the Italian race," are perhaps more indicative of the terminology of the age than a deeply held conviction.[42] Rather than a fascist, Riccobono was a

[41] Salvatore Riccobono Jr., "Un manoscritto inedito di Salvatore Riccobono: le lezioni tenute ad Oxford e Londra nel 1924," *Iura*, 29 (1978), p. 15.

[42] Cosimo Cascione, "Romanisti e fascismo," in Miglietta and Santucci, *Diritto romano e regimi totalitari nel '900 europeo*, p. 36; Mario Varvaro, "Gli 'studia humanitatis' e i 'fata iuris Romani' tra fascio e croce uncinata," *Index: quaderni camerti di studi romanistici = international survey of Roman law*, 42 (2014), 643–661. Quotation from Salvatore Riccobono, "Il diritto del impero," in Carlo Galassi Paluzzi (ed.), *La missione dell'impero di*

conservative Catholic, for whom ideas of culture and heritage were linked to the role of Christianity in European civilization.[43]

The cultural and historical connection between antiquity, ancient Rome and the present was a preoccupation for fascists and this became a theme in the fascist historical and Roman law scholarship. One of the most prominent scholars of the older generation to wholeheartedly embrace the fascist movement was Professor Pietro De Francisci (1883–1971).[44] He became one of the most prominent legal scholars in the fascist regime, serving as Mussolini's minister of justice from 1932 to 1935. As a member of parliament and minister, he advanced a very authoritarian agenda both in constitutional law and judicial procedure. His theories called for an open break with liberal ideas, using the Roman model as a guide in building the future. He argued for a strong state, guided by a sovereign national leader. As such, he was strictly against ideas such as humanity and cosmopolitanism that were inherent for instance in Roman Stoicism.[45] De Francisci's works on Roman legal history are perhaps not as openly political as some of his writings on legal reform but they are quite blatant in their use of history to justify present policies. De Francisci's 1941 book on the origins of the Principate of Augustus, for example, traces the constitutional and political processes from the republic to empire. While the book taken out of context would appear to be a simple historical work, it was anything but. The rule of Augustus had become one of the cornerstones of the

*Roma nella storia della civiltà* I (Rome: Istituto di Studi Romani, 1938), p. 42. On the relations, see Mantello, "La giurisprudenza romana fra Nazismo e Fascismo." Riccobono was also close to Edoardo Volterra, who was both Jewish and a member of the partisan resistance movement. For instance, he intervened in 1943 on Volterra's behalf to preserve his personal library from the fascist police. Pierangelo Buongiorno, "Die Ethik eines Juristen. Edoardo Volterra zwischen der Palingenesia Codicis, den *senatus consulta* und dem italienischen Faschismus (1929–1943)," *Philippika*, 105 (2017), 52.

43 This combination of law, conservatism and cultural Europeanism was fairly typical of Catholic conservatives of the era. On the role of Catholic conservativism in the human rights movement, see Samuel Moyn, *Christian Human Rights* (Philadelphia, PA: University of Pennsylvania Press, 2015).

44 On De Francisci, most recently, see Carlo Lanza, "La 'realtà' di Pietro De Francisci," in Italo Birocchi and Luca Loschiavo (eds.), *Giuristi e il fascino del regime* (Rome: Roma Tre-Press, 2015), pp. 215–236; Valerio Marotta, "Roma, l'Impero e l'Italia nella letteratura romanistica degli anni trenta," in Giovanni Cazzetta (ed.), *Retoriche dei giuristi e costruzione dell'identità nazionale* (Bologna: Il Mulino, 2013), pp. 425–460.

45 Cascione, "Romanisti e fascismo," pp. 18–21; Marotta, "Roma, l'Impero e l'Italia," pp. 437–439.

search for historical legitimacy for the new fascist empire. The massive celebrations and the scholarly production that accompanied the *bimillenario Augusteo* in 1938 were meant to exalt the leadership of Augustus that had resolved the problems of the Republica by instituting a new order. By some coincidence, the Fascist depictions of the new order had distinct traces of corporativism and other ideas of the fascist new order. De Francisci's book joined innumerable others, both in Italy and in Germany, that through history celebrated the present. Among these works were many that were sound historiography but others served a distinct agenda on the side. Even in Germany, Nazi scholars wrote extensively of Augustus as an authoritarian leader who would resolve issues that the republic could not.[46] In De Francisci's 1941 work, the very language of the text, which talks of the "new world that rises and the old that is extinguished" (p. 3) or the "revolutionary nature of the new regime" (p. 106) are direct parallels with fascist ideas. However, these parallels remained parallels in the sense that the works were still about ancient Rome and were founded on ancient Roman sources.[47]

[46] De Francisci, *Genesi e struttura del principato Augusteo*; Heinrich Siber, *Das Führeramt des Augustus* (Leipzig: S. Hirzel, 1940); Volkmann, *Zur Rechtsprechung im Prinzipat des Augustus*; Anton von Premerstein, *Vom Werden und Wesen des Prinzipats. Aus dem Nachlass herausgegeben von Hans Volkmann* (Munich: Verlag der Bayerischen Akademie der Wissenschaften, 1937); Biondo Biondi, "La legislazione di Augusto," in R. Paribeni and M. Canavesi (eds.), *Conferenze Augustee, nel bimillenario della nascita* (Milan: Vita e Pensiero, 1938), pp. 141–262; Francesco De Martino, *Lo stato di Augusto* (Naples: Tip. G. Barca, 1936); Pietro De Francisci, "La costituzione Augusteo," in *Studi in onore di Pietro Bonfante* (Milan: Fratelli Treves, 1930), pp. 13–43. Even Riccobono wrote on the matter earlier in Salvatore Riccobono, "Augusto e il problema della nuova costituzione," *Annali del Seminario giuridico di Palermo*, 15 (1936), 363–507. The main scientific product of the *bimillenario* was the stately opus *Augustus: Studi in occasione del Bimillenario Augusteo* (Rome: Tipografia della R. Accademia Nazionale dei Lincei, 1938). However, as Ernst Levy, at that point already in his American exile, pointed out, the book was far from a fascist propaganda tool, in fact it included many excellent articles as well as some more propagandist texts, and even the odd Jewish author, Arnaldo Momigliano. Ernst Levy, "Review of Augustus: Studi in occasione del Bimillenario Augusteo. (Rome: Tipografia della R. Accademia Nazionale dei Lincei. 1938)," *The American Historical Review*, 45 (1939), 106–107.

[47] This in 1945 allowed Vincenzo Arangio-Ruiz to write to Benedetto Croce, arguing against the plans to expel De Francisci from the Accademia dei Lincei, due to the separation he had always maintained between his politics and science. However, he also maintains that there might be things that he does not know about De Francisci. Letter from Vincenzo Arangio-Ruiz to Benedetto Croce on March 22, 1945, now in Valerio Massimo Minale, *Carteggio Croce – Arangio-Ruiz* (Naples: Il Mulino, 2012), pp. 43–45.

The Italian fascist obsession with ancient Rome and by extension Roman law was welcomed by one interest group in particular, namely Roman law scholars in Germany. With the new political, military and cultural alliance between Italy and Germany came all kinds of interactions, such as a German–Italian conference on fascism and law held in Vienna in 1938. Among its participants was Paul Koschaker, who talked about the foundational role of Roman law in the idea of the Roman Empire. This very short article reminds readers yet again of the long history of Roman law but the point of reference was different. He acknowledged that for Italians Roman law had a national significance but for Germans the situation was more complicated. While there was a question of legal heritage in German jurisprudence, the main issue was that of European legal science. Here Koschaker launches into praise of the "European cultural feeling" that is growing, the sense that civilization and culture were uniting the nations.[48] The occidentalist train of thought carried the implication that supranational elements such as Roman law were agents of civilization that carried the potential of progress. In the case of Roman law, this contact would have enabled German jurisprudence to develop.[49] What was surprising in his speech is how liberal and unfascist the outline was, allowing him to quote praising ideas like European identity and the value of humanity.[50]

However, beyond the position of Roman law, the Italian fascist ideas of law and justice were not fundamentally removed from Nazi legal thought. Their common enemies were the destructive ideas of individualism that they wished to replace with corporativism. They both sought to defend the position of the (racially pure) working people and strove for a social conception of justice. The methods were in many instances the same: the leadership principle of decision-making, the corporativist state, the submission of all interest to

[48] Paul Koschaker, "Deutschland, Italien und das römische Recht," in *Faschismus und Recht. Schriften des NS.-Rechtswahrerbundes in Österreich* (Vienna: Landesgeschäftsstelle des NS.-Rechtswahrerbundes, 1938), pp. 19–22.

[49] Koschaker, "Deutschland, Italien und das römische Recht," p. 21, Koschaker uses a distinctly racist parable to illustrate how only a *Kulturvolk* such as the Germans can assume civilized traits like the influences of Roman law: "Wenn ein Neger einen Frack anziecht, so ist dies eine Barbarei. Den der Frack bleibt hierbei Frack und sein Träger ein Neger." However, it is not a sign of lesser value when a *Kulturvolk* appropriates and makes its own a piece of a higher civilization.

[50] Koschaker, "Deutschland, Italien und das römische Recht," p. 22.

that of the state and, finally, the submission of law to being an instrument of state power.[51]

While De Francisci was hardly the only one of the older generation of legal scholars to jump on the fascist bandwagon, there were numerous older German-speaking legal academics who became ideologically fervent Nazi supporters. Among Roman law scholars, none was more so than the Austrian academic Ernst Schönbauer.[52] Even someone like Pringsheim, who went to extraordinary lengths to forgive former Nazis in academia after the war, stated that there was one whose behavior was so inexcusable that he could not forgive him and that was Schönbauer. He was an extraordinary character, describing himself even officially as both a professor and a "farmer in Eichberg." After the *Anschluss*, Schönbauer was appointed interim dean by the Nazis and proceeded to purge the faculty of Jews and "politically untrustworthy" characters, leading to the expulsion of roughly half of the faculty. This context makes it all the more notable how Schönbauer took Koschaker to task for writing the *Krise*. In a rebuttal that was published in 1939 in Koschaker's own Festschrift of all places, Schönbauer denied the very existence of a crisis. Instead, he outlined the great history of Roman law studies and how it had a promising future once it took into account the principles of National Socialism. For Schönbauer, the larger difficulty was not the fact that Roman law was nationally alien and that the party program demanded its removal. Rather, the main issue was that the main protagonists of Roman law in Germany had been non-Aryan (i.e., Jewish), whereas in Ostmark (the Nazi term for Austria) they had been national. To rescue Roman law, there had to be a purge on two fronts, both on the teachers and scholars and on the subject matter,

[51] See, for example, the speech of Arrigo Solmi, "Le nuove Direttive del diritto," in *Faschismus und Recht. Schriften des NS.-Rechtswahrerbundes in Österreich* (Vienna: Landesgeschäftsstelle des NS.-Rechtswahrerbundes, 1938), pp. 1–3.

[52] The divisiveness of Schönbauer extends to his description in recent biographies, see, for example, Johannes Kalwoda, "Ernst Schönbauer (1885–1966). Biographie zwischen Nationalsozialismus und Wiener Fakultätstradition," *Beiträge zur Rechtsgeschichte Österreichs*, 2 (2012), 282–316; Irmgard Schartner, *Die Staatsrechtler der juridischen Fakultät der Universität Wien im "Ansturm" des Nationalsozialismus. Umbrüche und Kontinuitäten* (Frankfurt, Berlin, Bern, Brussels, New York, Oxford and Vienna: Peter Lang, 2011), pp. 258–303; Meissel and Wedrac, "Strategien der Anpassung – Römisches Recht im Zeichen des Hakenkreuzes"; Theo Mayer-Maly, "Ernst Schönbauer zum Gedächtnis," *Zeitschrift der Savigny-Stiftung für Rechtsgeschichte. Romanistische Abteilung*, 84 (1967), 627–630; Gamauf, "Die Kritik am römischen Recht im 19. und 20. Jahrhundert," pp. 57–58, speaks of Schönbauer's "*Arisierungstaktik*."

where the "Jewish-oriental law" should be decisively rejected.[53] One should note that Koschaker's first interest had been in the laws of Mesopotamia and this was the subject that he had hoped to found his own institute in.

The controversies were, of course, not purely political but were more focused on scholarship. The disputes over interpolationism and the historical study of Roman law divided scholars and although many of the arguments might begin as scholarly discussions, they developed into political statements. For example, when Schönbauer condemned the interpolationist studies as inherently destructive, this was an opinion that he shared for example with Riccobono (whom he cites approvingly). Riccobono saw the overly critical approach to interpolationism as methodological nihilism, where the process became an end in itself and the practical gains were negligible. In contrast, Schönbauer maintained that if the supporters of interpolationism (who were to a large degree of Jewish origin) were right, then it would have meant that the Germans and other peoples who had received Roman law would have received a law that was Eastern and Oriental, not Aryan and Western. To Schönbauer this would have been simply wrong. Luckily, according to Schönbauer, new research had returned to focus solidly on the West and its law-creating force.[54]

In these discussions, the common thread was that culture creates law. The metaphor of blood or blood community was another expression of this cultural determinism. Thus, it mattered a great deal whether the origin of law was one of proud and virtuous Romans of the republic and Principate who conquered the Mediterranean, or one of degenerate Byzantine scheming involving Jews and Semites.

Schönbauer's criticism reflected a long-standing anti-Semitic trope that had been present at least since the nineteenth century.[55] However, the glorifying tones used by Riccobono and others about ancient Rome and its legacy to the modern world were quite common among ancient historians and especially those on the far right of the political spectrum. Conservatives had produced images of the ancient world as a utopia of military conquest and strict social order, where the realities of social movements and calls for reform did not disturb

[53] Schönbauer, "Zur 'Krise des römischen Rechts'," pp. 388, 410. Schönbauer rarely mentions Jewish Roman law scholars (Levy and Pringsheim are mentioned in passing), who are removed from the list of accomplished scholars.

[54] Schönbauer, "Zur 'Krise des römischen Rechts'," pp. 390–391.

[55] Gamauf, "Die Kritik am römischen Recht im 19. und 20. Jahrhundert."

the peace of the upper classes. Much like in the Nazi and fascist movements in Germany and Italy, these illusions of the ancient world were often mixed with racial undertones and sometimes with overt references. For instance, French historian of the ancient world Jérôme Carcopino (most famous for his *La vie Quotidienne à Rome à l'Apogée de l'Empire*, translated into English as *Daily Life in Ancient Rome*) became an ardent supporter of the collaborationist Vichy regime during the World War II. He was made minister of education and in this role he would promote racist and anti-Semitic policies such as the exclusion of Jews from universities. As part of the Vichy government, he was eager to contribute to its ideas of authoritarianism and ultranationalism. In accordance with the Vichy French policy, he executed a cultural polity that touted France and, with it, Continental Europe as the true successors of ancient culture.[56]

At the end of the war, the ethnic visions of Aryan peoples or *romanità* were promptly and wisely forgotten. Nationalism itself was tainted by association with the horrors of the war. For Koschaker, nationalism represented a new opportunity.

## Rewriting the Role of Roman Law and Europe

Koschaker does not really mention how and why he came to write *Europa*. In his autobiography, he simply mentions how he disliked Berlin and moved to the quiet of Tübingen in 1941. When the war ended, he retired in 1946. A year later, *Europa* was published. The years in Tübingen were marked by relatively quiet living. The university remained open and teaching went on almost until the end of the war. Koschaker moved to a house in the village of Walchensee, where he could enjoy both the peace and quiet missing in Berlin and the closeness of nature. The years in Berlin had been marked with academic strife and the resulting anger and disappointment were beginning to take a toll on his health.[57] In Tübingen, the atmosphere and cooperation with the

[56] Even his reputation was kept clean by students for a long time. See, for instance, the difference in the image given by Stéphanie Corcy-Debray, *Jérôme Carcopino, un historien à Vichy* (Paris: Éditions L'Harmattan, 2001) and in the earlier work by Pierre Grimal, Paul Ourliac and Claude Carcopino, *Jérôme Carcopino: un historien au service de l'Humanisme* (Paris: Les Belles Lettres, 1981). Despite his role in the Vichy government, he protected Jewish historian Marc Bloch, who was a member of the Resistance. On Bloch, see Carole Fink, *Marc Bloch: A Life in History* (Cambridge and New York: Cambridge University Press, 1989), p. 251.

[57] Beggio, *Paul Koschaker*, pp. 119–132.

university administration was easier. There were a few noteworthy incidences during the Tübingen years regarding whether this or that person could be hired as his assistant or whether he could bring a student from Berlin with him. One interesting name comes up, that of a student named Pierre Pescatore, the future ECJ judge, whom Koschaker wanted to hire as his scientific assistant.[58] The end of the war saw the policies of denazification followed by what Koschaker described as renazification. In a letter to Kisch, he complains that he is being pushed to retire and that he, a committed anti-Nazi, is going to be followed by either one of two Nazis.[59]

In *Europa*, Koschaker expanded the thoughts that he had earlier presented in *Krise*, building an imposing narrative of legal development and the European legal heritage. The book came at an opportune moment. Not only was the idea of Europe on the rise, with economic integration at its core but concrete steps were also being taken to define the new free Europe in contrast to the rising communist dictatorship in the East. The OECD was established in 1948, and the Marshall Plan spearheaded an American-led plan on the integration of European economies. At the same time, the Soviet bloc was formed and by the time *Europa* was published communists had taken over all the lands of former Central and Eastern Europe. The Soviet bloc rejected the Marshall Plan and its aid programs, leading to a new economic confrontation. While right-wing totalitarianism had been destroyed in Germany and Italy, a new totalitarian regime had taken over in the East. It was against this new threat that the former liberal and conservative forces of Western Europe would unite.[60]

Already in the *Krise*, Koschaker wrote of the function of Roman law as the foundation of European private law scholarship (*Privatrechtwissenschaft*) and the mediator between the nations of Europe.[61] For Koschaker in *Europa*, European culture was a combination of factors, a tableau of cultural elements derived from different sources. What clearly both troubled and amazed him was the durability of the cultural connections, through colonialist expansionism, nationalism, religious controversies, socialism

58 A letter from Professor Hans Erich Feine to Koschaker on April 20, 1943. Universitätsarchiv, Eberhard Karls Universität, Tübingen, Personalakten Juristische Fakultät, 601/42.

59 Koschaker to Kisch on November 27, 1947 (pp. 21–24), now in Kisch, *Paul Koschaker*.

60 Conservative authors such as Pannwitz noted this with satisfaction. See Vermeiren, "Imperium Europaeum," pp. 145.

61 Koschaker, *Krise*, p. 73.

and so forth. What the saving grace of Roman law would be was the inherent conservatism of private law, the reluctance to adopt rash innovation. There might be a time when Roman law would be consigned to a museum and the pure historical study of law would be a fine way to advance that but the mission would still be ongoing.[62]

It is evident from his teaching plans in Tübingen how the ideas behind *Europa* were already beginning to take form during the war. Even here, in 1942, the intention was to use the foundations of Roman private law as an introduction to European legal thinking. This conception was of course not in line with the ideas of either the old study plan or the new study plan of 1935, both of which were founded on the separation of Roman law and the European legal tradition.[63] In 1941, Koschaker had prepared his own plan for the reform of legal education and the role of Roman law in it, which he sent to the minister of education and presented to the conference of the deans of the German law schools on July 10, 1942. In it, Koschaker advocated reform of the teaching of Roman law as the most important foundation for European legal science, *Europäische Rechtswissenschaft*. In typical fashion, he presented different options, the first being the complete abolishment of Roman law and only the last was his own plan.[64] At the same time, Koschaker wanted to push strongly for the reform of Roman law as a European legal science but appeared to realize the extent of his temerity in making proposals that ran counter to Nazi ideology. For example, in responding to a request to write an article, he mentioned that he would like to write about the relationship between European legal science and legal science based on Roman law, *romanistische Rechtswissenschaft*, and the present mortal danger for the study of Roman law. However, he realized that in order to do this, he must be cautious and careful in order not to cause problems for both himself and the person making the request.[65]

While in the *Krise*, Europe was a strong presence tying the study of Roman law to the larger framework, in *Europa* it became a central

[62] Koschaker, *Europa*, pp. 350–352.

[63] Beggio, *Paul Koschaker*, pp. 132–145.

[64] Koschaker's proposal for a reform of Roman Law teaching in German universities. Universitätsarchiv, Eberhard Karls Universität, Tübingen, Personalakten Juristische Fakultät, 601/42. On the proposal, see Beggio, "Paul Koschaker und die Reform des romanistischen Rechtsstudiums in Deutschland."

[65] Letter from Koschaker to Fritz Brüggemann on November 20, 1943. Landesarchiv Nordrhein-Westfalen, Duisburg, NL Carl Schmitt, RW 265-8125.

theme. Koschaker begins the book by asking "What is Europe?" His answer is that Europe is a cultural phenomenon, an original combination of Germanic and Roman cultural elements. He rephrases many of the same points he laid out in the *Krise* but rearranges them around the theme of Europe. As a new starting point, Koschaker takes a heterogeneous sampling of the earlier Europeanist literature, beginning with Christopher Dawson's 1935 *The Making of Europe*. This selection of literature includes Catholic universalists like Dawson but also German nationalists and writers of the *Grossraum* ideological slant as well as medieval historians. Even Carl Schmitt makes an appearance as an author in the volume *Das Reich und Europa* (1941). Despite these numerous references, his own Europe is very clear. Europe as a legal community was simply a part of Europe as a cultural and religious community. Europe was a product of history.[66]

It is hard to tell how much Koschaker's turn toward Europe was due to favorable political circumstances. In the *Krise*, there was really no discussion on the definition of Europe nor its boundaries or even significance. Of course, the *Krise* has been compared to Husserl's crisis of European science and its European definitions. For Husserl, the concept of Europe was not only geographical but to a large degree one of philosophy. He drew from Hegel and Nietzsche, who both saw Europe as a mode of rationality, a spirit. For Hegel, Europe was a spiritual unity, an understanding of reason and rationality that reconciled individual freedom and institutions.[67] It is impossible to understand either Koschaker's concept of crisis or the concept of Europe without their multifarious contexts. While for philosophers, Europe could mean rationality, order, freedom and the triumph of the spirit, it was equally a symbol of crisis, the tired constraints of civilization and morality. For historians, Europe could be a symbol of an almost transcendent unity of religion and morality but at the same time a catchword of imperial ambitions and "natural" spheres of influence. Its crisis could be a cultural crisis, an economic crisis, a value crisis or even a crisis of identity or race. Both the

[66] Koschaker, *Europa*, pp. 2–4. Christopher M. Dawson, *The Making of Europe* (London: Sheed and Ward, 1932); Carl Schmitt and Fritz Hartung, *Das Reich und Europa* (Leipzig: Koehler & Amelang, 1941).

[67] Georg W. F. Hegel, *Lectures on the Philosophy of World History* (Cambridge: Cambridge University Press, 1975), p. 173; Timo Miettinen, *The Idea of Europe in Husserl's Phenomenology* (Helsinki: Philosophical Studies, 2013), pp. 29–33.

concept of crisis and the concept of Europe were thus easily adaptable for whatever purpose one could imagine.

In line with the cultural slant of the book, Koschaker begins it with the coronation of Charlemagne in Rome at Christmas in the year 800. Whatever the cultural surroundings with which Koschaker frames the book, it is very largely focused on the idea of empire as a foundational concept. The empire was not simply the Roman Empire or the Holy Roman Empire, it was also the Christian Roman Empire. All of these combined to form the idea of Rome or *Romidee*. The connection between Rome and Europe was one of culture and civilization. Others, like Betti, saw Europe as a cultural community, which was founded on shared values.[68]

The concept of *Romidee* struck a chord with reviewers but a number of them were skeptical of what they felt were Koschaker's enormous historical generalizations. For instance, Genzmer praised the concept of *Romidee* but criticized Koschaker's concept of reception, which made no distinction between the continuing influence and renaissance of Roman law in traditional Roman law countries like Italy, and the reception of Roman law in Germany.[69]

The Roman Empire or the idea of the Roman Empire were not in any way fixed concepts. In the conception of the Middle Ages, they were almost synonymous with the concept of Christian universality. This universality manifested itself in the *Romidee* and overshadowed the weak national inclinations of the time (p. 47). These were ideas that would later be adapted by Christian conservative movements. Especially important were actors such as the French political philosopher Jacques Maritain, who would in the 1930s and 1940s formulate the tenets that would be the foundation of postwar Christian Democratic parties. For the Europeanist movement, it became a crucial moment that Robert Schuman, one of the founders of European unification, was influenced by Maritain's ideas on a new foundation of Europe based on human rights and democracy inspired by Christian values. Some, like McCauliff, have maintained that the 1950 Schuman declaration was

68 Emilio Betti, *Das Problem der Kontinuität im Lichte der rechtshistorischen Auslegung* (Wiesbaden: Franz Steiner Verlag, 1961).

69 Erich Genzmer, "Rez. Paul Koschaker, Europa und das römische Recht. Biederstein Verlag. München und Berlin 1947. XII und 378 Seiten," *Zeitschrift der Savigny-Stiftung für Rechtsgeschichte: Romanistische Abteilung*, 67 (1950,) 595–611; Franz Wieacker, "Ursprünge und Elemente des europäischen Rechtbewusstseins," in Martin Göhring (ed.), *Europa, Erbe und Aufgabe. Internationaler Gelehrtenkongress Mainz 1955* (Wiesbaden: Franz Steiner, 1956), pp. 105–119.

inspired by Maritain.[70] The connection with Catholic intellectuals was one of the more difficult issues in Koschaker's *Europa*. Thus, while the emphasis on Roman law and the ideals of law such as universalism were tenets that had long been associated with Catholicism, the law that Koschaker was talking about was after all Roman private law, which had few or no direct connections with religion.

The outline of the historical development that Koschaker sketches in *Europa* is a very familiar one, as it is the narrative of a shared European legal heritage. He begins with the Glossators and continues with the Commentators, stressing their European credentials and outlook (p. 82). The law they developed was jurists' law (p. 99), which emerges as the unifying idea that links not only medieval jurists but also their Roman predecessors. From there Koschaker moves to the Humanists, to *mos italicus*, to the reception of Roman law in Germany and the French *Code Civil*. He also covers developments in other places and clearly has an interest in the position of Roman law in the US, where he specifically mentions the Riccobono seminar at the Catholic University in Washington, DC.[71] From there, one comes to the codifications and the BGB and the eradication of the practical applicability of Roman law in Europe (p. 141). In the build-up to the Historical School and Savigny, Koschaker outlines the importance of jurists' law in the making of a professional corps of jurists with shared ideals and values. The ideas of *Volksgeist* and *Professorenrecht* are for Koschaker simply imperfect manifestations of jurists' law. It was jurists' law that transported the learning of Roman law to the modern era (pp. 164–245). In that scheme, natural law had often been presented as an opponent of Roman law influence. This was only true to a very limited degree (p. 251) as natural law relied on Roman law teachings to a large extent. From there, Koschaker then ends up with Savigny and the Historical School, Pandectism and Neohumanism (pp. 254–311).

This exposition was a fairly typical outline of the history of European legal science, with the exception that Koschaker introduced British and North-American elements to the European narrative. In fact, some of

[70] Catherine McCauliff, "Union in Europe: Constitutional Philosophy and the Schuman Declaration, May 9, 1950," *Columbia Journal of European Law*, 18 (2012), 441–472. On Christian democrats as a Europeanist movement, see Wolfram Kaiser, *Christian Democracy and the Origins of European Union* (Cambridge: Cambridge University Press, 2007).

[71] Koschaker, *Europa*, p. 129. On the Riccobono Seminar, see Salvo Randazzo, "Roman legal tradition and American law. The Riccobono Seminar of Roman Law in Washington," *Roman Legal Tradition*, 1 (2002), 123–144.

the similarities may be due to the fact that much of it was reminiscent of the narrative recounted by Savigny himself. However, more importantly, Koschaker's interpretation inspired many of the later authors, especially Coing, to reengage with Savigny and his theories on the links between law and history. There are numerous ways in which the return to Savigny advocated by Koschaker was truer to Savigny than the Historical School itself. As an observant French author Gaudemet wrote, the early Historical School of Grimm and Savigny had a nostalgic view of history, meaning its conception of history was idealizing and anachronistic. What Koschaker sought to do was to make that idealizing anachronism the explicit aim of legal inquiry. In this legal discourse, it is notable that Koschaker's view of Savigny influenced that of Coing, who in turn inspired Zimmermann. Zimmermann in fact was the first to openly state that the history of Roman law in Europe is mostly about the reception of Roman law, which in turn had very little to do with the Romans themselves.[72]

Within this historical outline of the position of Roman law is also a very marked exposition of the fate of Roman law under the Nazi regime. While the outline in the *Krise* was programmatic, the narrative of *Europa* was primarily analytical, despite the reference to Roman law as relative natural law. According to Koschaker, the Nazi attack on Roman law was a logical continuation of the nationalistic tendencies of the nineteenth century. Some elements had been proved wrong, such as the lingering assertions that Roman law was Jewish. Prominent Nazi Romanists like Schönbauer would refute that claim (p. 157) and subsequent discussions on laws that were alien to the German people (*Artfremd*, p. 159). Koschaker even mentions how he himself pointed out that Roman law had not been in force in Germany for decades and thus point nineteen of the party program was no longer relevant. This appeared to be the case even for the NSDAP itself, because there was really nobody who would have suffered from Roman law, save for a few law students who had received bad grades (pp. 312–313). Then again, if Germany was to have a socialist or *volkstümlich* private law, it would really matter if Roman law was the basis of the old laws.

[72] Jean Gaudemet, "Histoire et système dans la méthode de Savigny," in *Hommage à/Hulde Aan René Dekkers* (Brussels: Bruylant, 1982), p. 121; Reinhard Zimmermann, "Roman law and the harmonization of private law in Europe," in Arthur S. Hartkamp, Martijn W. Hesselink, Ewoud Hondius, C. Mak and Edgar Du Perron (eds.), *Towards a European Civil Code* (Alphen aan den Rijn: Kluwer Law International, 2011), pp. 27–54.

As a result, there was really no consistent purge of Roman law or Romanists. As Koschaker ironically states, no professor "had the hair on his head twisted" even if he officially sang hymns in praise of Roman law. This was not due to the liberal tendencies of the regime but rather that Roman law was not a threat. He compares the attitude of the Nazi regime to that of the church toward heretics. They were generally tolerated unless they began to gain followers (p. 314).[73] In fact, many would be able to make a good career and be promoted. This did not, of course, include the numerous Romanists who were either driven into exile, lost their lives during the war or were killed in the concentration camps.

The Nazi regime would in fact gain a new appreciation of the Holy Roman Empire and the European dimension with the conquest of Europe. This was tied together with the idea of a Europe led by the Great German Reich (p. 316), and much scholarly energy was spent at the time to give it historical roots. However, these cultural theories mixed with racial theories were riddled with logical problems of continuities where there really were none, resorting to mythical constructions that basically attempted to prove a straight line from Wotan to Adolf Hitler (p. 324). For the Nazis as with many other radical movements, the lure of the past was one means of gaining legitimacy. Theories of great Germanocentric empires were easier to present if they could be supported by examples of earlier great European empires with Germany as their center. One should not of course forget that Nazi ideas about Europe were in essence ways in which the idea of German dominance in economics, politics and even law could be made more natural and palatable. It is hardly a surprise that one of the roots of the Nazi enthusiasm for Europe may be found in the SS and its push in 1941–1942 to incorporate allies and inhabitants of conquered territories in support of the German war effort.[74] However, not even the Nazi conceptions of Europe were uniform, as there were innumerable different ideas, from the reawakening of the European nobility to a unified European economic community and even a basic European

[73] In the same vein, Wieacker noted that despite what Koschaker wrote, the true catastrophe was not specifically about Roman law but about the Nazi attack on scholarship in general. Franz Wieacker, "Rezension Paul Koschaker: Europa und das römische Recht," *Gnomon*, 21(5/6) (1949), 190.

[74] There is considerable literature on the matter. See Jochen Böhler and Robert Gerwarth, *The Waffen-SS: A European History* (Oxford: Oxford University Press, 2016); Hans-Werner Neulen, *Europa und das Dritte Reich. Einigungsbestrebungen im deutschen Machtbereich 1939–1945* (Munich: Universitas, 1987).

unity in anticommunism, which were supported by elements within the Nazi elite.[75]

Koschaker ends *Europa* with a return to the idea of the crisis of Roman law and Europe. The great political upheavals of Europe and the political and military battles of the world wars had transformed Europe. The division of Europe and the altered spheres of influence had diminished Europe and changed its culture. What European culture was for Koschaker was a combination of Germanic, Christian and Latin influences. It was a universalist and unified cultural sphere that had spread throughout the world through colonization. Its opponent was the nationalism that had spread itself first through Western Europe and then elsewhere. Now with the competition of ideas with the other universalist ideology, socialism, it was possible that the ideas of culture and civilization, the idea of Rome, might begin to have currency again.[76] Koschaker pushed forward his own idea of Europe at a very opportune moment, a moment when European unification had begun to gain acceptance.

At the end of *Europa*, Koschaker moves to one of the most controversial remarks concerning the value of Roman law, namely that it functions as a kind of relative natural law (*relatives Naturrecht*). While he denies the possibility of an absolute natural law, the potential is still there for a European natural law (*europäisches Naturrecht*). Thus, while absolute natural law based on reason itself is simply speculative, European natural law would be based strictly on history and the comparative method, examining the common traits uniting European legal systems, thus enabling the legal rebuilding of Europe and the cultural world it leads (p. 346). Thus, for example, Beggio has argued that the foundation of European legal unity, for which this relative natural law would refer to, pertains more to a methodological than a substantive legal foundation.[77] The idea of relative natural law raises a number of

[75] On the transformation of ideologies, see for instance two articles from very different eras: Paul Kluke, "Nationalsozialistische Europa-Ideologie," *Vierteljahrshefte für Zeitgeschichte*, 3 (1955), 240–275; Thomas Sandkühler, "Europa und der Nationalsozialismus. Ideologie, Währungspolitik, Massengewalt," *Zeithistorische Forschungen/Studies in Contemporary History*, 9 (2012), 428–441; Ingo J. Hueck, "'Spheres of influence' and 'Völkisch' legal thought: Reinhard Höhn's notion of Europe," in Joerges and Ghaleigh, *Darker Legacies of Law in Europe*, pp. 71–86. The Nazis were influenced by all kinds of ideas circulating at the time and adopted them with contradictory results. See Gusejnova, *European Elites and Ideas of Empire, 1917–1957*.

[76] Koschaker, *Europa*, pp. 350–352.

[77] Beggio, *Paul Koschaker*, pp. 238–245.

issues, in addition to being illogical. As Fraenkel had already noted in his *Dual State*, despite its opposition to natural law and human rights, Nazi law claimed to exist as a kind of relative natural law in that it had raised the law of the blood community above the legal order itself.[78]

## The Nazi Legacy and the New Germany

Even though some of the non-Jewish professors were acutely aware of the plight of their Jewish colleagues, for many this invisible suffering did not appear to be very drastic. Especially émigrés who had left Germany before the war could be considered to have escaped the suffering of mass bombing, food shortages and the horrors of war and occupation that German civilians were subjected to during and after the war. Thus, even Koschaker wrote to one of his students, Guido Kisch, in 1947 and noted how he had simply escaped the Nazis whereas Koschaker himself was forced to experience the totalitarian regime in person. In his responses, Kisch reminded Koschaker of the fact that escape had come after untold suffering and deprivation at the hands of the Nazis and long years of uncertainty in exile. Kisch also reminded him that many of his loved ones had been brutally murdered.[79] This exchange of letters provides a telling link about life in postwar Germany and the new ideas of democracy.

One of the enduring questions about Koschaker has been his relationship with the Nazi regime. In earlier scholarship, some have presented him as an opponent to the regime, others as a bystander who became an accomplice due to his inaction.[80] In these letters with Guido Kisch, who was at the time in exile in the US, his position is quite clear. However, because the letters are mainly from the period after the war, such anti-Nazi convictions may of course be belated.

[78] Fraenkel, *Dual State*, pp. 109–150. On the Nazi notion of relative natural law, see Fabian Wittreck, *Nationalsozialistische Rechtslehre und Naturrecht. Affinität und Aversion* (Tübingen: Mohr Siebeck, 2008), pp. 35–55. Discussions on natural law did exist even in the Nazi legal journals, for example Franz Beyerle, "Der andere Zugang zum Naturrecht," *Deutsche Rechtswissenschaft*, 4 (1939), 1–20. On Beyerle as a reformer, see Liebrecht, *Die junge Rechtsgeschichte*, pp. 19–106.

[79] Kisch, *Paul Koschaker*, pp. 16, 58. It should be noted that Koschaker had not abandoned Kisch when the Nazi repression began, but had recommended him to numerous acquaintances in the US. Kisch, *Die Lebensweg eines Rechtshistorikers*, pp. 121, 128.

[80] In the most recent literature, a kind of middle ground appears to have been reached. See Beggio, *Paul Koschaker*.

The correspondence with Kisch is quite revealing about the myopia that reigned among people in academia about the plight of exiles. However, Kisch's letters to Koschaker form a stark contrast to Kish's correspondence with Salo W. Baron about going into exile. A recent émigré himself, Columbia professor Baron was a natural first point of contact for numerous exiled academics seeking a position in America, from Kisch to Hannah Arendt and Hans Kelsen. In almost all of these cases, the correspondence begins with a simple letter of introduction, stating their current position and the difficulties they are facing but continuing into discussions about science and publications, interspersed with notes about personal distress and difficulties with emigration. In the case of Baron, the letters to and from refugees are complemented with his innumerable letters of introduction on their behalf to potential employers and benefactors.[81] While there were many friends and former employers who undoubtedly wanted to and did help the persecuted, the overwhelming fact was that the scholars who went into exile were often simply abandoned to fend for themselves, being forced to grasp lifelines like Baron. Often, their academic work was literally eradicated by the Nazis. Kisch, for instance, wrote that the whole printing of his book on Jews at the University of Prague was literally destroyed when "Hitler's hordes" took over Czechoslovakia.[82]

The postwar correspondence between Koschaker and Kisch began in 1947, when Koschaker started to make inquiries about Kisch's whereabouts, not knowing whether he was alive or dead. This was the time of the "first letters," where tentative contacts were made after the war. Kisch responded, mentioning how the shock of learning about the Holocaust had taken away all his strength. When the war ended, they had waited to hear from their relatives who had stayed in Europe but had only received silence. Almost every one of their family had been killed by the Nazis. His house had also been ransacked by the Gestapo, his library stripped bare and the house later given to someone else. Though Kisch was one of the lucky ones, being able to work in New York and publish at an astonishing rate,

[81] Special Collections & University Archives, Stanford University Libraries, M0580 Salo W. Baron Papers, Series 1: Correspondence. In this collection, for example Box 22, folder 19 contains the numerous letters Baron sent to Franz Boas about the scholars coming over from Europe.

[82] Guido Kisch, *Die Universitäten und die Juden: eine historische Betrachtung zur Fünfhundertjahrfeier der Universität Basel* (Tübingen: Mohr, 1961), p. 3.

his sense of trauma was clearly apparent.[83] Kisch's appalled reaction was not uncommon among exiles. They had been persecuted, labeled as second-class citizens and physically and mentally abused. Their property had been taken and their relatives had been murdered. In making first contacts, they often found it galling that they were expected to sympathize with the suffering of the perpetrators and forget their own. Some, like Thomas Mann, were dumbfounded that everyone would ask for goods and parcels from America.[84]

What Koschaker reports was not an optimistic vision of Germany. Though the official denazification process was still ongoing, former Nazis were quickly reestablishing themselves. They requested letters to prove their blameless character, to show that they were only Nazis on the outside, and, as Koschaker writes with stinging sarcasm, stern antifascists on the inside. Koschaker's disappointment with the new democracy and German antifascism grew even more pronounced when it became apparent that Koschaker, a self-declared anti-Nazi, would be pushed into retirement to allow former Nazis to get his chair. One of them, Walter Erbe, was in fact appointed to his chair and ultimately became rector of the University of Tübingen.[85] The rise of former Nazis coincided with the rush to the center, where even card-carrying Nazi party members cleansed their previous records to appear neutral. This retroactive cleansing allowed them to return to their posts in universities, where they were now the only candidates with a sufficient track record to qualify for positions, for opponents to the regime were either abroad in exile or outside academia during the thirteen-year Nazi rule. Within postwar historiography, this has led to a curious phenomenon, where even the most blatant Nazis such as Ernst Schönbauer were presented as innocent bystanders who had upheld the rule of law despite Nazi pressure.[86] In most cases, the record within the university archives, showing simply the implementation of outside rules as the cause of the purges, had given the whitewashers, former students and Nazi followers, reason to claim their innocence. Reading the

[83] Letters Koschaker to Kisch on October 9, 1947 (p. 17), Kisch to Koschaker on November 23, 1947 (pp. 17–21), now in Kisch, *Paul Koschaker*.

[84] Krauss, *Heimkehr in ein fremdes Land*, pp. 42–43.

[85] Koschaker to Kisch on November 27, 1947 (pp. 21–24), now in Kisch, *Paul Koschaker*. On the successors, see Beggio, *Paul Koschaker*, p. 159. Despite Koschaker's judgment, Erbe's allegiance to the Nazi movement was not as solid as he thought.

[86] Kalwoda, "Ernst Schönbauer."

scholarship on the Nazi years, one sometimes wonders whether there were in fact any Nazis in academia.

One of the reasons for Koschaker's disappointment was that his own opposition to the Nazis was not recognized. However, this was hardly a surprise, as everyone attempted to present themselves as opponents to the Nazis. Additionally, a common approach appears to have been to at least publicly attempt to forget the Nazi years and move forward. Even Koschaker himself had worked for the Nazi regime, being employed by the *Gesellschaft für europäische Wirtschaftsplanung und Grossraumforschung* (the Society for European Economic Planning and Research) to study European law. This was a Nazi government agency dedicated to the planning of the new European economy as part of the Nazi reorganization of Europe after the final victory had been achieved. The term *Grossraum* (greater space or area) was of course famously utilized by Carl Schmitt, who also figured prominently in the leadership of the organization.[87] The nature of Koschaker's position is not known but it does diminish his aura as a committed anti-Nazi.

For Koschaker, the immediate years after the war were marked by his own retirement. The situation in Tübingen was difficult, with people surviving on hunger rations (1,075 calories per day). Koschaker himself spent much of his time in Walchensee, in part because his apartment in Tübingen had been taken by the occupying French troops.[88] Nevertheless, he managed to first obtain a post as a visiting professor in Munich and later in Ankara. In Munich, Koschaker was investigated in the denazification process in the *Spruchkammer* but unsurprisingly nothing incriminating was found.[89] His stay in Turkey, where exiled Romanists like A. B. Schwarz had

[87] *Bescheinigung* written for Koschaker about his activities, dated February 17, 1945. Universitätsarchiv, Eberhard Karls Universität, Tübingen, Personalakten Juristische Fakultät, 601/42. The document attests that Koschaker is working for a project titled "Untersuchung über europäisches Recht" at the *Gesellschaft für europäische Wirtschaftsplanung und Grossraumforschung*, coordinated by the *Reichsamtsleiter Gesandter* Daitz. Beggio, *Paul Koschaker*, pp. 143–144.

[88] Letter dated March 20, 1946. Universitätsarchiv, Eberhard Karls Universität, Tübingen, Personalakten Juristische Fakultät, 601/42; Letter from Koschaker to Salvatore Riccobono on October 6, 1946, Collection of correspondence by Professor Salvatore Riccobono, currently at the disposal of Professor Mario Varvaro, at the Faculty of Law of the University of Palermo; Beggio, *Paul Koschaker*, p. 157.

[89] Universitätsarchiv München, Personalakte der Juristischen Fakultät, L-IX-037.6, note of the public prosecutor of the Spruchkammer Bad-Tölz (April 24, 1947): on the basis of the information provided by Koschaker he will not be prosecuted under the *Gesetz zur Befreiung von Nationalsozialismus und Militarismus*.

taken refuge and taught Roman law, reinforced Koschaker's image as a Nazi opponent but the visit took place well after the war. The position in Ankara had been arranged by Schwarz, who had returned to Germany after the Nazi regime had fallen. Schwarz occupies an interesting role in this respect, having been like Koschaker a student of Mitteis and in Freiburg he had been a teacher of Wieacker along with Pringsheim.[90]

The stay in Ankara lasted for two years. One of the things that had lured Koschaker to take up the position was that Benno Landsberger, his former colleague and collaborator, worked there. However, due to an unfortunate coincidence, Landsberger was hired in Chicago just when Koschaker arrived in Turkey. The time in Turkey was marked by declining health, the coldness of the Turkish winters being balanced by the respect he enjoyed. He was clearly impressed by the interest of students and the great authority of professors in Ankara. In his communications, Koschaker presents himself as an exile in Turkey.[91]

After returning to Germany, he continued to teach, even though his health was clearly failing, this time in Bonn, where the faculty was exceptionally free of Nazis. He suffered a heart attack and died on June 1, 1951.[92]

## Koschaker and the Vision of a European Legal Heritage

The aim of Koschaker's famous works was quite clear and he makes no effort to hide it: it was nothing less that ensuring the future of

[90] Beggio, *Paul Koschaker*, p. 166. On Schwarz, see Breunung and Walther, *Die Emigration deutscher Rechtswissenschaftler ab 1933*, vol. 1, pp. 460–481. The Turkish government took advantage of the eviction of professors from Germany, offering dozens of professors from different fields a lifeline and a new career. On this see Bahar Öcal Apaydin and Marco Franchi, "L'importanza e la metodologia del corso di diritto romano nella formazione del giurista dall'impero ottomano ad oggi," in Isabella Piro (ed.), Scritti per Alessandro Corbino 5 (Tricase: Libellula, 2016), pp. 277–300.

[91] Letter from Koschaker to Riccobono on April 11, 1949. Collection of correspondence by Professor Salvatore Riccobono, currently at the disposal of Professor Mario Varvaro, at the Faculty of Law of the University of Palermo; Beggio, *Paul Koschaker*, pp. 166–171. Koschaker's influence in Turkey was lasting; his pupil Kudret Ayiter continuing to teach Roman law until 1982. Koschaker had prepared a textbook for his teaching in Ankara, which was then translated by Ayiter into Turkish. The original is in the University of Ankara Law Faculty Library, signature: Ayniyat: No. 25971. The last edition of the Turkish translation is Paul Koschaker and Kudret Ayiter, *Roma Ozel Hakukunun Ana Hatlari* (Ankara: Ankara Üniversitesi, 1993).

[92] Beggio, *Paul Koschaker*, p. 171.

Roman law. What happens next was to a large degree serendipitous. Europe became a dominant catchphrase of its era, a straw to which disillusioned scholars hung on to in search of a purpose. The publication of *Europa* coincided with the beginning of European integration and the general spirit of the era was that of seeking unifying visions of Europe. The political process of European integration proceeded at an astonishing pace during the postwar years. In 1949, the European Council was founded and it drafted the European Convention on Human Rights (ECHR), which was signed in 1950. Also in 1949, the North Atlantic Treaty Organization or NATO was formed. In 1951, the Treaty of Paris was signed by the original six parties, creating the European Coal and Steel Community (ECSC). The European Court of Justice (ECJ) was established in the same year. In 1957 the Treaty of Rome created the European Economic Community (EEC) and the European Atomic Energy Community (Euratom).

Koschaker's position in this development is one of the main alternatives presented concerning European integration. There were three main schools of thought on the foundations of integration: 1) functionalism or neofunctionalism, which emphasized economic integration; 2) federalism, which advocated a constitutional development where nation-states would relinquish their sovereignty; and 3) cultural integration, which reasoned that European integration would need to start with the cultural community and shared values. Of these, Koschaker's works emphasized the third alternative.

The model ultimately chosen for European integration was that advocated by Monnet and Schumann. It was based on the idea of functionalism, of pulling the European nations together, with economic integration and codependency as its leading ideas. This meant that national and cultural traits were by and large left aside, for instance the Treaty of Rome spoke almost exclusively of trade and the economy.[93] The choice of focusing on the economy rather than institutions or culture was not uncontroversial, however. There was, for instance, a strong faction of federalists who advocated the unification of Europe through a constitutional approach, namely the creation of the United States of Europe.

The most influential of the federalists was Italian Altiero Spinelli, who had during the war in 1941 drafted with Ernesto Rossi the Ventotene Manifesto (*Manifesto di Ventotene*). The name of the manifesto

[93] This was equally the choice of Schumann in the famous Schumann Declaration of 1950.

came from the place where they were interned, namely the island of Ventotene. Spinelli and Rossi were at the time members of the communist resistance movement but their vision for the future of Europe was of a progressive, free and united Europe. It rejected both the totalitarian state and its abuse of nationalism and the reactionary conservatism which promised to protect liberty but only advanced the class interests of the wealthy and privileged. Though the continuation of the work was left to Spinelli, the vision they outlined and later developed as politicians was federalist in the sense that they argued that national sovereignty would need to be curtailed in favor of European unity and cooperation. Spinelli and Rossi wanted an internationalist revolution, which would mold the pieces of a shattered Europe together into a new Europe that would correspond to their ideal of civilization, a movement that would bring about social reform and the end of predatory monopolistic capitalism.[94]

The many varieties of Europeanists had suffered different fates during the war. Spinelli and many others had led the resistance to totalitarianism. On the more aristocratic end of the Europeanist spectrum, Richard von Coudenhove-Kalergi, the Austrian count who was the founder and head of the Pan-Europa Movement, had wisely escaped during the *Anschluss*. He had perhaps calculated that as the proverbial rootless cosmopolite repeatedly denounced by Hitler, his future may not have been that promising under the Nazis. He fled first to France, then to the US, where he spent the war in New York drumming up support for European unification. After years of comparative neglect, the change within the internal dynamics of the allies shifted in 1945 and he returned to favor, gaining praise from both Roosevelt and Churchill. At the same time, other Europeanists such as Rudolf Pannwitz, a German aristocrat who had advocated a unified, traditionalist and anti-modernist Europe led by the nobility, continued to gather support from the far right.[95]

Koschaker's vision in *Europa* was of supranational historical trends; it spoke of universal values and culture. It placed Germany back into a common European framework and praised its contribution to the

[94] Altiero Spinelli and Ernesto Rossi, *The Ventotene Manifesto* (Ventotene: The Altiero Spinelli Institute for Federalist Studies, 2016), pp. 75–96. Rossi was a member of the liberal Partito D'Azione.

[95] Anita Prettenthaler-Ziegerhofer, "Richard Nikolaus Cloudenhove-Kalergi, Founder of the Pan-European Union, and the Birth of a 'New' Europe," in Hewitson and D'Auria, *Europe in Crisis*, pp. 89–110; Vermeiren, "Imperium Europaeum," pp. 144–145.

European cultural heritage. Among the competing visions of Europe, Koschaker offered a third alternative, one that sought European unity from the past, in the cultural and moral community that a Christian Europe had developed. Rather than develop an economic or political community, Koschaker's vision of the past invited the reader to envision a future where this shared past would serve as a foundation for European unity. This vision was, of course, very attractive to many political groups, chief among them the nascent Christian Democratic movement.

The calls for the appreciation of European culture and civilization were enthusiastically adopted by Nazi propaganda, especially after the beginning of Operation Barbarossa in the summer of 1941. The Nazis noted that they received a strong positive response around Europe to their anticommunistic press releases. One such release urged other nations to join the "European unity against communism," prompting the peoples of Europe to see Hitler not as a modern-day Genghis Khan but rather as a "military leader of Europe and its common culture and civilization," who struggles for the "recognition of the whole European world."[96] What the new cultural theories were emphasizing in contrast to the tainted Nazi references was an insistence on justice and law as the foundation of the new Europe.

The influence of Koschaker's *Europa* is hard to estimate. The book itself presented a very old narrative in a novel way, and the links between *Europa* and the European legal history that Franz Wieacker and many others promoted is obvious. The legal profession and the Romanists appreciated the flattery, for the history presented by Koschaker and later by Wieacker is one which emphasizes the importance of lawyers and jurisprudence in the formation of law.

The reception and criticism of Koschaker's theories are vividly displayed in his memorial collection published in 1954. Unlike the *Festschrift* from 1938, this work contained arguments from both exiles and former Nazis and even current fascists. The work demonstrated amply the way in which Koschaker's reputation was tied to *Europa*, as it was titled *L'Europa e il diritto romano*. While some like Wolfgang Kunkel engaged with Koschaker's theories on reception, others like Alvaro D'Ors went on the offensive. D'Ors contrasted Koschaker's theories on Roman law with those of Carl Schmitt, comparing their approaches to

[96] Press release (Propagandaministerium, Vertrauliche Information für Zeitschriften R. Spr. Nr. 317, Inf. Nr 49) on June 30, 1941, reprinted in Kluke, "Nationalsozialistische Europa-Ideologie," p. 259.

the idea of the continuity of jurisprudence from antiquity to the present. D'Ors shows a remarkable affinity with the ideas of concrete order and legal realism, which are perhaps surprising choices in a chapter in a memorial work dedicated to an anti-Nazi. He was a close friend of Schmitt and promoted his work in Spain. Where D'Ors is in agreement with Koschaker is in the central role of Christianity. However, he has a very different view on the issue of natural law, defending its universalism. He faults Koschaker's idea of a European natural law as reprehensible separatism because one should really be aspiring to a universal law, an ecumenical civil law, a *ius catholicum*.[97]

Salvatore Riccobono, Koschaker's friend to whom *Europa* was dedicated also spoke about universalism but unlike D'Ors, gave the role of universal law to Roman law or, more specifically, to Roman legal doctrine. Adolfo Plachy discussed Roman law as a European cultural value, promoting the role of Roman law as a guarantee of liberty and personal autonomy. What this meant was that most totalitarian regimes have at some point introduced measures against Roman law.[98]

While most of the chapters in some way or another mirrored Koschaker's main themes, the only one to seriously engage with the implications of what Koschaker's programmatic ideas of a return to Savigny would have meant was Wieacker. He had just published his *Privatrechtsgeschichte* and clearly did not see the value or applicability of Koschaker's theory. Criticizing Koschaker's ideas on Roman law and its history as essentializing, he sought to move beyond the old distinction between dogmatics and history. There simply wasn't a single "Roman law" that would have had a decisive role in European legal

[97] Wolfgang Kunkel, "Paul Koschaker und die europäische Bedeutung des römischen Rechts," in *L'Europa e il diritto romano. Studi in memoria di Paolo Koschaker*, I (Milan: Giuffrè, 1954), pp. 5–12; Álvaro d'Ors, "Jus Europaeum," in *L'Europa e il diritto romano. Studi in memoria di Paolo Koschaker*, I (Milan: Giuffrè, 1954), pp. 471, 476. D'Ors makes a curious remark about individualism and the need for a dynamic order in a manner that clearly mirrors the concrete order thought presented by Schmitt but gives particular thanks to a civil law scholar Gregorio Ortega Pardo for enlightening him on the issues. Ortega Pardo was Spanish and called himself a professor but as a member of Opus Dei he had been sent to Portugal to run the organization's banking business. In 1965, he was arrested in Venezuela with a suitcase full of money and jewels, leading to his suspicious disappearance in Spain. Filipe Ribeiro De Meneses, *Salazar: A Political Biography* (New York: Enigma Books, 2009), p. 595. I would like to thank my colleaque Dr Pedro Magalhaes for this lead.

[98] Salvatore Riccobono, "La universalità del diritto romano," in *L'Europa e il diritto romano. Studi in memoria di Paul Koschaker*, I (Milan: Giuffrè, 1954), p. 11; Plachy, "Il diritto romano come valore culturale nella storia dell'Europa," pp. 484–485.

development, rather there were numerous and often contradictory traditions which were utilized in different ways. Instead of pure dogmatism or pure philological or historical inquiry, Wieacker called for a legal historical inquiry that would be both dogmatically astute and contextually sensitive.[99] In a sense, for Wieacker the crisis of Roman law and its underlying causes and solutions were fundamentally different, and although he does not state it openly, to him Koschaker's way of defining them was irrelevant.

Another sign of the continuing importance of *Europa* was Calasso's translation into Italian in 1962. In his introduction, Calasso paints a vivid picture of Koschaker as the quiet and reticent scholar of cuneiform law, who was prompted into action by the psychological trauma caused by the attack on law during the Nazi years. Just like Savigny was prompted into action by the threat of codification and the Code Napoleon, Koschaker saw the threat to Roman law with the rise of Nazism.[100]

Finally, we must return to Koschaker's very curious idea in the final pages of *Europa*, where he describes Roman law as a kind of relative natural law (*relatives Naturrecht*). A relative natural law is of course a contradiction in terms but it shows the importance that the cultural heritage would be given in the post-totalitarian conceptions of law. Roman law was a central part of the cultural heritage of Europe and thus a natural link between the legal systems but the positioning of legal tradition as the foundation of law was a move that sought to give it preeminence. While Nazi jurists had vehemently opposed legal positivism and had spoken of a "people's law" or the "blood community," Koschaker turns the argument around. By taking the figure of Savigny as his arm and shield, he shows Roman law as a culturally embedded law which is inherent in the people.

The theory was perhaps developed into its final form as a reaction to Nazi jurisprudence but its roots in Koschaker's thinking go much deeper. A clue may be found in a letter sent by Koschaker to Francis de Zulueta at Oxford in 1930. In it, he describes himself as an opponent of the *antike Rechtsgeschichte*, the ancient legal history of Mitteis

99 Franz Wieacker, "Über 'Aktualisierung' der Ausbildung im Römischen Recht," in *L'Europa e il diritto romano. Studi in memoria di Paolo Koschaker, I* (Milan: Giuffrè, 1954), pp. 531–533.

100 Calasso, "Introduzione," pp. xii–xiii. This comparison naturally does not take into account the considerable differences between the threats posed by Napoleon and Hitler.

and Wenger. The main reason is that Roman law has a special position as the foundation of the European cultural community (*europäische Kulturgemeinschaft*), a position that is secured by Roman jurisprudence and the fact that it was the law of the Roman Empire.[101]

The need for such a cultural heritage or touchstone becomes apparent when one reads the way in which Koschaker describes the German people's situation. Words like horror, misery and boundless moral barbarity are used to describe the Germans and their state during the Nazi years. After the war, the perpetrators had made a radical U-turn and reemerged as good democrats. By 1948 the universities had been thoroughly renazified. In Koschaker's sarcastic turn of phrase, these professors were now deeply committed democrats, or "Nazimocrats" as they are called.[102]

Another factor that prompted the need for a deep commitment to justice was the reemergence of anti-Semitism in Germany. Like Nazism, it did not disappear from Germany with the fall of Hitler, and Koschaker warned Kisch, who was contemplating a return, that under a democratic cover both were resurging.[103] This shows how the situation in Germany was one of constant insecurity whether the democratic turn would prove to be permanent and what would be the fate of former Nazi scholars and opponents. In 1947, for instance, Erwin Seidl would write at length to Schiller in New York about what would happen to Koschaker. According to Seidl, there was a general resurgence in Roman law in all of Germany, making Koschaker's pessimism unfounded. He does note that Koschaker was always a pessimist.[104]

The cultural theory of European legal tradition remains the main contribution of Koschaker and his most lasting legacy. As a teacher, he influenced generations of jurists, who would in some cases have an immediate impact on European legal development. One such example was Pierre Pescatore (1919–2010), who was Koschaker's student in Tübingen when he was writing *Europa*. From Luxembourg, Pescatore

101 The letter is reprinted in Lorena Atzeri, "La 'storia del diritto antico' e una lettera inedita di Paul Koschaker," *Iuris Antiqui Historia*, 2 (2010), 191–222.

102 Koschaker to Kisch on April 3, 1948 (p. 27), Koschaker to Kisch on May 24, 1948 (p. 29), now in Kisch, *Paul Koschaker*.

103 Koschaker to Kisch on June 16, 1948 (p. 31), now in Kisch, *Paul Koschaker*. These ideas come up repeatedly in the later letters.

104 Rare Book and Manuscript Archive, Columbia University, New York, Arthur Schiller Papers, Uncatalogued correspondence, Box 6, Erwin Seidl to Schiller (October 2, 1947).

studied with Koschaker and worked as his assistant. After the war, he returned to work in the foreign affairs of Luxembourg, serving in the delegation for the negotiations leading to the Treaty of Rome. After a career as a law professor, he became a judge in the European Court of Justice, serving from 1967 to 1985. Pescatore, along with delegates from other Benelux countries and Germany, whose delegation was headed by Walter Hallstein, were in favor of a strong and independent European court, while Jean Monnet had initially suggested a mere ad hoc system of arbitration. Pescatore himself wrote that the court was a work in progress, staffed by judges who had a will to create a European court that was based on a certain idea of Europe. Both as a judge and an academic, Pescatore was central in the creation of the independent field of European law and maintaining its primacy over national law.[105] Of course, it is highly tentative to estimate what precise influence Koschaker had on Pescatore's thought.

## Conclusions

Crises and exceptional circumstances lead to rethinking. For some, this is prompted by the personal circumstances or the intellectual challenge resulting from the crisis. While exiles such as Schulz or Pringsheim were lucky to be alive after the war, having witnessed a cataclysm that proved to be a mortal threat to them, their families and loved ones, evaluating the impact of the Nazi revolution and the repressions that followed on someone like Paul Koschaker is difficult. Some (even himself) could even say that he was not under threat, and was at worst only mildly inconvenienced by the reforms and the war. Despite this, his response to the crisis of Roman law was one of the most deeply thought out and articulate in his day.

Even though Koschaker began his main texts, *Europa* and *Krise*, as responses to the crisis of Roman law, the main message concerned Europe and law. What was the role of the legal tradition in the formation of European culture and how was law a unifying factor in Europe? As such, the transformations that they intended concerning the

[105] Pierre Pescatore, "Fundamental rights and freedoms in the system of the European Communities," *The American Journal of Comparative Law*, 18 (1970), 343–351; Ditlev Tamm, "The history of the Court of Justice of the European Union since its origin," in *The Court of Justice and the Construction of Europe: Analyses and Perspectives on Sixty Years of Case-Law – La Cour de Justice et la Construction de l'Europe: Analyses et Perspectives de Soixante Ans de Jurisprudence* (The Hague: Springer, 2013), p. 20.

conceptions of law and nationalism in Europe were far reaching. They propagated the idea that the unit, the cultural whole, of European law and history was Europe, not the nation-states. In an age of hypernationalism, this was a contrarian stance that was successful mostly because of the defeat of Nazi Germany.

Koschaker's Europe was thus a combination of universalism and particularism. Regarding universalism, Koschaker drew both from the imperialist tradition of European exceptionalism in terms of civilization and culture and the Catholic tradition of universalizing the values of Europe. On the side of particularism, he spoke about European culture being the product of a specific historical and cultural fabric. Koschaker's conception of European legal tradition as a relative natural law is in a similar way a contradiction in terms, an idea of being both particular and universal at one and the same time. Therein also lies the difference between the Catholic Europeanism of d'Ors or even Riccobono and Koschaker, in that Koschaker rejected the universalizing claims of Catholic lawyers. For him the legal tradition was primary, not values or even culture.

On Koschaker's position with regard to the Nazi regime, the judgment of contemporary scholarship has been ambiguous. On the one hand, he has been rightly seen as an opponent of Nazi policies and a defender of academic freedom but on the other his involvement with Nazi reform plans and his occasional use of the code words of the Nazi regime have been seen as negative. The truth lies somewhere in between. He hoped that by being part of the planning process he would be able to save as much as possible of the field of Roman law, while at the same time keeping some of his ideas to himself. This was a typical strategy of the inbetweeners, who shied away from personal danger and opted to slow down the reforms and dull their effect.

The idea of crisis and renewal may also be seen through another viewpoint, namely the perseverance of an academic discipline. One may with some confidence suggest that one of the main motivations driving Koschaker in both of his major programmatic works, the *Krise* and *Europa*, was self-preservation of the field of study. Beggio also suggests this in an oblique manner.[106] One may also take the approach adopted by Alessandro Somma, who links Koschaker to a long line of scholars who have sought to preserve the field by giving it a new purpose. This includes Nazi and fascist era scholars such as Koschaker

[106] Beggio, *Paul Koschaker*, p. 274.

but also those allied with the regime, who sought in different ways and strategies to present a new mission in an era where one of the major regimes was expressly against Roman law. It also involves those who wrote about Roman law and the class struggle during the socialist period or scholars in the 1990s such as Reinhard Zimmermann, who were adamant in seeking a source for the unity of European private law in Roman law.[107] Continuing Somma's argument, it is possible to see the dangers of the will to survival in which a discipline unknowingly adopts positions that are reprehensible in their own right. One may ask, for instance, whether Koschaker and others were complicit in the crimes of totalitarianism by preparing plans and giving presentations for their benefit or were they merely acting as the voices of reason, defending a just cause of science and learning? Did in fact their willingness to appeal to the holders of power and their interests lead them to transform the field into one that supported ideas such as racism and the inherent supremacy of white Europeans?

This is a very difficult question to answer. However, there is one way to answer it, at least partially. In 2000, Pier Giuseppe Monateri published an article entitled "Black Gaius: a quest for the multicultural origins of the Western legal tradition" in which he essentially claimed that there had been a systematic cultural bias that had led to the removal of all mentions of Eastern influences in the Roman or even European legal tradition. In his criticism of Monateri's thesis, Santucci argues that the problem is that there is no evidence of the missing tradition and its crucial influence and that the elements of the Greco-Roman tradition within law are usually important for a reason. Thus, when Monateri attacks Schulz's conception of the Greek systematic framework that was imported into Roman law, he does so by using scholarship that was used to attack Roman law for having Eastern and Semitic influences, scholarship relied upon by the likes of Oswald Spengler and Nazi scholars.[108] The question then is whether someone like Koschaker fabricated or falsified Roman law or even the image of Roman law, or whether what he did simply

[107] Alessandro Somma, "'Roma madre delle leggi.' L'uso politico del diritto romano," *Materiali per una storia della cultura giuridica*, 32(1) (2002), 153–181.

[108] Gianni Santucci, "La scienza gaia e la strana idea del diritto romano non romano," *Europa e diritto private*, 4(4) (2007), pp. 1077–1078; Pier Giuseppe Monateri, "Black Gaius: a quest for the multicultural origins of the Western legal tradition," *Hastings Law Journal*, 51 (2000), 479–555.

demonstrated the different sides of the tradition which he wanted to emphasize?

In his numerous writings about Koschaker and the Nazi past, Giaro has noted that Koschaker's merits as a Nazi opponent are few and far between. He was not arrested and sent to a concentration camp after presenting the *Krise* but was instead given rousing applause and presumably taken for dinner. He was not unduly concerned that Poland had been the victim of German aggression. He was deeply occidentalist, giving positive valuations only to the culture of Western Europe not to mention his attitude toward non-European peoples and cultures and his approval of Western imperialism. To Giaro he was clearly opportunist and some of his statements about Jewish culture may be construed to be, if not anti-Semitic, at least acquiescent to language that was. Instead of having been removed from office, he was actually appointed to a different chair, not exactly an enormous demotion. On top of all this, Giaro reminds us, his idea for the renewal of law was to go back to the past.[109]

While it could be said that none of these accusations are very dramatic and such attitudes were common among men of Koschaker's time or even later, the fundamental issue remains whether there was an attempt to peddle Nazi ideas in his treatment of Roman law or the European legal tradition? Later apologists defending the works of Nazi scholars such as Carl Schmitt have often argued that ideas can have a value separated from their context and the values held by the people who present them. This, however, is a false premise. We can definitely say that Koschaker was no hero. He was spared the role of reluctant hero given by circumstances to people such as Schulz or Pringsheim. However, it is highly likely that their attitudes toward non-European peoples and cultures or even Eastern Europe were not particularly enlightened by modern standards. In his defense of the Roman law tradition, Koschaker sought to influence Nazi officials but this was due to the fact that they were in power at that time. In the process, he produced a novel theory, a theory that would give a new meaning to the discipline and to the whole of legal science.

For someone who wrote so much about the Roman law tradition, Koschaker did very little to clarify what he meant by it. This was in spite of the ongoing debate about the historical and the dogmatic orientations of Roman law and legal history, to which he participated

[109] Giaro, "Paul Koschaker sotto il Nazismo."

with gusto. From his works, it becomes clear that he viewed Rome as a foundational idea, an illusion rather than a concrete thing or even a normative system. Thus, for all his ponderings about the actualization of Roman law and returning to Savigny, it is sometimes hard to see whether he actually believed in the very project he was suggesting, namely the reawakening of a normative continuity from antiquity to the present day. What he envisioned was, on the contrary, a cultural continuity and a sequence or reappraisals, where the idea of Rome was used to promote a certain order of things.

The encounter with ideas on Europe was most likely serendipitous, the appropriation of a concept that both served to give his work the political relevance it needed but also had an explanatory value. The Pan-Europa Movement, the ideas of *Mitteleuropa* and the Nazi conceptions of *Neue Europa* combined together political, cultural and economic traits in search of a community. Koschaker's Europe was more expansive, bringing together the whole of the Western world. There was clearly a connection with his friend Riccobono and his notions of combining Christianity and the influence of ancient civilization as the tradition uniting the occidental world from Europe to the Americas. However, men like De Francisci, Schönbauer or Carcopino were offering a different kind of Europe, one based on authoritarianism, the reverence of ancient culture and Christianity as a closed and hostile system.

Thus, even though there were similarities, Koschaker's Europe was first and foremost one of cultural heritage and history. Despite the apparent Germanocentrism, his ideas had none of the sense of building a unity against foreign foes, be they Anglo-American or communistic. This sense of intellectualism and, if one may use the word, tolerance, was what separated Koschaker from the strict conservatives or fascists. Whatever influence there was in the fact that his original plans for his scientific future had been destroyed and his friends and allies had had to escape, it is difficult to say. The result was that his turn toward Europe was one of culture, not of exclusion.

This meant that for postwar Europeanism, the ideas presented by Koschaker were useful. From the economic functionalism of Monnet and Schuman to the federalism of Spinelli and others, only the cultural turn offered the foundation upon which a cultural cohesion could be founded.

# 5 Reconfiguring European Legal Tradition after the War


## Abstract

This chapter turns to the younger generation of scholars and the tortuous route by which they arrived to the idea of a European legal tradition. By looking at the so-called young lions of Nazi legal academia and their attempts at legal reform based on the racialized order, this chapter sets the stage for their conversion after the war. Through the works of Franz Wieacker, the chapter analyzes the return to tradition and the discovery of Europe and Roman law among German legal historians, seeing it as a reaction to the works of Koschaker, and the spread of these ideas in Europe. By tracing the careers and works of other scholars involved in the Nazi movement, it discusses the role of denazification and the continuities of Nazi policies in the formation of the role of Europe in legal culture.


## Introduction

The inconvenient truth about academia is that, above all, there is permanence. Once rooted, people stay for decades in the same university and continue working on topics that are often very similar to those they worked on when they started. Thus, when the Nazi regime expelled and drove into exile roughly a third of the professors in Germany, two major changes took place. First, the composition of German academia changed permanently. Many young professors were hired, the majority of whom were either supporters of the regime or willing to accommodate its ideology. Second, most of the exiles became permanent émigrés. Only a fraction would be reinstated and among the younger generation, those who were sidelined during the Nazi years were unable to catch up with those who had had thirteen years of official support to gain merits. In Italy, where the fascist takeover took place earlier, supporters of the regime had a decade more time to consolidate their position. As a result, during the postwar years, academia in much of continental Europe was in the hands of people who had supported or at least acquiesced to authoritarianism, totalitarianism or fascism.[1] Not only in Germany and Italy, but also in Austria and Spain, not to mention the Eastern European countries, most professors were solidly among this group.

How is it then possible that European legal academia would almost instantly become a supporter of freedom, the rule of law and democracy after WWII? The exiles discussed in the previous chapters were to a large degree either in the retirement phase or having integrated in the academic world in the US and Britain. As a result, they were often unwilling or unable to return to Germany. One explanation is that the former Nazis and fascists had a change of heart, abandoned their earlier ultranationalistic ideas and become converts to the new cause.

Franz Wieacker (1908–1994) was one of the most influential and learned legal historians of the twentieth century. His career is both striking and controversial. He entered academia as a pupil of Fritz Pringsheim, quickly making a promising start as a scholar. After the Nazi takeover, he was recruited to the movement and became one of the "young lions" of Nazi legal academia, forging long friendships with his peers and equally the great minds of the time like Carl Schmitt and Hans-Georg Gadamer. After the war, he was rehabilitated with Pringsheim's help and returned to work. He would fairly soon begin to reorient himself to the new order, fashioning the history of legal scholarship as a European development. But how much did his views change and how much continuity with earlier ideas was there?[2] If Koschaker can be credited with inventing the concept of European legal history, it was Wieacker who after World War II popularized the narrative of Europe in the academic world. Wieacker's Europe, however, was not the same as Koschaker's.

[1] Forner, *German Intellectuals*, p. 8. Tomasz Giaro has noted that even the so-called members of the resistance shared ideas (condemning democracy and equality, anti-Semitism, etc.) that could be considered conservative or even repugnant by today's standards. Giaro, "Paul Koschaker sotto il Nazismo."

[2] In this chapter, I will compare the European narratives between wartime works such as Wieacker, *Das römische Recht und das deutsche Rechtsbewußtsein* and Wieacker's main oeuvre, *Privatrechtsgeschichte der Neuzeit*.

The purpose of this chapter is to analyze the transition in Wieacker's thought from the Nazi period to the postwar era, especially through the lens of the idea of Europe. The underlying issue is one of the perceived turn in the thinking of former Nazi jurists toward Europe. Instead of an enlightened history of a turn toward the European liberal idea, what this chapter offers is a more nuanced and perhaps even a darker reading of the events that took place. Central in this development was the role of legal science and its continuity, both as an idea of tradition as a shared intergenerational ethos beyond the individual and the force of civilization as a binding element of the legal profession. Like many other members of the conservative academia, Wieacker initially welcomed the Nazi regime as a counter to the communist threat but eventually rejected the crude terror and oppression it represented. However, for conservative academics, the war was a disaster but the Bundesrepublik was likewise a threat to the established order. After the war, some of them would specifically refer to the "evil period" meaning the Allied occupation, not the Third Reich.[3] To most professors of law, the established order was more or less a means to maintain their preeminent position in the academic community. To explore these notions further, this chapter will compare Wieacker with both his colleagues but also with noted fascist scholars such as Emilio Betti, who shared his ideas on the role of history in law.

In Wieacker's thought, we will be following the development of the European idea through classicism. The idealization of Roman law and classical civilization was the thread that bound together such scholars as Schulz, Pringsheim and Wieacker despite their differences of opinion regarding the Nazi regime. Classicism was also a feature that represented a crucial difference between Nazi academia and Romanists, meaning that explaining Roman law through classical ideas was not without its problems. The main vehicle through which Wieacker advanced the European narrative was that of legal science and its continuity. For him, jurists formed a corps, a distinct group with an ethos and coherence both across national boundaries and also through history.[4]

[3] For example, attorney and Centre Party representative Bernhard Reismann in 1949, quoted in Norbert Frei, *Adenauer's Germany and the Nazi Past: The Politics of Amnesty and Integration* (New York: Columbia University Press, 2002), p. 14.

[4] Erkkilä, *Conceptual Change of Conscience*, argues that Wieacker understood lawyers as forming a community beyond national and historical boundaries. Winkler, *Der Kampf gegen die Rechtswissenschaft*, p. 103 sees behind this idea the influence of Hermann

The transformation of Wieacker's thought on Roman law is interesting because it reveals the processes of realignment that he and subsequently many other German scholars went through. As in the case of Schulz or Pringsheim, the discussion on ancient Roman law took the role of a surrogate stage, where one could discuss things that were too dangerous or painful to discuss otherwise. One looked far into the past in order to avoid facing the recent past. Thus looking at Roman law enabled an analysis of changes in ideas regarding law and justice in general, and was not simply concerned with ancient history.

However, Wieacker's main contribution, his *Privatrechtsgeschichte der Neuzeit*, was revolutionary because it combined many influential ideas into a single narrative that coalesced around the concept of Europe. The work transcended the boundary between Roman law and modern (German) law, initiating a discussion that brought new influences to both. Wieacker's idea of the rationalization process, a loan from Weber, was fused with Schmittian conceptions of European legal rationality. However, while Wieacker's deep knowledge of German law and legal history allowed him to address the concerns and interests of a German legal audience, his fertile imagination also produced novel ideas.[5]

While the main focus of this chapter is Wieacker, it also covers figures who formed his group of peers, both in Germany and elsewhere. Some, like Emilio Betti, shared his passion about hermeneutics and the theory of history. Betti also became a hardcore member of the fascist movement. Others, like Max Kaser, sought in their works to combine social theories with the Nazi movement's aims regarding communalism and nationalism.[6]

This chapter seeks to fill a gap in the scholarship surrounding the work of Franz Wieacker regarding Europe and the European legal tradition. Many of the early works were written by his students and portrayed him in the light of their personal relationships.[7] Then there are

Kantorowicz. On this, see also Reinhard Zimmermann, "Winkler, Viktor: Der Kampf gegen die Rechtswissenschaft. Franz Wieackers 'Privatrechtsgeschichte der Neuzeit' und die deutsche Rechtswissenschaft des 20. Jahrhunderts," *Rabels Zeitschrift für ausländisches und internationales Privatrecht*, 79 (2015), 686–694.

5 Winkler, *Der Kampf gegen die Rechtswissenschaft*, pp. 220–221.

6 Kaser, *Römisches Recht als Gemeinschaftsordnung*; Ziegler, "Max Kaser," pp. 79–80, notes that while Kaser attempted in a few works to adopt the racist language of Nazi jurisprudence, there was never an anti-Semitic slant in his writings. Winkler, *Der Kampf gegen die Rechtswissenschaft*, pp. 498–499 is much more skeptical of Kaser's apolitical nature.

7 Detlef Liebs, "Franz Wieacker (1908 bis 1994) – Leben und Werk," in Okko Behrends and Eva Schumann (eds.), *Franz Wieacker: Historiker des modernen Privatrechts* (Göttingen: Wallstein Verlag, 2010), pp. 23–48; Okko Behrends, "Franz Wieacker 5.8.1908–

some recent critical works by the younger generation, which seek to analyze Wieacker's studies through their connection with German legal and historical scholarship.[8] Some have even sought to see his works, especially the *Privatrechtsgeschichte*, through the lens of Nazi ideology.[9] The difference between these two strands is considerable. This chapter seeks to continue the analytical approach by looking at Wieacker as someone between two worlds, who after the Nazi years pressed for an understanding of jurisprudence as a uniting trait in Europe.[10]

In order to explore the transformation of Wieacker's thought and the change that encompassed not only him but also his colleagues, this chapter will analyze both Wieacker's published works and his correspondence with colleagues and friends during this period.[11]

17.2.1994," *Zeitschrift der Savigny-Stiftung für Rechtsgeschichte, Romanistische Abteilung*, 112 (1995), 13–62; Okko Behrends, "Franz Wieacker. Historiker und Jurist des Privatrechts (5.8.1908–17.2.1994)," in *A l'Europe du troisieme millenaire. Studi in onore di Giuseppe Gandolfi* (Milan: Dott. A. Giuffrè Editore, 2009), pp. 2341–2351; Joseph Georg Wolff, "Franz Wieacker (5. August 1908–17. Februar 1994)," in Stefan Grundmann (ed.), *Deutschsprachige Zivilrechtslehrer des 20. Jahrhunderts in Berichten ihrer Schüler. Eine Ideengeschichte in Einzeldarstellungen. Bd. 1* (Berlin: De Gruyter, 2007), pp. 73–86; Joachim Rückert, "Privatrechtsgeschichte der Neuzeit: Genese und Zukunft eines Faches?," in Okko Behrends and Eva Schumann (eds.), *Franz Wieacker: Historiker des modernen Privatrechts* (Göttingen: Wallstein Verlag, 2010), pp. 75–118; Joachim Rückert, "Geschichte des Privatrechts als Apologie des Juristen – Franz Wieacker zum Gedächtnis," *Quaderni Fiorentini per la storia del pensiero giuridico moderno*, 24 (1995), 531–562. On Wieacker and the Nazi movement, see Ralf Kohlhepp, "Franz Wieacker und die NS-Zeit," *Zeitschrift der Savigny-Stiftung für Rechtsgeschichte: Romanistische Abteilung*, 122 (2005), 203–223.

[8] Winkler, *Der Kampf gegen die Rechtswissenschaft* looks into Wieaker's *Privatrechtsgeschichte* and Erkkilä, *Conceptual Change of Conscience* analyzes Wieacker's concepts. Many of the articles in Okko Behrends and Eva Schumann (eds.), *Franz Wieacker: Historiker des modernen Privatrechts* (Göttingen: Wallstein Verlag, 2010) also belong to this later generation. Of these, see especially Martin Avenarius, "Verwissenschaftlichung als 'sinnhafter' Kern der Rezeption: eine Konsequenz aus Wieackers rechtshistorischer Hermeneutik," in Okko Behrends and Eva Schumann (eds.), *Franz Wieacker: Historiker des modernen Privatrechts* (Göttingen: Wallstein Verlag, 2010), pp. 119–180, and elsewhere Martin Avenarius, "Universelle Hermeneutik und Praxis des Rechtshistoriker und Juristen. Die Entwicklung ihres Verhältnisses im Lichte der Diskussion zwischen Gadamer und Wieacker," in *Juristische Hermeneutik zwischen Vergangenheit und Zukunft* (Baden-Baden: Nomos, 2013), pp. 59–103, and Marion Träger, "Methode und Zivilrecht bei Franz Wieacker (1908–1994)," in Joachim Rückert and Ralf Seinecke (eds.), *Methodik des Zivilrechts – von Savigny bis Teubner* (Baden-Baden: Nomos, 2012), pp. 235–260.

[9] Frassek, "Wege zur nationalsozialistischen 'Rechtserneuerung'," p. 365.

[10] Kohlhepp, "Franz Wieacker," p. 223, claims that Wieacker would have begun to propagate a European idea of law in late 1942.

[11] In the reading of Wieacker's letters, I gratefully acknowledge the help of Ms. Saara Uvanto, who deciphered Wieacker's illegible handwriting and transcribed the letters.

## The Stormtrooper and History

Though Wieacker was a student of Fritz Pringsheim, this did not stop him from taking up the Nazi cause. In the laudatio for Pringsheim's 70th birthday, he writes how Pringsheim's reputation was not enough to protect him from Nazi persecutions.[12] This phrasing is strange but revealing and shows the mechanisms that Wieacker used to shield himself from personal involvement in the happenings of the day. Like his later writings, where Wieacker does not deny his involvement in the Nazi movement, he nevertheless alienates himself from events taking place around him. While he was not personally involved in the ousting of Pringsheim, which took place to put into practice a law excluding a whole category of people from holding public office, that is not to say that his position was not compromised.

Wieacker's personal history may be seen to a large extent to be a product of the times. He was born in 1908. Much of his earliest memories were thus from World War I and an atmosphere steeped in nationalism and propaganda, which would change into the chaos of the early Weimar years, followed by an economic crisis.[13] He was only twenty-four years old when the Nazis took power and just thirty-six years old when the war ended. This means that his formative years were spent during times of unrest, making these circumstances a potentially critical factor in the emergence of his historical thinking. This was not unusual, and it has been noted that the experience of the war and especially that of frontline service, with its intense emotions of togetherness, unity and community were formative in the emergence of Nazi theories of law and state.[14]

Like many scholars in German academia, Wieacker was a member of the *Bildungsbürgertum*, an academic civil servant class that had begun to eclipse the old nobility in influence. His father was a president of the

[12] Franz Wieacker, "Fritz Pringsheim 70 Jahre," *Juristenzeitung* 7(19) (1952), p. 605.

[13] On the different interpretations of the war generation, see Koontz, *Nazi Conscience*, p. 49 and Ulrich Herbert, "'Generation der Sachlichkeit.' Die völkische Studentenbewegung der frühen zwanziger Jahre in Deutschland," in Frank Bajohr, Werner Johe and Uwe Lohalm (eds.), *Zivilisation und Barbarei, Die widersprüchlichen Potentiale der Moderne* (Hamburg: Hans Christians Verlag, 1991), pp. 115–144, where Koontz represents the view that it was actually the generation that had gone to war, those born in the 1880–1890s, while Herbert and others see it as those born around the 1900–1910s.

[14] Herlinde Pauer-Studer, "'Jenseits von Chaos und Interessenkonflikten.' Aspekte der Rechtsentwicklung im NS-System der 1930er Jahre," in Werner Konitzer (ed.), *Moralisierung des Rechts: Kontinuitäten und Diskontinuitäten nationalsozialistischer Normativität* (Frankfurt: Campus Verlag, 2014), p. 13.

district court (*Landsgericht*) of Stade and Wieacker went to the law faculty in Tübingen. There, he joined the student association of *Corps Rhenania Tübingen*, like many of his relatives. It was a typical male student association (resembling the more widely known *Burschenschaften*) with a long history, splendid settings and an appreciation of *Kameradschaft*, collegial male bonding. Wieacker remained a member all his life. After studies in Munich and Göttingen, he went to Freiburg to complete his doctoral thesis under Pringsheim, finishing it in 1930.[15] His educational foundation was not purely German because Wieacker studied in Palermo for a semester in 1931 with Salvatore Riccobono.[16] After that, Wieacker had temporary positions first in Freiburg and then in Frankfurt. During the years of the Nazi takeover 1933–1934, he was in Frankfurt, hoping to be made a professor in this dynamic faculty full of promising young scholars. Instead, the university became a dumping ground for expelled Jewish scholars. In his letters, he notes how his hopes were dashed as the situation became increasingly disturbing, with unwanted legal historians and Romanists like Gerhart Husserl and Fritz Schulz being transferred there.[17]

Wieacker ended up in Kiel in 1935, joining the so-called *Kieler Schule* with other young legal academics who were allied with or members of the Nazi party. This conglomeration of jurists became Wieacker's main group of friends and allies, both through the war years and beyond. In this group, his closest friends were Ernst Rudolf Huber, Karl Larenz, Karl Michaelis, Wolfgang Siebert, Georg Dahm and Friedrich Schaffstein. The question of

[15] The details of Wieacker's life are told in numerous works; here we mostly follow Liebs, "Franz Wieacker"; Detlef Liebs, "Franz Wieacker †," *Gnomon*, 67 (1995), 473–477; Dieter Nörr,"'Franz Wieacker 5.8.1908–17.2.1994," in Tiziana J. Chiusi, Wolfgang Kaiser and Hans-Dieter Spengler (eds.), *Dieter Nörr. Historiae Iuris Antiqui* (Goldbach: Keip Verlag, 2003), pp. 248–256; and Winkler, *Der Kampf gegen die Rechtswissenschaft*. On the meaning of *Bildung* for Wieacker, see Erkkilä, *Conceptual Change of Conscience*.

[16] Liebs, "Franz Wieacker," p. 24. Wieacker remained in lifelong contact with Riccobono, both via letters and through visits to Palermo, where he stayed at his house. Letter from Wieacker to Riccobono on March 10, 1951. Collection of correspondence by Professor Salvatore Riccobono, currently at the disposal of Professor Mario Varvaro, at the Faculty of Law of the University of Palermo.

[17] Erik Wolf had been Wieacker's mentor in Freiburg and their correspondence lasted a lifetime. Wieacker to Erik Wolf on April 18, 1934. Universitätsarchiv, Albert-Ludwigs-Universität, Freiburg im Breisgau, NL Erik Wolf. On the situation in Frankfurt, see Bernhard Diestelkamp, "Die Rechtshistoriker der Rechtswissenschaftlichen Fakultät der Johann Wolfgang Goethe-Universität Frankfurt am Main 1933-1945," in Stolleis and Simon, *Rechtsgeschichte im Nationalsozialismus*, pp. 84-85, 96-97. Of Wieacker's long-time associates, Wolff and Forsthoff were in Frankfurt at the same time.

Wieacker's connection with the Nazi regime remains a pressing one for this study. He was a member of the party, that is without doubt. His works mirror many of the themes of the movement and reflect its vocabulary. However, his writings, both public and private, betray no trace of the anti-Semitism or racism that was prevalent in Germany.[18] Even his choice of student association, the aristocratically minded *Corps*, was not as infused with the Nazi movement as the *Burschenschaften.*

Wieacker joined the Nazi party (NSDAP) on May 1, 1937, also joining the Nazi university teachers' union (*Nazionalsozialistische Deutschen Dozentenbund*). As early as 1933 he had been a member of the Nazi lawyers' union (*Nazionalsozialistische Bund Deutscher Juristen*) and on November 3, 1933 he had joined the Nazi drivers' corps (*Nazionalsozialistische Kraftfahrerkorps*) where there were already other members of the *Kieler Schule* such as K. A. Eckhardt. However, this did not help with his career prospects and Wieacker waited for many years for the call to become an ordinary professor. Finally, he accepted a professorial position in Leipzig in 1939. The fact that Wieacker was not a full professor in Kiel has led some to speculate that he should not be counted as a member of the *Kieler Schule*. In retrospect, this is something of a nonissue.[19] Though Wieacker was the youngest of the group and was thus not on some of the listings, this did not change the fact that he was both factually and emotionally bound to this group consisting of Ernst Rudolf Huber, Karl Larenz, Karl Michaelis, Friedrich Schaffstein and others. They became his closest friends and associates and remained so over the years.[20]

[18] Erkkilä, *Conceptual Change of Conscience* does not report a single instance where anti-Semitism would have been present in Wieacker's writings, including his private letters.

[19] Liebs, "Franz Wieacker," pp. 25–27; Winkler, *Der Kampf gegen die Rechtswissenschaft*, pp. 455–476. The central role of the *Kieler Schule* in developing the Nazi conceptions of justice becomes apparent from the collections of texts such as Herlinde Pauer-Studer and Julian Fink, *Rechtfertigungen des Unrechts. Das Rechtsdenken im Nationalsozialismus in Originaltexten* (Berlin: Suhrkamp, 2014), where all of them feature prominently. On scholarship about the *Kieler Schule*, see Winkler, *Der Kampf gegen die Rechtswissenschaft*, pp. 13–14, on its theories, pp. 264–312, and about its influence on Wieacker, pp. 465–494. Frassek, "Wege zur nationalsozialistischen 'Rechtserneuerung'," p. 358 names Martin Busse, Georg Dahm, Karl August Eckhardt, Ernst Rudolf Huber, Karl Larenz, Karl Michaelis, Paul Ritterbusch, Friedrich Schaffstein, Wolfgang Siebert and Franz Wieacker as members of the *Kieler Schule*. See also Jörn Eckert, "Was war die Kieler Schule," in Franz Säcker (ed.), *Recht und Rechtslehre im Nationalsozialismus* (Baden-Baden: Nomos, 1992), pp. 37–70; Christina Wiener, *Kieler Fakultät und "Kieler Schule" Die Rechtslehrer an der Rechts- und Staatswissenschaftlichen Fakultät zu Kiel in der Zeit des Nationalsozialismus und ihre Entnazifizierung* (Baden-Baden: Nomos Verlag, 2013).

[20] This is evident from the letters, where there is evidence of a close social interaction between them, including regular holidays together. Letters from Wieacker to Huber on November 20

This was no accident. The Nazi authorities had been well aware of the socializing aspects of the training programs. The camps to which future professors like Wieacker were sent aimed at transforming and bonding people through shared experiences, much like military training. Hartshorne, a contemporary American observer, noted how even the new rector of Berlin University was astonished how similar dress, simple food, common lodging and shared labor in a common effort developed genuine comradeship. All new professors were, in addition to having academic credentials, required to have proof of Aryan descent and to have attended community camp (*Gemeinschaftslager*).[21]

In the biographies, it becomes apparent how intellectual and personal loss through the emigration of his teachers and colleagues became an elephant in the room even before the war. The sense one has is that the former community was missing a vital element.[22]

Figure 5.1 Nazi Minister of Justice Kerrl on a visit to the Jüterbog camp for legal trainees, note the uniforms worn by the trainees. Source: Wikimedia Commons. Bundesarchiv, Bild 102–14898/CC-BY-SA 3.0

1957, from Huber to Wieacker on November 25, 1957, and from Wieacker to Huber on July 2, 1961. Das Bundesarchiv, Koblenz, NL Ernst Rudolf Huber, bestand 1505, 1529.

21 Hartshorne, *German Universities and National Socialism*, pp. 103–105.

22 Liebs, "Franz Wieacker," p. 27.

During the war, Wieacker, who had begun compulsory military service just before the war started, served in the Polish campaign in the artillery. He was then sent back to teach in his chair in Leipzig and only redrafted in the fall of 1944. Due to his knowledge of Italian, he was sent to the Italian front where he was captured on April 27, 1945 in Milan. After a few months in a POW camp, he was back in Germany, although he did not return to his chair or his ransacked apartment in Leipzig, which was in the Russian zone of occupation. After the call to Freiburg, Wieacker got the chair in Göttingen, where he stayed until the end of his career.[23]

It is an open question how much Wieacker wholeheartedly believed in the Nazi revolution. What is clear is that Wieacker was inducted into the circle of the *Kieler Schule* and was part of its efforts to transform German legal science into a model that followed Nazi principles. His work in Leipzig was part of this effort, as Leipzig was, in addition to Kiel, Breslau and Strassburg, a planned model faculty, a "Stormtroop Faculty" (*Stoßtrupp-Fakultät*). This work involved the practical application of the *Gleichschaltung* (uniformization) of legal culture with Nazi ideology, the creation of a New Legal Science that was antipositivistic and nationalistic and reflected the ideas of the "concrete order." However, at the same time Wieacker continued to advocate the value of *Bildung* and the tradition of Roman law, both of which were not favored by the Nazis and their obsession with racial "thinking with the blood."[24]

Wieacker's early works demonstrate how torn he was between traditional Roman law ideas of jurisprudence as an elite pursuit and the new Nazi legal ideology emphasizing life and social reality. Thus in 1935 he published both "Wandlungen in Eigentumsverfassungen" and another article, "Studien zur Hadrianischen Justizpolitik." The first was a study on the new conceptions of ownership advanced by Nazi policies, which emphasized the social and concrete nature of ownership as opposed to the strict legal definition of BGB §903. In "Wandlungen," Wieacker saw the users of property, such as farmers cultivating land, as a unit tied

[23] Liebs, "Franz Wieacker," pp. 28–29; Winkler, *Der Kampf gegen die Rechtswissenschaft*, pp. 475–476.

[24] Erkkilä, *Conceptual Change of Conscience*, pp. 91–99. On the extent of the ideological push within these universities on hiring, teaching and research, see on Strassburg Herwig Schäfer, *Juristische Lehre und Forschung an der Reichsuniversität Straßburg 1941–1944* (Tübingen: Mohr Siebeck, 1999). From the *Kieler Schule*, Dahm, Schaffstein and Huber were hired in Strassburg.

together with blood and contributing to the concrete order of the community of the people. This was a direct reflection of Nazi ideas that used socialist conceptions of ownership to appeal to small farmers and businesses. Wieacker's articles on the matter were just one of the numerous works in which radical Nazi jurists sought to present the contradiction between traditional capitalist and socially conscious Nazi legal policies. The second study reflected Pringsheim's studies on Hadrian and ideas of legal cosmopolitanism and the rule of law discussed in Chapter 3 of this book. There, Wieacker presented a similar idea of the idealized community of lawyers working under the benevolent ideal monarch.[25] This inner tension marked how much Wieacker was torn between the need to be in the vanguard of the new order, promoting the agenda of the renewal of law, and allegiance toward his *Doktorvater*. Two years later, he proposed items for the reform agenda with fellow members of the *Kieler Schule* such as Karl Larenz.[26]

## The Roots of the European Narrative in the Nazi Years

Despite his willingness to engage in the legal reforms of this time, Wieacker was mostly confined to historical developments even in his writings during the Nazi era. In his inaugural lecture in Leipzig, published as an article in 1939, the new vocabulary of the time was clearly visible. He addressed the law faculty by the Nazi era name, *Rechtswahrer* (roughly translatable as protectors of law), and he spoke of national characteristics using Nazi vocabulary. While the depiction of Roman

[25] Franz Wieacker, "Wandlungen der Eigentumsverfassung," in Christian Wollschläger (ed.), *Franz Wieacker. Zivilistische Schriften (1934–1942)* (Frankfurt: Vittorio Klostermann, [1935] 2000); Wieacker, "Studien zur Hadrianischen Justizpolitik." Wieacker's text on landed property has parallels in the other works of the Kieler Schule, for example Karl Michaelis, *Wandlungen des deutschen Rechtsdenkens seit dem Eindringen des fremden Rechts* (Berlin: Junker und Dünnhaupt Verlag, 1935), p. 9: "völkische Lebensordnung und Lebensgemeinschaft sind mit dem Rechte eins." On the discussions and the other literature, see Karl Kroeschell, "Die nationalsozialistische Eigentumslehre. Vorgeschichte und Nachwirkung," in Stolleis and Simon, *Rechtsgeschichte im Nationalsozialismus*, pp. 52–55. On Wieacker's later reconfiguring of the article, see Erkkilä, *Conceptual Change of Conscience*, pp. 14–15. The notion that the concrete living conditions would have direct normative consequences was a shared conviction among early Nazi lawyers, see Rüthers, *Die Unbegrenzte Auslegung*, p. 294.

[26] Franz Wieacker, "Der Stand der Rechtserneuerung auf dem Gebiete des bürgerlichen Rechts" *Deutsche Rechtswissenschaft*, 2 (1937), 3–27. *Deutsche Rechtswissenschaft* was one of the main outlets of the reform agenda, publishing important works by many of the leaders of the *Neue Rechtswissenschaft*. It was known as Eckhardt's journal as he was its founder, much like *Deutsches Recht* was Hans Frank's.

jurists he presents there is fairly standard, what is noteworthy is his exhortation to his colleagues: the Roman jurists were the *viva vox iuris civilis*, a reference to the *Digest of Justinian* (*Dig.* 1.1.8) which Wieacker translates as des "*völkischen Rechtes lebendige Stimme*" (the living voice of the people's law).[27] The translation summarizes the way in which during the Nazi years the vocabulary of the law and consequently the interpretation of the law gradually shifted. Thus, while the translation was not wrong in itself (even though the original Roman passage was about the role of the praetor in Rome in creating new law with his pronouncements), it includes two very weighty concepts of Nazi jurisprudence. The first was the living law or law that takes into account the political situation as opposed to law in books. The second was the concept of the people's law (*Volksrecht*) as opposed to an alien law. In consequence, within a single loose translation, Wieacker makes a reference to both the Nazi policy of the concrete order, which states that all law is secondary to politics, in which the ultimate statement was that the will of the Führer is the highest law, as well as the Nazi aim to replace all old law with the new "people's law."

These public declarations of allegiance proved to be an exception to the main strand in Wieacker's works, the continuity of jurisprudence. Wieacker early on read Coing's thesis about the reception of Roman law and incorporated it into his idea about the central role of humanists in legitimating and strengthening the reception of Roman law.[28] This became a central theme in his writings, where he sought to present the jurisprudential link between ancient and modern law as one of the fundamental traits of Western civilization.

Even in Wieacker's early works, the origin of the law and legal heritage was in ancient Rome. For example, Wieacker wrote in 1942 about Justinian's *Corpus Iuris* in a way that reflected a very strongly classicizing idea of Roman law. There had been an original creative spirit that had formed the original Roman law of the classical period, but the *Codex Justinianus* was simply a poor reflection of that. As someone fond of visual imagery, he would describe it as a herbarium, full of pressed dead plants. However, already here he presented the idea of

[27] Franz Wieacker, "Vom Römischen Juristen," *Zeitschrift für die gesamte Staatswissenschaft*, 99 (1939), 463.

[28] Franz Wieacker, "Einflüsse des Humanismus auf die Rezeption. Eine Studie zu Johannes Apels Dialogus," *Zeitschrift für die gesamte Staatswissenschaft*, 100 (4) (1940), 423–456.

the European spirit at work, developing and growing in the true tradition of Roman law and inspiring German development.[29]

In this article, Wieacker makes the distinction between the life of the law and the book form that carries it. It is very difficult to actually make sense of his organic imagery but it would appear that he makes a comparison between the vitality and self-esteem of "young peoples," a reference to Germanic peoples and the wisdom of the book, and how they would be joined in the reception of Roman law. Roman law, as transferred from the *Corpus Iuris*, would provide a mere skeleton, a rational framework through which the life of the nation would again flow.[30] These floral or organic theories of culture masked a desire to preserve the vitality of the law. While the interpolationist critique of the era had sought to perform an autopsy of the Justinianic compilation and to separate the authentic and the unauthentic, its critics like Koschaker demanded an actualization of the texts and their revitalization as part of the existing law, a kind of resurrection. What Wieacker proposed was a third way, an idea that he would later develop in the *Textstufen*, which was a textual analysis producing a truly historical understanding of law in its intellectual context and as part of the development of law.

According to Winkler, the alternative presented by Wieacker shows clear input from his main influences: Pringsheim, A. B. Schwarz, Hermann Kantorowicz and Max Weber. Its main points were the historicization of legal history, the focus on classical Roman law rather than the law of Justinian, the advanced methods of history such as hermeneutics and the connection between Roman law and newer legal history. However, with this Wieacker presents a degree of separation not only from the Koschakerian idea of dogmatic continuity but also to the dogmatic connection between ancient Rome and modern law made by scholars closer to the regime like Schönbauer, Kreller and Kaser.[31] In short, Wieacker offers a more historical understanding of Roman law as the foundation of the legal method.

There was another connection, to the work of Schulz, who was adamant in his depiction of Roman law as a living tradition that managed to avoid the petrification resulting from writing down the law and reducing it to a codification.[32] The fact that his strongest influences were nearly all

[29] Franz Wieacker, "Corpus Iuris," *Zeitschrift für die gesamte Staatswissenschaft*, 102 (1942), 444–445.
[30] Wieacker, "Corpus Iuris," p. 445.
[31] Winkler, *Der Kampf gegen die Rechtswissenschaft*, pp. 173, 179–180.
[32] This is the main theme in Schulz, *Roman Legal Science*.

Jewish authors (Schulz, Pringsheim, Kantorowicz and Schwarz) or liberals (Weber) makes his turn toward Nazi jurisprudence all the more remarkable.

This is not to say that there would not have been important influences from the Nazi side as well, from Carl Schmitt to the *Kieler Schule*, who stressed the social and political connectedness of law. The distinction between the life of the law and its form in books was equally significant in the theories of legal realism, which described the contradiction between law in books and law in action. While legal realism was most widely an American phenomenon, similar viewpoints were present even in Europe.[33] A particularly important perspective was Carl Schmitt's thinking on the concrete order. Ever since Wieacker joined the Kiel group, Schmitt was an important influence on him. The two were in constant contact until the end of the war, Schmitt often commenting on Wieacker's writings. One should not, however, try to reduce Wieacker's thinking to Schmitt's[34] but instead see how the ideas of the political order were carried over to Wieacker's thought and how the sensitivity to the political influence to law grew.

In a presentation given in 1943, Wieacker returned to the relationship between the Roman and the German legal consciousness. He would begin by acknowledging how the love for German cultural heritage and the spirit of freedom would earlier have led German legal historians to denounce the influence of Roman law ever since the national awakening in the nineteenth century. The development of the historical consciousness and the organic conception of the people led them to see Roman law as an alien implant. Somewhat later, Roman law had ceased to be seen as a national self-betrayal but was instead dismissed as an irrelevant relic in a modern world that had moved far beyond its limits, much like mathematics had outgrown Euclid. Here is it interesting to note how Wieacker uses the words un-German and un-European almost interchangeably. What Wieacker then presents as the great redemption of Roman law is almost something drawn from Savigny: to describe the use of Roman law in Europe as a foreign and ancient implant suppressing national law is an enormous misunderstanding of the Western

[33] On the fundamental differences between the various legal realisms, see Heikki Pihlajamäki, "Against metaphysics in law: the historical background of American and Scandinavian legal realism compared," *The American Journal of Comparative Law*, 52 (2004), 469–487.

[34] For example, Winkler, *Der Kampf gegen die Rechtswissenschaft*, p. 323 attempts to find an almost causal connection.

creative spirit. What Roman law was actually is more akin to the works of Homer and Aristotle, products of the common spirit of the West and of European destiny that would then form a basis for new developments.[35]

The references to contemporary language and the contemporary imaginary are startlingly clear. Wieacker equates the European and the German civilization, presents culture and people as the prime actors and refers to blood as a metaphor of the people. The organic conceptions of culture are very strong; cultures are either young and developing or they are mature and they grow much like plants nourished by influences. This idea is a central feature of the idea of reception as Wieacker presents it: Roman law and the idea of Rome were not something alien to the German people (*volksfremd*, *Undeutsches*, p. 26); they nourished learning and rationality and had been incorporated into the German and by extension European culture.[36] Wieacker's ideas were thus in stark contrast to the early Nazi theories where Roman law was a dangerous weed, something to be uprooted. While the standard response of the Roman law scholar had been to separate the earlier pure Roman law and the later Eastern and Semitic influences, Wieacker presented it all as a kind of continuum.

Wieacker's position in relation to the evolution of Nazi legal thought proved to be a wise one. Over time the opposition toward Roman law became more nuanced and focused on the later Justinianic law, from where different purportedly Semitic ideas were thought to have emerged. Even Hans Frank maintained that the Nazis had nothing against the teaching and research of the law of a proud and self-conscious nation,[37] meaning the Rome of the republic and early empire. This evolution of Nazi thought had of course in the background both the alliance with fascist Italy and the careful resistance by lawyers themselves, who consistently advocated for the preservation and value of Roman law.[38] A similar rehashing of priorities was undertaken by leading Nazi Roman law scholars such as Hans Kreller, who presented three points in which Roman law would be essential to lawyers in Nazi Germany: 1) the dogmatic continuity from Roman law to contemporary law means that Roman roots are essential; 2) the racial proximity between Germans and the old "master races" of the Mediterranean,

[35] Wieacker, *Das römische Recht und das deutsche Rechtsbewußtsein*, pp. 3–9.
[36] Wieacker, *Das römische Recht und das deutsche Rechtsbewußtsein*, pp. 10–27.
[37] Hans Frank, "Zur Reform des Rechtsstudiums," *Deutsches Recht*, 3 (1933), 23–24.
[38] On this, see Chapter 4.

the Greeks and the Romans, makes their history our history; and 3) the Romans are the classical authorities on law, which means that their history has to be known in order to surpass them.[39] As Stolleis has pointed out, in *Mein Kampf* Hitler himself had supported the study of Roman history and Greek culture, a fact that Roman law scholars were relieved to note.[40]

However, during the war years the issue of culture was very much a matter of demonstrating hegemony, the manifestations of German cultural superiority offering a way to argue for German dominance in Europe. During the war, Wieacker, Carl Schmitt and others gave lectures as part of the war effort. They went to allied countries like Hungary as well as to occupied Paris to give presentations on such topics as the superiority of German culture.[41]

In a book published in 1944, *Vom römischen Recht*, Wieacker returns to the problem of reception and the link between Roman law and Western legal science. In the section titled "Ratio scripta," he distinguishes two roles for Roman law, first as history and second as an idea. Roman law is seen as the mother of European legal science and as the root of legal concepts and thinking in the history of law. What Roman law then means to us, writes Wieacker, is a cultural heritage:

*Soweit das römische Recht uns angeht, is es ein Element nicht der Alten Geschichte, sondern des europäischens, besonders auch des deutchen Lebens und Denkens. Römisches Recht ist dem abendländischen Denken über Recht und Staat, das in der Schule der Antike begonnen hat, seit der frühesten Dämmerund des europäischen Bewusstseins zugesetz.*[42]

What Roman law means to us is not an element of ancient history, but rather a part of the European, especially German life and thought. For Western thought on law and the state, Roman law is the foundation laid in antiquity from the earliest beginnings of European consciousness.

[39] Hans Kreller, *Römische Rechtsgeschichte: eine Einführung in die Volksrechte der Hellenen und Römer und in das römische Kunstrecht* (Tübingen: Mohr Siebeck, 1936); Simon, "Die deutsche Wissenschaft vom römischen Recht nach 1933," pp. 162–163.

[40] Stolleis, "'Fortschritte der Rechtsgeschichte' in der Zeit des Nationalsozialismus?," pp. 180–181.

[41] Letter from Wieacker to Carl Schmitt on November 30, 1941. Landesarchiv Nordrhein-Westfalen, Duisburg, NL Carl Schmitt, RW 0265; Leipzig Universitätsarchiv, Personenakten/Dossiers Wieacker, Franz, PA-SG 0457: September 2, 1944, workorder from *Reichminister für Wissenschaft, Erziehung und Volksbild* to give a lecture in Hungary. On their travels, see Erkkilä, *Conceptual Change of Conscience*, p. 102; Winkler, *Der Kampf gegen die Rechtswissenschaft*, pp. 473–474.

[42] Wieacker, *Vom römischen Recht*, p. 196.

What Wieacker outlines here is a more complex process than a simple continuity, reception or rebirth. Again, true to form, he builds a parable out of the influence that *limes*, the fortified border between the Roman Empire and the Germans that ran mainly along the Rhine and Danube, had on Germanic peoples both inside and outside of the wall. Wieacker maintains that as a result of the shared cultural and material life and the innumerable instances of transfer, the people were ultimately both Romans and Germans at the same time. This, he claims, is the true source of the unity of Europe.[43]

Wieacker then presents at length the practical process of the reception with the glossators and so forth that appears as a secondary fulfillment of the promise made by the initial unity. The scientific process, the building of the new shared European tradition operated on the basis of canonistic, Germanistic and Romanistic scholarship. The result was both ideological and practical, and here Wieacker refers to Koschaker's idea of the "*kulturelle Romidee*."[44] It is perhaps not necessary to follow Wieacker's thought as it winds through the reception of Roman law, early modern humanist scholarship, Pandectism, the Historical School and finally to modern law. However, it is important to note that here, in under a hundred pages, is the form of historical narrative that would later be retold in the *Privatrechtsgeschichte*.

The main components of the European narrative were already present in Wieacker's early works published before the end of the war but the shaping of these ideas was a long process where both the historical facts and their implications changed over the years. Wieacker was clearly influenced by Nazi legal thinkers and their theories of culture but in important aspects he provided a completely opposite viewpoint. He presented very clearly the idea of reason and rationalism as the key ingredient of European legal thought. The process of rationalization as a key feature was of course something that Wieacker took from Weber. This connection between Wieacker and Weber was one of the elements that helped Wieacker's historical narrative gain acceptance.[45]

[43] Wieacker, *Vom römischen Recht*, pp. 196–199.
[44] Wieacker, *Vom römischen Recht*, p. 221.
[45] Winkler, *Der Kampf gegen die Rechtswissenschaft*, p. 115.

## The Right and Europe as a Historical Concept

One of the clearest differences between more senior scholars such as Schulz, Pringsheim or Koschaker and the new generation can be located in their theories of history. While the others were primarily lawyers and mainly interested in historical developments as a sequence of intellectual and dogmatic transformations, Wieacker had a deep interest in the relationship between social and legal development, the relationship between sources and interpretation and theories of philosophy and history, where his main focus was on historical hermeneutics. He had been influenced by Gadamer and they had been in correspondence over the years. What they shared was a deep appreciation of the ideas of *Bildung* and culture as creative and formative forces that shape the intellectual process. For them both, what defined Europe was its culture and civilization. Even in the apocalyptic final stages of the war, they would discuss the way in which history and historical consciousness shaped culture and how the past was present in one's culture. In March 1945, Wieacker would write to Gadamer from Italy, remarking how it is obvious how in Italy the classical and the present are intertwined regardless of the vicissitudes of the day.[46]

Interest in hermeneutics and its implications in the history of law were shared by other influential legal historians. Emilio Betti (1890–1968) was equally fascinated with Gadamer's ideas about hermeneutics. Betti became an enthusiastic supporter of the fascist regime but unlike many others did not become personally involved in the regime.[47] Betti had early on begun to discuss the relationship between Roman law and contemporary law, first describing and later criticizing the idea of a separation between a historical and a dogmatic or a historical and a scientific method. For Betti, legal phenomena were not divisible into separate historical and dogmatic sides

[46] Wieacker to Hans-Georg Gadamer on March 14, 1945. Deutsches Literatur Archiv, Marbach am Neckar, NL Hans-Georg Gadamer, Briefe von Franz Wieacker an Gadamer (from 1945 to 1991) – A: Gadamer; Erkkilä, *Conceptual Change of Conscience*, pp. 108–110; Avenarius, "Universelle Hermeneutik und Praxis des Rechtshistoriker und Juristen." On an unrelated note, it shows how much Wieacker was focused on culture as he was making remarks about classical culture as an officer of an occupying army.

[47] Pietro Costa, "Emilio Betti: dogmatica, politica, storiografia," *Quaderni Fiorentini*, 7 (1978), 311–393; Giuliano Crifò, "Emilio Betti (1890–1968)," in Rafael Domingo (ed.), *Juristas Universales, IV* (Madrid and Barcelona: Marcial Pons, 2004), pp. 217–222; Emilio Betti, *Notazioni autobiografiche* (Padova: CEDAM, 1953); Cascione, "Romanisti e fascismo," pp. 19–20; Massimo Brutti, "Emilio Betti e l'incontro con il fascismo," in Italo Birocchi and Luca Loschiavo (eds.), *Giuristi e il fascino del regime* (Rome: Roma Tre-Press, 2015), pp. 63–102.

but should be seen as unified wholes where historical or philosophical studies were equally relevant as studies on contemporary law in the understanding of law. In consequence, his solution to the perceived crisis of Roman law and its relation to modern law was the emphasis on the connection and the mutual interdependence of the historical and the contemporary.[48] Betti's interest in legal hermeneutics led him into a long and convoluted debate with Gadamer, in which Wieacker participated on occasion.[49]

Betti's involvement with fascism was intellectual in nature and belied the transformation of his ideas about constitutional thought. While his early works on the crisis of the Late Republic demonstrated his beliefs that it was the senatorial order that had begun to transgress the constitution, during the 1920s he focused on elements such as power, order, *imperium* and leadership. He joined the fascists in 1929 but the process of intellectual alignment had already begun earlier. His works would contain discussions on the nature of totalitarianism and the importance of maintaining the fascist alliance with Germany, even when defeat was imminent.[50] During the Italian liberation, Betti was arrested by the partisans in June 1944 and put on trial, where he would defend his choices. It has been said that his philosophical defense almost got him shot and he was only saved by the intervention of his hastily summoned defense attorney, who argued that Betti was clearly insane and was thus not responsible for his actions.[51]

The link between Betti and Wieacker is strongest in their discussions over the nature of history and law. For Betti as for Wieacker, jurisprudence was an autonomous tradition which resisted any revolutionary change. In the case of Betti, a good example of the type of interpretative traditionalism

[48] Emilio Betti, "Diritto romano e dogmatica odierna," *Archivio Giuridico*, 99 (1928), 129–150 and *Archivio Giuridico*, 100, 26–66; Emilio Betti, *Istituzioni di diritto romano, vol. 1* (Padova: CEDAM, 1942), p. xiv; Santucci, "Decifrando scritti," pp. 93.

[49] Much has been written on this, most recently Emilia Mataix Ferrandiz, "Betti vs. Gadamer. El debate acerca de método y verdad en la hermenéutica jurídica," in Lorenzo Gagliardi (ed.), *Antologia giuridica romanistica ed antiquaria, II* (Milan: Collana di Diritto romano del Dipartimento di Diritto privato e Storia del Diritto, Università degli Studi di Milano, 2018), pp. 575–610. On a practical level, Betti is a constant presence in the extensive correspondence between Wieacker and Gadamer, see Wieacker to Hans-Georg Gadamer on April 11, 1963. Deutsches Literatur Archiv, Marbach am Neckar, NL Hans-Georg Gadamer.

[50] Brutti, "Emilio Betti e l'incontro con il fascismo," pp. 71–102.

[51] A sanitized version of the story is told in Eloisa Mura, "Emilio Betti, oltre lo specchio della memoria," in Emilio Betti, *Notazioni autobiografiche (a cura di Eloisa Mura)* (Padova: CEDAM, 2014 [1953]), pp. ix–x, lii.

with regard to political power that was willing to institute rash reforms can be found in his early text on the crisis of the Roman Republic. Here he denounces the attempts to restrict the possibility of appeal (*provocatio*) as the abolition of liberty, which would have meant supplanting it with terror and absolutism.[52] This conviction that the interpretation of norms were tied not only to the historical context but even more importantly to the historical tradition was a lesson that hermeneutics could teach to legal history.

Even in his postwar debates with Gadamer, Betti questioned the traditional distinction in hermeneutics between a normative legal interpretation that sought to find the correct legal answer and a contemplative historical interpretation that aimed to track down the original intent and circumstances. He takes the example of Savigny, whose work traced the history of influences, interpretations and adaptations of Roman legal texts through the two millennia between the Romans and modern Germans, highlighting how the multitude of layers demanded that one approached the process of reception and interpretation as a whole.[53] In 1955 Betti would publish his own theory of interpretation, the *Teoria Generale dell'interpretazione*, which sought to universalize the ideas from the field of jurisprudence to other human sciences. His general theory of legal interpretation from 1943 had preceded this work.[54]

The hermeneutic thinking manifested in Wieacker's works emphasized the relationship between text and interpretation, and the difference between the past as a factual reality and contemporary interpretations of the past as a factor in the writing of history. In this sense, Wieacker's thought could be described as constructivist, inasmuch as the interpretation of history is not detachable from the context and intention of the author. Of course, Wieacker occupied a very specific position between the discussions on historical hermeneutics and legal hermeneutics, a position shared only by Betti. In Wieacker's writings, hermeneutical aspects were tied to the concept of reception and the continuing reinterpretation of the text though the ages.[55]

[52] Betti, *Crisi della repubblica*, pp. 148–153, 225–230, 304–306, returning repeatedly to the dangers of declaring a crisis in order to circumvent the constitution. See also Giuliano Crifò, *Materiali di storiografia romanistica* (Torino: G. Giappichelli Editore, 1998), p. 135.

[53] Emilio Betti, *Die Hermeneutik als allgemeine Methodik der Geisteswissenschaften* (Tübingen: J. C. B. Mohr (Paul Siebeck), 1962), pp. 46–54.

[54] Emilio Betti, *Teoria generale del negozio giuridico* (Naples: Edizioni scientifiche italiane, 2002).

[55] Avenarius, "Verwissenschaftlichung als 'sinnhafter' Kern der Rezeption," pp. 121–136.

The link between Gadamer, Wieacker and Betti is evident in the letters between Gadamer and Wieacker. Wieacker notes how much the example of Gadamer had helped him to sharpen his own thinking regarding historical and legal hermeneutics, especially in presenting his case against Betti.[56]

The interest in legal and historical hermeneutics was for most scholars of Roman law and legal history rooted in the concepts of tradition and reinterpretation, a continuous return to classical texts and rereading them from a new perspective. This was hardly a preoccupation that would have been consistent with the ideals of the new legal science advocated by the Nazis.

The relationship between Wieacker and Nazi ideology is a complicated one. On the one hand, the whole orientation toward the European history of private law that came to fruition in the *Privatrechtsgeschichte* was prompted by the new study order instituted by the Nazis. On the other hand, the Nazi interest in legal education and research was by and large fleeting and reforms were left to be carried out by those in the field. Whether the reformers were inspired by the ideology of racism and nationalism is hard to say but enthusiasm for implementing Nazi ideology may be too strong a word. While one may reject the idea that Wieacker was a critic of the regime who did not join the resistance but always maintained his loyalty to the ideals of justice and individual worth,[57] the issue was perhaps not that complicated. Overall it would appear to be true that the vast majority of legal academia lacked a deep political commitment. As Koschaker stated, they were by and large unimportant to the regime.[58] They often thought of the regime as vulgar and contrary to the widespread anti-Semitism did not agree with the exclusion of their Jewish or liberal colleagues. These were, however, things that were out of their control and they sought instead to make the best out of the situation.

For the Nazi regime, the main idea was to push through a reform agenda that would comprehensively revolutionize German society. To that end, they focused on the youth, including young academics. Among the older generation, passive acquiescence was tolerated while for the younger generation, the carrot was much more powerful than

[56] Letters from Wieacker to Gadamer, on January 26, 1962 and on July 6, 1965. Deutsches Literatur Archiv, Marbach am Neckar, Letters from Wieacker to Gadamer – A: Gadamer.

[57] As noted by Liebs, "Franz Wieacker," pp. 28–29. Liebs notes how Wieacker was by and large unpolitical and was unimpressed by Hitler himself. Wieacker would join later join the SPD.

[58] Koschaker, *Europa*, pp. 312–313.

the stick. Especially after the expulsion of Jewish academics from the faculties, ample opportunities to make a splendid career were possible. Max Kaser, for example, became a professor at the age of twenty-seven. The other so-called "young lions" of the Nazi legal academia, such as the *Kieler Schule*, were similarly successful.

Liebs maintains that the whole point of Wieacker's writings during the war was to provide a counterpoint to the Nazi narrative. While some would go along with the Nazis and co-opt their language, Wieacker by and large stuck to his own message despite its political unpopularity.[59] However, Wieacker's ideas were not as against the regime policies as some would like to present them. Neither were the young Romanists in a particularly disadvantaged position; in addition to Kaser many were appointed as professors at a relatively young age.[60]

The idea of the *Privatrechtsgeschichte* was rooted in the outline given in the 1935 reform, which instituted courses such as *Privatrechtsgeschichte der Neuzeit* and *Antike Rechtsgeschichte* (ancient legal history). There were others who sought to define the field as it emerged. Hedemann, for example, as early as 1935 give his own stab at the idea of how the new course should be developed.[61] It goes to show the degree to which purely structural changes in the educational system impacted on scholarship that some scholars have actually claimed that the change in the study plan became the starting point for the modern history of private law in Germany.[62] Wieacker's *Privatrechtsgeschichte* was thus not the first book to attempt to cover the field, and important works were published both before and after the war.[63] However, its coherent message would ensure its success for decades to come.

[59] Liebs, "Franz Wieacker," pp. 38–39.

[60] Wolfgang Kunkel to Göttingen in 1934, Hans Kreller to Tübingen in 1935, Kaser to Münster in 1937. Ernst Schönbauer, who was considerably older, was made dean at Vienna in 1938 (after the *Anschluss*). Romanists were even invited to the Akademie des deutschen Rechts (even Koschaker was there). Winkler, *Der Kampf gegen die Rechtswissenschaft*, p. 164.

[61] Justus Wilhelm Hedemann, "Privatrechtsgeschichte der Neuzeit. Ein Versuch," in *Festschrift für Rudolf Hübner* (Jena: Friedrich-Schiller-Universität Jena, 1935), pp. 5–18; Rückert, *Privatrechtsgeschichte der Neuzeit*, p. 79.

[62] Peter Landau, "Wieackers Konzept einer neueren Privatrechtsgeschichte: Eine Bilanz nach 40 Jahren," in Okko Behrends and Eva Schumann (eds.), *Franz Wieacker: Historiker des modernen Privatrechts* (Göttingen: Wallstein Verlag, 2010), pp. 49–74; Rückert, *Privatrechtsgeschichte der Neuzeit*, p. 77 also sees the reform as the creation of a new discipline in law.

[63] See Winkler, *Der Kampf gegen die Rechtswissenschaft*, pp. 157–161 on the discussions and the publications seeking to fill the need for new material.

While the course *Privatrechtsgeschichte der Neuzeit* was based on the ideas included in the Nazi reforms, its roots went deeper, to the complicated connections and distinctions between Roman and Germanic law in legal education. The study reform managed to solve a number of problems as well as create a historically oriented introduction to the legal tradition. The original aims of these Nazi-initiated legal study reforms, however, were different, the drafters having a clear political aim. K. A. Eckhardt, the main architect, was an early and a staunch Nazi, having joined the SA in 1931, the NSDAP in 1932 and the SS in 1933. He worked in a number of influential committees on education reform and was a member of Himmler's personal staff. He even edited a *Festschrift* for Himmler in 1941. The interesting point in the internal politics of the Nazi regime was that Eckhardt was part of the SS and thus in opposition to figures like Hans Frank and even Carl Schmitt, who also played a powerful role in the legal reforms.[64]

Along with many other members of the *Kieler Schule*, Wieacker took part in the *Aktion Ritterbusch*, a program named after the University of Kiel rector and dedicated Nazi Paul Ritterbusch. The aim of the program was to use the best minds in the German social sciences and humanities to advance the German war aims. Scholarship was explicitly used as a weapon of war. The different contributions were aimed to outline the New Europe that would emerge after the war under German leadership. As with his Kiel colleagues, Wieacker's contribution was listed under *Kriegseinsatz* and could be located on the narrow path between science and propaganda.[65]

The idea of Europe was by no means an exclusively liberal or progressive idea, indeed discourse on Europe included all sides of the political spectrum. During the war, even the Nazi regime became fascinated with the idea of Europe and began to propagate the idea of Europe as a wider community led by Germany, united by anticommunism and based on

[64] Winkler, *Der Kampf gegen die Rechtswissenschaft*, pp. 138–142; Niemann, "Karl August Eckhardt," pp. 164, 167–184. Eckhardt served in the Wehrmacht, for instance as Canaris's adjutant, reaching the rank of *Oberleutnant*. In the SS, he served in diverse roles, both in local organizations and in the *Sicherheitsdienst* under Heydrich, finally in the rank of *Sturmbannführer* (corresponding to a major in the military). His advancement in the SS was long hindered by the laudatory *Nachruf* he had written of his Kiel predecessor Max Pappenheim, despite his Jewish background. Nehlsen "Karl August Eckhardt," p. 514 notes how Eckhardt was in fact one of the most productive of the Germanist legal historians and was bound for a brilliant career before the Nazi rule.

[65] Frank-Rutger Hausmann, *"Deutsche Geisteswissenschaft" im Zweiten Weltkrieg: Die "Aktion Ritterbusch" (1940–1945)* (Heidelberg: Synchron, 2007); Erkkilä, *Conceptual Change of Conscience*, pp. 96–97.

ethnicity, i.e., Nordic supremacy (*Neue Europa*). This meant that instead of a purely German racial basis, there was a push to loosen the criteria of who would count as members of the Nordic race.[66]

Even within legal history in Germany, there were at least three competing visions of Europe and its legal heritage that were presented during and after the war. If Koschaker's conception rested on the idea of continuity of the legal tradition, namely the long arc of the jurist's law from ancient Rome to the modern world seen as a history of reception, Coing saw a dogmatic continuity in private law. In contrast, Wieacker's European legal community was a matter of legal method, a method that rested on the shared conviction of lawyers themselves.[67]

The idea of law presented by Wieacker was one that reflected the new conceptions of science. The new scholarship on law recognized social realities and sociological advances, and was imbued with a new sense of history as a science that operated under its own mechanisms. Wieacker's history of legal tradition in Europe drew completely different conclusions from a very similar factual basis as Koschaker's.

Wieacker refused the definitional accusation presented by Koschaker and others that the historicization of Roman law would have meant that it would become irrelevant for law today. Instead, Wieacker's aim was to present a methodological continuity from the ancient Romans to the present. At the same time, he rejected simplistic historical dogmatics, arguing for a history that was deeply contextual, a true definition of the living past. Such a perspective would see law as part of society and its social reality. In the long theoretical debate over the position of law between *Sollen* and *Sein* (Ought and Is), Nazi legal theory had taken a stand toward a kind of legal realism, seeing law as a part of political reality. Wieacker's new legal history was in many ways part of this new methodological orientation.[68]

The Nazi roots of Wieacker's methodological thinking are complex, traceable both to the *Kieler Schule* and to Schmitt. While it would be easy to discount them as purely youthful indiscretions, it is apparent that the idea of a new way of legal thinking strongly appealed to him. In a report on one of the camps organized for young teachers, the Kitzeberger Lager, where Wieacker attended the activities with many of his colleagues both from Kiel and elsewhere in Germany, the enthusiasm is

[66] On the Nazi idea of Europe, see Chapter 4.
[67] Winkler, *Der Kampf gegen die Rechtswissenschaft*, pp. 238–246.
[68] Winkler, *Der Kampf gegen die Rechtswissenschaft*, p. 189.

palpable. He talks of the community of "blood, life, fate and morale" that links the "concrete community of the people" (p. 166) in a shared theme. However, what Wieacker himself notes to be the true aim of the camp was the "fighting critique" directed toward the old legal science (p. 174). This was probably the feeling shared by the participants not only of the camp but of the early Nazi legal reform movement: they were the young, the future and the innovators who would sweep away the old.[69]

It is possible that Liebs may have been overly generous in distancing Wieacker from the Nazi regime but it is equally possible that he considered his assessment to be accurate. There are two potential explanations behind this, the first a legal one and the second a psychological one. The legal explanation is that within the Nazi regime, the bifurcated nature of the structure of governance, between the formal and the real, meant that for a very long time, the legal realm remained if not fully at least partially functional. Within the normative realm, the courts and the legal profession, the incursion of the Nazi regime was at first relatively benign. It sought to persuade and to lure, to convince the legal profession, especially its younger members, of the benefits of the new regime. What Meierhenrich has dubbed "the remnants of the *Rechtsstaat*," the institutions and norms that continued as before, obscured the violent tyranny from view, allowing the members of the legal profession to discount violent acts as excesses and exceptions. The law continued to exist and under its provisions even Jewish lawyers and professors continued to function. As Wieacker was one of those who was being lured, to whom the idea of a legal revolution as a remedy to the problems of legal positivism appealed and someone who would benefit from the professorial purge, he was perhaps unable to see the true nature of the regime. It is possible to believe that he felt his work would enhance the impact and social and political significance of legal scholarship. The second explanation, the psychological one, is much more conditional. In the same way as the changes in the legal system were normalized, Koontz has noted how the vast majority of Germans normalized the exclusion of Jews in their midst. Rules were rules. Thus while they may not have had any reason for supporting the ongoing repression, very few stood against it. As a result, Wieacker may have

[69] Franz Wieacker, "Das Kitzeberger Lager," in Christian Wollschläger (ed.), *Franz Wieacker. Zivilistische Schriften (1934–1942)* (Frankfurt: Vittorio Klostermann, 2000 [1936]), pp. 163–176.

rationalized that the exclusion and exile of Pringsheim, not to mention other friends and colleagues, was simply an unfortunate phenomenon that was beyond his control.[70]

Another possible explanation was the psychological mechanism associated with totalitarianism defined by Czesław Miłosz as the will to belong. Originally aimed at explaining the acquiescence of intellectuals to communist dictatorships, the will to belong can also be extended to Nazi Germany. In the face of a regime that employed the language of community, of belonging to a group, it is very hard to maintain a social detachment from the ideological pull of group dynamics.[71] Wieacker and other members of the new generation were not only persuaded to join the movement, they were also drawn to its social aspects, the will to be in the vanguard of reforms that would draw Germany out of the chaos and despair of the Weimar years.

During the war, Wieacker's *Privatrechtsgeschichte* was an ongoing project as is obvious from his letters. In his numerous letters to Erik Wolf, the themes later found in the *Privatrechtsgeschichte* come up frequently, even during the war. At the end of the war, just before his own redeployment, Wieacker uses the *Privatrechtsgeschichte* project as an excuse for not contributing to other projects.[72]

The work on the book project continued until Wieacker was redeployed in late summer 1944 and sent to Italy. He was captured in Northern Italy at the end of the war and sent to a POW camp. In the camp, he was the dean of the camp university, and lectured to fellow inmates.[73] In early 1946, he was back in Germany, taking care of his parents who had both survived the war. His university, Leipzig, was in the Russian sector and in his letters Wieacker grumbles about its transformation into a "worker's academy" (*Arbeitervolkshochschule*) where half of the students were actually members of the ruling party. These letters offer a rare glimpse of the mental state of academics like Wieacker after the war. Wieacker speaks, for instance, of the intolerance, egoism, small-minded dogmatism and servility induced by the Nazi regime but

[70] Koontz, *Nazi Conscience*, p. 11; Meierhenrich, *Remnants of the Rechtsstaat*, pp. 34–36.

[71] Czesław Miłosz, *The Captive Mind* (London: Secker & Warburg, 1953).

[72] Universitätsarchiv, Albert-Ludwigs-Universität, Freiburg im Breisgau, NL Erik Wolf, bestand C130, signum 562, especially letters from Wieacker to Wolf dated October 18, 1940, May 4, 1942, October 23, 1943; Universitäts- und Landesbibliothek, Bonn, NL Rothacker I.1, Briefe Rothacker, Erich von und an Wieacker, Franz, Leipzig July 8, 1944–October 6, 1952, letters from Wieacker to Erich Franz von Rothacker dated July 8, 1944 and August 8, 1944.

[73] Liebs, "Franz Wieacker," pp. 28–29.

also the brutality, suffering and inhumanity of the war. His office at the university had been destroyed during the war, and now he was actively seeking a new position outside the Russian zone. He was hoping to get a position in Göttingen but at this point things were still unclear.[74]

## After the War

One of the issues Wieacker faced after the war was the denazification process, which he was subjected to as a party member. In the end, Wieacker was rehabilitated fairly quickly. He was found guilty in one of the review panels (*Spruchkammer*) that sought to weed out the worst Nazi offenders but the sentence was merely one of *Mitläufer*, participant. He soon got a job at the University of Göttingen and began his career anew. In this, he was helped by a number of people who wrote letters of recommendation for him, vouching for his good name. Pringsheim wrote a letter, as did Gadamer. A very interesting addition to the writers of these letters was theoretical physicist and Nobel Prize winner Werner Heisenberg. In these processes, many of the *Kieler Schule* members, among them Huber, were condemned for participating in the Nazi regime, and also for their writings in which they had supported the persecution of Jews. Both in the process of denazification and in the resettling of academics displaced by war, the association with the group friends made in the *Kieler Schule* was highly beneficial. In the case of Wieacker, the fact that Rudolf Smend was rector of the University of Göttingen proved to be crucial because Smend was able to hire not only Wieacker but also Wolfgang Siebert and Karl Michaelis.[75] Wieacker wrote a heartfelt letter of thanks to Smend, describing himself and his colleagues as exiles who had to flee persecution. Erkkilä has aptly noted that for Wieacker to compare himself, Siebert and Michaelis as moral equivalents to Huguenots

[74] Letters of Wieacker to Erik Wolf on February 2, 1946 and on March 14, 1946. NL Erik Wolf, Albert-Ludwig-Universitätsarchiv, Freiburg im Breisgau.

[75] Leipzig Universitätsarchiv, Personenakten/Dossiers Wieacker, Franz, PA-SG 0457: March 17, 1947, "Eidesstattliche Erklärung" given by Hans-Georg Gadamer, *Rektor* of the University. The archival location of the letter from Pringsheim on May 12, 1947 defending Wieacker is not known, but copies have circulated and two matching copies have been seen and copied. Erkkilä, *Conceptual Change of Conscience*, pp. 148–149. Pringsheim's letter is also discussed and quoted in Behrends, "Franz Wieacker. Historiker und Jurist des Privatrechts," pp. 2349–2350.

fleeing France demonstrates how deeply ingrained their conviction of the rightness of their status as an elite was.[76]

What happened to Wieacker was in line with the process of denazification in general. The greatest issue was that of scale. Some 8.5 million individuals had belonged to the NSDAP, even more to associated organizations. This amounted to roughly two-thirds of the German population being part of the Nazi regime in some shape or form. In the process of trying to weed out the worst criminals, the torturers and mass murderers, there was also the question of rehabilitation. Throwing all Nazis in prison was impossible and because Nazi ideology and its anti-Semitism was still widely shared among Germans, the danger was that one could inadvertently strengthen a sense of solidarity among the major offenders and relatively nominal Nazis. Thus, the Allies opted to punish the worst offenders and let the Germans handle the rest.[77]

Of the Nazi scholars discussed in this book, most were given minor sentences. Hans Frank, minister and head of the *Akademie für deutsches Rechts*, was tried at Nürnberg. He was mostly accused of atrocities committed while he was the governor of occupied Poland. In his defense, he blamed evil demons for his actions but his pleas fell on deaf ears and he was hanged for his crimes on October 16, 1945.[78] For others, there was a period of exclusion that for some like Huber was shorter than for others such as Carl Schmitt. A similar permanent exclusion, but partly for health reasons, befell K. A. Eckhardt, who was removed from office by occupying powers and never reinstated.[79]

This was hardly the whole story. The renazification of German universities that, for example, Koschaker talks about, operated much along the lines of pure academic continuity. Jobs had to be filled, students taught and so forth. Within legal academia, there was public silence about the Nazi years. Stolleis talks about the silence of the 1950s, when law journals focused on technicalities, on the minutiae of the law, carefully

[76] Letter from Wieacker to Rudolf Smend on January 14, 1947. Niedersächsische Staats- und Universitätsbibliothek, Göttingen, NL Rudolf Smend: Allgemeine Korrespondenz. Cod. Ms. R. Smend A 960; Erkkilä, *Conceptual Change of Conscience*, p. 153.

[77] Of the denazification process, see Clemens Vollnhals, *Entnazifizierung. Politische Säuberung und Rehabilitierung in den vier Besatzungszonen 1945–1949* (Munich: Dtv, 1991). On the intellectual reasonings, see Forner, *German Intellectuals*, pp. 62–63, 170–171. A similar process took place in Italy, where the amnesty of 1946 (*Amnistia Togliatti*) on crimes committed during fascism led to corresponding results.

[78] Schudnagies, *Hans Frank*, p. 99.

[79] Frassek, "Eckhardt, Karl August," p. 1180; Niemann, "Karl August Eckhardt," pp. 164–165. Eckhardt was finally in 1948 declared to be in group 4, *Mitläufer onhe Berufsbeschränkung* but his heart condition meant that he was put on pension.

avoiding even the mention of what had happened during the Nazi years.[80] This silence was a part of a more general conscious denial and forgetting regarding the Nazi past that was already noted by the end of the 1940s in Germany. Frei called this phenomenon the triumph of silence, where discretion and privacy became so marked that the social integration of Nazi "fellow travelers" like Wieacker became possible.[81] Many offenders hid in plain sight, either shielded by the silence of others or by assuming a different name. This led to some curious incidents. For example, Hannah Arendt's editor in Germany at Piper Verlag was Hans Rössner, who had worked in the *Reichssicherheitshauptamt* (RSHA) Office III, the *Sicherheitsdienst* (SD), and had been a member of the SS.[82]

These matters of denazification and readmittance were hotly debated among scholars themselves. Erwin Seidl, in his 1947 letter to A. Arthur Schiller in New York, gave an overview of the fate of the former Nazi and anti-Nazi scholars. He mentioned Wieacker as one of those who had made a splendid career under the Nazis, being appointed to the highly coveted chair in Leipzig. According to Seidl, Wieacker was not wise enough to abstain from Nazi vocabulary in his scientific works, writing about *Gemeinschaftsgeist* and *Blut und Boden*. As a consequence, he was still a suspect person, even though he had managed to secure a tenuous position in Göttingen.[83]

In tandem with the extensive denazification effort, many of the exiles had returned and been reinstated. In Heidelberg, Karl Jaspers had been central in the denazification process, a role that had prompted much enmity. The exiles, especially those who had been involved in the American war effort, were privately vilified as traitors who had turned the world against Germany. While the West Germans wished to be model students in the school of democracy, as Kraus put it, the exiles served as surrogate enemies upon which the negative trauma could be projected.[84]

[80] Ville Erkkilä, "The metaphysics and legal history. An interview with Michael Stolleis," *European Legal Roots Online*, (2016), 14; Stolleis, *Law under the Swastika*, p. 10.

[81] Frei, *Adenauer's Germany*, p. xiv.

[82] Michael Wildt, *An Uncompromising Generation: The Nazi Leadership of the Reich Security Main Office* (Wisconsin: University of Wisconsin Press, 2010), p. 395.

[83] Rare Book and Manuscript Archive, Columbia University, New York, Arthur Schiller Papers, Uncatalogued correspondence, Box 6, Erwin Seidl to Schiller (October 2, 1947).

[84] Remy, *Heidelberg Myth*, pp. 169–170 maintains that Jaspers was in fact seeking to limit the investigations of the more ambitious American investigators; Krauss, *Heimkehr in ein fremdes Land*, p. 52. Krauss notes (pp. 63–64) that the role of exiles in the military administration has been exaggerated and in reality their numbers were fairly small compared with the total. The reason for this disconnect was that they operated in very visible roles such as the press corps.

Despite this, ideas of liberal democracy were being promoted within both political and legal discourse. There was the official Allied propaganda and efforts for reeducation but equally the adoption of the language of democracy by the German elites themselves. The official reeducation program and the purging of the education system of Nazism and militarism had been one of the chief points of the Potsdam Declaration of 1945. However, skeptics such as Franz Neumann claimed that "To attempt to re-educate Germans by military government action is to attempt the impossible."[85]

The denazification and renazification processes involved a number of complex calculations in which Nazi professors were just one part of the equation. The leaders of the recreation of universities such as Jaspers in Heidelberg had to first determine what kind of university they would strive for. A large part of the problem in 1933 had actually been the students, who eagerly took up the Nazi cause. For Jaspers, the solution was to reject the mass university and return to the elite university. According to the professors, the causes of the disaster in 1933 had been the encroachment of the state on the autonomy of the university along with the mass of students infused with Nazi ideology. In the elite university, one could support the intellectual development of students and carefully select them. By supporting the intellectual and academic freedom of professors, one could protect the university from a return to Nazi policies.[86]

In contrast, Franz Neumann and others were equally convinced that the professors and their sheltered position was part of the problem. Professors were naturally conservative and reactionary, perpetuating the ruling classes and their ideological bias. In the face of the denazification efforts, the professors had closed ranks and sought to maintain the rigid caste system they had created within higher education. On the part of the student population, there were two issues: the students were overwhelmingly from the upper and middle classes and the majority of them had voted for the Nazi party.[87]

Hartshorne, who had been a houseguest with the Schulz family during the 1930s, returned to Germany in 1945 and became part of the US

[85] Franz Neumann, "Re-educating the Germans," *Commentary*, 3 (1947), 517; On the reeducation efforts, see Thomas Alan Schwartz, *America's Germany: John J. McCloy and the Federal Republic of Germany* (Cambridge, MA: Harvard University Press, 1991).

[86] These ideas were expressed in Jaspers' famous 1946 *Die Idee der Universität*. In his letters to Arendt, Jaspers notes that the book was written in April–May 1945 and by 1946 seemed to be almost outdated. Jaspers to Arendt on October 28, 1945 and June 9, 1946 in Köhler and Saner, *Hannah Arendt/Karl Jaspers*, pp. 58, 78; Remy, *Heidelberg Myth*, p. 124.

[87] Neumann, "Re-educating the Germans," pp. 519–521; Remy, *Heidelberg Myth*, p. 127.

military government effort in reopening the German universities. He was convinced that the Germans themselves should be set the task of reforming universities and the American effort should be secondary. A series of questionnaires would be used to gather information and to form a basis of the reorganization. The Allied task was, as Hartshorne put it, to put up the mirror and let the Germans draw their own conclusions.[88]

In practice, the military administration was not interested in the universities and the efforts at denazification were stymied by German resistance. The investigations were hampered by accusations by German professors made against the few diligent people who sought to perform a thorough investigation, as well as a general lack of enthusiasm by the German public to accuse anyone beyond the main culprits. For the Americans, the most baffling aspect was the apparently sincere sense of victimization that was shared by the Germans. Even former Nazis perceived themselves to be the victims of Nazis and they now felt that that they were being victimized by denazification. Nobody was taking responsibility for the millions of Jews who had been killed. In the postwar public discussions, the sense of German victimhood grew and the balancing of German suffering and German crimes became normalized in arguments based on "whataboutism." Here, the curious yet psychologically understandable process resulted in the declarations where culpability for the war and the Holocaust was externalized to the Nazis and the suffering of German civilians became a central preoccupation.[89]

A similar process also took place in Italy, where some members of the fascist leadership were held accountable but at universities very little was done to sanction or remove fascist professors. Thus scholars close to fascism such as Emilio Betti decried the barbarism of the victors, who had under the guise of liberty and peace spread destruction. The winners were, as a consequence, responsible for the destruction of cities, civilian deaths and the "loss of the millenarian European patrimonium of art and culture."[90]

For the former exiles who were now part of the military administration or simply observing the situation in the US, the situation appeared tragicomic. Edgar Bodenheimer recounted how every former Nazi was

[88] Remy, *Heidelberg Myth*, p. 129.

[89] Remy, *Heidelberg Myth*, pp. 147–152; Forner, *German Intellectuals*, pp. 170–172; Caroline Sharples, *Postwar Germany and the Holocaust* (London: Bloomsbury, 2016).

[90] Betti, *Teoria generale*, p. 4.

whitewashing himself, presenting themselves as opponents to the regime. A collective amnesia and active forgetting were the main ways in which Germans dealt with the past.[91]

Nowhere else was the whitewashing more prominent than in the process leading to the amnesty laws issued in West Germany. While the most serious Nazi offenders were tried at the Nuremberg trials, hundreds of thousands more were tried in different courts, ranging from the *Spruchkammern* where Wieacker was tried (the status of these varied in the different Allied occupation zones) to Allied military courts and German courts. In total, some 3.6 million persons were processed in the West German occupied zones, of which 1,667 were considered major culprits and 23,060 were "majorly incriminated." Roughly one million were deemed "fellow travelers." However, due to the amnesty laws, these sentences were reduced or commuted, and by 1951 nearly eight hundred thousand sentences were reduced, most of them to small fines or prison sentences. While the majority of these cases were minor offenses, especially the German courts would engage in a creative legal interpretation, extending amnesties to Nazi bosses who had participated in torture. In these amnesties, countless members of the SA, the SS and other organizations who kidnapped people to be tortured and killed were released. Simultaneously with the amnesties, there was a concerted campaign to liberate Nazi war criminals who were held by the Allies. All in all, this amounted to a coordinated effort by the old elites of Germany, operating through networks of legal specialists, politicians and leaders of the church, to not only grant amnesty to its members but also to rehabilitate the German military and to consolidate their own power.[92]

The fact that former Nazis and supporters of the regime were not held accountable may appear incomprehensible. However, one explanation revolves around the concept of zero hour (*Stunde Null*), a moment of complete and utter renewal from which the only possibility is to go forward and leave the past behind. The human suffering and moral

[91] Bodenheimer, *Edgar and Brigitte*, pp. 123–130.

[92] The figures cited are based on Vollnhals, *Entnazifizierung*; Frei, *Adenauer's Germany*, pp. 5–9, 22–25, 94–95; Konrad H. Jarausch, *After Hitler: Recivilizing Germans, 1945–1995* (New York: Oxford University Press, 2006), p. 54. In the British zone, the *Spruchgerichte* were special courts that dealt with expressly criminal activities, such as participation in criminal organizations like the SS or Gestapo, while the American *Spruchkammern* were denazification tribunals. On the German trials, see Nathan Stoltzfus and Henry Friedlander (eds.), *Nazi Crimes and the Law* (Cambridge: Cambridge University Press, 2008).

bankruptcy that the Third Reich represented was best left forgotten. In this sense, May 1945 was a moment of optimism and a new beginning.[93]

For the cultural elite, the sense of reckoning was in many ways a process of reimagination and revitalization of German culture. To intellectuals, part of the question was the role of the masses and elites: Were the people to be trusted with the democratic process? This was not to say that there were no democrats in Nazi Germany. Most of the non-Jewish activist democrats had spent the war in "inner exile," staying put and weathering out the war without taking part in active resistance. For democratic intellectuals, culture and humanism were catchwords that signified a commitment to the freedom of the spirit in opposition to the mindless obedience of Prussian militarism.[94]

The need for a clear and strong intellectual foundation for a new Germany was evident. The discussions regarding the amnesties offered to Nazi criminals and war criminals had demonstrated how strong the undercurrent of former ideologies was. A mass demonstration in Landsberg am Lech against the execution of war criminals in January 1951, where speakers had equated the killing of Jews and the execution of condemned Nazi war criminals, had culminated in the crowd beginning to chant "Juden raus!" to the counterdemonstrators. Tellingly, only the Jewish newspaper reported the incident, the *Frankfurter Allgemeine* only mentioning the disturbance caused by Jewish counterdemonstrators.[95] Marita Krauss maintains that in Germany the resurfacing of anti-Semitism against returning Jews was one of the taboos relating to the reemergence of German democracy.[96]

The process of denazification, the reeducation efforts and the attempts to imprint upon Germans a new democratic conviction is not easy to see as a success story. The most prominent German reaction to the efforts appeared to be resistance and irritation to the patronizing tone and a reluctance to abide by the distinctions between minor "nominal Nazis" and the main culprits. The Allies, of course, were not really interested in these distinctions as their main concern was to prevent a future war of aggression by Germany. The Allied observers were deeply troubled by the signs of denialism, including the denial of "true" military defeat and the denials of the Holocaust. This increased the pressure for a more decisive action and the initial denazification

[93] Forner, *German Intellectuals*, p. 1.
[94] Forner, *German Intellectuals*, pp. 11, 53, 125.
[95] Frei, *Adenauer's Germany*, p. 158.
[96] Krauss, *Heimkehr in ein fremdes Land*, p. 17.

process reflected this. However, the process ended up being highly bureaucratic and led to the categorization of people in ways that were felt to be unjust and counterproductive.[97]

In the field of law, nowhere was the contradiction between the magnitude of the offenses and the lack of responsibility greater than in the German justice system. While there had been some efforts to prosecute judges who had served in the people's courts and had condemned innocent people to death, most were let off without any consequences. Müller, in his 1987 book, notes how murderers had gone free and their crimes declared to be lawful actions. Their careers had continued unhindered, their pensions paid on time and their reputation remained spotless. For example, in 1952 the *Landgericht* of Wiesbaden came to the conclusion that the decision by the Ministry of Justice to transfer Jewish, Russian and Ukrainian prisoners to the SS to be killed through labor (*Vernichtung durch Arbeit*) was not unlawful and was thus not punishable.[98]

The ultimate result after denazification and reeducation was, as we now know, that Germany emerged as a democratic country committed to upholding human rights and opposing totalitarianism. In the years after the war, this result was hardly certain. Many of the exiles would debate the reasons why Hitler was able to gain power and why Germany, the land of *Dichter und Denker* ("poets and thinkers") could turn into a land of torturers and mass murderers. Theodor Adorno in his Los Angeles exile developed a theory of the authoritarian personality, which was easily persuaded by fascism. Max Horkheimer identified traits of authoritarianism even in bourgeois democracies, maintaining that a similar will existed for the repression of the popular will.[99]

[97] Jarausch, *After Hitler*.

[98] Ingo Müller, *Furchtbare Juristen: die unbewältige Vergangenheit unserer Justiz* (Munich: Kindler, 1987), pp. 7, 285. Wildt, *Uncompromising Generation*, pp. 444–448 notes how most of the members of the Nazi security apparatus were actually able to return to normal civil life after the war.

[99] Jarausch, *After Hitler*, p. 167. The contradictory notions of America and the Americans that puzzled the émigrés processing their experience of Europe are notable in their recollections. For example, Adorno's typical stance would be seen to portray the Americans as shallow and uncultured when compared to Germans. Anthony Heilbut, *Exiled in Paradise: German Refugee Artists and Intellectuals in America, from the 1930s to the Present* (New York: Viking Press, 1983), pp. 160–161. In private recollections, he would on the contrary praise their generosity and democratic spirit that far exceeded the narrow-minded meanness of Europeans. Adorno, "Scientific experiences of a European scholar in America." A similar notion of contradictions is evident in Arendt. For example, in her letter to Jaspers on January 29, 1946, she writes how in America the notion of republic is no empty letter and public life is celebrated. Köhler and Saner, *Hannah Arendt/Karl Jaspers*, p. 66.

Critics, especially those on the political left, were adamant that the American aim was not to promote democracy but to push American models and values, ultimately the American form of capitalism.[100]

After the war, the political situation, especially among students, took a turn that baffled liberals and conservatives alike. Far from accepting the new liberal state, radical students began to advocate authoritarianism, this time from the Left. The new generational battle was fought between the old liberals and the students of the far Left, who began boycotts and verbal assaults on teachers in a manner reminiscent of the Nazi years. The alliance of liberals and the Left, held together in the 1950s by their common battle against the old Nazis and other anti-liberal forces that had rejected democratic ideas, began to break down.[101] In academia, part of this process was the gradual rehabilitation of even the worst of the Nazi academics. For example, the amity between Wieacker and Pringsheim was threatened by the fact that Wieacker had helped his *Kieler Schule* friend and Nazi jurist Huber be selected for Freiburg.[102]

In all this, one of the major side effects was that the princely role of professors as the undisputed authority at universities also broke down. During the 1960s, a new public discourse and criticism directed toward former Nazis like Wieacker began.[103] In the case of Wieacker, this meant that for all his success in academia, radical students would see him as a Nazi.

## The Great European Narrative from Roman Law to Germany

Although Wieacker's first main work, *Privatrechtsgeschichte*, was typical of the postwar reorientation, it took shape during the war and was

[100] On a reevaluation of these criticisms that peaked during the sixties, see Diethelm Prowe, "Democratization as conservative restabilization," in Jeffry M. Diefendorf, Axel Frohn and Hermann-Josef Rupieper (eds.), *American Policy and the Reconstruction of West Germany, 1945–1955* (Cambridge: Cambridge University Press, 1993), pp. 305–329.

[101] A. Dirk Moses, *German Intellectuals and the Nazi Past* (Cambridge, MA: Cambridge University Press, 2007), p. 49.

[102] Ewald Grothe, *Zwischen Geschichte und Recht: Deutsche Verfassungsgeschichtsschreibung 1900–1970* (Oldenbourg: Wissenschaftsverlag, 2005), p. 322; Letter from Pringsheim to Erich Weniger on September 21, 1952. Niedersächsische Staats- und Universitätsbibliothek, Göttingen, NL Erich Weniger, Cod. Ms. E Weniger, 1:676.

[103] Moses, *German Intellectuals*, p. 186; Erkkilä, *Conceptual Change of Conscience*, p. 265.

influenced by Nazi ideology and their reformulation of the law curriculum. The work was interrupted by the final stages of the war but Wieacker managed to continue it in Göttingen, writing to Riccobono in 1950 that he had now finished the book. The aim of the book, as he wrote to Riccobono, was to put textual criticism on a more secure foundation: "It will be a very conservative book."[104] However, in the same letter he mentions how, inspired by Riccobono, he wishes to celebrate Justinian's service to European legal culture. Thus, at the same time, *Privatrechtsgeschichte* was inspired by the Nazi reforms, an input into the debates over interpolationism and a book about European legal culture.

For Wieacker, the outline of the *Privatrechtsgeschichte* gave new currency to the idea of German dominance in intellectual development. Though he purportedly developed a European narrative of the development of law, in practice the historical development he presented was a teleology of German legal heritage. What Wieacker's *Privatrechtsgeschichte* and innumerable other essays demonstrate is the strength of the narrative construct in his mind, the narrative of the *translatio studii* from antiquity to the present, from Justinian to Bologna, to the humanists and finally to Germany. Thus while the book sets out to explore the emergence of European culture, the culture it describes is fairly German as becomes clear from the division of Wieacker's materials: 1) the foundations of European legal culture in medieval legal science; 2) its reception in Germany and the *usus modernus;* 3) the era of the law of reason or natural law and the first codifications; 4) the Historical School and Pandectism; and 5) legal positivism and its crisis. In all of these chapters, the focus is on Germany, the outside world being mentioned either as a source or recipient of influences. The second clear focus was Roman law as a dominant feature of legal culture from the medieval beginnings to the modern day. In this sense, Wieacker closely follows Koschaker and others who saw the history of law in Europe and in Germany especially as primarily a history of Roman law and its continuing influence.[105]

When many of Wieacker's contemporaries returned to natural law after World War II, his response was skeptical. While he acknowledged the need for a safeguard against unjust law and violent repression when these were performed using formally correct means, natural law would

[104] Letter from Wieacker to Riccobono on January 10, 1950. Collection of correspondence by Professor Salvatore Riccobono, currently at the disposal of Professor Mario Varvaro, at the Faculty of Law of the University of Palermo.

[105] Wieacker, *Privatrechtsgeschichte der Neuzeit*, (1952), pp. 16–37.

not provide the answer. In an article written as a response to four recent books, Wieacker maintains that natural law was still subject to the same problems that led to its rejection earlier on. In practical cases it provides little help for the judge, who has to juggle contradictory claims of legal principle and moral worth. Referring to Coing's 1947 book on legal principles (*Die Oberste Grundsätze*), Wieacker points out that safeguarding law rests on the strengthening of the will of justice and the understanding of the overly positive principles of justice among the people. Otherwise one just raises one moral, ethical or social conception over others and here Wieacker curiously raises the Nuremberg trials and the Nazi persecutions.[106] This singular example demonstrates how skewed Wieacker's moral compass was. This is not to say that it would have been in any particular way different from the general tendencies of this period because the Nuremberg trials were not very well regarded in Germany at the time. Even among legal exiles like David Daube the trials were heavily criticized, both as victor's justice and being based on retroactive law.[107] Despite this, what the reference to the perceived equivalence underlines is that what is now understood as good or bad was not necessarily so during the early years of the Bundesrepublik.

The first edition of the *Privatrechtsgeschichte* appeared in 1952. It was, like the second edition would be, dedicated to Fritz Pringsheim. The historical narrative of the book revolved around two concepts, scientification and rationalization. The historical contours of the book, the development from Bologna to the present, were to a large degree similar to the earlier drafts but the historical meaning given to the changes had changed. The idea of science that was so central in the conception of the reception of Roman law, had distinct roots in Schulz's and Pringsheim's theories about Roman law as an autonomous science but also in theories developed in the *Kieler Schule* discussions. These revolved around the attempts to reconcile the German and Roman elements within the reception of Roman law, preferably without giving either of them an inferior position. The concept of rationalization was similarly drawn from two roots: first the scientific rationality of Roman law and its exclusion of ulterior elements such as religion; and second the methodological input of Max Weber's theory of rationalization as

[106] Franz Wieacker, "Zur Erweckung des Naturrechts," *Süddeutsche Juristenzeitung*, (1949), 295–301.
[107] Carmichael, *Ideas and the Man*, p. 82.

a typically Western process.[108] There was, of course, a distinct similarity in the conception of the European sphere and its progression as the expansion of rationality that was typical of works such as Schmitt's *Der Nomos der Erde*. At the end of *Privatrechtsgeschichte*, Wieacker returns to the issues of positivism, naturalism and neo-Kantianism. This then grows into a wholesale condemnation of the degeneration of legal positivism, aided by naturalism, that enabled the Nazi tyranny:

*Wir finden uns nun in der Ethik des Tierreichs, wo die Art um ihr Dasein kämpft, und in einem Rechtsbild, dem sich die Geschichte darstellt wie dem Zoologen die Überwältigung der Hausratte durch die stärkere Wanderratte, und keine Unschuld des vormenschliches Daseins entsühnt die Taten eines überhellen Bewusstseins. Hier wird folgerichtig Recht, was "dem Volke" (oder irgendeinem anderen Interesse, etwa der Rasse) nützt. Wie die Wirklichkeit dieser Formel aussieht, lehren die fürchterlichen Triumphe des Naturalismus im Gesetzesrecht oder in der Routine der jüngsten Vergangenheit. Dass die Ausmordung der Geisteskranken dem Haushalt der "Volksgemeinschaft," die Vernichtung anderer Rassen der Herrenrasse, die Sippenhaftung dem Wohlverhalten der Familienväter, die Belohnung von Denunzianten der Herrschaft einer Minderheit "nützt": diese kurzbeinigen Wahrheiten als "Rechts"wahrheiten dem öffentlichen Bewusstsein eingeprägt zu haben, sind die Verirrungen eines angewandten Naturalismus, der sich des Gedankens Blässe entschlug und vom wissenschaftlichen Beobachten der Wirklichkeit zum Experimentieren mit Menschen überging.*

These are the ethics of the animal world, where the "species" fights for survival and the conception of law where history is shown almost like zoology, where the house rat is gradually suppressed by the more powerful brown one. And it is all done with full consciousness, not in the innocence of the world before man. When "law" was whatever was said to be good for "the people," society, progress or any other tin idol such as race, we learnt the reality behind these formulas, the terrible triumphs of naturalistic purposive legislation and other day-to-day application in times not long past. We learnt to exterminate the weak-minded to improve the biological stock of the "community of the people," to eliminate other races for the "benefit" to the "master-race," to make the family liable to ensure the political correctness of the *paterfamilias*, to encourage delation to ensure the rule of the minority. Public opinion swallowed such trash as legal facts but could do so, misled as it was, only because naturalism took to action, decided to pay the devil because it was tired of words, and abandoned scientific explanation of reality for experimentation in living flesh and blood.[109]

[108] Wieacker, *Privatrechtsgeschichte der Neuzeit*, (1952). On influences from the reception studies of *Kieler Schule* notables such as Schaffstein, Michaelis and Dahm, see Stolleis, "'Fortschritte der Rechtsgeschichte' in der Zeit des Nationalsozialismus?," pp. 192–193.

[109] Wieacker, *Privatrechtsgeschichte der Neuzeit*, (1952), p. 347. The translation is adapted from the second edition, Wieacker, *History of Private Law in Europe*, p. 461.

Wieacker was naturally not the only one to present criticism of Nazi jurisprudence and practice but for him the Nazi idea of naturalism, of raising the idea of the people above everything else, was the root of the problem.[110] Considering that Wieacker himself had been an integral part of the same Nazi jurisprudence, these passages may be read in two ways – either as indirect self-criticism or as distancing himself from his previous actions.

The themes Wieacker outlined in the *Privatrechtsgeschichte* were further developed in an article on the origins of European legal consciousness in 1956. There, he made a clear statement against English-language scholarship and its claims to represent the Western tradition. In contrast, Wieacker argued that the European tradition had three constitutive elements: 1) the concept of law and legal order which derived from the *imperium Romanum*; 2) the continuity of these and their unique relationship with metaphysics and social ethics was the work of the church; and 3) the vitality and will to develop social and state structures should be credited to the Germans. Though there were many subsequent developments, such as the idea of freedom, these were more in the nature of sediments that accumulated on top of these foundations.[111]

Even here Wieacker returns to the issue of natural law, positivism and the problem of tyrants. While in all ages there had been tyrants, positivistic thought held no distinction between a law and an unjust law as long as formal criteria were fulfilled, a reference to the postwar criticism of Kelsen and Radbruch. The problem with naturalism was that if one changed the yardstick, the protection offered would be nullified. The only solution, and here Wieacker would make a strange excursus into Chinese thought, is the higher community of law. What he envisions is a feeling, a community and experience that would transcend not only abstract principles but also demagoguery and political conferences. In short, what he calls for is the appreciation of the tradition of European legal thought and its long constitutive force.[112]

110 Joachim Rückert, "Der Rechtsbegriff der Deutschen Rechtsgeschichte in der NS-Zeit: der Sieg des 'Lebens' und des konkreten Ordnungsdenkens, seine Vorgeschichte und seine Nachwirkungen," in Joachim Rückert and Dietmar Willoweit (eds.), *Die Deutsche Rechtsgeschichte in der NS-Zeit ihre Vorgeschichte und ihre Nachwirkungen* (Tübingen: Mohr Siebeck, 1995), pp. 180–181.

111 Wieacker, "Ursprünge und Elemente des europäischen Rechtbewusstseins." Franz Wieacker, *Vulgarismus und Klassizismus im Recht der Spätantike* (Heidelberg: C. Winter, 1955), p. 63 shows the same idea in a nutshell.

112 Wieacker, "Ursprünge und Elemente des europäischen Rechtbewusstseins," pp. 115–118.

In a 1963 essay on the continuing impact of ancient legal culture on the European world, he returns to the themes of organic succession and inheritance from antiquity to the present in ways that are surprisingly similar to those presented in 1944 in *Vom römischen Recht.* Aside from the transmission of learning, he takes up the issues of administrative practices and their continuities, for example the idea of impersonal magistracy and its material capabilities that is central to the Western idea of the state. Wieacker claims that though there had been Oriental, Hellenistic and Roman precedents, the true inventors of the magistracies were the Byzantine centralized monarchies, which developed the hierarchical administrative structures necessary for this to operate. What then followed was the long dispute between the Roman and Germanic concepts of magistracies, the first focusing on their material scope, the second on the person of the magistrate.[113]

This idea of history as a long process of tradition formation was best outlined in the second edition of the *Privatrechtsgeschichte* (1967, English translation 1995). The second edition was twice as long as the first but contained largely the same historical outline. Wieacker's theoretical framework in this edition is best defined as continuity. Continuity here means the continuing process of interaction between old and new law, responses to the ancient traditions and so forth. He wishes to overcome simplistic notions like influence or inheritance in favor of a more complex and nuanced idea of organic development. Wieacker again resorts to biological analogies of the transmission of life between generations as a model for legal tradition.[114]

We do not need to revisit Wieacker's historical narrative from antiquity to the present day, but what is interesting in the second edition is the way he comes back to the criticism of positivism and naturalistic ideas of suprapositive norms. Wieacker is fundamentally critical of the idea of constitutional guarantees and fundamental rights and considers them ultimately useless as safeguards. What use is a constitutional guarantee if the whole constitution might be negated and put on hold? He is equally critical of the introduction of values and interests, having seen how they too could be turned

[113] Franz Wieacker, "Die Fortwirkung der antiken Rechtskulturen in der europäischen Welt," in *Vom Recht* (Hannover: Niedersächsische zentrale für Politische Bildung, 1963), p. 83.

[114] Wieacker, *History of Private Law in Europe*, pp. 25–26; Wieacker, *Privatrechtsgeschichte der Neuzeit*, (1967), pp. 43–44.

into tools of repression.[115] The condemnation of legal positivism, present already in the first edition, became stronger and his choice of wordings even more pronounced. In the section quoted above, for example, many passages lack scholarly detachment. Elsewhere in the text, naturalism is replaced by a reference to purposive legislation and "secret laws," dictators are mentioned and the practice of executing petty thieves because the metal they stole was needed for war is added.[116]

As a consequence, Wieacker points out, all should be extremely wary whenever someone uses good intentions as arguments in constitutional debates, even for innocent or desirable purposes.[117] This is an argument that Wieacker would develop during the postwar period. In 1957 in Karlsruhe he gave a lecture to judges of the German supreme constitutional court about judges and the law when legal order is outside the law. Wieacker underlined the ethical responsibility of the practicing lawyer to maintain the limits of the law because an interpretation that was too loose or too purpose oriented would lead to dangerous precedents.[118] This was a not too subtle reference to the Nazi idea of political will being the sole legal criterion as well as the dangers of general principles raised earlier by Pringsheim.

The fact that the Nazi past would be taken up in earnest only in the 1967 second edition comes as no surprise. While the Nazi past had been swiftly forgotten after the enthusiasm for denazification subsided, a new generation of students were not willing to let such memory loss take place. Radical students confronted their teachers about the Nazi years and led debates about what had happened and why, forcing the resignation of Nazi professors such as Forsthoff.[119] In 1968 Bernd Rüthers demolished the myth that judges were largely innocent about

[115] Wieacker, *History of Private Law in Europe*, pp. 444–460; Wieacker, *Privatrechtsgeschichte der Neuzeit*, (1967), pp. 559–585.

[116] Wieacker, *History of Private Law in Europe*, p. 461; Wieacker, *Privatrechtsgeschichte der Neuzeit*, (1967), pp. 585–586.

[117] Wieacker, *History of Private Law in Europe*, p. 461. Even before the Nazi years this idea was presented by none other than Hedemann, *Die Flucht in die Generalklauseln*.

[118] Franz Wieacker, *Gesetz und Richterkunst. Zum Problem der außergesetzlichen Rechtsordnung* (Karlsruhe: Verlag C. F. Müller, 1958); Liebs, "Franz Wieacker," p. 40.

[119] Moses, *German Intellectuals*, pp. 186–218; Erkkilä, *Conceptual Change of Conscience*, pp. 8–9, 260–267 notes that for Wieacker the 1960s was a time of self-reflection and self-criticism.

Nazi crimes, being victims of legal positivism that meant that they were bound to follow the law regardless of its content.[120]

What Wieacker raises as a solution is the idea of legal conscience, the unique and distinctive mandate of justice concerning the conduct one adopts in relation to others.[121] The attack on legal positivism can be traced in part to the postwar theories of Radbruch that traced the roots and the blame for the legal nihilism of the Nazi years to excessive positivism.[122]

Much like Koschaker, Wieacker would return to the figure of Savigny time and again, in a way that may be seen as both analytical and normative. On the other hand, he engages with the historical Savigny and his context, but on the other, the relentless focus on Savigny and the Historical School served to legitimate the role of history in jurisprudence.[123] The narrative of the Historical School was in many ways a vehicle through which to discuss the importance of history to law. In contrast to many others, Wieacker considered Hugo's importance at best marginal, while Savigny is raised onto a pedestal. Following Koschaker, Wieacker downplayed the fundamental difference between the Historical School and the natural law thinkers which had been Savigny's main claim. In fact, both Wieacker and Koschaker discussed learned law, *Professorenrecht*, emanating from the writings of the professors of law, and both had Roman law as their main source. He was equally critical of Puchta and his attempt at a conceptual balancing between the systematic and the historical approach. However, the true difference between Koschaker's and Wieacker's vision of the history of law was the interpretation of the period between 1880 and 1930. For Koschaker, the codification process and the enactment of the BGB started a downward slide for scholarship on Roman law, a fall from which it never recovered. In contrast, to Wieacker the period between 1880 and 1930 was the pioneering age, where studies

[120] Rüthers, *Die Unbegrenzte Auslegung*; Stolleis, *Law under the Swastika*, pp. 8–9; Jerry Z. Muller, *The Other God that Failed: Hans Freyer and the Deradicalization of German Conservatism* (Princeton, NJ: Princeton University Press, 1987) expanded this criticism to the legal profession in general.

[121] Wieacker, *History of Private Law in Europe*, pp. 478–481.

[122] Landau, "Wieackers Konzept," p. 71; Gustav Radbruch, "Gesetzliches unrecht und übergesetzliches Recht," *Süddeutsche Juristenzeitung*, 1 (1946), 105.

[123] Franz Wieacker, *Gründer und Bewahrer. Rechtslehrer der neueren deutschen Privatrechtsgeschichte* (Göttingen: Vandenhoeck & Ruprecht, 1959); Franz Wieacker, "Friedrich Carl von Savigny," in Hermann Heimpel (ed.), *Die grossen Deutschen III* (Berlin: Ullstein, 1956), pp. 39–51.

followed a common agenda of the historification of normative interpretations, setting them in their historical contexts and the combination of legal and historical knowledge.[124]

At the same time as Wieacker was rewriting the history of the European legal tradition, he was actively engaged in debates about the history of ancient Roman law. Only later would he write his magnum opus about Roman legal history but throughout the years his works would reflect the ongoing reevaluation of the Roman tradition and its role in the development of legal science. For instance, in his 1969 article on the work of the Roman jurist Quintus Mucius Scaevola, Wieacker dismissed the earlier interpretations that Quintus Mucius would have begun the systematic study of law through the adoption of Greek scientific methods. According to Wieacker, the debate shows more the preoccupation that has reigned about the role of the Greek and Roman heritages in Western legal tradition, namely the need to pursue theories in which the origins of the tradition would extend to the ancient Romans.[125]

Stolleis has noted that even though the Nazi propaganda and the attacks on Roman law were a threat to the study of Roman law, it also produced something positive. The criticism that social realities and political circumstances had been neglected proved to be an impulse that led Roman law scholars to new ways of inquiry and resulted in a new image of Roman law.[126] This may be the case but one wonders whether the social scientific turn which reached the historical sciences in the 1960s would not have had the same result.

Wieacker's central contribution to the narrative of European law and the reorientation of scholarship to the "foundations of European legal culture" are best summarized in his article in the *American Journal of Comparative Law* in 1990. In the introduction, Wieacker presents a defense of the law against claims of repressiveness and oppression by Marxist and postcolonialist critics but soon takes up the unity of European legal culture. What he defines as Europe is in fact quite telling: Wieacker's Europe is the wider Atlantic–European world, including

[124] Franz Wieacker, *Römische Rechtsgeschichte I* (Munich: C. H. Beck, 1988), pp. 45, 49–51; Wieacker, *History of Private Law in Europe*, pp. 284–302, 316–318; Koschaker, *Europa*, pp. 269, 275–291.

[125] Franz Wieacker, "Uber das Verhaltnis der romischen Fachjurisprudenz zur griechisch-hellenistischen Theorie," *Iura*, 20 (1969), 460–469.

[126] Stolleis, "'Fortschritte der Rechtsgeschichte' in der Zeit des Nationalsozialismus?" p. 188.

even the offshoots of European culture as far as the antipodes. After a brief nod to the distinctiveness of the common law system, Wieacker takes up the familiar themes of historical development from Rome to the middle ages and onwards. The role of the church is underlined in developing the "modern" traits of European legal culture but the true hero of the narrative is the autonomous legal science of jurists. The story then culminates in the "essential constants of European legal culture": personalism, legalism and intellectualism. Personalism meant the primacy of the individual in law, as the subject, end and point of reference. Individual association and individual relationship with deities produced the same results as the emphasis on freedom and self-determination. Based on these ideas, Wieacker explains why the emphasis on freedoms and thus rights is so pervasive in European legal culture.

The principle of legalism rested on the exclusive power of the legal rule over others, in the way that relationships are objectified through law and law is separated from social and ethical norms. Legalism was introduced along with the idea of rationalism, the strict removal of law from the ideas of social equality. The final principle was that of intellectualism, where legal science is just that, a science where systematic and conceptual reasoning rules.[127]

The narrative created by Wieacker has some peculiarities that are not really reducible to any particular scholarly choice. For example, the decision to limit observations almost solely to the civilian tradition dating to Bologna is odd. This omits, for example, nearly all of the canon law tradition.[128]

The concept of culture was a key element in the postwar discussions, where the idea of culture and the *Kulturnation* were utilized as touchstones of German identity. Culture could be the one clean sphere where German achievement and superiority could be safely touted. For democrats and conservatives alike, resorting to Goethe gave them a neutral way of describing values and national identity.[129]

To Wieacker, the grand narrative of the development of law from antiquity to the modern day was clearly a historical development

[127] Franz Wieacker, "Foundations of European legal culture," *The American Journal of Comparative Law*, 38 (1) (1990), 1–29. This is a translation of his earlier essay titled "Voraussetzungen europäischer Rechtskultur," presented originally in Helsinki in 1983. The essay was translated and introduced by Bodenheimer, himself an exile.

[128] Landau, "Wieackers Konzept," pp. 57–58.

[129] Forner, *German Intellectuals*, pp. 119–120.

that encompassed the legal profession and its evolution. Wieacker had little understanding of the ideas presented, for instance, by Koschaker about the legal dogmatic continuity from the past to the present but emphasized that law was a living culture not some sort of textual transmission. This same conception guided his reservations and resistance to both the renaissance of natural law and legal positivism. Both were easily circumvented by unscrupulous interpreters working for totalitarian rulers, either by raising another superior principle over that of human dignity or by simply stopping the constitution from being applied. The only lasting value was the legal conscience, the internal conviction of lawyers in maintaining law and justice.

## Conclusions

It may be surprising that the most influential book about the new narrative of European legal history and the shared legal heritage was published by a card-carrying member of the Nazi party who had actively participated in the ideological work of the new Nazi legal science. On closer inspection, it is less surprising. There are several reasons for this: one being strong continuities on ideas about Europe, the impetus for change being shared by former Nazis and conceptions about legal science were jointly held at this time.

While his involvement in the Nazi movement has been explained as a nominal membership, Franz Wieacker joined the movement early on and found friends and a common purpose in the reform of German law according to the new principles. This was true despite his *Doktorvater* Fritz Pringsheim being persecuted by the regime and the obvious contradictions between the teachings of the movement and the ideals of law. However, there were strong continuities, for after the war most former Nazis continued to serve as professors despite their earlier activities. Moreover, especially after Operation Barbarossa and the war on the Eastern Front had begun, the Nazi movement began a strong push toward Europeanism. The Nazi conceptions of Europe were of course united against communism and perceived Jewish ideas and took advantage of Christian cultural theories of European civilization. This meant that even after the war, promotion of the Europeanist ideas fell on receptive ground.

Wieacker served in the German army during the war, from the Polish campaign to the North Italian battles in 1945. Especially during the last months of the war battles took the form of annihilation: over a million German soldiers died during the last five months of the war in Europe. That leaves a mark. When the war ended, Wieacker's home had been destroyed and his university had been taken over by Soviet occupiers. Ending up in Göttingen, Wieacker considered himself to be an exile as well.

Finally, Wieacker's conception of law and legal science, especially the role given to tradition and Roman law, was never a good fit with the Nazi party ideology. Even during the war, he wrote about Roman law as the foundation of Western thinking on law and the state and about the idea of legal science as a cumulative process taking place within the legal profession. Legal rationalism, the idea of an autonomous science unconnected with politics and ideology, was diametrically opposed to Nazi ideas on law as an extension of politics.

The great achievement of Wieacker was, without doubt, the *Privatrechtsgeschichte*. It tied together the conception of European legal science with the idea of its shared roots in the Roman past. It is a book about law as a science, ultimately, a book about the noble past. Behrends, for instance, noted how Wieacker built the link between early modern legal concepts and the idea of the reception of the Greek ideas of concept and system into Roman jurisprudence into a model of how law should be.[130] Thus, the Greco-Roman origin story was in its simplest form a mandate for the future, an idea of what the European legal tradition both is and should be.

However, the narrative formulated by Wieacker was the result of two competing and mutually hostile traditions: one representing the ideas of autonomous jurisprudence as a scientific pursuit; the other seeing law as a component of social, political and cultural order. It would be facile to claim that this would have been a battle between the influences of Pringsheim and Schmitt because the elements that formed Wieacker's thinking are much more complex. There was, for example, his ongoing fixation with Savigny, which provided a completely different reading than the one presented by Koschaker. For Wieacker, Savigny had successfully bridged the chasm between the science of law, the Roman law tradition and the demands of

[130] Behrends, "Franz Wieacker. Historiker und Jurist des Privatrechts," p. 2343.

contemporary society and its Germanic foundations. Riccobono also exerted a strong influence and contributed to his vision of the long continuity of the legal tradition from antiquity to the present day. The group formed by his friends in the *Kieler Schule*, moreover, were a powerful presence both socially and intellectually, compelling him to adopt a sensitivity toward social and political realities. Schmitt and Gadamer, as well as Weber, led him in a more theoretical direction from strictly legal beginnings.

One should not overestimate the influence of the Nazi thinking in Wieacker, though there were other important issues which contributed to his ideas. Beyond the initial stage of the first years of the Nazi revolution, his time in Kiel and Frankfurt, the pull of Nazi theories diminish and by the time of his wartime writings, he begins to formulate his idea of reception. In and by themselves, many of his works begin to undermine the official Nazi policy of criticizing Roman law influences.

The concept of reception and its reformulation with the hermeneutical theories of interpretation formed the foundation of the concept of the Western legal tradition as outlined in the *Privatrechtsgeschichte*. With Betti and Gadamer, Wieacker engaged in a long debate over what the difference between historical and legal interpretation meant, especially in the case of the legal tradition. In the case of reception, the concept of rationality and its advancement became a thread through which legal science would develop.

In addition to his personal involvement with the Nazi movement, the approach that Wieacker developed proved to be well suited to another Nazi-era invention, the reform of law studies. The narrative of the *Privatrechtsgeschichte* was drafted to correspond to a course of the same name in the study plan. This had a crucial significance because it gave the book an instant audience and selling point. Thus it could be said that the Nazi revolution gave him both a position at the university and a platform upon which to present his ideas.

Despite this, the turn toward Europe after the war ended was not a given. The *Privatrechtsgeschichte* was a postwar book that incorporated both old and new, appealing to both former Nazis, which were still in numerous in academia, as well as the demands of the new political situation. Wieacker himself was rehabilitated as a minor player and through his connections joined the academic community. In this community of silence, being a former member of the Nazi legal academia may even have been an asset.

The turn toward Europe, much like the turn toward democracy and the rule of law, may be seen as an external factor, one of the circumstances which scholars would need to adapt to. Here, the will to belong worked in the opposite direction as it had done in the 1930s, leading not only Wieacker but also most of the legal academia to discover the shared roots of European legal science.

# 6 The European Narrative and the Tradition of Rights


## Abstract

This chapter approaches the reconfiguring of the legal tradition through the work of Helmut Coing and his idea of the tradition of rights as a jurisprudential construct. This is contextualized through the rise of the rights tradition in human rights scholarship and the central role that human rights came to have in the initial stages of the European project. This emphasis, resulting in the creation of the European Convention of Human Rights, was mirrored by the commitment of the new German state to democracy and rights. The chapter concludes with an analysis of the spread of the European narrative about the role of Roman law and its greatest proponents, among them Reinhard Zimmermann.


## Introduction

For all the writings about a European legal tradition or European legal culture in the works of such scholars as Koschaker or Wieacker, among researchers today there is a clear agreement that no such singular tradition or culture actually existed. The idea, present in literature from World War II onward and in almost every textbook of European legal history, that there would have been a shared legal culture at some point in European history, is considered to be wishful thinking at best, a historical invention promoted for the benefit of contemporary needs. What one may talk about, with some confidence even, are legal traditions that may or may not be reduced to a central principle. Within the European legal tradition, they are often reduced to two competing alternatives: natural law and cultural theories. The ideas of natural law and the concept of legal culture are broadly speaking related to the concepts of universalism and particularism. The first of these traditions, that of universal natural law, gained prominence during the French Revolution: it includes elements such as the universal rights of man, British theories of rights, the nascent human rights movement of the 1930s and so forth. The second, the cultural theory, was based on the ideas of romanticism that were given legal form by authors like F. C. von Savigny or Jacob Grimm. They saw law as part of culture and spoke of a Germanic legal culture.[1]

How the division between the two has been made is unclear and depends on the people making these definitions but one critical issue is noticeable. The tradition of universal rights has more often been emphasized in discussions through public law or the relationship between the individual and the state, whereas the emphasis on legal culture is present in discussions on private law.

Within the German discourse of 1933–1945, the disputes over tradition took on very curious overtones as Nazi legal thought sought to present itself as an alternative to the liberal order. Even in *Mein Kampf*, Hitler lambasted the false equality of the French Revolution as the root cause of the Jewish menace. People simply did not know their place. In its stead Nazi thinkers offered community, the orderly dignity of a culture based on race. However, Nazi thought was very much against the idea of tradition as long as that tradition was based on Roman law. In fact, Nazi thought contained much in the way of social progressivism, reformism and the idea of sweeping away the old order.[2] In contrast, after the war a veritable renaissance of interest in natural law emerged parallel with the emergence of modern human rights thought.

The traditional narrative of Roman law and European legal history was very much a conservative narrative of tradition and continuity, where culture and belonging formed the basis of the legal system. Its roots lay in romanticist thought and the Historical School, but in order to gain larger acceptance, it needed to break out of that model. Wieacker argued that a tradition began in the Roman period where jurists would have developed the law autonomously and that autonomy and self-guidance was the root of its claim to be the true European legal heritage. In contrast, Coing sought to extend this tradition further,

[1] This notion underlies most textbooks of European legal history.

[2] On the juxtaposition of Nazi thought and the notions of rights and dignity, see Whitman, "On Nazi honor and the new European dignity"; Rüthers, *Die Unbegrenzte Auslegung*, pp. 336–351.

maintaining that the tradition of rights was equally derived from Roman law heritage.

The purpose of this chapter is to analyze this dichotomy between culture and rights through the thinking of Helmut Coing (1912–2000), one of the most influential legal historians in postwar Europe, who in his early works attempted to combine the historical and the natural law tradition into one. In these works, Coing fused together the emphasis on freedom and rights, while grounding them in a narrative of culture and tradition.[3] A medievalist, Coing built his impressive post-WWII career on the basis of the idea of European legal history, as a researcher and as long-time director of the Max Planck Institute for European Legal History. The main question is how Coing pivoted from a fairly traditional conservative position both toward human rights and European legal heritage.

The reinterpretation of tradition also had real-life consequences. Coing was one of the persons who acted as adviser to important EU officials such as Walter Hallstein. Hallstein was a friend of Coing's, who became the president of the EEC commission. He was enthusiastic about the potential of law and legal tradition as a unifying factor in Europe and saw in law a cultural force that would create a European community.[4]

One of the enduring issues about the spread of the idea of a tradition of rights as the foundation of European legal heritage is the impact of transatlantic influences, especially those of exiled scholars after WWII. We will explore this through the examples of scholars such as Neumann and Strauss, who became influential both in the US and Germany in the postwar years. Another parallel process was the spread of human rights thought after 1948 and the creation of the European Convention on Human Rights. This process, spearheaded by conservative politicians such as Winston Churchill, led to a particular emphasis on political rights. I will also analyze the spread of European narratives about the role of Roman law in conjunction with the deepening of European integration. Central figures in this respect are Reinhard Zimmermann

[3] Coing, "Zum Einfluss der Philosophie des Aristoteles auf die Entwicklung des römisches Rechts"; Coing, "Römisches Recht in Deutschland"; Coing, "Die ursprüngliche Einheit der europäischen Rechtswissenschaft."

[4] *Thomas Duve, "European legal history – global perspectives," Max Planck Institute for European Legal History Research Paper Series*, No. 2013-06 (2013), p. 9. Available at SSRN: https://ssrn.com/abstract=2292666 or http://dx.doi.org/10.2139/ssrn.2292666.

and a number of continental legal historians, who spread the idea of a European tradition as a model for the future.[5]

Despite Coing's importance in the shift toward rights and a common European heritage in the postwar discussions, he has not been studied to any great extent. One partial explanation is that Coing did not leave much of an archive beyond the official papers stored at the Max Planck Gesellschaft. The most interesting part of the archive is an autobiography composed in the early 1990s,[6] of which an edited version has recently been published.[7] A couple of recent articles, such as by Duve (2013), trace Coing's importance to the turn in legal history toward Europe.[8] Lena Foljanty has traced the role of Coing in the resurgence of natural law in postwar Germany.[9] This chapter is mostly based on Coing's published works, with some references to the correspondence between Coing and his colleagues. The reason for this is that there is very little in the way of archival material relating to Coing's early years.[10]

Coing started out as a typical product of the nationalistic bourgeoisie, an intellectual and a reserve officer, someone who would have easily fitted into both the Wilhelmine Empire as well as postwar West Germany. His career may be defined as one of an opportunist but behind the façade it is evident that the Nazi years had taken their toll. What

[5] Zimmermann, *Roman Law, Contemporary Law, European Law.*

[6] Archiv der Max-Planck-Gesellschaft, Berlin, Abteilung III, Repositur 103 (NL Helmut Coing 1912–2000), 21–1: Autobiographie Coing. There is also a minor official archive at the Bibliothek des Max-Planck-Instituts für europäische Rechtsgeschichte, Frankfur (NL Coing – MPI – Dritte Mappe).

[7] Coing, *Für Wissenschaften und Künste.*

[8] Of the obituaries, the most substantial were Klaus Luig, "Helmut Coing (28.2.1912–15.8.2000)," *Zeitschrift der Savigny-Stiftung für Rechtsgeschichte: Romanistische Abteilung*, 119 (2002), 662–678 and Dieter Simon, "Zwischen Wissenschaft und Wissenschaftspolitik: HelmutCoing (28.2.1912–15.8.2000)," *Neue Juristische Wochenschrift*, 54 (2001), 1029–1032. On the historical side, see also Dieter Nörr, "Über das Geistige im Recht: ein Nachruf auf Helmut Coing," *Juristenzeitung*, 56 (2001), 449–452; Michael Stolleis, "Helmut Coing 28.2.1912–15.8.2000," *Jahrbuch der Max-Planck-Gesellschaft*, (2001), 873–874. Most recently Coing's role has been explored by Thomas Duve, "Von der Europäischen Rechtsgeschichte zu einer Rechtsgeschichte Europas in globalhistorischer Perspektive (From a European legal history towards a legal history of Europe in a global historical perspective)," *Rechtsgeschichte Legal History. Zeitschrift des Max Planck-Instituts für Europaische Rechtsgeschichte*, 20 (2012), 18–71. Available at SSRN: https://ssrn.com/abstract=2139312 and Duve, "European legal history – global perspectives."

[9] Lena Foljanty, *Recht oder Gesetz: Juristische Identität und Autorität in den Naturrechtsdebatten der Nachkriegszeit* (Tübingen: Mohr Siebeck, 2013), pp. 175–224.

[10] Coing's extant papers are in the archives of the Max Planck Society. Archiv der Max-Planck-Gesellschaft, Berlin, Abteilung III, Repositur 103 (NL Helmut Coing 1912–2000).

Coing's trajectory shows is first a drift toward nationalistic historiography, followed by the postwar turn to natural law and finally a return to tradition and Europe.

## Toward a Postwar Reckoning

The end of the war led to a number of different academic outcomes, to put it mildly, both on a disciplinary and on an individual level. In the case of the two traditions on the origins of rights, the Germanic theory of law and culture was unsurprisingly shunned due to its links with the Nazi regime. Along with the discrediting of Nazi jurisprudence and Nazi jurists, there was equally a backlash against theories of ultranationalism. The unfortunate collateral damage was the field of *Germanistik*, the history of German law, which had become tainted by association with Nazi theories. However, this extended to individual scholars only on a very selective basis.

For scholars who had participated in the intellectual pursuits of the Nazi era, the postwar period was one of cleansing of reputations and offering apologies and explanations for prior positions. As we saw in Chapter 5, the processes of rehabilitation were fairly uniform: innumerable scholars were processed through the various systems of *Spruchkammern* and other organizations. In these processes, character statements from colleagues were sought and evidence in different forms was presented. In practice, the defense sought to demonstrate that the accused might not have been a real Nazi after all, but rather had joined after coercion or persuasion. There was even an association for the perceived "victims of denazification."[11]

For most of the accused, the process of denazification was relatively short, mostly due to the enormous scale of the process and the will to focus on the worst offenders. For Coing, the entire process of denazification is unremarkable. Though autobiographies are notoriously unreliable as evidence, it would appear that he was never an openly political person. In his autobiography, the nuances of the description of his relationship with the Nazi party are revealing in that they describe a long gradual development. At first, he describes his upbringing as a child in a conservative family that had roots in the Protestant

[11] Michael Stolleis, "Reluctance to glance in the mirror: the changing face of German jurisprudence after 1933 and post-1945," in Joerges and Ghaleigh, *Darker Legacies of Law in Europe*, p. 6.

Huguenots. Coing's family and its social circle belonged to the *Bildungsbürgertum*, which meant according to Coing that all family acquaintances were public servants, teachers, officers and the like. The men were NCOs or officers in the reserve, as was typical of the class. His father had died as an officer in World War I. Coing himself would follow the same path as the majority of his family, into academia and, at the same time, into voluntary military service, leading to a position in the peacetime reserves in the infantry, where he developed lasting bonds (*Kameradschaft*) with his fellow soldiers. This outline of his autobiography is mirrored by the obituaries written soon after his death, which emphasize that he belonged to a class of public servants where loyalty and service were valued.[12]

In his autobiography, Coing describes his realization of the coming Nazi takeover while witnessing a SA parade through the small university town of Göttingen. His membership of the Nazi party is never mentioned directly, he simply externalizes it by noting how he was preparing to defend his thesis when an older professor told him that all doctors within the law faculty should be members of the party. The fact that Coing was only twenty years old when the Nazis took power (and thirty-three when the war ended) partially explains why his involvement in the movement did not present a considerable change from his previous commitments. Whether or not he was a party member is something of an open question. Feldkamp notes that as a student Helmut Coing held a NSDAP party card in 1933 but as an officer he would not have needed to be a member in order to have a career.[13]

Coing defended his thesis in law at Göttingen in 1935 with Wolfgang Kunkel about the reformation in Frankfurt, continuing with a habilitation thesis with medieval historian Erich Genzmer at the University of Frankfurt, completing it in 1938. The habilitation thesis on the reception of Roman law in Frankfurt was Coing's first work to gain wider attention, and it is cited by Wieacker as an example of the continuing role of Roman law in legal science.[14]

[12] Coing, *Für Wissenschaften und Künste*, pp. 13–55; Luig, "Helmut Coing," pp. 662–663.

[13] Coing himself does not say anything about his own possible membership but remarks on his admiration for those who opposed the Nazis, such as Genzmer. Feldkamp notes that in the registers of the party, of which 80 percent are preserved, Coing is not mentioned. Coing, *Für Wissenschaften und Künste*, pp. 45–47, 56–57.

[14] Coing, Für Wissenschaften und Künste, pp. 41–52; Helmut Coing, *Die Rezeption des römischen Rechts in Frankfurt am Main. Ein Betrag zur Rezeptionsgeschichte* (Frankfurt: Vittorio Klostermann, 1962 [1939]).

During the war, Coing was on the front lines with his unit, serving in both the attack on France in 1940 and the Eastern front, reaching the rank of captain. He was most likely saved by a transfer. A week before his unit was sent to Stalingrad, he was assigned as an adjutant officer and moved to a new unit. This experience and the loss of his friends was clearly traumatic to Coing.[15]

At the end of the war, Coing was made a prisoner of war on the Western front and ended up in a camp in France. He was released from the POW camp in September 1945 and returned to his position at the University of Frankfurt, where he was made full professor in 1948.[16]

Although official documents on Coing no longer exist, we do have some information about his prewar activities. Coing participated, with many other academics, in the training camps (*Referendarlager*) organized by the Nazis, where healthy outdoor activities were combined with academic discussions about the new order (see Figure 5.2). Coing was an enthusiastic participant, spending two months in a camp in 1938, where he was praised for his academic excellence.[17]

In short, Coing was not a natural champion for European legal heritage based on rights. He started out as a conservative, possibly a card-carrying member of the Nazi party, working in a field where Nazi influence was strong. He was clearly a conservative academic from a conservative background. However, it is equally clear how strong an impact the experience of war had on him and the traumatic consequences it had.

## The Rise of Natural Law and Rights Theories?

Although the reasons for it were rarely openly discussed, the end of the war signaled a crucial change in legal scholarship with the emergence of natural law and ideas of human rights and universalism. Unlike the majority of his colleagues, Coing would later reflect on the intellectual turns in his life. For example, in his autobiography, Coing mentions how the end of the war and the realization what unfettered power could do inspired him to take up natural law again. Similarly, Stolleis wrote

[15] Coing, *Für Wissenschaften und Künste*, pp. 59–74.
[16] Coing, *Für Wissenschaften und Künste*, pp. 74–75.
[17] Folker Schmerbach, *Das "Gemeinschaftslager Hanns Kerrl" für Referendare in Jüterbog 1933–1939* (Tübingen: Mohr Siebeck, 2008), pp. 127–128; Coing, *Für Wissenschaften und Künste*, p. 54.

how Western values of idealism and natural law were the only possible path after the Nazis. Natural law would be the only bulwark against violence and political power. Coing was not alone in returning to natural law and it is possible to talk about a renaissance of natural law studies in Germany after WWII. As noted in Chapter 5, the issue was also hotly contested and Wieacker, for instance, continued to reject the premise that natural law would have been an effective foil to tyranny.[18]

During the Nazi years natural law was a contested issue among those who resisted the Nazis. Although Fraenkel and Neumann took divergent paths, for both of them natural law provided the justification for resistance. This was a crucial change for Neumann, who had earlier sought to present natural law as inherently conservative and against the interests of the left. While Neumann sought to build his criticism of Nazi law through classical liberalism, Fraenkel resorted to rational natural law, drawing from the religious resistance of sects such as Jehovah's Witnesses the importance of conscience. For both of them, natural law was not an easy fit, due to its religious and class connotations. However, the incorporation of the universal idea of reason and the liberal rule of law allowed them to have the benefits of natural law without elevating an ethical value system above the law. Both would ultimately embrace the idea of the liberal rule of law and democracy as a way of securing the values of equality, liberty and security against the threat of totalitarianism.[19]

However, when Coing or his peers begin to talk about rights, they approach it in a very different way than what one might do in the Anglo-American or French traditions. For them, rights were seen to be

[18] Coing, *Für Wissenschaften und Künste*, p. 140; Luig, "Helmut Coing," p. 664; Stolleis, "Reluctance to glance in the mirror," p. 2; Kristian Kühl, "Rückblick auf die Renaissance des Naturrechts nach dem Zweiten Weltkrieg," in Gerhard Köblerl, Meinhard Heinze and Jan Schapp (eds.), *Geschichtliche Rechtswissenschaft: ars tradendo innovandoque aequitatem sectandi; Freundesgabe für Alfred Söllner zum 60. Geburtstag am 5.2.1990. Giessener rechtswissenschaftliche Abhandlungen, Bd. 6* (Brühl: Giessen, 1990), pp. 331–357; Foljanty, *Recht oder Gesetz.*

[19] On this, see Douglas Morris, "Write and resist: Ernst Fraenkel and Franz Neumann on the role of natural law in fighting Nazi tyranny," *New German Critique*, 126 (2015), 197–230. The dilemma that natural law represented to progressives is evident in Kerwin's review of Fraenkel's *Dual State*, where he points out how the earlier progressive rejection of natural law was enthusiastically embraced by Nazi theorists, who used it to prove that their racial theory was correct. Jerome G. Kerwin, "Review of the Dual State: a contribution to the theory of dictatorship. By Ernst Fraenkel. New York: Oxford University Press, 1940" *The University of Chicago Law Review*, 8 (1941), 616–618.

inherent in humanity itself through natural law and only secondarily guaranteed in constitutions, declarations and conventions. Coing wished to lay the foundations for a third way of approaching rights and natural law. First, one would begin the inquiry through the origins within the tradition; in the case of Coing, this meant returning to Donellus, a French legal humanist of the sixteenth century. Second, in Coing's early works, there was no talk of the rights of man, either in the French or the American sense, or even the UN Declaration of Human Rights. In his 1950 speech on human rights theory, Coing maintained that the German tradition of natural law scholarship had always omitted the political meaning of human rights.[20] From the modern perspective, this amounted to a very peculiar tradition of rights, one that was quite distinct from either the French or the transatlantic tradition of rights.[21]

Despite this omission, in 1947 Coing would write an important work on the responsibility of judges in cases where natural law was violated. This was a convoluted way of referring to cases during the Nazi years where judges had sentenced people to death based on the Nazi laws of treason. As these laws were clearly against natural law, could the judge be held accountable if he applied unjust law? For Coing, the ethical obligation of the judge was to resist but whether he could be punished was another matter.[22]

In the same year, Coing published a curious small book on legal philosophy titled "The Highest Foundations of Law" (*Die obersten Grundsätze des Rechts. Ein Versuch zur Neugründung des Naturrechts,* 1947). In it, he addressed the problem of statutory law and power. The book is a peculiar attempt at combining natural law and statutory law and by extension legal positivism, by demonstrating how natural law

[20] Coing, *Die Rezeption des römischen Rechts*, pp. 63–67. The idea of Donellus's derivation of rights, including rights to life, liberty, property, from Roman law has been picked up by authors such as Stein, *Roman Law in European History*, pp. 82–83.

[21] On the competing and sometimes contradictory origin stories of human rights and their evolution, see Samuel Moyn, *The Last Utopia: Human Rights in History* (Cambridge, MA: Belknap Press of Harvard University Press, 2010), pp. 17–43.

[22] Helmut Coing, "Zur Frage der strafrechtlichen Haftung der Richter für die Anwendung naturrechtswidriger Gesetze," *Süddeutsche Juristenzeitung*, 2 (1947b), 61–64. This was a response to the article by Gustav Radbruch in the previous year (Radbruch, "Gesetzliches unrecht und übergesetzliches Recht"); Helmut Coing, "Der Jurist und das unsittliche Gesetz," in *Gesammelte Aufsätze, Band 2. Naturrecht als wissenschaftliches Problem* (Wiesbaden: Franz Steiner Verlag, 1965), pp. 50–66; Helmut Coing, *Naturrecht als wissenschaftliches Problem* (Wiesbaden: F. Steiner, 1966 [1965]). On these, see Luig, "Helmut Coing," p. 665.

principles are embedded in the legal system. In it, values and ideals shared in the culture gained legal form. Using examples such as the BGB §242 about good faith and justice, Coing seeks to demonstrate how much the law has elements that are not reducible to the text of the law.

In the beginning of the book, Coing describes it as a new foundation of natural law after what had just happened. It is noteworthy that the Nazi regime or its perversion of justice are not mentioned, in a manner typical of the era, beyond a very oblique reference. The issue is stated as obvious: while natural law had for a long time been neglected and met with skepticism, now it had become obvious that legal science should free itself from legal positivism and turn to a new concept of law based on the idea of law. It had become clear that only natural law was able to respond to the challenge of political power and raw violence.[23]

What Coing is outlining is not the natural law of eighteenth-century rationalism but rather the new connection between legal science and philosophy (p. 8). The end result is something different altogether. A combination of cultural theories, sociological observations, moral statements, historical facts and elliptical sentences, *Die obersten Grundsätze* spins together a theory that links together law, religion, morality, values and ideals to form an edifice that relies not only on ideals and law but also on established social norms and values. Coing's foundations of law thus work on many different levels, allowing him to demonstrate how they are in reality embedded in the law.

Though the book makes no explicit mention of rights, it discusses their content exhaustively. Freedom is one of the core elements in Coing's theories, it becomes ultimately the foundation of an entire theory of law. In it, freedom incorporates not only personal freedom but the whole spectrum of rights currently categorized under the classical liberty rights. It included the freedom of conscience, the freedom of expression in spheres such as art, and the freedom of moral and religious life (p. 15). Freedom was also used as an expression of human value and dignity (p. 41).

Thus, it is apparent that for Coing, the concept of freedom evolves into a general concept that included numerous principles, such as the idea of equality of all. These ideas he traces to sources in Roman law such as the *Digest of Justinian* (p. 43):

[23] Helmut Coing, *Die obersten Grundsätze des Rechts: ein Versuch zur Neugründung des Naturrechts* (Heidelberg: Schriften der Süddeutschen Juristen-Zeitung, 1947), p. 7.

*Freiheit is das Wesen alles echten geistigen Lebens, ist Ausdrück der Personwürde des Menschen. Darum ist Freiheit das höchste Rechtsgut, das einem Jedem zukommt; "libertas inaestimabilis est"* (*D*. 50.17.106).[24]

Freedom is the essence of all real spiritual life, it is the expression of the value of the person. Therefore freedom is the highest legal value that is to be assigned to each and everyone; "freedom is immeasurable" (*Dig*. 50.17.106).

Using the Weimar Constitution, Coing seeks to demonstrate how these ideals have permeated into the legal system, being guaranteed not only in the constitution but equally in the private law system (p. 25).

The formulation of the analogies that Coing builds up shows how he talks about rights through foundational principles. Thus, one can derive the right of education from the notion of freedom of thought. What Coing does is build these conceptions through the legal goods that are to be protected, ending up with a fairly long list of fairly conventional rights that are justified through law, morality and values: legal status, life and health, honor, freedom and protection of the domestic sphere, protection of property and freedom from want, protection of privacy, freedom of expression and creativity, freedom of conscience, freedom of education and freedom of association. All of these are the foundational rights and freedoms of the individual as a human being.[25]

What distinction Coing then makes between his own theory and what he calls classical French human rights is not really clear (p. 73). Like Koschaker, Coing's thesis has a strong Christian character; it sees the foundations of basic rights in Christianity and the humanists (p. 119). The issue of religion was also a matter of contention. In private, Coing stressed the connection between political freedom and the social acceptance of authority but at the same time he opposed the politicization of religion that would mix the spiritual and the political.[26]

The cultural boundedness of law and the foundations of law are evident in the way Coing introduces elements of legal primitivism into the discourse. There are numerous references to indigenous peoples and their customs as well as the historical primitivism of Europeans, with examples such as revenge presented frequently. The

[24] Coing, *Die obersten Grundsätze des Rechts*, pp. 41–42.

[25] Coing, *Die obersten Grundsätze des Rechts*, pp. 69–70. However, Luig, "Helmut Coing," sees Coing's theory of natural law as based on value ethics and their scientific basis.

[26] Letter from Coing to Sternberger on January 23, 1959. Deutsches Literatur Archiv, Marback am Neckar, A: Sternberger/FAZ/Zuschriften Ekeland. Freiheit. 2 Mappe 4450 1989.10.8998. Coing was a Protestant.

purpose of these references is mainly to serve as counterpoints to the connection between law and culture.[27]

In the latter part of the book, Coing's argument moves closer to the traditional human rights claims, maintaining that one of the chief roles of basic rights is to protect against state power. Recalling, though not naming, the use of exceptional degrees and the power of exception, Coing notes that dictatorial power transforms legal relations into a power relation. With the limitations of basic rights power becomes tyrannical and despotic. Unlimited power is in itself an aberration of law.[28]

The book contains numerous instances of concepts that have ambiguous reference points. For example, the concepts of honor and dignity were a staple of Nazi thinking and jurisprudence, where they acted as kinds of protected individual traits. While the individual did not have secured rights but rather duties, the Nazi state sought to guarantee the honor and dignity of every German. However, the concept of dignity had an equally central place in the language of Christian conservatism, where it served a very different purpose.[29]

As we have seen in our previous examples, that a scholar would start thinking of the foundations of a discipline and begin a new line of inquiry into its structural assumptions is very rare. Within the research of legal history, Coing notes that true explorations of the foundations of legal traditions have been the utmost rarities. According to Coing, "Fritz Schulz's *Principles of Roman law* stands alone" (p. 138). That Coing himself would embark on a similar enterprise was unusual at the very least.

The natural law theory of Coing also has parallels with Wieacker. Both operate with the concepts of *Rechtsgefühl* and *Rechtsbewusstsein* (crudely translated as the feeling of law and legal consciousness). For Coing, both are in essence concepts of justice. Here, Coing returns to Ulpian's formulation on the foundations of law (*Dig.* 1.1.10), which he raises as the foundations of justice in general, namely to live honestly (preserving one's one dignity), not hurting others (and here Coing refers to humanity in general) and, finally, giving each their due (which is expanded as the principle of equality and the rule of law). The original text, *honeste vivere, alterum non laedere, suum cuique tribuere,* contains many of the same expressions but the content they are given in Coing is

[27] Coing, *Die obersten Grundsätze des Rechts*, pp. 67, 74, 118 et passim.
[28] Coing, *Die obersten Grundsätze des Rechts*, pp. 85, 88.
[29] On this distinction, see Whitman, "On Nazi honor and the new European dignity."

modern.[30] This is what one could describe a use of a Roman law text in an anachronistic interpretation.

Though his book is about law and its foundations, it makes constant references to social life, business practices and other forms of real-life organization and how law will need to adjust to them. In a manner, it links with theories of legal realism or even those of concrete order thinking of Nazi theorists but equally to the value base of the *Bildungsbürgertum*.

In his works, Coing would make a very slow movement toward the theory of rights, writing in 1959 an important article about the history of subjective rights.[31] However, the issues now understood under the realm of rights (freedom of speech, personal freedom, equality under the law, the right to privacy, freedom of religion, ownership and so forth), were formulated as legal principles, as values rather than rights.[32] In this, there is continuity with the theories outlined in the *Oberste Grundsätze*.

Earlier, in a 1950 speech, Coing tied the idea of human rights to two origins, the theories of fundamental subjective rights either in Enlightenment natural law thinking or in Christianity. While the first origin story was based on the fact that the British or the US tradition saw rights as inalienable; the second was derived from the very concept of humanity. In contrast, Coing argued for a third way, to approach rights from the perspective of personality and morality, positing the person as a moral subject. Thus Donellus, for example, separated four natural rights: life, physical immunity, liberty and honor. However, these subjective rights were about private law, not political rights by themselves.[33]

What this meant was that ideas of restoring the rule of law after the Nazi injustice, of making a clean break from legal repressions and the submission of law to the caprice of political power, the rule of

[30] Coing, *Die obersten Grundsätze des Rechts*, pp. 29–36. These notions were popularized in Max Friedrich Gustav von Rümelin, *Rechtsgefühl und Rechtsbewusstsein, Rede gehalten bei der Akademischen Preisverteilung am 6. November 1925* (Tübingen: J. C. B. Mohr, 1925).

[31] Helmut Coing, "Zur Geschichte des Begriffs 'subjektives Recht'," in Helmut Coing, Frederick H. Lawson and Kurt Grönfors (eds.), *Das subjektive Recht und der Rechts- schutz der Persönlichkeit* (Frankfurt: Alfred Metzner, 1959), pp. 7–23.

[32] Helmut Coing, *Grundzüge der Rechtsphilosophie* (Berlin: de Gruyter, 1993 [1950]), pp. 127–129.

[33] Coing, *Die Rezeption des römischen Rechts*, pp. 66–67. Later, Heribert Waider, "'Ars iuris' und 'suum in persona ipsa' bei Hugo Donellus," *Archiv für Geschichteds der Philosophie*, 43 (1961), 60–62 would link Donellus' list of natural rights to both the 1776 US Declaration of Independence and the Universal Declaration of Human Rights and the European Convention of Human Rights.

dictatorship, were clearly there. What was the most peculiar aspect from the contemporary perspective is not what was done but rather how it was done. Instead of referring to rights, human rights or civil rights, as much of the world had been doing at the time, Coing started to look for answers in the legal tradition itself, from legal history. Applying a characteristically Germanic way of argumentation, the issue was where would one find sources of law that are *überpositiv*, beyond statutory law?

One of the explanations might be that German legal tradition had often been wary of making claims to individual liberties and rights. Some, like Stolleis, have argued that in the German tradition, constitutional norms were rather concessions of the sovereign power of the state to accept limitations rather than formative agreements that founded the state as a polity.[34] What this meant was that the constitutional guarantees provided by rights enshrined in the constitution were only as valuable as the constitution itself. And Hitler's Germany had famously declared a state of exception, revoking the application of the constitution. The way in which Nazi constitutional scholars approached the matter was nothing less than an attempt at removing the ideas of constitution and state in the traditional sense from the equation.[35]

Even after the war, some have claimed that German constitutional law scholars were very apprehensive about the whole conception of rights, resisting the creation of the new constitution (the 1949 *Grundgesetz* or Basic Law) and its emphasis on rights. The influence of Nazi-era constitutional law scholars like Schmitt or Smend continued and faculties would fiercely resist the reintroduction of expelled scholars, be they leftists or Jews. In addition to this, anti-Semitism continued rampant within the field. This tendency took on surprising forms. Hans Kelsen, for example, was attacked for his legal positivism due to the fact that in the interpretations of opponents, the theory made no distinction between just law and unjust law, or it left law without defense against tyranny. In their view, positivism was responsible for the Nazi perversion of law. This attack was made even stranger by the fact that many of the attackers were scholars who had been deeply compromised during the Nazi years.[36]

[34] Michael Stolleis, *Public Law in Germany 1914–1945* (Oxford: Oxford University Press, 2004), p. 59.

[35] Lepsius, "The problem of perceptions of National Socialist Law," p. 29.

[36] Frieder Günther, "The neglect of Hans Kelsen in West German public law scholarship, 1945–1980," in D. A. Jeremy Telman (ed.), *Hans Kelsen in America – Selective Affinities and the*

Thus, it is hardly surprising that constitutional law scholars were not among the first to embrace the new liberal theory of rights or the ideas of exiles in general. Like in many other fields of law, the true breaking point happened only much later, in the 1960s.

It is clear that the transformation of Coing's work after the war can be grouped together with other studies that made up the reemergence of natural law. Coing's approach to the ideas of natural law and human rights was to propose a third way with two different meanings. First, as opposed to the founding of rights either through natural law or through declarations or conventions, he argued for tracing them through tradition. Second, as opposed to Enlightenment ideas of inalienability or Christian ideas of humanity, he claimed that subjective rights are derived from the position of a person as a moral subject. The idea of a long tradition, tracing themes through the historical development extending to the Roman law roots, was central to his thesis. Another key point was the linkage between rights and the legal goods they were meant to protect, seeing law connected to values and morality. In a sense, Coing chose to see law as part of a coherent whole, where the totality of this conception formed the true bulwark against the aggression and violence represented by totalitarianism.

## European Legal History?

The way in which Coing and others focused on European legal history and its reinterpretation may thus be seen almost as a constitutional project without a constitution. Through the construction or the discovery of a tradition of principles, rights and legal dogma, German legal scholars emphasized the long tradition through which the law had developed. Tradition and history were in a sense *überpositiv*, beyond and above positive law. Since there was no real concept of an original contract on rights (as supposed by the French or Anglo-Saxon tradition), the tradition took its place in the equation.

The European legal history project may also be seen as very much a German project. Indeed, scholars like Osler have famously ridiculed it

*Mysteries of Academic Influence* (Dordrecht: Springer, 2016), pp. 217–228. On the strange intellectual atmosphere relating to positivism and natural law, see Foljanty, *Recht oder Gesetz*, pp. 23–31. On the Kelsen–Radbruch debate over the nature of Nazi law, see Frank Haldemann, "Gustav Radbuch vs. Hans Kelsen: a debate on Nazi law," *Ratio Juris*, 18(2) (2005), 162–178.

as the universalization of the German tradition.[37] Even early critics such as Alvaro d'Ors were skeptical but his criticism was more on the Germanic and nonreligious nature of the tradition as he would have preferred a religious foundation of the European tradition.[38]

The European legal heritage as an intellectual project thus had many roots and legal science was only one of them. The different versions of this project had a number of both similarities and distinctions, as noted earlier in the differences between Koschaker's and Wieacker's Europe. Coing's version of the European tradition was distinct from both of the aforementioned, linking not only statutory law, the writings of the jurists or the culture of the jurists but also values and moral and philosophical foundations. In fact, for Coing the legal rules in themselves appear more as manifestations of those values rather than foundational texts themselves.

If we look at one of the more influential iterations of the project, Hans Hattenhauer's massive book on European legal history, the implications are clear. The idea of civil and human rights only appears at the very end, as part of the things that were imported from the US into West Germany during reconstruction after the war.[39]

The foundation of law in the civilian tradition and in private law scholarship was also peculiar considering the German constitutional tradition after the war. Under the new constitution, Germany was given a constitutional court with wide authorities. The protection of the constitution was a fundamental feature of the political and legal culture in West Germany. Even the successor to the Gestapo, the new domestic intelligence service, was called *Verfassungsschützsamt*, or office for the protection of the constitution. The constitution itself protected a wide variety of basic freedoms that were framed according to the models provided by international human rights treaties.[40]

But how did this tie in with the tradition of law advocated by the scholars of Roman and civil law tradition? What kind of Europe did this tradition represent?

[37] See, for example, Osler, "The fantasy men."
[38] d'Ors, "Jus Europaeum."
[39] Hans Hattenhauer, *Europäische Rechtsgeschichte* (Heidelberg: Müller Juristischer Verlag, 1992), pp. 752–753.
[40] The Basic Law for the Federal Republic of Germany, May 23, 1949; www.verfassungsschutz.de. This complete reversal made it all the more curious by the fact that, as mentioned earlier, a considerable part of German constitutional law scholars after WWII were former Nazis and students of Carl Schmitt. Grothe, *Zwischen Geschichte und Recht*, pp. 409–415.

Some had of course seen the long tradition extending to Rome as containing in essence the foundations of the rule of law. Fritz Schulz had famously described principles like freedom, humanity and security as the principles of Roman law. Pringsheim also represented Hadrian's Rome as an empire where the rule of law was observed and the weak were protected.

What Coing wanted to do was to present the European tendencies, rights and tradition combined. In his important essay on the task of the legal historian from 1976, he quotes F. A. Hayek: "it is impossible to rebuild the foundational values of our civilization, we may only develop them from the inside." What this meant was that the European tradition would have to be rebuilt from the existing materials by reinterpreting the things that were already there.[41]

For Coing, there were two important shared traditions: 1) the private law tradition of 2,000 years of Roman law scholarship, which formed the foundation of the civilian tradition; 2) the natural law tradition, which gave Europe the ideas of democracy, human rights and the rule of law. These traditions were intermingled, but separate.

In his autobiography, Coing notes how ancient culture had a foundational role in his intellectual life and personal culture, it presented a kind of blueprint for humanity. In this he was inspired early on by Werner Jaeger's idea of Paideia, of a culture and civilization as formational concepts.[42] Jaeger would later continue in his exile in the US to remind others of the humanistic tradition and the distressing rejection of the very principles of liberty that the US and the West was founded on. In 1936, Jaeger wrote:

> The disruption of Western civilization which we are witnessing, with the rise of the doctrine that culture and knowledge are nationalistic possessions, dividing group from group, rather than expressions of kinship binding the heirs of a common heritage into closer union, dismays not only disinterested philosophers and educators, but men of foresight and good will in all walks of life.[43]

What Jaeger points out was that even those on the sidelines, apparently out of harm's way, would be affected by the kind of cataclysmic events that had already taken place in Germany. In 1936, Jaeger did not foresee even more drastic events such as the war and the Holocaust.

[41] Helmut Coing, *Aufgaben des Rechtshistorikers* (Wiesbaden: Franz Steiner Verlag, 1976), p. 163.

[42] Coing, *Für Wissenschaften und Künste*, pp. 22, 28.

[43] Werner Jaeger, "Classical philology and humanism," *Transactions and Proceedings of the American Philological Association*, 67 (1936), 363.

Jaeger thus links the concept of civilization and the idea of a cultured state to the concept of the rule of law and liberty. It was a common idea at the time to see the rise of Nazism not only as a crisis of politics or justice but also as a crisis of civilization and culture. To exiled legal theorist Edgar Bodenheimer, for example, the conception of justice was intimately tied to the idea of civilization.[44] Thus the collapse of the rule of law was ultimately a consequence of the crumbling of civilization under Nazi rule.

Coing's outline of legal history developed gradually, but included the same elements as Koschaker's and Wieacker's. The rediscovery of Roman law in Italy, the Glossators and the Commentators, the French and Dutch Humanists, leading to the natural law revolution and to modern law, were the foundational stones of a European legal science. In Coing's major rewriting of the European tradition, a massive handbook for the sources and literature of European history of private law, this approach was the main narrative connecting the historical outline. Coing stated that while individual national histories might have particularities and exceptional issues, this was the great history of European legal development.[45]

Later, in the first issue of *Ius Commune*, the journal of the Max Planck Institute, Coing traces the European approach to Curtius and his study on medieval literature. Much like Curtius, Coing's idea was to create a unity from disparate parts and to see the whole cultural entity that had eluded previous observers. The connection to Curtius was something that Coing shared with Genzmer, who was also interested in the role of European legal history as a new field.[46]

In the 1950 textbook of legal philosophy, Coing presents a similar understanding of law and tradition that he sketched in the *Obersten Grundsätze*. There is a strong realistic bent in the philosophical outline,

[44] W. Cole Durham (Jr.), "Edgar Bodenheimer: conservator of civilized legal culture," in Lutter, Stiefel and Hoeflich, *Der Einfluß deutscher Emigranten auf die Rechtsentwicklung in den USA und in Deutschland*, pp. 127–143.

[45] Helmut Coing, "Einleitung," in Helmut Coing (ed.), *Handbuch der Quellen und Literatur der neueren europäischen Privatrechtsgeschichte. Vol. 1: Mittelalter (1100–1500): Die gelehrter Rechte und die Gesetzgebung* (Munich: Beck Verlag, 1973), p. 5.

[46] Helmut Coing, "Die europäische Privatrechtsgeschichte der neueren Zeit als einheitliches Forschungsgebiet. Probleme und Aufbau," *Ius Commune*, 1 (1967), 1–33; Ernst Robert Curtius, *Europäische Literatur und lateinisches Mittelalter* (Bern: A. Francke, 1948). Coing first wrote about the idea of European legal history in his 1952 review of Curtius. On Coing, Curtius and Genzmer, see Duve, "Von der Europäischen Rechtsgeschichte zu einer Rechtsgeschichte Europas in globalhistorischer Perspektive," p. 40; Luig, "Helmut Coing," p. 669.

a reliance on human psychology or sociology as explanatory factors in the ways that law operated in society. His theory of natural law was, however, one founded on morality, on ideas of virtue and the inherent value of the human being. While Coing does discuss the principles of natural law and human rights, what is particular and peculiar is his idea of cultural law (*Kulturrecht*). The point of cultural law is that certain legal ideas are part of the legal culture.[47] In the sphere of European tradition, the term cultural law could be understood as a reference to the specific characteristics of European legal culture. The concept is central to the whole proposition since it makes possible the combination of universal norms and European culture.

To discuss the role that human rights and the legal guarantees and balances that they contain, Coing returns time and again to the spectre of totalitarianism. He mentions the legality of terror when positive law itself has gone astray.[48] This was one of the central criticisms that were leveled against legal positivism and especially at Hans Kelsen. Coing even mentions how the Platonic principle of the rule of the best could be construed in a way that enabled the fascists and the Nazis to ruthlessly take power under the claim of good intentions.[49] In all these examples, good intentions are used to justify abuses of power, the exceptions to the foundations of law.

As a legal philosopher, Coing would, in typical German fashion, feel the need to address and define the fundamental issues. While these are rarely interesting in the sense that another definition of law would really be needed, what these definitions do serve is to indicate the priorities and value judgements of their makers. Coing argued that the meaning of the law was clearly one that needed the two traditions, natural law and Roman law, in order to:

1) preserve peace and security in society;
2) promote order among different interests, including the state's, to promote cooperation and to channel conflicts; and
3) do that effectively.[50]

In short, a balanced account of the rule of law, where the natural law tradition would account for the public sphere and the Roman law tradition would account for matters between individuals. What is

[47] Coing, *Grundzüge der Rechtsphilosophie*, p. 169 and passim.
[48] Coing, *Grundzüge der Rechtsphilosophie*, p. 175.
[49] Coing, *Grundzüge der Rechtsphilosophie*, p. 208.
[50] Coing, "Aufgaben des Rechtshistorikers," pp. 156–157.

noteworthy is that the definition of law was deeply humanistic; it concerned the individual perspective and protecting the individual.

The redefinition of fundamental concepts was also a necessity in that the legal profession and the legal academia were still full of people who had been very much involved in the Nazi regime and formulated their theories based on Nazi principles. After the war, many had reinvented themselves but others continued to present ideas that were not that different from those they had published during the Nazi years. In a letter to Karl Larenz, Coing defended the idea that the law should have both the function of resolving conflicts and maintaining order (*ordo*). The correspondence itself was on the nature of the jurisprudence of interests (*Interessenjurisprudenz*) and thus the role of the material in the legal analysis. Larenz, of course, was a former member of the *Kieler Schule* and one of the main ideologues of the Nazi new legal science. What Larenz in his methodological texts argued was a continuation of the Nazi era idea of the concrete order, which he transformed after the war into an interest in the life order and the societal interests visible in law. What Coing argues is that materialism and thus the jurisprudence of interest loses sight of the spiritual, the feeling of right and justice that is so central in the activity of judges. In a similar way, he maintains that the concept of order should be seen as open, a sum of principles that informs decisions, including ethical precepts.[51] The legal debates over the nature of the law and the foundational principles were masked in obscure language with references to Kant and Hegel. Issues of vital principled importance were debated through sometimes minute definitional challenges.

Why Coing is so important for an understanding of European legal historical tradition is not due to his achievements as a scholar but because he was a skilled administrator. Coing's teacher Erich Genzmer, a medievalist, had prepared a plan for a new Max Planck Institute for comparative legal history but was no longer interested in taking up the task when already close to retirement, and so after some shuffling the position fell to Coing. Coing took Gentzmer's original idea of a center for comparative legal history and turned it into a European one. Many of Gentzmer's plans, such as the insistence on methodological rigor and the focus on medieval Roman law, were taken up, but the resulting plan of the Institute was all Coing.[52] The comparison with

[51] Letter from Coing to Karl Larenz on June 18, 1952. Universitätsbibliothek München, NL Karl Larenz, 18.06.1952, Frankfurt, Coing an Larenz, Karl.

[52] The founding of the Institute was also offered to Kunkel, who had other ideas about the direction it should take. On the history of the MPI of European Legal History, see Frank

Genzmer and distinguishing his influence may be impossible due to the long collaboration between the two. For example, in his 1950 review of Koschaker's *Europa*, Genzmer maintains how Koschaker's main discovery is how the reception of Roman law can only fruitfully be explored through a true European focus.[53] This was, probably not coincidentally, one of the early concentration points of the new Institute.

The way that Coing outlined his own research plans and interests as well as those of the MPI were not only politically highly relevant but also ideologically inspired. He was among the first to make a direct link between human rights thought and the European tradition, linking the project of European integration with the exploration of its past.

The genius of his plan was the way in which it linked national tradition and internationalism. Seeing the obvious need to accept and integrate the values and rights of the West, the tradition of rights, he nevertheless managed to turn it into a plan that required greater interpretation of the past. European legal unity would be a combination of the Anglo-American and the French tradition of rights with the Germanic tradition of private law.

Coing's main programmatic text on the idea of a continuing legal tradition from 1968 was fittingly titled "The original unity of European legal science." In it, he claimed that from the medieval Glossators to the school of natural law in the late eighteenth century there was a sense of scientific unity within European legal science. In it, the systematization and the pedagogical presentation of law was fundamentally uniform throughout Europe, inspired and influenced as it was by Roman law and canon law doctrines. These doctrines were then adopted by natural law scholarship and *ius commune* legal science. The fundamental issue was that a coherent way of thinking and writing about law emerged that enabled legal scholars to overcome whatever borders there were, aided of course by the use of Latin as the lingua franca.[54]

Coing's idea of European tradition was in many ways similar to Koschaker's theory about Roman law as a "*relatives Naturrecht*," a relative natural law of Europe. However, on closer inspection the

L. Schäfer, "Visionen und Wissenschaftsmanagement. Die Gründung eines Max-Planck-Instituts für europäische Rechtsgeschichte," *Zeitschrift für Europäisches Privatrecht*, 17 (2009), 517–535. On the role of the different founders, see Luig, "Helmut Coing"; Coing, *Für Wissenschaften und Künste*; Simon, "Zwischen Wissenschaft und Wissenschaftspolitik."

[53] Genzmer, "Rez. Paul Koschaker, Europa und das römische Recht," p. 598.

[54] Coing, "Die ursprüngliche Einheit der europäischen Rechtswissenschaft."

similarities appear superficial in that Koschaker's unity was that of a dogmatic methodology, while Coing saw in it values and ideals such as the freedom reflected in legal tradition.[55] He connected the concepts of culture, civilization and tradition as the fundaments of legal culture, from which ideas such as rights and freedoms were to be traced. Like many others, Coing argued that concepts such as human rights had ultimately been imported into German tradition. Their significance in the constitutional environment was only beginning to emerge and thus the centrality of the new constitution is not visible in his early works. The connection between law and civilization enabled him to see the Nazi rule not only as a crisis of law and politics but also as a crisis of civilization. In this crisis, a return to roots was a logical corrective. Thus, the premise of reaching out to tradition, in the case of public law to the natural law tradition and in private law to the Roman law tradition, was both a way forward and a corrective from the past.

## Return to Liberty

The idea of freedom became a central theme in political discourse during WWII, and this was also reflected in the legal debates. The emergence of the Cold War after 1948 saw the language of freedom being directed more as a critique of the Soviet sphere of influence, where a new wave of repression was taking shape. The erection of the Berlin Wall in 1961 made concrete the permanence of this division.

In the first outlines of the philosophy of law written after the war, Coing justifies the return to the theories of natural law by pointing to the failure of the legal system in the face of totalitarianism. The foundation of the new theory was the idea of freedom as an overarching conception from which rights and duties were derived. In Coing's early texts, the framework built to support this presupposition was founded on references to legal theory, statutory law and legal and philosophical examples from European legal history.[56]

The question is what if any influence did the émigrés have in the return to theories of natural law, human rights and the connection between the European tradition along with them? What was the role of anti-totalitarianism in this process?

[55] As Beggio, *Paul Koschaker*, pp. 230, 236 notes, Koschaker's influences were more in neoscholasticism than philosophy.

[56] Coing, *Die obersten Grundsätze des Rechts*, p. 7.

Of course, the linkages can be difficult to demonstrate and one is often left with the conundrum of parallel developments and the question what was the relationship between the two. In the issue of natural law and human rights, the parallels are obvious. In the post-WWII world, the rise of the human rights discourse and the preparation of the treaties and declarations, such as the European Convention of Human Rights (agreed on 1950, in force since 1953) or the Universal Declaration of Human Rights (adopted in 1948), meant that human rights were very much on the agenda.

The second issue, the rise of anti-totalitarianism, is linked with the start of the Cold War from the years 1947 to 1948 and the consolidation of Soviet power in Eastern Europe.

One of the open questions is that what, if any, influence there was back in Germany from the anti-totalitarian theories of Arendt, Neumann and Strauss? Did they have a lasting impact in the US? In Germany, the reception of their works happened much later, namely with the 1960s generation. There is, of course, a long-lasting debate over the influence of German exiles in the US in the turn toward democracy but in the following we shall focus specifically on the ideas of human rights and the legal tradition.[57]

The reconstruction of Germany after WWII is hailed as one of the great miracles of the twentieth century. It saw in a few years the transformation of a totalitarian state in ruins into a prosperous democracy with strong institutions. Scholars have presented two conflicting views on what accounted for this change. Some credit the vast American effort on reconstruction, reeducation and propaganda that sought to counter the Soviet threat. Others claim that the real achievers were the Germans themselves, who chose the path to democracy often despite transparent American propaganda.[58] Both explanations contain a kernel of truth and suggest a complex process of interaction.

There were numerous contradictory trends, ranging from attempts to impose and indoctrinate mixed with movements to revive the German prewar traditions of democracy and the rule of law. While there was a marked tendency to think of 1945 as a zero hour and a clean slate upon which the new Germany was founded, this excludes many continuities.

[57] See, for instance, Alfons Söllner, "Normative Verwestlichung. Der Einfluß der Remigranten auf die politische Kultur der frühen Bundesrepublik," in Heinz Bude and Bernd Greine (eds.), *Westbindungen. Amerika in der Bundesrepublik* (Hamburg: Hamburger Edition, 1999), pp. 72–92; Strote, *Lion and Lambs*.

[58] Greenberg, *Weimar Century*, pp. 6–7.

As Forner writes, for the elite, their careers continued mostly uninterrupted and they were able to reestablish themselves after the war. For the common people, the postwar era formed a continuity of suffering with the last war years. There was a shared sense of German victimhood that overshadowed all talk of complicity with the Nazis. In these first years, the returning exiles were a rare sight, as travel to occupied Germany still needed many permits that were not easily acquired, and they made their presence felt more through letters and packages sent from abroad.[59] Within this equation of guilt and suffering, the émigrés were a complicated addition, having collaborated with the victors and in many cases being seen as having escaped the suffering that those who stayed had gone through.

The German emigrants who were recruited into US academia and administration were a decisive influence in the formation of anti-Soviet ideas such as the theories of totalitarianism or militant democracy. Greenberg maintains that their views on democracy and totalitarianism were rigid, dualistic and paranoid and contributed to the hysterical reaction against communism in the US.[60] This was hardly a surprise because many of them had been involved in the study of the emergence of totalitarianism in Germany and they had been influenced by their work in agencies such as the OSS. From the American background, one may also see the motivation for the reliance on concepts such as freedom as the foundation of the anti-totalitarian ethos.

This view is based on a fairly limited sample because the roles of German exiles were different in the US and in Germany. In the German discussions, they returned in many cases to a similar role as they had had before the Nazi years, while in the US they had to carve a new niche for themselves in the public discussions. However, the legalistic concerns of the German exiles about constraining state power, which were forged in the political debates of the Weimar years and the bitter experiences of the Nazi takeover of power, were not immediately successful in the American discussions.[61]

In his 1953 article for the *Columbia Law Review*, Neumann argues strongly against a nihilistic interpretation of the legitimacy of an existing political system, presenting a legal argument for political freedom as an ideology. In it, he repudiates the idea of the enemy or fear as

59 Forner, *German Intellectuals*, pp. 5–9, 35.
60 Greenberg, *Weimar Century*, p. 23.
61 Kornhauser, *Debating the American State*, p. 96.

a driving force of politics as contrary to democracy. Instead, he launches into an analysis of the heritage of liberty as a legal ideal, beginning from the traditional concept of freedom as the absence of restraints. What he develops is the view of the liberal theory of freedom following after the collapse of a totalitarian state. He offers a criticism of the positivistic approaches to the rule of law or *Rechtsstaat*, i.e., the conservation of freedom and civil rights as a means of preserving freedom. What the protection of liberty through law is incapable of is protection against the law itself, either through the law or through escape clauses. What he argues is precisely that the ways in which Truman's Loyalty Program or the Taft-Hartley Act operated are comparable to the totalitarian state's mode of operation in subverting freedoms. Its only true remedy is active political democracy and shared values.[62] During the entire thesis, Neumann relates the argument to the Western philosophical tradition from Socrates onwards. That is the true crux of his message, the reliance of law and political systems on tradition as a guide in interpretation. For Neumann, the concentration of power was as much a threat to the rule of law in a democracy as anywhere else.

However, the story is quite different regarding Germany. The returning émigrés were a crucial influence in the postwar debates on democracy and the rule of law. Here, their ideas were tempered by the fact that the intellectual atmosphere was shaped by different kinds of political forces. Leftist students did not embrace democracy but authoritarian ideas from the left. Left-wing parties in Germany themselves underwent a radical transformation, shown in 1959 by the SDP renouncing Marxism and the economic theories of nationalization, and opting instead to support democratic reforms and the rule of law. This transformation was brought about by a combination of changes in the internal dynamics of the party and also by returning exiles such as Fraenkel, who argued forcefully for the transformation based on his American experiences. Fraenkel was central in the redefinition of the ideas behind the concept of *Rechtsstaat*, namely linking social aims and recent thinking on natural law to produce a just society.[63] In a similar way, Neumann was instrumental in the refounding of the study of politics in Berlin, insisting that the new institutions should be committed to the

[62] Franz Neumann, "The concept of political freedom," *Columbia Law Review*, 53 (7) (1953), 901–935, now in William E. Scheuerman (ed.), *The Rule of Law Under Siege: Selected Essays of Franz L. Neumann and Otto Kirchheimer* (Berkeley, Los Angeles, London: University of California Press, 1996), pp. 195–230.

[63] On this, see Greenberg, *Weimar Century*, pp. 76–78, 83–85.

study of democracy. However, Söllner argues that the impact of German intellectual émigrés and the US influence should be seen not only as an input into the system but rather as a process of negotiation and adaptation.[64]

The two groups of émigrés were unevenly balanced. Of the scholarly exiles, only a tiny minority returned, in some fields none of the senior scholars driven into exile abroad came back after 1945. In law and social sciences, the number was fairly high but one is still talking of a small minority. Those who did return, such as Pringsheim, were often driven by an urge to help Germany back to normalcy, while those who did not were prone to describe renazified Germany as a lost cause. However, despite the fact that few returned at least permanently, many of the connections were rekindled and ideas and correspondence moved across the Atlantic and the English Channel.

In this climate, the liberals and the conservatives found a new understanding. Many of the former émigrés embarked on an educational campaign to promote democracy as an inborn German tradition rather than as an imposed framework.[65] As an intellectual endeavor, this was similar to the ideas espoused by Coing and Koschaker, namely that the tradition already contained in essence the framework necessary for the rule of law and the success of the rights to be recognized.

Among the exiles the idea that Germany could be rescued from itself was an idea that had limited support. While they had personal experience of the persecutions that accompanied their flight, this was overshadowed by the knowledge of the Holocaust that began to spread in late 1942 but was only uncovered fully by May 1945. Arendt, Horkheimer and Adorno had all written at length about anti-Semitism and its causes but the sheer scale and cruelty of the extermination led them to question the very concept of humanity. Assimilation and the trappings of civilization had done nothing to prevent or even limit the carnage.[66]

To claim that democratic ideas or conceptions of the rule of law would have been imposed on Germany by the Allied powers after the war does not really bear closer inspection. There had been certain ideas about such an intervention but nothing really came of it. In fact, one of

[64] Söllner, "Normative Verwestlichung."

[65] Greenberg, *Weimar Century*, p. 8.

[66] Anson Rabinbach, "The Frankfurt School and the 'Jewish Question,' 1940–1970," in Ezra Mendelsohn, Stefani Hoffman and Richard Cohen (eds.), *Against the Grain: Jewish Intellectuals in Hard Times* (New York: Berghahn Books, 2013), pp. 262–263.

the many exiles working with the American military administration, comparative lawyer Max Rheinstein later said in an interview that it was good that nothing came of these plans since the whole idea that outside forces would reform German law was simply absurd.[67]

There are, after all, a number of similarities in the postwar developments within Germany and in the works written at the same time. For instance, in 1949 Leo Strauss gave a series of lectures that resulted in the 1953 book titled *Natural Right and History*. In it, he sought to reevaluate the issue of natural law and by extension universal human rights. While the criticism of natural right as a philosophical doctrine had been the realm of the Historical School, the juxtaposition was by and large similar to the debates between the other Historical School, the Historical School of Jurisprudence, which was against universalism and natural law.[68] The second great similarity between Strauss and Coing is that both sought to argue by appealing to historical tradition, emphasizing long-term developments as signs of maturity and acceptance. Thus, when Strauss quotes Roderich Stinzing, the great historian of jurisprudence, that pure natural rights must be diluted to secondary natural rights in order to be applicable in civil society, this brings about an argument through history that even legal historians such as Coing might have approved.[69]

During the interwar period, the concepts of natural law and natural right were in essence dead. Even under the onslaught of Nazi repression, people such as Franz Neumann or Ernst Fraenkel were clearly uncomfortable about using the notion of natural law as a criticism of Nazi policies. Strauss's history of natural right is a very different one to the traditional histories of natural law that normally begin with an exploration of the Stoic cosmopolis. He placed Hobbes's natural right at the center of the very ideal of civilization. This was in a sense a supplanting of aristocratic virtue by bourgeois morality, where most of the traditional human rights such as the protection of security, mind or property have their roots, according to Tanguay.[70]

67 Wolfgang Freiherr von Marschall, "Max Rheinstein," in Lutter, Stiefel and Hoeflich, *Der Einfluß deutscher Emigranten auf die Rechtsentwicklung in den USA und in Deutschland*, p. 337.

68 Strauss, *Natural Right and History*, pp. 13–14 describes the historical school of philosophy in remarkably similar terms as the one in jurisprudence: emerging as a reaction to the French Revolution, emphasizing local and historically based variants over universals and so forth.

69 Strauss, *Natural Right and History*, p. 153.

70 Daniel Tanguay, *Leo Strauss: An Intellectual Biography* (New Haven, CT: Yale University Press, 2007), p. 102.

All in all, the convergence of the émigrés and their anti-totalitarian ideas, the emergence of the human rights regime and the coming of the Cold War and ideological competition with the communist regimes formed a crucial set of influences upon which the turn toward rights and tradition was formed. Much like during the Nazi years, there was a *Gleichschaltung* where a gradual shift began to occur as a result of numerous simultaneous factors. The traumatic experiences during the Nazi years and the war meant that new ideas coming from both abroad and from the democrats within met with fertile ground. As a result, the concept of freedom was embraced as the mantra of anti-totalitarianism but with numerous different connotations from political freedoms to freedom rights. Ideas such as democracy and the rule of law were adapted as cornerstones of the state.

Strauss's relationship with this development was complicated. His *Natural Right and History* is a reworking of tradition, an attempt at determining the line between Cicero, Machiavelli, Hobbes, Locke and Rousseau. In a lecture presented in 1940, Strauss notes that the German philosophy stems from a criticism of civilization and science and an emphasis on nature and history.[71] Strauss's own work works through a similar mode, namely the notion of history as a cumulative process. However, it is simultaneously a historical, legal and philosophical process that produced the modern concept of natural right. That thought process in Strauss belies any explicit link with the experience of exile or totalitarianism but both its preconditions and its conclusions are conditioned by it.

## The European Tradition in Transition

While the adaptation of the ideas of liberty, democracy and human rights can be seen as a reaction to Nazi totalitarianism, American influence and self-definition against communism, how does the concept of a European legal tradition fit into this narrative?

The legal history of Europe and the European legal tradition were not in any way the same thing. Certain ideas and practices, and a number of methodological and dogmatic similarities, were to be found in many European countries and were central to the development of the legal cultures of Europe.

[71] Leo Strauss, "The living issues of German postwar philosophy," in Heinrich Meier (ed.), *Leo Strauss and the Theologico-political Problem* (New York: Cambridge University Press, 2006), pp. 115–139.

In postwar Europe, the whole concept of shared values, history and institutions gained a new market seeking to place law and human rights at the center of the nascent European project. In the absence of a cultural component in the initial idea of European integration, a need arose to seek justification for the unification from within shared fundamental values. As mentioned earlier, the chosen form of the early integration, the neo-functionalist idea of focusing on economic integration had sidelined the earlier ideas of constitutional integration through federalism. Because law was thought to crystallize the fundamental values of society, the link between law and culture was a natural continuation in seeking a firmer foundation for the integration process.[72]

The European narrative in law became not only an interpretation of the past but also a vision for the future. In the writings of Coing, much like in the later writings of Reinhard Zimmermann and others, the common past would form a basis for a common future. According to Zimmermann, common law or rather the emerging common law of Europe should be informed by the shared tradition of the reception of Roman law not ancient Roman law itself. Thus Roman law or rather its history has both nothing and everything to do with the new common law, showing how a common legal tradition may be established through intellectual unity. A shared legal culture based on legal science was born through a series of exchanges and transmissions across Europe, where both scholars and texts moved in unprecedented ways. Inspired by this historical precedent, a new *ius commune* could be formed based on shared values, methods and principles. Zimmermann maintains that

[72] The focus on the economy is prevalent not only in the founding documents of European integration but equally in the histories of European integration. In the fundamental works (the historiography of the early history began with the opening of the archives in the early 1980s), the focus is on steel production and coal, tariffs and trade: Raymond Poidevin (ed.), *Histoire des débuts de la construction européenne (Mars 1948–Mai 1950)* (Brussls: Bruylant, 1984); Alan S. Milward, *The Reconstruction of Western Europe, 1945–51* (London: Methuen, 1984); Frances M. B. Lynch, Alan S. Milward, Ruggero Ranieri, Federico Romero and Vibeke Sørensen, *The Frontier of National Sovereignty: History and Theory 1945–1992* (London: Routledge, 1994). For example, Milward, *Reconstruction of Western Europe*, pp. 491–504 argued in his criticism of neo-functionalist theories that while the shared aim was economic prosperity gained through increased trade, nation-states did not relinquish their sovereignty and political, let alone cultural, integration was not on the agenda. In contrast, recent works such as Wilfried Loth, *Building Europe: A History of European Unification* (Berlin: De Gruyter Oldenbourg, 2015), see even in the early stages the foundations of social and political harmonization among European states.

this creation is a complex process where the involvement of judges, legislators and professors is crucial. In the numerous books and articles that Zimmermann has devoted to the subject, there is a clear emphasis on the historical demonstration of the European influences in English private law tradition and hence the links between England and Europe.[73] In short, his European tradition is one that joins Britain with the continent.

This teleological narrative of Europe and its private law has attracted its share of critics, most prominently Pierre Legrand, who in numerous articles argued that there was hardly a kind of convergence as Zimmermann envisions. On the contrary, lawyers still think in very national ways, even when dealing with European statutes. The unification that was envisioned is simply not happening.[74] More critically minded lawyers have noted that the whole concept of European private law appears less a statement of fact than a project. Its proponents like Hondius see it as a long and inevitable process of harmonization that gradually envelops the field of private law.[75] In contrast, historians such as Wijffels have already earlier noted how there may or may not be a European private law but there is increasingly more disagreement on what exactly it is. Not coincidentally, the often-stated historical precedent of *ius commune* has itself come under criticism from scholars who have doubted whether such a unity existed historically.[76]

The historical debate of a shared European legal heritage has in consequence become a hostage to the contemporary debate over the future of the European private law project and the drive for a European Civil Code. While the debates have often been simplified and framed as one between the "harmonizer Ole Lando and the defender of national traditions Pierre Legrand,"[77] the field as a whole is much more fragmented. In fact, there have been numerous large projects beside Lando's *Commission on European Contract Law*, such as Bussani's and Mattei's *Trento*

[73] Zimmermann, "Roman law and the harmonization of private law in Europe."

[74] One example is Pierre Legrand, *Fragments on Law-as-Culture* (Deventer: W. E. J. Tjeenk Willink, 1999), pp. 76–77.

[75] Ewoud Hondius, "Towards a European Civil Code," in Arthur S. Hartkamp, Martijn W. Hesselink, Ewoud Hondius, C. Mak and Edgar Du Perron (eds.), *Towards a European Civil Code* (Alphen aan den Rijn: Kluwer Law International, 2011), p. 3.

[76] Alain Wijffels, "European private law: a new software-package for an outdated operating system?," in Mark van Hoecke and François Ost (eds.), *The Harmonisation of European Private Law* (Oxford: Hart, 2000), pp. 101–106.

[77] Thomas Wilhelmsson, "Introduction: harmonization and national cultures," in Thomas Wilhelmsson, Elina Paunio and Annika Pohjolainen (eds.), *Private Law and the Many Cultures of Europe* (Alphen aan den Rijn: Kluwer Law International, 2007), p. 4.

*Common Core Project* or the *Study Group on a European Civil Code*. There are considerable disagreements whether the process should be top down or bottom up with different initiatives presenting different approaches.[78]

In all of this, it is unclear where the historical foundation of the European project or even the idea of shared roots stands in this constellation. In their influential criticism on the *Draft Common Frame of Reference*, Eidenmüller et al. (including Zimmermann), cite Coing by name in recognizing how earlier legal historians have "helped us to recognize the common ground shared by Europe's modern national legal systems."[79] The former unity informed the current unifiers and the process of seeking a common ground for European legal systems. However, the narrative of the tradition extending from Roman law to European legal tradition spread out far beyond the writings of Coing.

The European narrative of the second life of Roman law was by no means a completely new invention even in Britain. There, this line of argument had been presented already by another exile (from Russia), Paul Vinogradoff, in his 1909 *Roman Law in Medieval Europe*. In the introduction to the second edition, Peter Stein ties the book not only to F. C. von Savigny and Hermann Conrat but also to the postwar resurgence of the theory by the likes of Francesco Calasso.[80] Vinogradoff wrote how the second, ghost life of Roman law was frankly quite puzzling: Why do students still need to learn about the basics from ancient Roman manuals? One of the interesting features about Vinogradoff is that he connects English jurisprudence such as Bracton directly to the Roman law tradition, a feature that was later picked up by Schulz.[81]

Another important work in bringing the European narrative to an English-speaking audience was Hermann Kantorowicz's *Studies in the Glossators of the Roman Law*.[82] Originally a part of the History of Legal

[78] For a rare level-headed introduction to these different initiatives, see Lucinda Miller, "The notion of European private law," in Michael Lobban and Julia Moses (eds.), *The Impact of Ideas on Legal Development* (Cambridge: Cambridge University Press, 2014), pp. 265–285.

[79] Horst Eidenmüller, Florian Faust, Hans Christoph Grigoleit, Nils Jansen, Gerhard Wagner and Reinhard Zimmermann, "The common frame of reference for European private law – policy choices and codification problems," *Oxford Journal of Legal Studies*, 28(4) (2008), 659–708.

[80] Peter Stein, "Foreword," in Paul Vinogradoff, *Roman Law in Medieval Europe* (Oxford: Clarendon Press, 1968), pp. x–xii.

[81] Paul Vinogradoff, *Roman Law in Medieval Europe* (Oxford: Clarendon Press, 1968), pp. 11, 101–106.

[82] Kantorowicz, *Studies in the Glossators of the Roman Law*.

Science project, which produced Schulz's *History,* it presents the refounding of the legal tradition by the glossators on Roman sources.

What was new about the narrative formed by Coing was the consolidation of the bridge between the traditions and the focus on Europe as the frame of reference. This combined many of the works written earlier by Schulz and Pringsheim about the link between certain ideals and the legal tradition, as well as Koschaker's focus on tradition and Wieacker's emphasis on the self-referentiality of legal scholarship. The connection between the continental and the British legal traditions, between civil law and common law, entered into Coing's work fairly late in the 1980s. In his attempts at finding a common ground, he again draws from the foundations of Christianity and Greco-Roman civilization. The areas of research he proposed were, to a large degree, ones where a common thread could be found arising from the Roman law tradition and thus an inherent unifying theme could be established. While he sought to present the aim of this comparative exercise as an intellectual one where the differences and similarities of the solutions developed by different legal cultures could be explored, the study also had a practical element linked to European integration. For instance, in the area of law and industrialization, "the study of these developments is especially interesting because it has a bearing on our understanding of modern European economic law and, in my view, is able to facilitate the necessary unification of economic law in the European communities."[83]

The most influential disseminators of the narrative of the shared roots of European law and jurisprudence are not only German or British. One of the crucial voices had been that of Raoul van Caenegem, who presented the European story in many of his works such as the *Historical Introduction to Private Law* (1992), which connects the legal and intellectual developments between Britain, the Benelux, France and Germany and the shared foundation in the *ius commune*. Caenegem presented the influence of Roman law as one of returning to a modernity that was lost: "Romanization therefore meant modernization." In contrast to the backwards feudal and agrarian society, Roman law "appeared to be a modern system, progressive, oriented to the future."[84] Italian scholar Aldo Schiavone has

[83] Helmut Coing, "Common law and civil law in the development of European civilization. Possibilities of comparisons," in Helmut Coing and Knut Wolfgang Nörr (eds.), *Englische und kontinentale Rechtsgeschichte: ein Forschungsprojekt* (Berlin: Duncker & Humblot, 1985), p. 40.

[84] Raoul C. van Caenegem, *An Historical Introduction to Private Law* (Cambridge: Cambridge University Press, 1992), p. 71.

argued in a similar fashion for the proto-modernity of ancient Roman law and society, where concepts, rules and theories emerged that would later form the foundations of not only the legal system but modern ideas of democracy and human rights. Ancient Roman society was naturally incapable of developing the implications of these ideas such as the equality of man.[85]

Within this historical tradition, some, like Grossi, have protested against the way that the common roots narrative "privileges the thread of the Roman law tradition," when other influences such as the medieval tradition have been equally significant.[86] Padoa-Schioppa has argued, much in the vein of Koschaker and Wieacker, that the convergence in the field of law of the three main inheritances from antiquity, namely Greek philosophy, Roman law and Christianity, only took place in medieval European jurisprudence. In part, he continues a similar argument that was presented earlier by Harold Berman in *Law and Revolution,* which traces the whole creation of modern science to medieval jurisprudence and canon law. However, his main thesis is that it was the polyvalence of the works of Roman jurists and the malleable usability that they demonstrated which gave them such success in the future formation of the legal profession. For Padoa-Schioppa, medieval jurisprudence and the practice of the church laid the groundwork for the "events that formed the modern European states and their legal systems."[87]

The emergence of the European narrative in legal history parallels the rise of human rights language in post-WWII Europe and consolidation of the idea that human rights were a particularly European concept.

In the basic works of human rights history, European nations are mostly portrayed as resisting their introduction.[88] In contrast, Marco

[85] Aldo Schiavone, *The Invention of the Law in the West* (Cambridge, MA and London: The Belknap Press of Harvard University Press, 2005), pp. 458–459. In other recent works, a similar historical narrative has been linked with the development, adaptation and transmission of legal knowledge. See, for example, Karl-Heinz Ladeur, *Der Anfang Des Westlichen Rechts: Die Christianisierung Der Romischen Rechtskultur Und Die Entstehung Des Universalen Rechts* (Tübingen: Mohr Siebeck, 2018).

[86] Paolo Grossi, "Historical models and present plans in the formation of a future European law," in Antonio Gambaro and Alfredo Mordechai Rabello (eds.), *Towards a New European Ius Commune* (Jerusalem: The Hebrew University of Jerusalem, 1999), p. 4.

[87] Antonio Padoa-Schioppa (ed.), *A History of Law in Europe. From the Early Middle Ages to the Twentieth Century* (Cambridge: Cambridge University Press, 2017), pp. 70, 294–295; Harold J. Berman, *Law and Revolution: The Formation of the Western Legal Tradition* (Cambridge, MA: Harvard University Press, 1983).

[88] Lynn Hunt, *Inventing Human Rights: A History* (New York: W. W. Norton, 2007), p. 202.

Duranti has lately argued that the traditional narrative of the emergence of human rights should be amended and that the true key players of the post-WWII construction of the European human rights regime were in fact conservatives such as Winston Churchill, whose involvement precedes the generation of EU founders like Monnet and Schumann. For conservatives, the promise of Europeanism and human rights was founded on a number of different motivations. One of the most important causes was opposition to totalitarianism, where fascism and communism were but two sides of the same coin. At the same time, conservatives were deeply distrustful of the tyranny of the majority and the dangers of populism in democracy. Pluralism and securing the rights of minorities were central concerns in this regard. To secure these rights, it had become clear that the national courts were unable to uphold the rule of law and thus international guarantees were needed. However, the conservative idea of free and united Europe was not necessarily a superstate, but rather a "return to tradition and older forms of community."[89]

Among the conservatives was also a large contingent of Catholics, for whom the idea of justice beyond the nation-state and the unification of Europe was appealing for religious reasons. For many Catholics, Roman law and canon law were such legal orders, drawing their validity not from the word of a legislator but from the cultural tradition. Many, like Koschaker, saw the Roman and the medieval Christian tradition as parts of the same continuum and an inherent part of the European heritage. In contrast, the human rights regime offered a different promise, strengthening the freedoms of Catholic associations and churches. However, on a more general level, the historical legal orders and the human rights order could be seen as part of the same process, where a higher law would constrain the excesses of national governments and legislators. For these Catholic conservatives, the new European unification gave a promise for a rebirth of the lost unity that was not only cultural but also spiritual. The traditional orders of justice and reason were at the heart of the Catholic worldview and the values and morals that underlay it.[90]

[89] Duranti, *Conservative Human Rights Revolution*, pp. 4–5.

[90] Within the human rights realm, see Duranti, *Conservative Human Rights Revolution*, p. 8; Moyn, *Christian Human Rights*, pp. 86–87. On the reorientation of Catholicism, see recently James Chappel, *Catholic Modern; The Challenge of Totalitarianism and the Remaking of the Church* (Cambridge, MA: Harvard University Press, 2018).

In the Europeanist discussion, Catholic voices had been some of the earliest to propose a new foundation to replace the nation-state. Maritain would emerge as a voice of Christian conservatives but similar ideas on the connections between European law, culture and civilization having a religious foundation were presented earlier by Riccobono and others. There was naturally a precedent in the earlier discussions, for instance the ideas such as *Abendland* promoted among Catholic conservatives, but these ideas did not figure for instance in the works of Coing. During the war Maritain and Dawson, whom Koschaker would cite approvingly, turned toward the ideas of human rights and democracy, conflating them with the protection of human persons, their individual freedoms and with it religion.[91] Even here, the émigré community was crucial, the Catholic sections actively promoting the combination of the ideas of anti-totalitarianism, democracy and the rule of law as a political, spiritual and legal policy.[92] The intellectual connection formed by Coing was one that focused on lawyers and their scholarship, not a dictate given by a ruler or a state legislator, thus making it more palatable for the nations concerned about their sovereignty and national traditions. A unity based on already shared traits and the common striving toward a unity of minds was thus easier to accept both politically and culturally than the limitations of sovereignty advocated by federalists.

The combination of Europe and rights was initially not easy to make. For one, Nazi collaborators and the Nazi occupation of much of Europe had framed the event as a pan-European struggle against communism. The resistance toward Nazism had been under the banner of patriotic nationalism against the foreign oppressor. At the same time, Allied powers had rejected Nazi ideology and maintained their commitment toward human rights as international and universal standards. The whole postwar era had been one of cosmopolitan internationalism, where the nation-state would be a component part of the international order. Thus, the initial reaction toward European unity and the legal unity of Europe was not necessarily positive. The postwar European

[91] Moyn, *Christian Human Rights*, pp. 84–85. On Riccobono, Koschaker and Maritain, see Chapter 4. On Coing's relationship with earlier Europeanism, see Duve, "Von der Europäischen Rechtsgeschichte zu einer Rechtsgeschichte Europas in globalhistorischer Perspektive," p. 44.

[92] See Greenberg, *Weimar Century*, pp. 147–149 on the ideas and people behind the *Manifesto on the War* published in 1942 by forty-three Catholic thinkers from different backgrounds from Hildebrand to Maritain.

governments, not to mention peoples, would, as a rule, support the reconstruction of a strong state in the service of the people. The people were here primarily understood as the nation, a popular sovereignty established through national sovereignty.[93]

The European conservatives advocating for unification would seek to transfer nationalistic feelings toward a European community. They stressed the long history and cultural unity but added to this a novel component, human rights. As Duranti maintains, they argued that the European community of peoples was linked by "a shared commitment to individual freedom and the rule of law." Thus their Europe was at the same time a return to an idealized past unity where Christianity and humanism reigned over the civilized cultures of Europe but also a liberal idea of human rights. In this configuration, human rights themselves became an expression of European heritage and its commitment to freedom and rights. Churchill himself would in his famous "Iron Curtain" speech in 1946 refer to the "great principles of freedom and the rights of man," which were the "joint inheritance of the English-speaking world and which through the Magna Carta, the Bill of Rights, Habeas Corpus, trial by jury and the English common law find their most famous expression in the American Declaration of Independence."[94] Thus the ideas of human rights and freedom were initially a legacy of the English-speaking peoples, which should then be bestowed upon the rest of Europe and the world.

Within the human rights discourse, Churchill's conception of human rights as freedoms that were shared by a community such as Europe that had a common culture, values and political system was in itself a conservative proposition. His human rights were thus not inherently universal and pointedly excluded, for example, the European colonies. In contrast, the leftist and communist conceptions of human rights, which the Soviet Union had advocated since the 1930s both directly and through its front organizations in Europe, focused on social rights and economic rights. Within their ambit, the liberal conception of human rights as well as liberal democracy itself was simply a sham that masked the real inequality and iniquity of capitalistic societies.[95]

Churchill, in his post-WWII speeches, pivoted toward anticommunism, starting from his "Iron Curtain" speech, where he presented the

[93] Duranti, *Conservative Human Rights Revolution*, pp. 348–349.
[94] Winston Churchill, *Iron Curtain* speech, on March 5, 1946, at Westminster College, Fulton, Missouri; Duranti, *Conservative Human Rights Revolution*, p. 350.
[95] Duranti, *Conservative Human Rights Revolution*, p. 355.

juxtaposition between the free peoples of the West and the dictatorships in the East. In this division, European unity was the unity of democratic, civilized nations that were part of a European family. Within this conception, human rights provided the moral, ethical and cultural foundations. Even during the war, Churchill was one of the first leaders of the Great Powers to refer to human rights. In his message to a rally in London in support of Jews in Germany, he predicted that the worldwide struggle against fascism would "end with the enthronement of human rights."[96]

The fact that human rights were presented as a European notion helped to resolve one of the fundamental problems of human rights, the question which Hannah Arendt posed as "the right to have rights." If the original Enlightenment notion of human rights was framed as the rights within a political community, these rights were dependent on membership in that community and "the spaces of citizenship in which rights were accorded and protected," as Moyn defined it. Thus, as one of the Nazi policies had been the stripping away of citizenship and the purposeful creation of lawless places, the new post-1945 human rights thought focused on the universalism of human rights and their capacity to limit the sovereignty of the state. With the creation of a European convention and a European human rights regime, its framers were intent on achieving the universal effect of human rights within the particular European area.[97]

It was at this political and ideological moment that the narrative of European legal heritage, the theory of the common legal roots, struck. It combined numerous traits, from Catholic conservatism and the ideas of universal law based on the cultural foundation of Christianity, the anticommunism of conservatism and the enthusiasm for private law as an instrument that secured property and transactions rather than social equality and the distribution of wealth.

Duve has criticized Coing's approach as Eurocentric. He argues that Coing, together with Wieacker and Koschaker, began the concept of European legal history as a successor to the project of Savigny and the Historical School, a project that revolved around the dogmatic core of legal science in the geographic core of Europe, an essence of law in the essence of Europe. This made it possible to focus on the unity of the idea rather than the complexities of the actual historical situation. Its law

[96] Loeffler, *Rooted Cosmopolitans*, p. 91; Duranti, *Conservative Human Rights Revolution*, p. 357.
[97] Moyn, *Last Utopia*, pp. 12–15.

was the law of jurists, of dogmatic civil law, a science of law that was at the same time historical and ahistorical, unified and particular.[98]

This is true in a certain sense but even Duve's criticism is Germanocentric. The grand narratives of the kind written by Harold Berman, Manlio Bellomo or Paolo Grossi are not reducible to the German project begun by Savigny. For example, Berman's *Law and Revolution*, which traces the origins of the whole of Western law to the beginnings of canon law, has a very different aim and purpose when compared with the German projects. Thus, while Duve rightly points out that in all of these cases, the themes of science, professionalization, secularization, rationalization and so forth are prominent,[99] they have more to do with the general self-definition of Europe that transcends German lawyers or even some of its most famous authors such as Weber.

The background of the new revitalization of Roman law in the European context was clearly in the deepening of European integration in the 1990s. It shared traits from the older revivalist movements, in that one of its primary motivations was the self-preservation of the field of study. The ideas of the new *ius commune* and the revival of Roman law stemmed from different backgrounds. In the case of the ideas of Zimmermann and Pichonnaz, Roman law had a role much like comparative law, it had a dogmatic utility in contemporary law. Scholars of this persuasion took up cases such as mixed legal systems (most famously South Africa, Scotland and Louisiana) as success stories.[100] During the debates that went on during the 1990s and early 2000s, others pointed out that Roman law had an underlying continuity in things such as legal concepts or principles,[101] and while issues such as human rights were clearly beyond its grasp, it could have value as a methodological tool for analysis.[102] The issues of method, analysis and case material were incidentally not only presented in terms of the relevance of ancient law for the European integration, but also as justifications for the continued teaching of Roman law.[103]

[98] Duve, "European legal history - global perspectives," pp. 3–11.

[99] Duve, "Von der Europäischen Rechtsgeschichte zu einer Rechtsgeschichte Europas in globalhistorischer Perspektive," p. 24.

[100] Reinhard Zimmermann, "'Double cross': Comparing Scots and South African law," in Reinhard Zimmermann, Daniel Visser and Kenneth Reid (eds.), *Mixed Legal Systems in Comparative Perspective* (Oxford: Oxford University Press, 2004), pp. 1–33.

[101] Massimo Vari, "Diritto romano 'ius commune' europeo?," *Index: quaderni camerti di studi romanistici = international survey of Roman law*, 30 (2002), 183–185.

[102] Franco Casavola, "Diritto romano e diritto europeo," *Labeo*, 40 (1994), 161–169.

[103] David Johnston, "The renewal of the old," *Cambridge Law Journal*, 56(1) (1997), 80–95.

For the European legal tradition and European legal history, the issue of unity and pluralism has both a dogmatic and an intellectual relevance. Is there a unity in the European legal tradition? If so, what is this legal tradition? Within the realms of human rights regimes, claims of unity and universality have been made with some regularity, even though with ample criticism. However, within private law regimes, claims of past unity have lost much of their relevance. An analytical way of understanding the connection between the past and the future leads inevitably to the rejection of the ideas of the actualization of the past as a foundation for the future. However, as noted by Carbonnier, even in the earlier usages of ancient law, for example in medieval Germany or early modern France, the point was not about historical accuracy, but about invention. Inventions are seldom created in a vacuum and legal invention in particular is a result of texts being read and reread. Thus, the significance of ancient ideas is in their role in legal discourse as ideas, concepts, cases and solutions.[104]

An even more fundamental issue behind the European narrative and the shared past of European legal tradition is its self-imposed link to the teleological nature of European integration. The deeply problematic notion of the teleology that underlay early European ideas of integration, even to the extent that it was presented as a principle of interpretation in EU law, was based on the premise that the union would experience only a deepening of integration. With the ongoing crises and the criticism that the negative side effects of integration have faced, this teleology of deepening integration may not be the safest of foundations for a historical understanding. In a similar manner, when scholars such as Zimmermann were drafting theories of the deep underlying shared tradition that tied together continental Europe and Britain, this was done in a political climate where issues such as Brexit were scarcely imaginable.

This means that the discussion today may lead to a similar conundrum as that which provoked the debates over *Antike Rechtsgeschichte* or ancient legal history and the crisis of Roman law during the first decades of the twentieth century: what is the value of history and thus

[104] Jean Carbonnier, "Usus hodiernus pandectarum," in Ronald H. Graveson, Karl Kreuzer, André Tunc and Konrad Zweigert (eds.), *Festschrift für Imre Zajtay. Mélanges en l'honneur d'Imre Zajtay* (Tübingen: J. C. B. Mohr (Paul Siebeck), 1982), p. 113. As Aldo Mazzacane, "'Il leone fuggito dal circo': pandettistica e diritto comune europeo," *Index: quaderni camerti di studi romanistici = International Survey of Roman Law*, 29 (2001), 97–111 already noted, even Savigny's Roman law was in no way faithful to the original.

tradition? The idea of using history as a vehicle for advancing contemporary policies may appear sound but the danger is that when the policy with or without its historical justification is rejected, what happens to history? In his 1999 article on the relationship between Roman law, comparative law and legal history, David Johnston argued that pure history is of no use, that it should in fact have a purpose, even as simple a purpose as enriching our understanding of the law.[105] However, what does it mean for history to support the European project if or when the European project is no more? A few years earlier, Zimmermann himself wrote how the discovery of the European dimension of law is largely due to the works of Koschaker, Wieacker and Coing. They taught jurists to see Roman law and legal science not simply as past or history but "as one of the essential cornerstones of European law and legal science."[106]

## Conclusions

Coing's main contribution was to link the rights tradition with the idea of a European legal heritage. While his own field had been more recent legal history, he embraced the idea of Roman foundations and its role in European legal science. Even though Coing's works can be seen as part of the renaissance of natural law in the postwar period, he was even more important in the institutionalization of the European legal narrative, both within legal academia and in the European political sphere. Recently, this influence has grown through the work of Reinhard Zimmermann, who has promoted Coing as a precursor.

Coing's background was in the German *Bildungsbürgertum*, where ideas about learning, civilization and service were valued. There is some confusion regarding his membership in the Nazi party but his ideological involvement left no trace in his works. In contrast, the experience of the war, in which he served in frontline units as a reserve officer, made a lasting impression and formed with the aftermath of totalitarianism a crucial starting point for his postwar works on natural law and rights.

[105] David Johnston, "Roman law, comparative law and legal history," *Zeitschrift für Europäisches Privatrecht*, 3 (1999), 562–564.

[106] Reinhard Zimmermann, "Roman and comparative law: the European perspective (some remarks apropos a recent controversy)," *The Journal of Legal History*, 16(1) (1995), 28; Reinhard Zimmermann, "Europa und das römische Recht," *Archiv für die civilistische Praxis*, 2 (2002), 243–316.

The turn toward natural law and legal philosophy in general was in line with the general turn toward discussing the implications of totalitarianism and Nazism in general. In the German legal world still dominated by former Nazi scholars, facing the past was not popular. Natural law was heavily criticized, as was legal positivism, in a discussion that can only be described as perverted. Exiles such as Kelsen were being blamed for their intellectual support for the Nazis and ideas such as human rights were shunned. In this atmosphere, Coing's approach of laying out a foundation for rights through tradition was a success as it used existing legal tradition for the justification of rights.

One of the fundamental tenets of Coing's thought was the idea of freedom and drawing rights from that basic premise. In a sense, Coing was building a third way for rights. He argued that rights may be founded through tradition, not through nature or through a convention. Human rights are thus something that is based on personhood and morality, not as inalienable rights as suggested by Enlightenment thought or humanity itself.

However, the philosophical side of Coing's thought was inseparable from his historical works, which focused on the later reception of Roman law. Klaus Luig, in his obituary on Coing, remarked that Coing's view of history was fundamentally about experience. Instead of the remarkable and the scandalous, he wanted to approach history through the concept of possibilities, in that historical examples demonstrate not simply answers but problems and alternative solutions. Thus, social, political and legal history should be approached as a whole, where the role of law was to provide peace and security not only between individuals but also between people and the state. This meant that each historical moment was at the same time a part of a continuum but also its own unique legal culture.[107]

When writing about the reception of Roman law, Coing described it as a purely unhistorical process in which beginning from the eleventh century the texts and rules of Roman law were applied with little care for their proper context. The medieval emperors were identified with the Roman emperors, Italian cities with Roman cities and so forth. Roman law was, as Kantorowitz had stated, a treasure chest of solutions which were applied with no concern for the proper legal context.[108]

107 Luig, "Helmut Coing," p. 220.

108 Helmut Coing, "Klassizismus in der Geschichte des römischen Rechts," in G. E. von Grunebaum and Willy Hartner (eds.), *Klassizismus und Kulturverfall* (Frankfurt: Vittorio Klostermann, 1960), p. 72.

The project of European legal history appears in Coing both as a conception of reception as an anachronistic reuse of ancient law but equally as a constitutive factor. In a sense, European legal history began to resemble a constitutional project without a constitution, where tradition operates at the same time as a justification and context. However, the legal rules were themselves more like manifestations of values inherent in the European tradition rather than these values themselves.

Within the postwar debates on constitutional law, Coing's idea of the rebuilding of tradition through the reworking of existing material appealed to scholars wary of innovations such as human rights. He gradually expanded the idea of European legal tradition to combine two traits: the natural law tradition and the Roman law tradition, where the first would be more about public law and the second about private law. Linking these was the idea of civilization, in which he was influenced by thinkers such as Werner Jaeger. Combined, these formed a *Kulturrecht*, a law of culture, which encompassed virtue, morality and the inherent value of the human person.

Within the emerging European discussion, Coing's ideas about a European tradition were taken by Zimmermann and others to a new level to form the foundation of a European legal tradition that would both explain the past and lay out the future of European law. In this, Coing's role resembled that of conservatives in the postwar human rights debates.

# 7 Conclusions

In one of the first studies on scholarly migration, Theodor Adorno very candidly described his own experience in America and what he had learned in America. He described at length the various shocks that he had endured coming in 1938 from Britain to New York to work on the Princeton Radio Project, not really understanding what the project was about and the strange statistical methods it used. Through all of his experiences, he began to see the limitations of his own mind, the things that he had taken for granted. This he defined as a kind of de-provincialization: "In America I was liberated from a certain naïve belief in culture and attained the capacity to see culture from the outside."[1]

The narrative of the shared tradition of European law, the idea that the legal heritage of Europe was an inherent source of unity and was traceable all the way back to antiquity and Roman law took shape in a long process, beginning from the 1930s. This book was the story of that process.

There was, even before the Nazi takeover of power, a sense of crisis in Europe. One should perhaps speak of crises in the plural because the pervasive sense of crisis had spread to so many issues, ranging from the crisis of science to the crisis of values or even the crisis of reason. Beginning in 1933, the Nazi persecution of opponents and people of Jewish descent turned the crisis into a personal one, not only one of maintaining one's position as a scholar but ultimately a battle for survival as repression turned to annihilation in the Holocaust.

How scholars reacted to the crisis is wholly another matter. For most of them, there was a separation between science and the personal, where scientific inquiry remained unaffected by the circumstances where that inquiry took place. In these cases, personal issues were

[1] Adorno, "Scientific experiences of a European scholar in America," quote from p. 367.

detectable only in the prefaces of books or in personal memoirs. This book was not about them.

This book was about the people whose experience of totalitarianism carried over to the way that they conducted their scientific work and transformed the questions and methods that were considered relevant. For example, philosopher Karl Popper turned from logic and the philosophy of science to the crisis of Western democracy and the challenge of totalitarianism in his exile in New Zealand, publishing his most famous work *Open Society and Its Enemies* in 1945.

However, it remains an open question whether crises really produce new solutions or whether they only make existing ones more acceptable. In the case of the researchers we have been following during this book, people such as Fritz Schulz, Fritz Pringsheim, Paul Koschaker, Franz Wieacker and Helmut Coing, the solution was not looking elsewhere but rather looking at the Western legal and intellectual tradition to rediscover what they considered to be the true meaning of that tradition. This was, in a way, a similar method as that utilized by Popper, to return to the tradition and to reread it for new meanings to find answers to new questions raised by the political and intellectual crisis.

In his seminal book *Atlantic Crossings*, Rodger maintains that crises are not truly moments where novel solutions are discovered but rather moments where existing solutions are tested and put to use: "The policy ideas pressed into service in the emergency are, as often as not, old, formulated in other circumstances to meet other conditions. They are an eruption of the past into the present."[2] In the transatlantic world, crises were moments of intellectual transmission and adaptation of ideas and practices across continents. While the interwar years had been marked by a gradual recognition of emerging American superiority in the economy and military power, there was equally an emergent intellectual challenge in the novel understanding of society and law produced in the political, social and legal sciences in the US. Within European academia, the recognition of this was as slow as was the realization of American power by European states. The slow and often painful experience of this realization and the critique of American society and science it contained was a clear consequence of how deep seated the ideas of European superiority were.

[2] Rodger, *Atlantic Crossings*, 414.

Many of the exiles did not reach American shores but the British experience tied them to the transatlantic world of ideas. Although they did not recognize it as such, what many of the exiles ended up doing was not only a reaction to the totalitarian challenge, but also a self-reflection of the fundamental values of Europe and a self-examination of the European tradition. Exposure to new ideas, traumatic experiences and feelings of marginalization were powerful impulses for rethinking.

Back in Europe, Nazi thought was not only a hyperdriven version of German nationalism and its inherent quest for cultural dominance but also a symptom of a wider intellectual and political reaction to social change and the perceived threat from communist movements. Within the nationalist movements in Europe, there was a fundamental disconnect between exclusionary nationalistic thoughts and the idea of Europe, ranging from the discussions of shared and indigenous traits to the notions of a common European culture and the role of elements such as the classical past or Christianity within it. During the war, these discussions were transferred to the search for unity in the face of the common enemy, not only Soviet Russia but also the Anglo-American world. While they were nominally shoring up support for the Nazi regime, in doing so they began to distribute notions of European unity and a new Europe.

For exiles such as Schulz and Pringsheim, the fall from a position of status and respect was debilitating. They survived with only their immediate family members and some belongings. Their life, as it had been, was destroyed. They began to reimagine and to reinvent, using their acquired knowledge, to build a new future. While many other exiles departed for America and took up permanent residence there, their eyes were on Europe.

At the same time, Koschaker, Wieacker and Coing were in different ways involved with the Nazi revolution in German society and science, taking part with varying degrees of enthusiasm. For them, the end of the war, the massive death toll and the loss of position and status were equally shocking.

The Nazi challenge had been one of fundamental reorganization of German law and society based on completely different criteria than the liberal Weimar Constitution. However, the racial and hierarchical ideology was in the end a marginal pursuit even within German legal science. When the totalitarian regime that supported it collapsed, there were few that would seriously advocate the model. For European legal thought, a deeper challenge was the same development that the Nazi movement had been a symptom of, that of the emerging industrial mass society and its problems. The social, legal, economic and other challenges were vast and many of the legal reform movements such as legal realism sought to answer them.

The solution that the Europeanist legal thought presented, the return to tradition and the fundamentals shaped by the tradition, was thus an unlikely answer to the challenges of the new society. The European tradition and the ideas of relative natural law were not the answers that would have been sufficient to resolve the pressing social questions, the ideological challenge of socialism or even the ills of industrial society. It may even be said that the alternative that returning to tradition posed would perhaps not have been worth considering without the fact that Nazi policies had made many of the alternatives unpalatable by association. Thus distributive social policies and economic and social rights remained in the margins due to their association with socialism and Nazism.

The ideals presented by postwar thinkers, the primacy of the independence of law from politics and the ideals of human rights, especially traditional liberty rights, were by and large conservative ideals. They sought to safeguard the individual from the oppression of the state, a notion that in itself contained the premise that the state as the wielder of sovereign power would need to be curtailed. Whether this premise was in opposition to a nascent totalitarian or authoritarian rule or the rise of socialism or populism through democratic means, was a matter that was often left undiscussed.

The role of Roman law in this construct was a historical oddity, a matter of tradition and heritage that was not easily explained logically. However, for the purpose of defending property rights and the established system of private law and contracts, the position of Roman law was quite suitable. It placed law in the realm of tradition, away from political discussion and most certainly away from the demands of a more equitable division of wealth.

The nascent role of European legal heritage and with it the historical claims of the Roman law tradition shared another trait with the emerging human rights regime. Both were sidelined by the Nazi regime, which was in principled opposition to the values and ideas that they contained and the Nazis sought to replace them with a more palatable alternative. For Roman law, this Nazi alternative was a national German legal system based on the idea of blood community; for human rights;

the Nazi alternative was the idea of a system of protecting the dignity of the members of the blood community.

For their revival, both were in a different shape and form driven by the personal experience of their defenders under totalitarianism. In both cases, there was a reticence about talking about these experiences. Schulz and Pringsheim were notoriously unwilling to discuss or write about them, the same was true for the founders of the modern human rights system such as Hersch Lauterpacht. Coming from the city of Lemberg, now called Lviv, he experienced at first hand the terrifying pogroms following World War I. He was not present during the horrendous repetition during World War II, an infamous event captured in gruesome detail on film. Both of the carnages were not even something that would be blamed solely on the Germans, because those who turned on the Jewish inhabitants of Lemberg were their Polish and Ukrainian neighbors.

The issue of trauma as a motivating factor has been under some discussion recently, with Lauterpacht's personal history as a focus.[3] Whether the traumatic experience prompts someone to act and someone else to write is naturally a question of personality.

What was quite beyond doubt was the role of European integration, both as a reaction to German aggression and Nazi terror as well as the growing realization of the threat posed by the Soviet Union and its satellite states. Human rights and European heritage formed the intellectual foundation of the Western European narrative: rights, the rule of law and economic prosperity were the catchphrases that were presented in opposition to the socialist demands for social and economic equality. For these purposes, the narratives presented against Nazi totalitarianism were equally suitable against communist totalitarianism as the same central argument was the separation of law and politics.

The narrative of European legal heritage and the shared common roots that European legal traditions had in the long development of jurisprudence formed were also much more than a political message. The European narrative drafted by Koschaker, Wieacker and Coing was a narrative of science and its development. At its core was the heritage of Roman law and Roman jurists; the ideas and the professional identity they developed were repurposed by generations of jurists in Europe. As such, it was a narrative that described the development of private law where the method and the independence of law were praised. Through

[3] Loeffler, *Rooted Cosmopolitans*.

the idea of the reception of ancient law, the narrative bridged the gap between the traditional disciplinary boundaries separating the Roman and the native legal heritages.

The two strands of the narrative, the exile and the German, form two parts of the whole. The narrative formed by the exiles was one of liberty and scientific integrity, while the narrative of those who remained was about culture and tradition, the long roots of the conventional interpretations in the thoughts and practices of the countries. The exile narrative proved to be extraordinarily influential in Britain, where the émigrés prompted a veritable renaissance of Roman law. As in areas of democracy, the rule of law and in human rights, the exile narratives were reincorporated after the war, leading to a novel interpretation of the tradition of legal history. Their interpretations were also integrated by many of those who did not become exiles, such as Wieacker or Coing, who sought to provide a new beginning for the history of law.

However, these narrative reformulations may have been for nothing had a political imperative for this work emerged through the deepening of European integration. While there had been a political process of integration, it, or its supporters, sought to strengthen its legitimacy by seeking to provide a historical foundation, a lineage.

Through this seeking of lineages, the narratives of Roman law were integrated with the changing conceptions of European self-understanding, one that was transformed by the inclusion of exile scholarship of other kinds as well. Ideas from Leo Strauss, Franz Neumann, Hans Kelsen, Hannah Arendt and others, who had revolutionized the conceptions of law and politics, democracy and authoritarianism, were also incorporated into the European narrative. With the nascent theories of human rights and natural law, the political and legal thought of exiles became a central tenet in European tradition.

Thus, when Coing began to formulate the theory of a European legal heritage, his inclusion of both the Roman law tradition and the natural law tradition proved to be prescient. Together, they were to form the European heritage and the background for European integration. Though the initial course chosen for integration was that of functionalism or neofunctionalism, integration through economic connections and rising prosperity, there was equally a need to find precedents for integration. One possibility for these precedents was European history and its shared past. While much of that history was one of antagonisms and war, the cultural and legal continuities were a good template for the argument of natural unification. Of these, the shared legal past was also important because unlike the reception of classical literature in general, it could have direct significance in the functioning of the integration as a legal process.

However, all of this could be seen as a secondary issue to the larger question of what do we mean by a shared heritage. Of the over two and a half millennia of continuity from ancient Greece and Rome to the present day do we choose to call our past, our heritage?

The answer depends, quite naturally, on the present: what we recognize from the past as our heritage depends on how we see ourselves in the present. This means that we unconsciously or consciously emphasize the things we value most and seek to trace them to the past as if to say that this is what we have always been and always will be. The past and our relationship with it is a part of our identity and hence is subject to the vagaries of identity politics and the aspirational side of identity.

The constructivist idea of the relationship between past and present does not in any way mean that phenomena such as the classical tradition or the Roman law tradition were not real. In the case of Roman law, there is a two and half millennia-long historical continuity of legal research, writing and application of law that utilizes ancient Roman texts, concepts and rules. This continuity is to a high degree self-referential and there are innumerable continuities between historical phenomena associated with it and contemporary European legal systems. However, what is interesting in the constructivist sense is the way in which value judgements are associated with these phenomena.

The fact that the Greco-Roman past is commonly called "classical" in itself shows the valuation embedded in the historical period in question. However, the usages of classics in identity politics have very recent iterations that pertain to the central issue of this book. Among far right movements, there has been a long-standing practice of the use of classical imagery and tropes to emphasize European hegemony and the supposed racial order that they wish to reinforce. These include so-called identitarian movements that present orderly white European culture as a counterpoint to the masses in the East and South. For that purpose, images of Spartans at Thermopylae are presented with approximately the same frequency as among interwar far right movements or governments. Images of the Roman military order are juxtaposed with barbarian hordes, the rectangular order of Roman roads, fields and cities with indigenous societies, etc. What this entails is not merely an innocent comparison but a push for a certain social order under the guise of ancient precedents. Unquestioning allegiance to the state, militarism, conceptions of outsiders as barbarian enemies and opposition as traitors are peddled as the true way of the political order. At the same time, they are mixed with ideas of racial and ethnic tropes that had very little or no foundation in the classical past. In Europe, these ideas have come to the fore as a consequence of the 2015 refugee crisis and its aftermath; in America and elsewhere they have benefited from the political turns of the 2016 elections.

The far right was, of course, not the only political group to have used the classical past as legitimation; it was also heavily used in the different campaigns relating to European integration. In its drive to present narratives of Europe and especially narratives that would act as justifications for the past and future unity of Europe, there has been a strong reliance on cultural heritage and the uniting traits of European culture. In it, classics and to a lesser extent medieval history has acted as a shared legacy, where continuities such as the reception of ancient culture have been emphasized. Art, literature and science and their shared roots have been embraced by institutions such as universities and museums.

In all of this, there have been strong links and continuities from the interwar period. In the uses and abuses of the past, the affinity of Italian fascism and ancient Rome has often been noted but this is not the only example. The reliance on classical imagery and tropes emphasizing heroism and sacrifice was shared by all right-wing, nationalist regimes in Europe. What has been forgotten is that there were also popular conservative and liberal uses of the classical past. As we have noted in the preceding chapters, numerous contesting utopian visions of the past and the future were presented, where the past was used as a surrogate stage for battles about the future.

The Nazi movement relied on the idea of the German blood community as the foundation of their ideal state; for the fascists, it was the notion of *Romanità*. This underwent a gradual and incomplete change after the attack on the Soviet Union began in 1941. The need for allies and soldiers to fill the ranks prompted the invention of the *Neue Europa*, the European alliance led and dominated by Germany. In some of the occupied countries, such as Vichy France, the notion of a European heritage was mixed with French nationalism, where the idea of a European community meant a Christian nationalism based on Greco-Roman culture, where the enemies were both communism and the Anglo-American alliance. The Nazi visions of the classical past were colored by their racial theories. On one hand the conquering Greeks and Romans were hailed as the former master races, on the other the perceived Semitic influences and the cosmopolitanism of the empire were shunned. This was also the basis of point 19 of the Nazi party program.

Some of the ideas presented in Vichy France were more commonly shared among conservative circles, which led to the curious mixture of ideas that underlie postwar conservatism in Europe. Christian conservatives saw in the classical past the origin of European cultural heritage, mixing traditionalism with the emphasis on classical culture and literature. Thus, cultural theories and the idea of Rome were easily combined with notions of Christian heritage, Rome signifying for Catholics at least both ancient Rome and the Catholic Church. It was also the position of the church that led to their postwar transformation and to favoring supranationalism and inalienable rights as well as the protection of minorities, especially religious minorities. These notions were heavily present among Roman law scholars in the making of the narrative of a shared past; the works of Koschaker and Riccobono, but also Wieacker, show these elements. Ideas such as anticommunism, as well as anti-totalitarianism, were also popular among conservatives, with notions such as democracy and property rights being traced all the way back to the classical past.

What is often forgotten is that there was also the liberal use of the classical past, one that focused on its cosmopolitanism and multiculturalism. This tradition was visible in the works of Schulz, Momigliano and Pringsheim. They emphasized the values of reason and liberty, the rule of law and equality for all. While the ideas of civilization and learning were often presented in opposition to the totalitarian conceptions of knowledge and the state, this was one of the areas where conservative and liberal visions of the classical past and the preferred future coincided. Only after the war did the notions of tolerance and nonethnic ideas of community and citizenship become shared themes among liberals and conservatives, due to the totalitarian experience.

While the continuities from Nazi and fascist ideas to the present far right are the most obvious, the point is that there are continuities from all of them in the present discourse. It is just that the resurgence of Nazi ideas is the most shocking as they had been in the shadows for so long. It is, of course, completely possible that after the Nazi and fascist ideas became unpalatable, support for them was channeled into conservative notions of the connection between the past and the present.

The basic premise of constructivism is that the text and thus the past have no innate meanings but rather that they are all given or constructed by interpreters. The connection of the classical past and Europe is thus something of an imagined community. This means that there are undoubtedly lines of continuities and reception but the underlying idea is to present value judgments on historical events and ideas. The functioning of the community simile means that through definitions, one can present judgments on what to include and what to exclude as part of the community. The community is thus a matter of choice as is its justification through history. The lineages that are traced are a part of the construction of the past, a reverse teleology or projection.

The past, classics, Roman law and European narratives are thus all a part of a normative realm of value statements and the setting of hierarchies. They are used in what could be defined as a process of historical utilitarianism, in which tradition and usage are seen as signs of correctness and legitimacy. What is included is, however, not as informative as what is not talked about. Issues of class, gender and race are embedded in these discussions but seldom openly debated.

While we have discussed at length exclusionary references to the classical past, it is important to note that the debate on these terms relates to a very thin slice of Europe, namely the culture and population that is white, conservative and nationalist. It is a policy of othering through race, culture and language. Should one want to present a different kind of vision, one could do worse than a return to the ideas presented by Schulz: the notions of humanity, equality, the rule of law, security and a sense of inclusion. Just an idea.

# Bibliography


Adorno, Theodor W. "Scientific experiences of a European scholar in America," in Bernard Bailyn and Donald Fleming (eds.), *The Intellectual Migration: Europe and America, 1930–1960* (Cambridge, MA: Belknap Press of Harvard University Press, 1969), pp. 338–370.

Anderson, Benedict. *Imagined Communities: Reflections on the Origin and Spread of Nationalism* (London: Verso, 1991).

André, J.-M, "La conception de l'État et de l'Empire dans la pensée gréco-romaine des deux premiers siècles de notre ère," *Aufstieg und Niedergang der römischen Welt*, 2.30.1 (1982), 3–73.

Apaydin, Bahar Öcal and Franchi, Marco. "L'importanza e la metodologia del corso di diritto romano nella formazione del giurista dall'impero ottomano ad oggi," in Isabella Piro (ed.), *Scritti per Alessandro Corbino 5* (Tricase: Libellula, 2016), pp. 277–300.

Arangio-Ruiz, V. (ed.). *Augustus: Studi in occasione del bimillenario Augusteo* (Rome: Tipografia della R. Accademia nazionale dei Lincei, 1938).

Archi, Gian Gualberto. "Fritz Schulz," *Studia et Documenta Historiae et Iuris*, 24 (1958), 451–459.

Arena, Valentina. *Libertas and the Practice of Politics in the Late Roman Republic* (Cambridge: Cambridge University Press, 2012).

Arendt, Hannah. "Exiles, enemies, or emigrants," in M. Anderson (ed.), *Hitler's Exiles: Personal Stories of the Flight from Nazi Germany to America* (New York: The New Press, 1998), pp. 253–262.

Arendt, Hannah. *The Origins of Totalitarianism* (London: Penguin, 2017 [1st ed. 1951, reprint of 1967]).

Arendt, Hannah. "We refugees," *Menorah Journal*, 31 (1943), 69–77.

Arendt, Hannah and Kohn, Jerome. *Essays in Understanding, 1930–1954: Formation, Exile, and Totalitarianism* (New York: Harcourt, Brace & Co., 1994).

Armon, Adi. "Leo Strauss reading Karl Marx during the Cold War," in Ezra Mendelsohn, Stefani Hoffman and Richard Cohen (eds.), *Against the Grain: Jewish Intellectuals in Hard Times* (New York: Berghahn Books, 2013), pp. 32–50.

Arzt, Donna E. "Otto Kirchheimer: critic of the administration of justice," in Marcus Lutter, Ernst C. Stiefel and Michael H. Hoeflich (eds.), *Der Einfluß deutscher Emigranten auf die Rechtsentwicklung in den USA und in Deutschland. Vorträge und Referate des Bonner Symposions im September 1991* (Tübingen: Mohr Siebeck, 1993), pp. 33–56.

Ash, Mitchell G. and Söllner, Alfons (eds.). *Forced Migration and Scientific Change: Émigré German-Speaking Scientists and Scholars after 1933* (Cambridge: Cambridge University Press, 1996).

Ash, Mitchell G. and Söllner, Alfons. "Introduction," in Mitchell G. Ash and Alfons Söllner (eds.), *Forced Migration and Scientific Change: Émigré German-Speaking Scientists and Scholars after 1933* (Cambridge: Cambridge University Press, 1996), pp. 1–20.

Atzeri, Lorena. "Francis de Zulueta (1878–1958): an Oxford Roman lawyer between totalitarianisms," in Kaius Tuori and Heta Björklund (eds.), *Roman Law and the Idea of Europe* (London: Bloomsbury, 2019), pp. 53–71.

Atzeri, Lorena. "La 'storia del diritto antico' e una lettera inedita di Paul Koschaker," *Iuris Antiqui Historia*, 2 (2010), 191–222.

Avenarius, Martin. "Bernhard Windscheid (1817–1892). Der Spätpandektist und seine Wirkung auf das Rechtsdenken des europäischen Auslands," *Zeitschrift für Europäisches Privatrecht*, 25 (2017), 396–418.

Avenarius, Martin. "Universelle Hermeneutik und Praxis des Rechtshistoriker und Juristen. Die Entwicklung ihres Verhältnisses im Lichte der Diskussion zwischen Gadamer und Wieacker," in Stephan Meder, Gaetano Carlizzi, Christoph-Eric Mecke and Christoph Sorge (eds.), *Juristische Hermeneutik zwischen Vergangenheit und Zukunft* (Baden-Baden: Nomos, 2013), pp. 59–103.

Avenarius, Martin. "Verwissenschaftlichung als 'sinnhafter' Kern der Rezeption: eine Konsequenz aus Wieackers rechtshistorischer Hermeneutik," in Eva Schumann and Okko Behrends (eds.), *Franz Wieacker – Historiker des modernen Privatrechts* (Wallstein Verlag GmbH, 2010), pp. 119–180.

Balakrishnan, Gopal. *The Enemy: An Intellectual Portrait of Carl Schmitt* (London: Verso, 2000).

Bartocci, Ugo. *Salvatore Riccobono, il Diritto Romano e il valore politico degli Studia Humanitatis* (Torino: G. Giappichelli Editore, 2012).

Beatson, Jack and Zimmermann, Reinhard. *Jurists Uprooted: German-Speaking Émigré Lawyers in Twentieth-Century Britain* (Oxford: Oxford University Press, 2004).

Becher, Tony and Trowler, Paul. *Academic Tribes and Territories: Intellectual Enquiry and the Cultures of Disciplines* (Ballmoor: Society for Research into Higher Education & Open University Press, 2001).

Beggio, Tommaso. "Un commento alla proposta di riforma degli studi romanistici di Paul Koschaker in un documento inedito di Ulrich von Lübtow," *Index: quaderni camerti di studi romanistici = international survey of Roman law*, 46 (2018), 589–622.

Beggio, Tommaso. "La 'Interpolationenforschung' agli occhi di Paul Koschaker: la critica a Gradenwitz e alla cosiddetta 'neuhumanistische Richtung' e lo sguardo rivolto all'esempio di Salvatore Riccobono," in Martin Avenarius,

Christian Baldus, Francesca Lamberti and Mario Varvaro (eds.), *Gradenwitz, Riccobono und die Entwicklung der Interpolationenkritik* (Tübingen: Mohr Siebeck, 2018), pp. 121–155.

Beggio, Tommaso. "Paul Koschaker and the Path to 'Europa und das römische Recht' (1936–1947)," *Legal Roots*, 6 (2017), 291–326.

Beggio, Tommaso. *Paul Koschaker (1879–1951). Rediscovering the Roman Foundations of European Legal Tradition* (Heidelberg: Winter Verlag, 2018).

Beggio, Tommaso. "Paul Koschaker und die Reform des romanistischen Rechtsstudiums in Deutschland. Ein unveröffentlichtes Dokument," *Zeitschrift der Savigny-Stiftung für Rechtsgeschichte: Romanistische Abteilung*, 135 (2018), 645–680.

Behr, Charles A. (ed.). *P. Aelius Aristides: The Complete Works, vols. 1–2* (Leiden: Brill, 1981–1986).

Behr, Charles A. "Studies on the Biography of Aelius Aristides," *Aufstieg und Niedergang der römischen Welt*, 2.34.2 (1994), 1140–1233.

Behrends, Okko. "Franz Wieacker 5.8.1908 - 17.2.1994," *Zeitschrift der Savigny-Stiftung für Rechtsgeschichte: Romanistische Abteilung*, 112 (1995), 13–62.

Behrends, Okko. "Franz Wieacker. Historiker und Jurist des Privatrechts (5.8.1908–17.2.1994)," in *A l'Europe du troisieme millenaire. Studi in onore di Giuseppe Gandolfi* (Milan: Dott. A. Giuffrè Editore, 2009), pp. 2341–2351.

Below, Karl-Heinz. "Paul Koschaker," *Zeitschrift der Deutschen Morgenländischen Gesellschaft*, 104 (1954), 1–44.

Below, Karl-Heinz and Falkenstein, Adam. "Paul Koschaker," *Zeitschrift der Savigny-Stiftung für Rechtsgeschichte: Romanistische Abteilung*, 68 (1951), ix–xix.

Benhabib, Seyla. *Exile, Statelessness, and Migration: Playing Chess with History from Hannah Arendt to Isaiah Berlin* (Princeton, NJ: Princeton University Press, 2018).

Benson, Carolyn and Fink, Julian. "New perspectives on Nazi law," *Jurisprudence*, 3 (2012), 341–346.

Berlin, Isaiah. *Two Concepts of Liberty: An Inaugural Lecture Delivered before the University of Oxford, On 31 October 1958* (Oxford: Clarendon Press, 1958).

Berman, Harold J. *Law and Revolution: The Formation of the Western Legal Tradition* (Cambridge, MA: Harvard University Press, 1983).

Bernstein, Arnie. *Swastika Nation: Fritz Kuhn and the Rise and Fall of the German-American Bund* (New York: St. Martin's Press, 2013).

Bernstein, Richard B. *The Founding Fathers Reconsidered* (Oxford: Oxford University Press, 2009).

Bessner, Daniel. *Democracy in Exile: Hans Speier and the Rise of the Defense Intellectual* (Ithaca and London: Cornell University Press, 2018).

Betti, Emilio. *La crisi della repubblica e la genesi del principato in Roma* (Rome: Lateran University Press/Pontificia Universitas Lateranensis, 1982).

Betti, Emilio. "La crisi odierna della scienza romanistica in Germania," *Rivista di Diritto commerciale*, 37 (1939), 120–128.

Betti, Emilio. "Diritto romano e dogmatica odierna," *Archivio Giuridico*, 99 & 100 (1928), 99: 129–150, 100: 26–66.

Betti, Emilio. *Die Hermeneutik als allgemeine Methodik der Geisteswissenschaften* (Tübingen: J. C. B. Mohr (Paul Siebeck), 1962).

Betti, Emilio. *Istituzioni di diritto romano, vol. 1* (Padova: CEDAM, 1942).

Betti, Emilio. "Methode und Wert des heutigen Studiums des römischen Rechts," *Tijdschrift voor Rechtsgeschiedenis/Legal History Review*, 15 (1937), 137–174.

Betti, Emilio. *Notazioni autobiografiche (a cura di Eloisa Mura)* (Padova: CEDAM, [1953] 2014).

Betti, Emilio. *Das Problem der Kontinuität im Lichte der rechtshistorischen Auslegung* (Wiesbaden: Franz Steiner Verlag, 1957).

Betti, Emilio (ed.), *Teoria generale del negozio giuridico* (Naples: Edizioni scientifiche italiane, 2002).

Beyerle, Franz. "Der andere Zugang zum Naturrecht," *Deutsche Rechtswissenschaft*, 4 (1939), 1–20.

Biondi, Biondo. "La legislazione di Augusto," in R. Paribeni and M. Canavesi (eds.), *Conferenze Augustee, nel bimillenario della nascita* (Milan: Vita e Pensiero, 1938), pp. 141–262.

Biondi, Biondo. "Romanità e Fascismo," *Annuario della R. Università degli Studi di Catania*, 7 (1929 [repr. 2001]), 756–770.

Birley, Anthony R. *Hadrian: The Restless Emperor* (London: Routledge, 1997).

Bleicken, Jochen. *Lex publica: Gesetz und Recht in der römischen Republik* (Berlin, New York: de Gruyter, 1975).

Bleicken, Jochen. *Senatsgericht und Kaisergericht. Eine Studie zur Entwicklung des Prozeßrechtes im frühen Prinzipat* (Göttingen: Vanderhoeck & Ruprecht, 1962 [1961]).

Bodenheimer, Rosemarie. *Edgar and Brigitte: A German Jewish Passage to America* (Tuscaloosa, AL: The University of Alabama Press, 2016).

Boehm, Max. "Die Krise des Nationalitätenrechts," in *Festschrift für Rudolf Hübner* (Jena: Friedrich-Schiller-Universität Jena, 1935), pp. 172–189.

Böhler, Jochen and Gerwarth, Robert. *The Waffen-SS: A European History* (Oxford: Oxford University Press, 2016).

Bonfante, Pietro. "Verso la Confederazione Europea," *Scientia*, 18 (1915), 326–342. Now also in Pietro Bonfante (ed.), *Scritti giuridici vari, Studi generali IV* (Rome: Sanpaolesi, 1925).

Bowersock, Glen W. *Greek Sophists in the Roman Empire* (Oxford: Oxford University Press, 1969).

Bowersock, Glen W. and Cornell, T. J. (eds.), *A. D. Momigliano: Studies on Modern Scholarship* (Berkeley: University of California Press, 1994).

Breuilly, John. "Historians and the nation," in Peter Burke (ed.), *History and Historians in the Twentieth Century* (Oxford: Oxford University Press, 2002), pp. 55–87.

Breunung, Leonie and Walther, Manfred. *Biographisches Handbuch der Emigration deutschsprachiger Rechtswissenschaftler ab 1933. Band 1* (Göttingen: De Gruyter, 2012).

Breunung, Leonie and Walther, Manfred. *Biographisches Handbuch der Emigration deutschsprachiger Rechtswissenschaftler ab 1933. Band 2* (Göttingen: De Gruyter, forthcoming).

Broszat, Martin. *Die Machtergreifung. Der Aufstieg der NSDAP und die Zerstörung der Weimarer Republik* (Munich: Deutscher Taschenbuch-Verlag, 1984).

Brunt, Peter Astbury. "Laus imperii," in P. D. A. Garnsey and C. R. Whittaker (eds.), *Imperialism in the Ancient World* (Cambridge: Cambridge University Press, 1978), pp. 159–191.

Brunt, Peter Astbury. "Libertas in the Republic," in Peter Astbury Brunt (ed.), *The Fall of the Roman Republic and Related Essays* (Oxford: Clarendon Press, 1988), pp. 281–350.

Brutti, Massimo. "Emilio Betti e l'incontro con il fascismo," in Italo Birocchi and Luca Loschiavo (eds.), *Giuristi e il fascino del regime* (Rome: Roma Tre-Press, 2015), pp. 63–102.

Buckland, William Warwick. "Review of Fritz Schulz's *Principles of Roman Law* (1936)/*Prinzipien des römischen Rechts* (1934)," *The University of Toronto Law Journal*, 2 (1938), 392–393.

Bund, Elmar. "Fritz Pringsheim (1882–1967). Ein Großer der Romanistik," in Helmut Heinrichs, Hans-Harald Franzki, Klaus Schmalz and Michael Stolleis (eds.), *Deutsche Juristen Jüdischer Herkunft* (Munich: Beck, 1993), pp. 733–744.

Buongiorno, Pierangelo. "Die Ethik eines Juristen. Edoardo Volterra zwischen der Palingenesia Codicis, den *senatus consulta* und dem italienischen Faschismus (1929–1943)," *Philippika*, 105 (2017), 43–56.

Buongiorno, Pierangelo. "'Ricordi di anni lontani e difficili'. Romanisti a Leiden nella lunga estate del 1939," *Index: quaderni camerti di studi romanistici = international survey of Roman law*, 44 (2016), 479–490.

Burckhardt, Jacob. *Griechische Kulturgeschichte* (Berlin: Spemann, 1898).

Burdick, William L. *The Principles of Roman Law and Their Relation to Modern Law* (Rochester: The Lawyers Co-operative Publishing Co., 1938).

Burke, Peter. *Exiles and Expatriates in the History of Knowledge, 1500–2000* (Waltham, MA: Stanford University Press, 2017).

Burke, Peter. *The Fabrication of Louis XIV* (New Haven, CT: Yale University Press, 1992).

Calasso, Francesco. "Introduzione," in *L'Europa e il diritto romano. Studi in memoria di Paolo Koschaker* (Florence: Sansoni, 1962).

Calasso, Francesco. *L'unità giuridica dell'Europa* (Soveria Mannelli: Rubbettino Editore, 1985).

Calliess, Christian. "Europe as transnational law," *German Law Journal*, 10 (2009), 1367–1382.

Campbell, A. H. "Review of Fritz Schulz's *Principles of Roman Law*," *Times Literary Supplement* (June 19, 1936 and February 6, 1937).

Camurri, Renato. "The exile experience reconsidered: a comparative perspective in European cultural migration during the interwar period," *Transatlantica*, 1 (2014) http://journals.openedition.org/transatlantica/6920.

Canovan, Margaret. *Hannah Arendt: A Reinterpretation of Her Political Thought* (Cambridge: Cambridge University Press, 1992).

Carbonnier, Jean. "Usus hodiernus pandectarum," in Ronald H. Graveson, Karl Kreuzer, André Tunc and Konrad Zweigert (eds.), *Festschrift für Imre Zajtay. Mélanges en l'honneur d'Imre Zajtay* (Tübingen: J. C. B. Mohr (Paul Siebeck), 1982), pp. 107–116.

Carmichael, Calum. *Ideas and the Man: Remembering David Daube* (Frankfurt: Vittorio Klostermann Verlag, 2004).

Carr, David. "Narrative and the real world: an argument for continuity," in Brian Fay, Philip Pomper and Richard T. Vann (eds.), *History and Theory: Contemporary Readings* (Oxford: Wiley-Blackwell, 1998), pp. 137–152.

Carrelli, Odoardo. "A proposito di crisi del diritto romano," *Studia et Documenta Historiae et Iuris*, 9 (1943), 1–20.

Carsana, C. *La teoria della costituzione mista nell'età imperiale romana* (Como: Edizioni New Press, 1990).

Casavola, Franco. "Diritto romano e diritto europeo," *Labeo*, 40 (1994), 161–169.

Cascione, Cosimo. "Romanisti e fascismo," in Massimo Miglietta and Gianni Santucci (eds.), *Diritto romano e regimi totalitari nel '900 Europeo* (Trento: Università degli studi di Trento, 2009), pp. 49–51.

Chapoutot, Johann. "The denaturalization of Nordic law: Germanic law and the reception of Roman law," in Kaius Tuori and Heta Björklund (eds.), *Roman Law and the Idea of Europe* (London: Bloomsbury, 2019), pp. 113–126.

Chapoutot, Johann. *Der Nationalsozialismus und die Antike* (Darmstadt: Philipp von Zabern, 2014).

Chappel, James. *Catholic Modern; The Challenge of Totalitarianism and the Remaking of the Church* (Cambridge, MA: Harvard University Press, 2018).

Chappel, James. "The Catholic origins of totalitarianism theory in interwar Europe," *Modern Intellectual History*, 8 (2011), 561–590.

Clark, Jonathan C. D. "National identity, state formation and patriotism: the role on history in the public mind," *History Workshop Journal*, 29 (1990), 95–102.

Coing, Helmut. *Aufgaben des Rechtshistorikers* (Wiesbaden: Franz Steiner Verlag, 1976).

Coing, Helmut. "Common law and civil law in the development of European civilization. Possibilities of comparisons," in Helmut Coing and Knut Wolfgang Nörr (eds.), *Englische und kontinentale Rechtsgeschichte: ein Forschungsprojekt* (Berlin: Duncker & Humblot, 1985), pp. 31–41.

Coing, Helmut. "Zum Einfluss der Philosophie des Aristoteles auf die Entwicklung des römisches Rechts," *Zeitschrift der Savigny-Stiftung für Rechtsgeschichte: Romanistische Abteilung*, 69 (1952), 24–59.

Coing, Helmut. *Die Rezeption des römischen Rechts in Frankfurt am Main. Ein Betrag zur Rezeptionsgeschichte* (Frankfurt: Vittorio Klostermann, 1962 [1939]).

Coing, Helmut. "Einleitung," in Helmut Coing (ed.), *Handbuch der Quellen und Literatur der neueren europäischen Privatrechtsgeschichte. Vol. 1: Mittelalter*

*(1100–1500): Die gelehrter Rechte und die Gesetzgebung* (Munich: Beck Verlag, 1973), pp. 3–38.

Coing, Helmut. "Die europäische Privatrechtsgeschichte der neueren Zeit als einheitliches Forschungsgebiet. Probleme und Aufbau," *Ius Commune*, 1 (1967), 1–33.

Coing, Helmut. "Zur Frage der strafrechtlichen Haftung der Richter für die Anwendung naturrechtswidriger Gesetze," *Süddeutsche Juristenzeitung*, 2 (1947), 61–64.

Coing, Helmut. "Zur Geschichte des Begriffs 'subjektives Recht'," in Helmut Coing, Frederick H. Lawson and Kurt Grönfors (eds.), *Das subjektive Recht und der Rechts- schutz der Persönlichkeit* (Frankfurt: Alfred Metzner, 1959), pp. 7–23.

Coing, Helmut. *Grundzüge der Rechtsphilosophie* (Berlin: de Gruyter, 1993 [1950]).

Coing, Helmut. "Der Jurist und das unsittliche Gesetz," in *Gesammelte Aufsätze, Band 2. Naturrecht als wissenschaftliches Problem* (Wiesbaden: Franz Steiner Verlag, 1965), pp. 50–66.

Coing, Helmut. "Klassizismus in der Geschichte des römischen Rechts," in G. E. von Grunebaum and Willy Hartner (eds.), *Klassizismus und Kulturverfall* (Frankfurt: Vittorio Klostermann, 1960).

Coing, Helmut. *Naturrecht als wissenschaftliches Problem* (Wiesbaden: F. Steiner, 1966 [1965]).

Coing, Helmut. *Die obersten Grundsätze des Rechts: ein Versuch zur Neugründung des Naturrechts* (Heidelberg: Schriften der Süddeutschen Juristen-Zeitung, 1947).

Coing, Helmut. "Römisches Recht in Deutschland," *Ius Romanum Medii Aevi*, 5.6 (1964), 26–28.

Coing, Helmut. "Die ursprüngliche Einheit der europäischen Rechtswissenschaft," in *Gesammelte Aufsätze zu Rechtsgeschichte, Rechtsphilosophie und Zivilrecht: Band 2* (Frankfurt: Vittorio Klostermann, 1982), pp. 137–156.

Coing, Helmut. *Für Wissenschaften und Künste. Lebensbericht eines europäischen Rechtsgelehrten, hrsg., kommentiert und mit einem Nachwort von Michael F. Feldkamp* (Berlin: Duncker and Humblot, 2014).

Colognesi, Luigi Capogrossi. *Le radici della modernità, Max Weber 1891–1909* (Rome: La Sapienza Editrice: 1997, 2nd ed.).

Constant, Benjamin. *Political Writings* , translated and edited by Biancamaria Fontana (Cambridge and New York: Cambridge University Press, 1988).

Corcoran, Simon. *The Empire of the Tetrarchs: Imperial Pronouncements and Government AD 284–324* (Oxford: Clarendon Press, 2000).

Corcy-Debray, Stéphanie. *Jérôme Carcopino, un historien à Vichy* (Paris: Éditions L'Harmattan, 2001).

Cornish, William Rodolph and Clark, Geoffrey de N. *Law and Society in England: 1750–1950* (London: Sweet & Maxwell, 1989).

Costa, Pietro. "Emilio Betti: dogmatica, politica, storiografia," *Quaderni Fiorentini*, 7 (1978), 311–393.

Crawford, Sally, Ulmschneider, Katharina and Elsner, Jas (eds.). *Ark of Civilization: Refugee Scholars and Oxford University, 1930–1945* (Oxford: Oxford University Press, 2017).
Crifò, Giuliano. "Emilio Betti (1890–1968)," in Rafael Domingo (ed.), *Juristas universales, IV* (Madrid and Barcelona: Marcial Pons, 2004), pp. 217–222.
Crifò, Giuliano. *Materiali di storiografia romanistica* (Torino: G. Giappichelli Editore, 1998).
Crifò, Giuliano. "Pandettisti e storicisti nel diritto romano oggi," *Diritto romano attuale*, 1 (1999), 11–28.
Cumin, David. *Carl Schmitt* (Paris: Cerf, 2005).
Curtius, Ernst Robert. *Europäische Literatur und lateinisches Mittelalter* (Bern: A. Francke, 1948).
*Das Judentum in der Rechtswissenschaft 1, Die deutsche Rechtswissenschaft im Kampf gegen den jüdischen Geist. 3. und 4. Oktober 1936* (Berlin: Deutscher Rechts-Verlag, 1935).
Daube, David. *Appeasement or Resistance and Other Essays on New Testament Judaism* (Berkeley, Los Angeles, London: University of California Press, 1987).
Dawson, Christopher M. *The Making of Europe* (London: Sheed and Ward, 1932).
De Francisci, Pietro. "La costituzione Augusteo," in *Studi in onore di Pietro Bonfante* (Milan: Fratelli Treves, 1930), pp. 13–43.
De Francisci, Pietro. *Genesi e struttura del principato Augusteo* (Rome: Reale Accademia D'Italia, 1941).
De Francisci, Pietro. "Paul Koschaker (1879–1951)," *Studia et Documenta Historiae et Iuris*, 17 (1951), 384–388.
De Martino, Francesco. *Lo stato di Augusto* (Naples: Tip. G. Barca, 1936).
de Meneses, Filipe Ribeiro. *Salazar: A Political Biography* (New York: Enigma Books, 2009).
Diamond, Sander A. *The Nazi Movement in the United States, 1924–1941* (Ithaca: Cornell University Press, 1974).
Diestelkamp, Bernhard. "Die Rechtshistoriker der Rechtswissenschaftlichen Fakultät der Johann Wolfgang Goethe-Universität Frankfurt am Main 1933–1945," in Michael Stolleis and Dieter Simon (eds.), *Rechtsgeschichte im Nationalsozialismus. Beiträge zur Geschichte einer Disziplin* (Tübingen: Mohr Siebeck, 1989), pp. 79–106.
d'Ors, Alvaro. "Jus Europaeum," in *L'Europa e il diritto romano. Studi in memoria di Paolo Koschaker, I* (Milan: Giuffrè, 1954), pp. 449–476.
Dreier, Horst. "Hans Kelsen (1881–1973). 'Jurist des Jahrhunderts?'," in Helmut Heinrichs, Hans-Harald Franzki, Klaus Schmalz and Michael Stolleis (eds.), *Deutsche Juristen Jüdischer Herkunft* (Munich: Beck, 1993), pp. 705–732.
Duff, P. W. "Review of Fritz Schulz's *Principles of Roman Law* (1936)," *The Classical Review*, 51(6) (1937) 238–239.
Duranti, Marco. *The Conservative Human Rights Revolution. European Identity, Transnational Politics, and the Origins of the European Convention* (Oxford: Oxford University Press, 2017).

Durham, W. Cole (Jr.). "Edgar Bodenheimer: conservator of civilized legal culture," in Marcus Lutter, Ernst C. Stiefel and Michael H. Hoeflich (eds.), *Der Einfluß deutscher Emigranten auf die Rechtsentwicklung in den USA und in Deutschland. Vorträge und Referate des Bonner Symposions im September* 1991 (Tübingen: Mohr Siebeck, 1993), pp. 127–143.

Duve, Thomas. "Von der Europäischen Rechtsgeschichte zu einer Rechtsgeschichte Europas in globalhistorischer Perspektive (From a European legal history towards a legal history of Europe in a global historical perspective)," *Rechtsgeschichte Legal History. Zeitschrift des Max Planck-Instituts für Europaische Rechtsgeschichte*, 20 (2012), 18–71.

Duve, Thomas. "European legal history - global perspectives," *Max Planck Institute for European Legal History Research Paper Series,* No. 2013-06 (2013).

Eckert, Jörn. "Was war die Kieler Schule," in Franz Säcker (ed.), *Recht und Rechtslehre im Nationalsozialismus* (Baden-Baden: Nomos, 1992), pp. 37–70.

Ecklund, John E. *The Origins of Western Law from Athens to the Code Napoleon. 2 Vols* (Clark, NJ: The Lawbook Exchange, Ltd., 2014).

Edgcomb, Gabrielle Simon. *From Swastika to Jim Crow: Refugee Scholars at Black Colleges* (Malabar, FL: Krieger Publishing Company, 1993).

Eidenmüller, Horst, Faust, Florian, Grigoleit, Hans Christoph, Jansen, Nils., Wagner, Gerhard and Zimmermann, Reinhard. "The common frame of reference for European private law - policy choices and codification problems," *Oxford Journal of Legal Studies*, 28(4) (2008), 659–708.

Elsner, Jas. "Paideia: ancient concept and modern reception," *International Journal of the Classical Reception*, 20 (2013), 136–152.

Epstein, Catherine. *A Past Renewed: A Catalog of German-Speaking Refugee Historians in the United States After 1933* (Cambridge: Cambridge University Press, 2002 [1993]).

Eriksen, Thomas Hylland. *Ethnicity and Nationalism* (London: Pluto Press, 1993).

Erkkilä, Ville. *The Conceptual Change of Conscience: Franz Wieacker and German Legal Historiography* (Tübingen: Mohr Siebeck, 2019).

Erkkilä, Ville. "The metaphysics and legal history. An interview with Michael Stolleis," *European Legal Roots Online*, (2016), 3–17.

Ernst, Wolfgang. "Fritz Schulz (1879–1957)," in Jack Beatson and Reinhard Zimmermann (eds.), *Jurists Uprooted* (Oxford: Oxford University Press, 2004), pp. 105–203.

Evans, Richard J. *The Coming of the Third Reich* (London: Allen Lane, 2003).

Fanizza, Lucia. *Autorità e diritto. L'esempio di Augusto* (Rome: L'Erma di Bretschneider, 2004).

Fanizza, Lucia. "I Principi di Fritz Schulz," *Studia et Documenta Historiae et Iuris*, 72 (1996), 543–549.

Fermi, Laura. *Illustrious Immigrants: The Intellectual Migration from Europe 1930–1941* (Chicago: University of Chicago Press, 1968).

Ferrandiz, Emilia Mataix. "Betti vs. Gadamer. El debate acerca de método y verdad en la hermenéutica jurídica," in Lorenzo Gagliardi (ed.), *Antologia giuridica romanistica ed antiquaria, II* (Milan: Collana di Diritto romano del

Dipartimento di Diritto privato e Storia del Diritto, Università degli Studi di Milano, 2018), pp. 575–610.
Ferro, Marc. *The Use and Abuse of History or How the Past Is Taught* (London: Routledge, 1984).
Fezzi, Luca. *Il rimpianto di Roma. Res publica, libertà "neoromane" e Benjamin Constant, agli inizi del terzo millenio* (Milan: Mondadori Education, 2012).
Fink, Carole. *Marc Bloch: A Life in History* (Cambridge and New York: Cambridge University Press, 1989).
Finkenauer, Thomas and Herrmann, Andreas. "Die Romanistische Abteilung der Savigny-Zeitschrift im Nationalsozialismus," *Zeitschrift der Savigny-Stiftung für Rechtsgeschichte: Romanistische Abteilung*, 134 (2017), 1–48.
Fitzpatrick, Peter. *The Mythology of Modern Law* (London and New York: Routledge, 1992).
Flinterman, Jaap-Jan. "Sophists and emperors: a reconnaissance of sophistic attitudes," in B. E. Borg (ed.), *Paideia. The World of the Second Sophistic* (Berlin and New York: De Gruyter, 2004), pp. 359–376.
Flume, Werner. *Fritz Schulz. Gedenkrede, gehalten bei einer von der Rechts- und Staatswissenschaftlichen Fakultät der Universität Bonn am 25.7.1958 veranstalteten Gedächtnisfeier* (Bonn: Hanstein, 1959).
Foerster, Marc. "Wolfgang Kunkel," in Mathias Schmoeckel (ed.), *Die Juristen der Universität Bonn in "Dritten Reich"* (Köln: Böhlau, 2004), pp. 456–519.
Foljanty, Lena. *Recht oder Gesetz: Juristische Identität und Autorität in Den Naturrechtsdebatten der Nachkriegszeit* (Tübingen: Mohr Siebeck, 2013).
Forner, Sean A. *German Intellectuals and the Challenge of Democratic Renewal Culture and Politics after 1945* (Cambridge: Cambridge University Press, 2014).
Forsthoff, Ernst. *Der Totale Staat* (Hamburg: Hanseatische Verlagsanstalt, 1933).
Fraenkel, Ernst. *The Dual State: A Contribution to the Theory of Dictatorship* (New York: Oxford University Press, 1940).
Frank, Hans. "Zur Reform des Rechtsstudiums," *Deutsches Recht*, 3 (1933), 23–24.
Frank, Hans. "Die Zeit des Rechts," *Deutsches Recht*, 6 (1936), 1–3.
Frassek, Ralf. "Steter Tropfen höhlt den Stein – Juristenausbildung im Nationalsozialismus und danach," *Zeitschrift der Savigny-Stiftung für Rechtsgeschichte: Germanistische Abteilung*, 117 (2000), 294–361.
Frassek, Ralf. "Wege zur nationalsozialistischen 'Rechtserneuerung' – Wissenschaft zwischen 'Gleichschaltung' und Konkurrenzkampf," in Hans-Georg Hermann, Thomas Gutmann, Joachim Rückert, Mathias Schmoeckel and Harald Siems (eds.), *Von den "leges barbarorum" "bis zum ius barbarum" des Nationalsozialismus* (Cologne: Böhlau Verlag, 2008), pp. 351–377.
Frei, Norbert. *Adenauer's Germany and the Nazi Past. The Politics of Amnesty and Integration* (New York: Columbia University Press, 2002).
Gamauf, Richard. "Die Kritik am römischen Recht im 19. und 20. Jahrhundert," *Orbis Iuris Romani*, 2 (1995), 33–61.
Garofalo, Luigi. "Carl Schmitt e la 'Wissenschaft des römischen Recths.' Saggio su un cantore della scienza giuridica europea," *Anuario da Facultade de Dereito da Universidade da Coruña*, 11 (2007), 299–323.

Garofalo, Luigi, "L'humanitas tra diritto romano e totalitarismo hitleriano," *Teoria e storia di diritto private*, 7 (2015), 687–713.

Gaudemet, Jean. "Histoire et système dans la méthode de Savigny," in *Hommage à/Hulde Aan René Dekkers* (Brussels: Bruylant, 1982), pp. 117–133.

Gaughan, Judy E. *Murder Was Not a Crime: Homicide and Power in the Roman Republic* (Austin: University of Texas Press, 2010).

Gelzer, Matthias. "Prinzipien des Römischen Rechts," *Gnomon*, 11 (1935), 1–6.

Gemie, Sharif, Humbert, Laure and Reid, Fiona. *Outcast Europe. Refugees and Relief Workers in an Era of Total War 1936–48* (London: Bloomsbury, 2012).

Genzmer, Erich. "Rez. Paul Koschaker, Europa und das römische Recht," *Zeitschrift der Savigny-Stiftung für Rechtsgeschichte: Romanistische Abteilung*, 67 (1950), 595–611.

Genzmer, Erich. "Was heißt und zu welchem Ende studiert man antike Rechtsgeschichte?," *Zeitschrift der Akademie für Deutsches Recht*, 3 (1936), 403–408.

Georgescu, Valentin. *Exista o crisä a studilor de Drept Roman?* (Czernowitz: Institutul de arte grafice si editura Glasul Bucovinei, 1937).

Giaro, Tomasz. *Aktualisierung Europas: Gespräche mit Paul Koschaker* (Genova: Name, 2000).

Giaro, Tomasz. "Paul Koschaker sotto il Nazismo: un fiancheggiatore 'malgré soi'," in *Iuris Vincula. Studi in onore di M. Talamanca, IV* (Naples: Jovene, 2001), pp. 159–187.

Giaro, Tomasz. "Der Troubadour des Abendlandes," in Horst Schröder and Dieter Simon (eds.), *Rechtsgeschichtswissenschaft in Deutschland 1945 bis 1952* (Frankfurt: Klostermann, 2001), pp. 31–76.

Gibbon,. *The Decline and Fall of the Roman Empire, vol. 1* (New York: International Book Company, 1845).

Gibbon, Edward. *The Decline and Fall of the Roman Empire, vol. 3* (New York: International Book Company, 1845).

Giltaij, Jacob. "Fritz Schulz, refugee scholarship, and the Riccobono Seminar," *Roman Legal Tradition*, 12 (2016), 1–19.

Giltaij, Jacob. *Mensenrechten in het Romeinse Recht* (Nijmegen: Wolf Legal Publishers, 2011).

Giltaij, Jacob. *Reinventing the Principles of Roman Law* (April 24, 2019) (SSRN, 2019), https://ssrn.com/abstract=3377309 or http://dx.doi.org/10.2139/ssrn.3377309.

Giltaij, Jacob and Erkkilä, Ville. "An interview with Tony Honoré," *Forum Historiae Iuris* (February 26, 2015).

Giltaij, Jacob and Tuori, Kaius. "Human rights in antiquity? Revisiting anachronism and Roman law," in Pamela Slotte and Miia Halme-Tuomisaari (eds.), *Revisiting the Origins of Human Rights* (Cambridge: Cambridge University Press, 2015), pp. 39–63.

Göppinger, Horst. *Juristen jüdischer Abstammung im "Dritten Reich": Entrechtung und Verfolgung* (Munich: Beck, 1990).

Gordley, James. *The Jurists: A Critical History* (Oxford: Oxford University Press, 2013).

Göring, Hermann. *Die Rechtssicherheit als Grundlage der Volksgemeinschaft* (Hamburg: Hanseatische Verlagsanstalt, 1935).

Gourevitch, Victor and Roth, Michael S. "Introduction," in Leo Strauss (ed.), *On Tyranny* (Chicago: University of Chicago Press, repr. 2000 [orig. 1948]), pp. i–xxii.

Graham, Kyle. "The refugee jurist and American law schools, 1933–1941," *American Journal of Comparative Law*, 50 (2002), 777–818.

Greenberg, Udi. *The Weimar Century: German Émigrés and the Ideological Foundations of the Cold War* (Princeton, NJ: Princeton University Press, 2015).

Gregorovius, Ferdinand. *Geschichte des römischen Kaisers Hadrian und seiner Zeit* (Königsberg: Bon, 1851).

Grimal, Pierre, Ourliac, Paul and Carcopino, Claude. *Jérôme Carcopino: un historien au service de l'Humanisme* (Paris: Les Belles Lettres, 1981).

Großfeld, Bernhard and Winship, Peter. "Der Rechtsgelehrte in der Fremde," in Marcus Lutter, Ernst C. Stiefel and Michael H. Hoeflich (eds.), *Der Einfluß deutscher Emigranten auf die Rechtsentwicklung in den USA und in Deutschland. Vorträge und Referate des Bonner Symposions im September 1991* (Tübingen: Mohr Siebeck, 1993), pp. 183–200.

Grossi, Paolo. "Historical models and present plans in the formation of a future European law," in Antonio Gambaro and Alfredo Mordechai Rabello (eds.), *Towards a New European Ius Commune* (Jerusalem: The Hebrew University of Jerusalem, 1999).

Grosso, Giuseppe. "Rec. di Koschaker, Die Krise des römischen Rechts und die romanistische Rechtswissenschaft, München/Berlin 1938," *Studia et Documenta Historiae et Iuris*, 5 (1939), 505–520, now also in Giuseppe Grosso, *Scritti storico giuridici, IV* (Torino: Giappichelli, 2001), pp. 101–116.

Grothe, Ewald. *Zwischen Geschichte und Recht: Deutsche Verfassungsgeschichtsschreibung 1900–1970* (Oldenbourg: Wissenschaftsverlag, 2005).

Gruchmann, Lothar. *Justiz im Dritten Reich 1933–1940: Anpassung und Unterwerfung in der Ära Gürtner* (Munich: De Gruyter, 2001).

Guarino, Antonio. "Cinquant'anni dalla 'Krise'," *Labeo*, 34 (1988), 43–56, now in Antonio Guarino (ed.), *Pagine di Diritto romano, I* (Naples: Jovene, 1993), pp. 276–291.

Günther, Frieder. "The neglect of Hans Kelsen in West German public law scholarship, 1945–1980," in D. A. Jeremy Telman (ed.), *Hans Kelsen in America – Selective Affinities and the Mysteries of Academic Influence* (Dordrecht: Springer, 2016), pp. 217–228.

Gusejnova, Dina. *European Elites and Ideas of Empire, 1917–1957* (Cambridge: Cambridge University Press, 2016).

Haferkamp, Hans-Peter. "'Byzantium!' – *bona fides* between Rome and 20th century Germany," in Kaius Tuori and Heta Björklund (eds.), *Roman Law and the Idea of Europe* (London: Bloomsbury, 2019), pp. 145–157.

Haferkamp, Hans-Peter. *Georg Friedrich Puchta und die "Begriffsjurisprudenz"* (Frankfurt: Klostermann, 2004).

Haferkamp, Hans-Peter. *Die historische Rechtschule* (Frankfurt: Klostermann, 2018).

Haferkamp, Hans-Peter, Thiessen, Jan and Waldhoff, Christian (eds.). *Deutsche Diktatorische Rechtsgeschichten? Perspektiven auf die Rechtsgeschichte der DDR. Gedächtnissymposium für Rainer Schröder (1947–2016)* (Tübingen: Mohr Siebeck, 2018).

Haldemann, Frank. "Gustav Radbuch vs. Hans Kelsen: a debate on Nazi law," *Ratio Juris*, 18(2) (2005), 162–178.

Hardwick, Lorna. *Reception Studies* (Oxford: Published for the Classical Association by Oxford University Press, 2003).

Harris, William V. and Holmes, Brooke (eds.), *Aelius Aristides between Greece, Rome, and the Gods* (Leiden and Boston: Brill, 2008).

Hartshorne, Edward Y. *German Universities and National Socialism* (Cambridge, MA: Harvard University Press, 1937).

Hattenhauer, Hans. *Europäische Rechtsgeschichte* (Heidelberg: Müller Juristischer Verlag, 1992).

Hattenhauer, Hans. "Das NS-Volksgesetzbuch," in Arno Buschmann, Gerhard Otte, Werner Schubert and Franz-Ludwig Knemeyer (eds.), *Festschrift für Rudolf Gmür* (Bielefeld: Gieseking Verlag, 1983), pp. 255–279.

Hausmann, Frank-Rutger. *"Deutsche Geisteswissenschaft" im Zweiten Weltkrieg: Die "Aktion Ritterbusch" (1940–1945)* (Heidelberg: Synchron, 2007).

von Hayek, Friedrich A. *The Road to Serfdom* (Chicago: University of Chicago Press, 1944).

Hedemann, Justus Wilhelm. *Die Flucht in die Generalklauseln: eine Gefahr für Recht und Staat* (Tübingen: Mohr Siebeck, 1933).

Hedemann, Justus Wilhelm. "Privatrechtsgeschichte der Neuzeit. Ein Versuch," in *Festschrift für Rudolf Hübner* (Jena: Friedrich-Schiller-Universität Jena, 1935), pp. 5–18.

Hedemann, Justus Wilhelm. *Das Volksgesetzbuch der Deutschen. Ein Bericht* (Munich: Beck, 1941).

Hegel, Georg Wilhelm Friedrich. *Lectures on the Philosophy of World History* (Cambridge: Cambridge University Press, 1975).

Heilbut, Anthony. *Exiled in Paradise: German Refugee Artists and Intellectuals in America, from the 1930s to the Present* (New York: Viking Press, 1983).

Henderson, Bernard W. *The Life and Principate of the Emperor Hadrian* (London: Methuen, 1923).

Herbert, Ulrich. "'Generation der Sachlichkeit.' Die völkische Studentenbewegung der frühen zwanziger Jahre in Deutschland," in Frank Bajohr, Werner Johe and Uwe Lohalm (eds.), *Zivilisation und Barbarei, Die widersprüchlichen Potentiale der Moderne* (Hamburg: Hans Christians Verlag, 1991), pp. 115–143.

Hewitson, Mark and D'Auria, Matthew (eds.). *Europe in Crisis: Intellectuals and the European Idea, 1917–1957* (Oxford: Berghahn Books, 2012).

Hildebrandt, Heinz. *Rechtsfindung im neuen deutschen staate: ein Beitrag zur Rezeption und den Rechtsquellen, zur Auslegung und Ergaenzung des Gesetzes* (Berlin: W. de Gruyter, 1935).

Hobbes, Thomas. *Leviathan* (Oxford: Oxford University Press, 2012).

Höbenreich, Evelyn. "À propos 'Antike Rechtsgeschichte': Einige Bemerkungen zur Polemik zwischen Ludwig Mitteis und Leopold Wenger," *Zeitschrift der Savigny-Stiftung für Rechtsgeschichte: Romanistische Abteilung*, 109 (2013), 547–562.

Hodgson, Louise. *Res Publica and the Roman Republic: "Without Body or Form"* (Oxford: Oxford University Press, 2017).

Hoeflich, Michael H. "Legacy," in Marcus Lutter, Ernst C. Stiefel and Michael H. Hoeflich (eds.), *Der Einfluß deutscher Emigranten auf die Rechtsentwicklung in den USA und in Deutschland. Vorträge und Referate des Bonner Symposions im September 1991* (Tübingen: Mohr Siebeck, 1993), pp. 15–17.

Hondius, Ewoud. "Towards a European Civil Code," in Arthur S. Hartkamp, Martijn W. Hesselink, Ewoud Hondius, C. Mak and Edgar Du Perron (eds.), *Towards a European Civil Code* (Alphen aan den Rijn: Kluwer Law International, 2011), pp. 3–26.

Honoré, Tony. *Emperors and Lawyers: With a Palingenesia of Third-Century Imperial Rescripts 193–305 AD* (Oxford: Clarendon Press, 1994).

Honoré, Tony. "Fritz Pringsheim (1882–1967)," in Jack Beatson and Reinhard Zimmermann (eds.), *Jurists Uprooted* (Oxford: Oxford University Press, 2004), pp. 205–232.

Honoré, Tony. *Ulpian: Pioneer of Human Rights* (New York: Oxford University Press, 2002).

Hueck, Ingo J. "'Spheres of influence' and 'Völkisch' legal thought: Reinhard Höhn's notion of Europe," in Christian Joerges and Navraj Singh Ghaleigh (eds.), *Darker Legacies of Law in Europe* (Oxford and Portland, OR: Hart Publishing, 2003), pp. 71–86.

Hunt, Lynn. *Inventing Human Rights: A History* (New York: W. W. Norton, 2007).

Jacobson, Arthur J. and Schlink, Bernhard. *Weimar: A Jurisprudence of Crisis* (Berkeley: University of California Press, 2000).

Jaeger, Werner. "Classical philology and humanism," *Transactions and Proceedings of the American Philological Association*, 67 (1936), 363–374.

Jarausch, Konrad H. *After Hitler: Recivilizing Germans, 1945–1995* (New York: Oxford University Press, 2006).

Jay, Martin. *Permanent Exiles: Essays on the Intellectual Migration from Germany to America* (New York: Columbia University Press, 1985).

Jellinek, Walter. "Le droit public en l'Allemagne en 1933," *Annuaire de L'Institut International de Droit Public*, (1934), 52–53.

von Jhering, Rudolf. *Geist des römischen Rechts auf den verschiedenen Stufen seiner Entwicklung. Teil 1–2* (Aalen: Scientia, 1993).

Joas, Hans and Wiegandt, Klaus. *The Cultural Values of Europe* (Liverpool: Liverpool University Press, 2008).

Joerges, Christian and Ghaleigh, Navrag Singh (eds.). *Darker Legacies of Law in Europe: The Shadow of National Socialism and Fascism over Europe and Its Legal Traditions* (Oxford: Hart Publishing, 2003).

Johnston, David. "The renewal of the old," *Cambridge Law Journal*, 56(1) (1997), 80–95.

Johnston, David. "Roman law, comparative law and legal history," *Zeitschrift für Europäisches Privatrecht*, 3 (1999), 560–569.
Jolowicz, Herbert F. *Roman Foundations of Modern Law* (Oxford: Clarendon Press and Oxford University Press, 1957).
Kaelble, Hartmut. *Europäer über Europa: Die Entstehung des europäischen Selbstverständnisses im 19. und 20. Jahrhundert* (Frankfurt and New York: Campus Verlag, 2001).
Kaiser, Wolfram. *Christian Democracy and the Origins of European Union* (Cambridge: Cambridge University Press, 2007).
Kalman, Laura. *Legal Realism at Yale 1927–1960* (Chapel Hill and London: University of North Carolina Press, 1986).
Kalwoda, Johannes. "Ernst Schönbauer (1885–1966). Biographie zwischen Nationalsozialismus und Wiener Fakultätstradition," *Beiträge zur Rechtsgeschichte Österreichs*, 2 (2012), 282–316.
Kantorowicz, Hermann. "Savigny and the Historical School of Law," *Law Quarterly Review*, 209 (1937), 326–343.
Kantorowicz, Hermann. *Studies in the Glossators of the Roman Law* (Cambridge: Cambridge University Press, 1938).
Kantorowicz, Hermann. *Was ist uns Savigny?* (Berlin: C. Heymanns Verlag, 1912).
Kantorowicz, Hermann and Schulz, Fritz (eds.). *Thomas Diplovatatius: De claris iuris consultis* (Berlin Leipzig: De Gruyter, 1919).
Kaser, Max. *Römisches Recht als Gemeinschaftsordnung* (Tübingen: Mohr Siebeck, 1939).
Keedus, Liisi. *The Crisis of German Historicism. The Early Political Thought of Hannah Arendt and Leo Strauss* (Cambridge: Cambridge University Press, 2015).
Kelsen, Hans. *Allgemeine Staatslehre* (Berlin: J. Springer, 1925).
Kelsen, Hans. "Foundations of democracy," *Ethics*, 66(1:2) (1955), 1–101.
Kerwin, Jerome G. "Review of the dual state: a contribution to the theory of dictatorship. By Ernst Fraenkel. New York: Oxford University Press, 1940" *The University of Chicago Law Review*, 8 (1941), 616–618.
Kettler, David. *The Liquidation of Exile: Studies in the Intellectual Emigration of the 1930s* (London and New York: Anthem Press, 2011).
King, Richard H. *Arendt and America* (Chicago: The University of Chicago Press, 2015).
Kisch, Guido. *Die Lebensweg eines Rechtshistorikers* (Sigmaringen: Thorbecke, 1975).
Kisch, Guido (ed.). *Paul Koschaker, Gelehrter, Mensch, Freund. Briefe aus den Jahren 1940 bis 1951* (Basel: Helbing und Lichtenbahn, 1970).
Kisch, Guido. *Die Universitäten und die Juden: eine historische Betrachtung zur Fünfhundertjahrfeier der Universität Basel* (Tübingen: Mohr, 1961).
Klein, Richard A. *Die Romrede des Aelius Aristides* (Darmstadt: Wissenschaftliche Buchgesellschaft, 1981).
Klein, Richard A. "Zum Kultur- und Geschichtsverständnis in der Romrede des Aelius Aristides," in B. Kühnert, V. Riedel and R. Gordesiani (eds.), *Prinzipat und Kultur im 1. und 2. Jahrhundert* (Bonn: R. Habelt, 1995), pp. 283–292.

Klein, Richard A. "Zur Datierung der Romrede des Aelius Aristides," *Historia*, 30 (1981), 337–350.

Kleßmann, Christoph. "Der Generalgouverneur Hans Frank," *Vierteljahrshefte für Zeitgeschichte*, 19 (1971), 245–260.

Kluke, Paul. "Nationalsozialistische Europa-Ideologie," *Vierteljahrshefte für Zeitgeschichte* 3 (1955) 240–275.

Kmak, Magdalena. "The impact of exile on law and legal science 1934–64," in Kaius Tuori and Heta Björklund (eds.), *Roman Law and the Idea of Europe* (London: Bloomsbury Academic, 2019), pp. 15–34.

Koenen, Andreas. *Der Fall Carl Schmitt* (Darmstadt: Wissenschaftliche Buchhandlung, 1995).

Köhler, Lotte and Saner, Hans (eds.). *Hannah Arendt/Karl Jaspers: Correspondence, 1926–1969* (Munich: Piper, 1993).

Kohlhepp, Ralf. "Franz Wieacker und die NS-Zeit," *Zeitschrift der Savigny-Stiftung für Rechtsgeschichte: Romanistische Abteilung*, 122 (2005), 203–223.

Koontz, Claudia. *The Nazi Conscience* (London and Cambridge, MA: The Belknap Press, 2003).

Kornhauser, Anne M. *Debating the American State: Liberal Anxieties and the New Leviathan, 1930–1970* (Philadelphia: University of Pennsylvania Press, 2015).

Koschaker, Paul. "Contributo alla storia ed alla dottrina della convalida nel diritto romano," *Iura*, 4 (1953), 1–89.

Koschaker, Paul. "Deutschland, Italien und das römische Recht," in *Faschismus und Recht. Schriften des NS.-Rechtswahrerbundes in Österreich* (Vienna: Landesgeschäftsstelle des NS.-Rechtswahrerbundes, 1938), pp. 19–22.

Koschaker, Paul. *Europa und das römische Recht* (Munich and Berlin: Beck, 1966 [1947]).

Koschaker, Paul. *Die Krise des römischen Rechts und die romanistische Rechtswissenschaft* (Munich and Berlin: C. H. Beck'sche Verlagsbuchhandlung, 1938).

Koschaker, Paul. "Die Krise des römischen Rechts und romanistische Rechtswissenschaft," *Schriften der Akademie für Deutsches Recht: Römisches Recht und fremde Rechte*, 1 (1938), 1–86.

Koschaker, Paul. "Probleme der heutigen romanistischen Rechtswissenschaft," *Deutsche Rechtswissenschaft*, 5 (1940), 110–136.

Koschaker, Paul. "Rez. Georgescu, Exista o crisä a studilor de Drept Roman? (Gibt es eine Krise des Studiums des römischen Rechts?), Czernowitz 1937," *Zeitschrift der Savigny-Stiftung für Rechtsgeschichte: Romanistische Abteilung*, 58 (1938), 425–427.

Koschaker, Paul. "Selbstdarstellung," in Nikolaus Grass (ed.), *Österreichische Geschichtswissenschaft der Gegenwart in Selbstdarstellungen, II* (Innsbruck: Wagner, 1951), pp. 105–125.

Koschaker, Paul and Ayiter, Kudret. *Roma Ozel Hakukunun Ana Hatlari* (Ankara: Ankara Üniversitesi, 1993).

Koskenniemi, Martti. "Hersch Lauterpacht 1897-1960," in Jack Beatson and Reinhard Zimmermann (eds.), *Jurists Uprooted* (Oxford: Oxford University Press, 2004), pp. 601–662.

Krauss, Marita. *Heimkehr in ein fremdes Land. Geschichte der Remigration nach 1945* (Munich: C. H. Beck Verlag, 2001).

Kreller, Hans. *Römische Rechtsgeschichte: eine Einführung in die Volksrechte der Hellenen und Römer und in das römische Kunstrecht* (Tübingen: Mohr Siebeck, 1936).

Kroeschell, Karl. "Die nationalsozialistische Eigentumslehre. Vorgeschichte und Nachwirkung," in Michael Stolleis and Dieter Simon (eds.), *Rechtsgeschichte im Nationalsozialismus. Beiträge zur Geschichte einer Disziplin* (Tübingen: Mohr Siebeck, 1989), pp. 43–62.

Kühl, Kristian. "Rückblick auf die Renaissance des Naturrechts nach dem Zweiten Weltkrieg," in Gerhard Köblerl, Meinhard Heinze and Jan Schapp (eds.), *Geschichtliche Rechtswissenschaft: ars tradendo innovandoque aequitatem sectandi; Freundesgabe für Alfred Söllner zum 60. Geburtstag am 5.2.1990. Giessener rechtswissenschaftliche Abhandlungen, Bd. 6* (Brühl: Giessen, 1990), pp. 331–357.

Kunkel, Wolfgang. "Paul Koschaker und die europäische Bedeutung des römischen Rechts," in *L'Europa e il diritto romano. Studi in memoria di Paolo Koschaker, I* (Milan: Giuffrè, 1954), pp. 5–12.

Kunkel, Wolfgang. "Ernst Levy zum Gedächtnis," *Zeitschrift der Savigny-Stiftung für Rechtsgeschichte: Romanistische Abteilung*, 86 (1969), xiii–xxxii.

Kunkel, Wolfgang. "Der Professor im Dritten Reich," in Helmut Kuhn (ed.), *Die Deutsche Universität im Dritten Reich* (Munich: Piper, 1966), pp. 103–133.

Ladeur, Karl-Heinz. *Der Anfang Des Westlichen Rechts: Die Christianisierung Der Romischen Rechtskultur Und Die Entstehung Des Universalen Rechts* (Tübingen: Mohr Siebeck, 2018).

Landau, Peter. "Wieackers Konzept einer neueren Privatrechtsgeschichte: Eine Bilanz nach 40 Jahren," in Eva Schumann and Okko Behrends (eds.), *Franz Wieacker – Historiker des modernen Privatrechts* (Wallstein Verlag GmbH, 2010), pp. 49–74.

Langbein, John H. "The influence of the German emigrés on American law: the curious case of civil and criminal practice," in Marcus Lutter, Ernst C. Stiefel and Michael H. Hoeflich (eds.), *Der Einfluß deutscher Emigranten auf die Rechtsentwicklung in den USA und in Deutschland. Vorträge und Referate des Bonner Symposions im September* 1991 (Tübingen: Mohr Siebeck, 1993), pp. 321–332.

Lange, Heinrich. "Deutsche Romanistik? Grundsätzliche Bemerkungen zu Fritz Schulz, 'Prinzipien des römischen Rechts'," *Deutsche Juristen Zeitung*, (1934), 1493–1500.

Lanza, Carlo. "La 'realtà' di Pietro de Francisci," in Italo Birocchi and Luca Loschiavo (eds.), *Giuristi e il fascino del regime* (Rome: Roma Tre-Press, 2015), pp. 215–236.

Laudani, Raffaele. *Secret Reports from Nazi Germany* (Princeton, NJ: Princeton University Press, 2013).

Laughland, John. *Tainted Source: The Undemocratic Origins of the European Idea* (London: Sphere, 1998).

Lauria, Mario. "Rec. Fritz Schulz *Prinzipien des römischen Rechts*," *Studia et Documenta Historiae et Iuris*, 1 (1935), 219–226.

Lauterpacht, Hersch. *International Law and Human Rights* (New York: Frederick A. Praeger, Inc., 1950).

Lautner, J. G. "Rec. Fritz Schulz, Principles of Roman Law," *Internationalen Zeitschrift für Theorie des Rechts*, 9 (1938).

Lefort, Elisabeth. "Arriving at justice by a process of elimination: Hans Kelsen and Leo Strauss," in Jeremy Telman (ed.), *Hans Kelsen in America – Selective Affinities and the Mysteries of Academic Influence* (Berlin: Springer Verlag, 2016), pp. 116–122.

Legrand, Pierre. "A diabolical idea," in Arthur S. Hartkamp, Martijn W. Hesselink, Ewoud H. Hondius, Chantal Mak, Edgar du Perron and Christian von Bar (eds.), *Towards a European Civil Code* (Nijmegen: Kluwer Law International, 2004), pp. 245–272.

Legrand, Pierre. "European legal systems are not converging," *International and Comparative Law Quarterly*, 45 (1996), 52–81.

Legrand, Pierre. *Fragments on Law-as-Culture* (Deventer: W. E. J. Tjeenk Willink, 1999).

Lepsius, Oliver. "The problem of perceptions of National Socialist law or: was there a constitutional theory of National Socialism?," in Christian Joerges and Navraj Singh Ghaleigh (eds.), *Darker Legacies of Law in Europe* (Oxford and Portland, OR: Hart Publishing, 2003), pp. 19–41.

Lerner, Robert E. *Ernst Kantorowicz: A Life* (Princeton, NJ: Princeton University Press, 2017).

Levy, Ernst. "Review of Augustus: Studi in occasione del Bimillenario Augusteo. (Rome: Tipografia della R. Accademia Nazionale dei Lincei. 1938)," *The American Historical Review*, 45 (1939), 106–107.

Levy, Ernst. "Review of Die Krise des römischen Rechts und die romanistische Rechtswissenschaft by Paul Koschaker," *The Classical Weekly*, 33 (1939), 91–92.

Levy, Ernst. "Natural Law in the Roman Period," in A. L. Scanlan (ed.), *University of Notre Dame Natural Law Institute Proceedings 2* (Notre Dame: Notre Dame Law School, 1949), pp. 43–72.

Liebrecht, Johannes. *Junge Rechtsgeschichte. Kategorienwandel in der rechtshistorischen Germanistik der Zwischenkriegszeit* (Tübingen: Mohr Siebeck, 2018).

Liebs, Detlef. "Franz Wieacker †," *Gnomon*, 67 (1995), 473–477.

Liebs, Detlef. "Franz Wieacker (1908 bis 1994) – Leben und Werk," in Eva Schumann and Okko Behrends (eds.), *Franz Wieacker – Historiker des modernen Privatrechts* (Wallstein Verlag GmbH, 2010), pp. 23–48.

Loeffler, James. *Rooted Cosmopolitans. Jews and Human Rights in the Twentieth Century* (New Haven, CT: Yale University Press, 2018).

Loth, Wilfried. *Building Europe: A History of European Unification* (Berlin: De Gruyter Oldenbourg, 2015).

Lowe, Keith. *Savage Continent: Europe in the Aftermath of World War II* (London: Picador, 2013).

Luig, Klaus. "Helmut Coing (28.2.1912–15.8.2000)," *Zeitschrift der Savigny-Stiftung für Rechtsgeschichte: Romanistische Abteilung*, 119 (2002), 662–678.

Lupoi, Maurizio. *The Origins of the European Legal Order* (Cambridge: Cambridge University Press, 2000).

Lutter, Marcus, Stiefel, Ernst C. and Hoeflich, Michael H. (eds.). *Der Einfluß deutscher Emigranten auf die Rechtsentwicklung in den USA und in Deutschland. Vorträge und Referate des Bonner Symposions im September 1991* (Tübingen: Mohr Siebeck, 1993).

Lynch, Frances M. B., Milward, Alan S., Ranieri, Ruggero, Romero, Federico and Vibeke Sørensen. *The Frontier of National Sovereignty: History and Theory 1945–1992* (London: Routledge, 1994).

MacMillan, Margaret. *The Uses and Abuses of History* (London: Profile Books Ltd, 2009).

Mantello Antonio. "Salvatore Riccobono," in Paola Luigia Carucci and Loredana Di Pinto (eds.), *"Romanisti lateranensi nel Novecento," Studia et Documenta Historiae et Iuris*, 68 (2002), pp. xvi–xxi.

Mantello, Antonio. "La giurisprudenza romana fra Nazismo e Fascismo," *Quaderni di Storia*, 13 (1987), 23–71.

Mantello, Antonio. "L'immagine di Jhering fra nazionalsocialismo e fascismo: analisi d'una vicenda ideologica," *Index: quaderni camerti di studi romanistici = international survey of Roman law*, 23 (1995), 215–250.

Marotta, Valerio. "'Mazziniano in politica estera e prussiano in interna.' Note brevi sulle idee politiche di Pietro Bonfante," in Italo Birocchi and Luca Loschiavo (eds.), *Giuristi e il fascino del regime* (Rome: Roma Tre-Press, 2015), pp. 267–288.

Marotta, Valerio. "Roma, l'Impero e l'Italia nella letteratura romanistica degli anni trenta," in Giovanni Cazzetta (ed.), *Retoriche dei giuristi e costruzione dell'identità nazionale* (Bologna: Il Mulino, 2013), pp. 425–460.

von Marschall, Wolfgang Freiherr. "Max Rheinstein," in Marcus Lutter, Ernst C. Stiefel and Michael H. Hoeflich (eds.). *Der Einfluß deutscher Emigranten auf die Rechtsentwicklung in den USA und in Deutschland. Vorträge und Referate des Bonner Symposions im September 1991* (Tübingen: Mohr Siebeck, 1993), pp. 333–341.

Marrone, Matteo. "Romanisti professori a Palermo," *Index: quaderni camerti di studi romanistici = international survey of Roman law*, 25 (1997), 587–616.

Marrus, Michael R. "Three Jewish émigrés at Nuremberg: Jacob Robinson, Hersch Lauterpacht, and Raphael Lemkin," in Ezra Mendelsohn, Stefani Hoffman and Richard Cohen (eds.), *Against the Grain: Jewish Intellectuals in Hard Times* (New York: Berghahn Books, 2013), pp. 240–254.

Maschke, Günter. "Vorwort," in Carl Schmitt (ed.), *Staat, Grossraum, Nomos: Arbeiten aus den Jahren 1916–1969* (Berlin: Duncker & Humblot, 1995), pp. xix–xxvi.

Mattei, Ugo. "Why the wind changed: intellectual leadership in Western law," *The American Journal of Comparative Law*, 42 (1994), 195–217.

Mayer-Maly, Theo. "Ernst Schönbauer zum Gedächtnis," *Zeitschrift der Savigny-Stiftung für Rechtsgeschichte: Romanistische Abteilung*, 84 (1967), 627–630.

Mazzacane, Aldo. "'Il leone fuggito dal circo': pandettistica e diritto comune europeo," *Index: quaderni camerti di studi romanistici = international survey of Roman law*, 29 (2001), 97–111.

McCauliff, Catherine. "Union in Europe: constitutional philosophy and the Schuman Declaration, May 9, 1950," *Columbia Journal of European Law*, 18 (2012), 441–472.

McNeill, William. "Mythistory, or truth, myth, history, and historians," *The American Historical Review*, 91 (1986), 1–10.

Mehring, Reinhard. *Carl Schmitt: Aufstieg und Fall* (Munich: Beck, 2009).

Meierhenrich, Jens Reinhard. *The Remnants of the Rechtsstaat. An Ethnography of Nazi Law* (Oxford and New York: Oxford University Press, 2018).

Meinel, Florian. *Der Jurist in der industriellen Gesellschaft: Ernst Forsthoff und seine Zeit* (Berlin: Akademie Verlag, 2011).

Meissel, Franz-Stefan. "Deutsche Rechtsgeschichte im nationalsozialistischen Staat," in Ulrike Davy, Helmut Fuchs, Herbert Hofmeister, Judith Marte and Ilse Reiter (eds.), *Nationalsozialismus und Recht* (Vienna: Verlag A. Orac, 1990), pp. 412–426.

Meissel, Franz-Stefan and Wedrac, Stefan. "Strategien der Anpassung – Römisches Recht im Zeichen des Hakenkreuzes," in Franz-Stefan Meissel, Thomas Olechowski, Ilse Reiter-Zatloukal and Stefan Schima (eds.), *Vertriebenes Recht – Vertreibendes Recht. Die Wiener Rechts- und Staatswissenschaftliche Fakultät 1938–1945* (Vienna: MANZ Verlag, 2012), pp. 35–78.

Michaelis, Karl. *Wandlungen des deutschen Rechtsdenkens seit dem Eindringen des fremden Rechts* (Berlin: Junker und Dünnhaupt Verlag, 1935).

Miettinen, Timo. *The Idea of Europe in Husserl's Phenomenology* (Helsinki: Philosophical Studies, 2013).

Miglietta, Massimo and Santucci, Gianni (eds.). *Diritto romano e regimi totalitari nel '900 Europeo* (Trento: Università degli studi di Trento, 2009).

Millar, Fergus. *The Emperor in the Roman World* (London: Duckworth, 1977, 2nd ed. 1992).

Miller, Lucinda. "The notion of European private law," in Michael Lobban and Julia Moses (eds.), *The Impact of Ideas on Legal Development* (Cambridge: Cambridge University Press, 2014), pp. 265–285.

Miłosz, Czesław. *The Captive Mind* (London: Secker & Warburg, 1953).

Milward, Alan S. *The Reconstruction of Western Europe, 1945–51* (London: Methuen, 1984).

Milza, Pierre and Peschanski, Denis (eds.). *Exils et migration. Italiens et Espagnols en France, 1938–1946* (Paris: L'Harmattan, 1994).

Minale, Valerio Massimo. *Carteggio Croce – Arangio-Ruiz* (Naples: Il Mulino, 2012).

Mohler, Armin. *Die Konservative Revolution in Deutschland 1918–1932: Ein Handbuch* (Darmstadt: Wissenschaftliche Buchgesellschaft, 1989).

Moll, W. L. "Review of Fritz Schulz's *Principles of Roman Law*," *Virginia Law Review*, 5 (1937), *858*.

Momigliano, Armando. "Ancient biography and the study of religion," in Armando Momigliano (ed.), *Ottavo contributo alla storia degli studi classici e del mondo antico* (Rome: Edizioni di Storia e Letteratura, 1987), pp. 193–210.

Momigliano, Armando. "Peace and liberty in the Ancient World," in Riccardo Di Donato, *Decimo contributo alla storia degli studi classici e del mondo antico* (Rome: Edizioni di Storia e Letteratura, 2012), pp. 4–105.
Monateri, Pier Giuseppe. "Black Gaius: a quest for the multicultural origins of the Western legal tradition," *Hastings Law Journal*, 51 (2000), 479–555.
Monateri, Pier Giuseppe, Giaro, Tomasz and Somma, Alessandro (eds.). *Le radici comuni del diritto europeo* (Rome: Carocci editore, 2005).
Morris, Douglas. "Discrimination, degradation, defiance: Jewish lawyers under Nazism," in A. E. Steinweis and Robert D. Rachlin (eds.), *The Law in Nazi Germany: Ideology, Opportunism, and the Perversion of Justice* (New York: Berghahn Books, 2013), pp. 124–128.
Morris, Douglas. "Write and resist: Ernst Fraenkel and Franz Neumann on the role of natural law in fighting Nazi tyranny," *New German Critique*, 126 (2015), 197–230.
Moses, A. Dirk. *German Intellectuals and the Nazi Past* (Cambridge: Cambridge University Press, 2007).
Mosse, George L. *The Crisis of German Ideology: Intellectual Origins of the Third Reich* (New York: H. Fertig, 1998 [1964]).
Mosse, George L. *The Fascist Revolution: Toward a General Theory of Fascism* (New York: Howard Fertig Pub, 1999).
Moyn, Samuel. *Christian Human Rights* (Philadelphia, PA: University of Pennsylvania Press, 2015).
Moyn, Samuel. *The Last Utopia: Human Rights in History* (Cambridge, MA: Belknap Press of Harvard University Press, 2010).
Müller, Ingo. *Furchtbare Juristen: die unbewältige Vergangenheit unserer Justiz* (Munich: Kindler, 1987).
Muller, Jerry Z. *Conservatism* (Princeton, NJ: Princeton University Press, 1997).
Muller, Jerry Z. *The Other God that Failed: Hans Freyer and the Deradicalization of German Conservatism* (Princeton, NJ: Princeton University Press, 1987).
Müller, Manfred. "Paul Koschaker (1879–1951). Zum 100. Geburtstag des Begründers der Keilschriftrechtsgeschichte," *Altorientalische Forschungen*, 9 (1982) 271–284.
Mura, Eloisa. "Emilio Betti, oltre lo specchio della memoria," in Emilio Betti (ed.), *Notazioni autobiografiche (a cura di Eloisa Mura)* (Padova: CEDAM, [1953] 2014), pp. ix–lxiv.
Murray, Oswyn. "Arnaldo Momigliano on Peace and Liberty," in Sally Crawford, Katharina Ulmschneider and Jas Elsner (eds.), *Ark of Civilization: Refugee Scholars and Oxford University, 1930–1945* (Oxford: Oxford University Press, 2017), pp. 202–207.
Mussgnug, Dorothee (ed.). *Ernst Levy und Wolfgang Kunkel. Briefwechsel 1922–1968* (Heidelberg: Universitätsverlag Winter, 2005).
Mussgnug, Dorothee. "Die juristische Fakultät," in Wolfgang Uwe Eckart, Volker Sellin and Eike Wolgast (eds.), *Die Universität Heidelberg im Nationalsozialismus* (Heidelberg: Springer, 2006), pp. 301–302.

Nasti, Fara. "Pensiero giuridico romano e tradizione europea nei *Prinzipien* di Fritz Schulz," in Pierre Bonin, Nader Hakim, Fara Nasti and Aldo Schiavone (eds.), *Pensiero giuridico occidentale e giuristi romani. Eredità e genealogie* (Torino: Giappichelli, 2019), pp. 225–247.

Nehlsen, Hermann. "In memoriam: Karl August Eckhardt," *Zeitschrift der Savigny-Stiftung für Rechtsgeschichte: Germanistische Abteilung*, 104 (1987), 497–536.

Nelis, Jan. "Constructing Fascist identity: Benito Mussolini and the myth of Romanità," *Classical World*, 100 (2007), 391–415.

Nelson, William E. *The Legalist Reformation: Law, Politics, and Ideology in New York, 1920–1980* (Chapel Hill, NC: University of North Carolina Press, 2001).

Neulen, Hans-Werner. *Europa und das Dritte Reich. Einigungsbestrebungen im deutschen Machtbereich 1939–1945* (Munich: Universitas, 1987).

Neumann, Franz. *Behemoth: The Structure and Practice of National Socialism 1933–1944* (New York: Harper & Row, 1966 [1944]).

Neumann, Franz. "The concept of political freedom," 53 *Columbia Law Review*, (7) (1953), 901–935.

Neumann, Franz. "The concept of political freedom," in William E. Scheuerman (ed.), *The Rule of Law Under Siege: Selected Essays of Franz L. Neumann and Otto Kirchheimer* (Berkeley, Los Angeles, London: University of California Press, 1996), pp. 195–230.

Neumann, Franz. "Re-educating the Germans," *Commentary*, 3 (1947), 517–525.

Neumann, Georg. "Paul Koschaker in Tübingen (1941–1946)," *Zeitschrift für altorientalische und biblische Rechtgeschichte*, 18 (2012), 23–36.

Niemann, Martin. "Karl August Eckhardt," in Mathias Schmoeckel (ed.), *Die Juristen der Universität Bonn in "Dritten Reich"* (Cologne: Böhlau, 2004), pp. 160–184.

Noailles, Pierre. "La crise du droit romain," in *Mémorial des études latines offert à J. Marouzeau* (Paris: Belles Lettres, 1943), pp. 387–415.

Nora, Pierre and Kritzma, Lawrence D. (eds.), *Realms of Memory. The Construction of the French Past* (New York: Columbia University Press, 1996).

Nörr, Dieter. "Franz Wieacker 5.8.1908–17.2.1994," in Tiziana J. Chiusi, Wolfgang Kaiser and Hans-Dieter Spengler (eds.), *Dieter Nörr. Historiae Iuris Antiqui* (Goldbach: Keip Verlag, 2003), pp. 248–256.

Nörr, Dieter. "Über das Geistige im Recht: ein Nachruf auf Helmut Coing," *Juristenzeitung*, 56 (2001), 449–452.

Nutton, Vivian. "The beneficial ideology," in Peter D. A. Garnsey and C. R. Whittaker (eds.), *Imperialism in the Ancient World* (Cambridge: Cambridge University Press, 1978), pp. 209–223.

Olechowski, Thomas. "Hans Kelsen, the Second World War and the US Government," in Jeremy Telman (ed.), *Hans Kelsen in America – Selective Affinities and the Mysteries of Academic Influence* (Berlin: Springer Verlag, 2016), pp. 101–112.

Oliver, James H. "The ruling power. A study of the Roman Empire in the second century after Christ through the Roman Oration of Aelius Aristides," *Transactions of the American Philosophical Society*, 43 (1953), 871–1003.

Orestano, Riccardo. "L''animus' di Salvatore Riccobono," *Iura*, 29 (1978), 1–8.

Ortu, Rosanna. "Salvatore Riccobono nell'Università di Sassari," *Diritto@Storia*, 3 (2004).

Osler, Douglas. "The fantasy men," *Rechtsgeschichte*, 10 (2007), 169–192.

Osler, Douglas. "The myth of European legal history," *Rechtshistorisches Journal*, 16 (1997), 393–410.

Osterkamp, Ernst, "The legacy of the George Circle," in David Kettler and Gerhard Lauer (eds.), *Exile, Science and Bildung. The Contested Legacies of German Emigre Intellectuals* (Berlin: Springer, 2005), pp. 19–26.

Padoa-Schioppa, Antonio (ed.). *A History of Law in Europe. From the Early Middle Ages to the Twentieth Century* (Cambridge: Cambridge University Press, 2017).

Pagden, Anthony. "Introduction," in Anthony Pagden (ed.), *The Idea of Europe. From Antiquity to the European Union* (Cambridge: Cambridge University Press, 2002), pp. 1–32.

Panofsky, Erwin. "Three decades of art history in the United States: impressions of a transplanted European," *College Art Journal*, 14(1) (1954), 7–27.

Pauer-Studer, Herlinde. "'Jenseits von Chaos und Interessenkonflikten'. Aspekte der Rechtsentwicklung im NS-System der 1930er Jahre," in Werner Konitzer (ed.), *Moralisierung des Rechts: Kontinuitäten und Diskontinuitäten nationalsozialistischer Normativität* (Frankfurt: Campus Verlag, 2014), pp. 11–34.

Pauer-Studer, Herlinde and Fink, Julian. *Rechtfertigungen des Unrechts. Das Rechtsdenken im Nationalsozialismus in Originaltexten* (Berlin: Suhrkamp, 2014).

Peachin, Michael. *Iudex vice Caesaris: Deputy Emperors and the Administration of Justice during the Principate* (Stuttgart: Franz Steiner Verlag, 1996).

Pernot, Laurent. "Aelius Aristides and Rome," in William V. Harris and Brooke Holmes (eds.), *Aelius Aristides between Greece, Rome, and the gods* (Leiden and Boston: Brill, 2008), pp. 175–201.

Perry, Matthew. "The *paterfamilias* and the family council in Roman public law," in Kaius Tuori and Laura Nissin (eds.), *Public and Private in the Roman House and Society* (Portsmouth, RI: Journal of Roman Archaeology Supplement Series, 2015), pp. 77–86.

Pescatore, Pierre. "Fundamental rights and freedoms in the system of the European Communities," *The American Journal of Comparative Law*, 18 (1970), 343–351.

Pettit, Philip. *Republicanism: A Theory of Freedom and Government* (Oxford: Oxford University Press, 1997).

Pieler, Peter E. "Das römische Recht im nationalsozialistischen Staat," in Ulrike Davy, Helmut Fuchs, Herbert Hofmeister, Judith Marte and Ilse Reiter (eds.), *Nationalsozialismus und Recht* (Vienna: Verlag A. Orac, 1990), pp. 427–444.

Pihlajamäki, Heikki. "Against metaphysics in law: the historical background of American and Scandinavian legal realism compared," *The American Journal of Comparative Law*, 52 2004, 469–487.

Plachy, Adolfo. "Il diritto romano come valore culturale nella storia dell'Europa," in *L'Europa e il diritto romano. Studi in memoria di Paolo Koschaker, I* (Milan: Giuffrè, 1954), pp. 477–491.

Plachy, Adolfo. "Rec. di Koschaker, Die Krise des römischen Rechts und die romanistische Rechtswissenschaft (1938)," *Rivista di Storia del Diritto Italiano*, 12 (1939), 388–394.

Pocock, John G. A. *The Machiavellian Moment* (Princeton, NJ: Princeton University Press, 1975).

Poidevin, Raymond. *Histoire des débuts de la construction européenne (Mars 1948-Mai 1950)* (Brussels: Bruylant, 1984).

Pound, Roscoe. "The call for a realist jurisprudence," *Harvard Law Review*, 44 (1930–1931), 697–711.

Prettenthaler-Ziegerhofer, Anita. "Richard Nikolaus Cloudenhove-Kalergi, founder of the Pan-European Union, and the birth of a 'new' Europe," in Mark Hewitson and Matthew D'Auria (eds.), *Europe in Crisis: Intellectuals and the European Idea, 1917–1957* (Oxford: Berghahn Books, 2012), pp. 89–110.

von Premerstein, Anton. *Vom Werden und Wesen des Prinzipats. Aus dem Nachlass herausgegeben von Hans Volkmann* (Munich: Verlag der Bayerischen Akademie der Wissenschaften, 1937).

Pringsheim, Fritz. "Aequitas und bona fides," in *Gesammelte Abhandlungen 1* (Heidelberg: Carl Winter & Universitätsverlag, 1961 [1930]), pp. 154–172.

Pringsheim, Fritz. *The Greek Law of Sale* (Weimar: Hermann Böhlaus Nachfolger, 1950).

Pringsheim, Fritz. "Die Haltung der Freiburger Studenten in den Jahren 1933–1935," *Die Sammlung*, 15 (1960), 532–538.

Pringsheim, Fritz. "Höhe und Ende der Römischen Jurisprudenz," in *Gesammelte Abhandlungen 1* (Heidelberg: Carl Winter & Universitätsverlag, 1961 [1930]), pp. 53–62.

Pringsheim, Fritz. "Legal policy and reforms of Hadrian," *Journal of Roman Studies*, 24 (1934), 141–153.

Prowe, Diethelm. "German democratization as conservative restabilization: the impact of American policy," in Jeffry M. Diefendorf, Axel Frohn and Hermann-Josef Rupieper (eds.), *American Policy and the Reconstruction of West Germany, 1945–1955* (Cambridge: Cambridge University Press, 1993), pp. 305–329.

Pugliese, Giovanni. "Diritto romano e scienza del diritto," *Annali dell'Università di Macerata*, 15 (1941), 5–48.

Pugliese, Giovanni. "Diritto romano e scienza del diritto," in Giovanni Pugliese (ed.), *Scritti giuridici scelti, III* (Naples: Jovene, 1985), pp. 159–204.

Rabinbach, Anson. "The Frankfurt School and the 'Jewish Question,' 1940–1970," in Ezra Mendelsohn, Stefani Hoffman and Richard Cohen (eds.), *Against the Grain: Jewish Intellectuals in Hard Times* (New York: Berghahn Books, 2013), pp. 255–276.

Rachlin, Robert D. "Roland Freisler and the Volksgerichthof," in A. E. Steinweis and Robert D. Rachlin (eds.), *The Law in Nazi Germany: Ideology, Opportunism, and the Perversion of Justice* (New York: Berghahn Books, 2013), pp. 63–87.

Radbruch, Gustav. "Gesetzliches unrecht und übergesetzliches Recht," *Süddeutsche Juristenzeitung*, 1 (1946), 105–108.

Radin, Max. *Cartas Romanisticas (1923–1950)* (Naples: Jovene, 2001).

Ramage, Edwin S. *The Nature and Purpose of Augustus' "Res Gestae"* (Wiesbaden: Franz Steiner Verlag, 1987).

Randazzo, Salvo. "Roman Legal Tradition and American Law. The Riccobono Seminar of Roman Law in Washington," *Roman Legal Tradition* 1 (2002) 123–144.

Remy, Steven P. *The Heidelberg Myth: The Nazification and Denazification of a German University* (New Haven, CT: Harvard University Press, 2003).

Rhodes, P. J. *Ancient Democracy and Modern Ideology* (London: Duckworth, 2003).

Riccobono, Salvatore. "Augusto e il problema della nuova costituzione," *Annali del Seminario giuridico di Palermo*, 15 (1936), 363–507.

Riccobono, Salvatore. "Dal diritto romano classico al diritto moderno," *Annali del Seminario Giuridico della R. Università di Palermo*, 3–4 (1917), 165–729.

Riccobono, Salvatore. "Il diritto del impero," in Carlo Galassi Paluzzi (ed.), *La missione dell'impero di Roma nella storia della civiltà* I (Rome: Istituto di Studi Romani, 1938), p. 39–51.

Riccobono, Salvatore. "Outlines of the evolution of Roman law," *University of Pennsylvania Law Review*, 74 (1925), 1–19.

Riccobono, Salvatore. "La universalità del diritto romano," in *L'Europa e il diritto romano. Studi in memoria di Paul Koschaker* (Milan: Giuffrè, 1954), pp. 1–11.

Riccobono, Salvatore Jr. "Un manoscritto inedito di Salvatore Riccobono: le lezioni tenute ad Oxford e Londra nel 1924," *Iura*, 29 (1978), 9–16.

Ries, Gerhard. "Paul Koschaker," *Neue Deutsche Biographie*, 12 (1980), 608–609.

Ritter, Gerhard. "Der deutsche Professor im Dritten Reich," *Die Gegenwart*, 1.1 (1945), 23–26.

Robinson, Olivia F., Fergus, David T. and Gordon, William M. *European Legal History: Sources and Institutions* (London: Butterworths, 2000).

Rodgers, Daniel T. *Atlantic Crossings: Social Politics in a Progressive Age* (Cambridge, MA: Harvard University Press, 2000).

Rösch, Felix. *Emigre Scholars and the Genesis of International Relations: A European Discipline in America?* (Basingstoke: Palgrave MacMillan, 2014).

Rückert, Joachim. "Geschichte der Privatrechts als Apologie des Juristen – Franz Wieacker zum Gedächtnis," *Quaderni Fiorentini*, 24 (1995), 531–562.

Rückert, Joachim. "Privatrechtsgeschichte der Neuzeit: Genese und Zukunft eines Faches?," in Eva Schumann and Okko Behrends (eds.), *Franz Wieacker – Historiker des modernen Privatrechts* (Wallstein Verlag GmbH, 2010), pp. 75–118.

Rückert, Joachim. "Der Rechtsbegriff der Deutschen Rechtsgeschichte in der NS-Zeit: der Sieg des 'Lebens' und des konkreten Ordnungsdenkens, seine Vorgeschichte und seine Nachwirkungen," in Joachim Rückert and Dietmar Willoweit (eds.), *Die Deutsche Rechtsgeschichte in der NS-Zeit ihre Vorgeschichte und ihre Nachwirkungen* (Tübingen: Mohr Siebeck, 1995), pp. 177–240.

von Rümelin, Max Friedrich Gustav. *Rechtsgefühl und Rechtsbewusstsein, Rede Gehalten Bei der Akademischen Preisverteilung Am 6. November 1925* (Tübingen: J. C. B. Mohr, 1925).

Rüsen, Jörn. "Tradition: a principle of historical sense-generation and its logic and effect in historical culture," *History and Theory*, 51(4) (2012), 45–59.

Rüthers, Bernd. *Entartetes Recht* (Munich: Beck, 1989).

Rüthers, Bernd. *Die Unbegrenzte Auslegung. Zum Wandel der Privatrechtsordnung im Nationalsozialismus* (Tübingen: Mohr Siebeck, 2005).

Sandkühler, Thomas. "Europa und der Nationalsozialismus. Ideologie, Währungspolitik, Massengewalt," *Zeithistorische Forschungen/Studies in Contemporary History*, 9 (2012), 428–441.

Sanfilippo, Cesare. "In memoriam. Salvatore Riccobono," *Iura*, 9 (1958), 123–133.

Santucci, Gianni. "'Decifrando scritti che non hanno nessun potere'. La crisi della romanistica fra le due guerre," in Italo Birocchi and Massimo Brutti (eds.), *Storia del diritto e identità disciplinari: tradizioni e prospettive* (Torino: Giappichelli, 2016), pp. 63–102.

Santucci, Gianni. "La scienza gaia e la strana idea del diritto romano non romano," *Europa e diritto private*, 4 (2007), 1057–1093.

von Savigny, Friedrich Carl. *System des heutigen römischen Rechts, vol 1* (Berlin: Bei Veit und Comp., 1840).

Schäfer, Herwig. *Juristische Lehre und Forschung an der Reichsuniversität Straßburg 1941–1944* (Tübingen: Mohr Siebeck, 1999).

Schäfer, Frank L. "Visionen und Wissenschaftsmanagement. Die Gründung eines Max-Planck-Instituts für europäische Rechtsgeschichte," *Zeitschrift für Europäisches Privatrecht*, 17 (2009), 517–535.

Schartner, Irmgard. *Die Staatsrechtler der juridischen Fakultät der Universität Wien im "Ansturm" des Nationalsozialismus. Umbrüche und Kontinuitäten* (Frankfurt, Berlin, Bern, Brussels, New York, Oxford and Vienna: Peter Lang, 2011).

Schermaier, Martin Josef. "'Fritz Schulz' *Prinzipien*. Das Ende einer deutschen Universitätslaufbahn im Berlin der Dreißigerjahre," in Stefan Grundmann, Michael Kloepfer and Christoph G. Paulus (eds.), *Festschrift 200 Jahre Juristische Fakultät der Humboldt-Universität zu Berlin* (Berlin: Humboldt-Universität zu Berlin, 2010), pp. 683–700.

Scheuerman, William E. (ed.). *The Rule of Law Under Siege: Selected Essays of Franz L. Neumann and Otto Kirchheimer* (Berkeley, Los Angeles, London: University of California Press, 1996).

Schiavone, Aldo. *The End of the Past. Ancient Rome and the Modern West* (Cambridge, MA, London, England: Harvard University Press, 2000).

Schiavone, Aldo. *The Invention of the Law in the West* (Cambridge, MA and London: The Belknap Press of Harvard University Press, 2005).

Schildt, Axel. *Zwischen Abendland und Amerika* (Oldenbourg: Wissenschaftsverlag, 1999).

Schiller, A. Arthur. "Review of the *Principles* [et al.]," *American Bar Association Journal*, 24 (1938), 1015–1017.

Schlegel, John Henry. *American Legal Realism and Empirical Social Science* (Chapel Hill: University of North Carolina Press, 1995).

Schmerbach, Folker. *Das "Gemeinschaftslager Hanns Kerrl" für Referendare in Jüterbog 1933–1939* (Tübingen: Mohr Siebeck, 2008).
Schmitt, Carl. "Die Auflösung der europäischen Ordnung im 'International Law' (1890–1939)," *Deutsche Rechtswissenschaft*, 5 (1940), 267–278.
Schmitt, Carl. "Die Verfassung der Freiheit," *Deutsche Juristen-Zeitung*, 40 (1935), 1133–1135.
Schmitt, Carl and Hartung, Fritz. *Das Reich und Europa* (Leipzig: Koehler & Amelang, 1941).
Schmidt, Katharina Isabel. "Law, modernity, crisis: German free lawyers, American legal realists, and the transatlantic turn to 'life,' 1903–1933," *German Studies Review*, 39 (2016), 121–140.
Schönbauer, Ernst. "Zur 'Krise des römischen Rechts'," in *Festschrift Paul Koschaker mit Unterstützung der Rechts- und Staatswissenschaftlichen Fakultät der Friedrich-Wilhelms-Universität Berlin und der Leipziger Juristenfakultät zum 60. Geburtstagüberreicht von seinen Fachgenossen, II* (Weimar: Verlag Hermann Böhlaus, 1939), pp. 385–410.
Schönwälder, Karen. *Historiker und Politik. Geschichtswissenschaft im Nationalsozialismus* (Frankfurt, New York: Campus Verlag, 1992).
Schudnagies, Christian. *Hans Frank. Aufstieg und Fall des NS-Juristen und Generalgoverneurs* (Frankfurt: Peter Lang, 1989).
Schulz, Fritz. *Einführung in das Studium der Digesten* (Tübingen: Verlag von J. C. B. Mohr (Paul Siebeck), 1916).
Schulz, Fritz. *Die epitome Ulpiani des Codex vaticanus reginæ 1128* (Bonn: A. Marcus und E. Weber, 1926).
Schulz, Fritz. *Principles of Roman Law* (Oxford: Clarendon Press, 1936).
Schulz, Fritz. *Prinzipien des römischen Rechts* (Berlin: Duncker & Humblot, 1954 [1934]).
Schulz, Fritz. *Roman Legal Science* (Oxford: Oxford University Press, 1946).
Schulz, Fritz. *Sabinus-Fragmente in Ulpians Sabinus-Commentar* (Halle: M. Niemeyer, 1906).
Schulz, Fritz. "System der Rechte auf den Eingriffserwerb," *Archiv für die civilistische Praxis*, 105 (1909), 1–488.
Schulz-Forberg, Hagen and Stråth, Bo. *The Political History of European Integration: The Hypocrisy of Democracy-Through-Market* (London: Routledge, 2010).
Schumann, Eva. "Die juristische Fakultäten in der NS-Zeit," in Thilo Ramm and Stefan Saar (eds.), *Nationalsozialismus und Recht* (Baden-Baden: Nomos, 2014), p. 39–154.
Schwartz, Thomas Alan. *America's Germany: John J. McCloy and the Federal Republic of Germany* (Cambridge, MA: Harvard University Press, 1991).
Sharples, Caroline. *Postwar Germany and the Holocaust* (London: Bloomsbury, 2016).
Siber, Heinrich. *Das Führeramt des Augustus* (Leipzig: S. Hirzel, 1940).
Simon, Dieter. "Die deutsche Wissenschaft vom römischen Recht nach 1933," in Michael Stolleis and Dieter Simon (eds.), *Rechtsgeschichte im Nationalsozialismus. Beiträge zur Geschichte einer Disziplin* (Tübingen: Mohr, 1989), pp. 171–176.

Simon, Dieter. "Ernst Levy," in Bernhard Diestelkamp and Michael Stolleis (eds.), *Juristen an der Universität Frankfurt am Main* (Baden-Baden: Nomos, 1989), p. 94.
Simon, Dieter. "Levy, Ernst," *Neue Deutsche Biographie*, 14 (1985), 403–404.
Simon, Dieter. "Zwischen Wissenschaft und Wissenschaftspolitik: Helmut Coing (28.2.1912–15.8.2000)," *Neue Juristische Wochenschrift*, 54 (2001), 1029–1032.
Skinner, Quentin. *Liberty before Liberalism* (Cambridge: Cambridge University Press, 1998).
Skinner, Quentin. *Visions of Politics III* (Cambridge: Cambridge University Press, 2002).
Smits, Jan, *The Making of European Private Law: Toward a Ius Commune. Europaeum as a Mixed Legal System* (Antwerp: Intersentia, 2002).
Snyder, Timothy. *Black Earth: The Holocaust as History and Warning* (London: Vintage, 2015).
Söllner, Alfons. "Ernst Fraenkel under die Verwetlichung der politischen Kultur in der Bundesrepublic Deutschland," in *Fluchtpunkte, Studien zur politischen Ideengeschichte des 20. Jahrhunderts* (Baden-Baden: Nomos Verlag, 2006), pp. 223–223.
Söllner, Alfons."Normative Verwestlichung. Der Einfluß der Remigranten auf die politische Kultur der frühen Bundesrepublik," in Heinz Bude and Bernd Greine (eds.), *Westbindungen. Amerika in der Bundesrepublik* (Hamburg: Hamburger Edition, 1999), pp. 72–92.
Söllner, Alfons. *Political Scholar: Zur Intellectuallengeschichte des 20. Jahrhunderts* (Hamburg: Europäische Verlagsanstalt, 2018).
Solmi, Arrigo. "Le nuove Direttive dell diritto," in *Faschismus und Recht. Schriften des NS.-Rechtswahrerbundes in Österreich* (Vienna: Landesgeschäftsstelle des NS.-Rechtswahrerbundes, 1938), pp. 1–3.
Somma, Alessandro. *I giuristi e l'Asse culturale Roma-Berlino: Economia e politica nel diritto fascista e nazionalsocialista* (Frankfurt: Klostermann, 2005).
Somma, Alessandro. "'Roma madre delle leggi.' L'uso politico del diritto romano," *Materiali per una storia della cultura giuridica*, 32 (2002), 153–181.
Somma, Alessandro. "L'uso del diritto romano e della romanistica tra Fascismo e Antifascismo," in Massimo Miglietta and Gianni Santucci (eds.), *Diritto romano e regimi totalitari nel '900 Europeo* (Trento: Università degli studi di Trento, 2009), pp. 113–114.
Spantigati, Federico. "La discontinuità nella continuità (commento a Leo Peppe)," *Diritto romano attuale*, 4 (2000), 89–94.
Spinelli, Altiero and Rossi, Ernesto. *The Ventotene Manifesto* (Ventotene: The Altiero Spinelli Institute for Federalist Studies, 2016 [1941]).
Stahlmann, Ines. "Vom Despoten zum Kaiser. Zum deutschen Augustusbild im 19. Jahrhundert," in Karl Christ and Armando Momigliano (eds.), *L' Antichita nell'Ottocento in Italia e Germania* (Bologna: Società editrice il Mulino, 1988), pp. 303–319.
Stein, Peter. "Foreword," in Paul Vinogradoff (ed.), *Roman Law in Medieval Europe* (Oxford: Clarendon Press, 1968), pp. x–xii.

Stein, Peter. *Roman Law in European History* (Cambridge: Cambridge University Press, 1999).
Steinwenter, Artur. "Rezension: Prinzipien des römischen Rechts von Fritz Schulz," *Historische Zeitschrift*, 152 (1935), 115–116.
Stertz, Stephen A. "Aelius Aristides' Political Ideas," *Aufstieg und Niedergang der römischen Welt*, 2.34.2 (1994), 1248–1270.
Stiefel, Ernst C. and Mecklenburg, Frank. *Deutsche Juristen im amerikanischen Exil (1933–1950)* (Tübingen: Mohr Siebeck, 1991).
Stirk, Peter M. R. (ed.). *European Unity in Context: The Interwar Period* (London: Bloomsbury, 1989).
Stolleis, Michael. "'Fortschritte der Rechtsgeschichte' in der Zeit des Nationalsozialismus?," in Michael Stolleis and Dieter Simon (eds.), *Rechtsgeschichte im Nationalsozialismus. Beiträge zur Geschichte einer Disziplin* (Tübingen: Mohr Siebeck, 1989), pp. 177–197.
Stolleis, Michael. *Geschichte des öffentlichen Rechts in Deutschland. 3. Band, Staats- und Verwaltungsrechtswissenschaft in Republik und Diktatur 1914–1945* (Munich: Beck, 1999).
Stolleis, Michael. "Helmut Coing 28.2.1912–15.8.2000," *Jahrbuch der Max-Planck-Gesellschaft* (2001), 873–874.
Stolleis, Michael. *The Law under the Swastika. Studies on Legal History in Nazi Germany* (Chicago London: University of Chicago Press, 1998).
Stolleis, Michael. *Public Law in Germany 1914–1945* (Oxford: Oxford University Press, 2004).
Stolleis, Michael. "Reluctance to glance in the mirror: the changing face of German jurisprudence after 1933 and post-1945," in Christian Joerges and Navraj Singh Ghaleigh (eds.), *Darker Legacies of Law in Europe* (Oxford and Portland, OR: Hart Publishing, 2003), pp. 1–18.
Stolleis, Michael and Simon, Dieter (eds.), *Rechtsgeschichte im Nationalsozialismus. Beiträge zur Geschichte einer Disziplin* (Tübingen: Mohr, 1989).
Stoltzfus, Nathan and Friedlander, Henry (eds.). *Nazi Crimes and the Law* (Cambridge: Cambridge University Press, 2008).
Strauss, Leo. "The living issues of German postwar philosophy," in Heinrich Meier (ed.), *Leo Strauss and the Theologico-political Problem* (New York: Cambridge University Press, 2006), pp. 115–139.
Strauss, Leo. *Natural Right and History* (Chicago: University of Chicago Press, repr. 1963 [orig. 1953]).
Strauss, Leo. *Persecution and the Art of Writing* (Chicago: University of Chicago Press, 1988).
Strauss, Leo. *On Tyranny* (Chicago: University of Chicago Press, repr. 2000 [orig. 1948]).
Streck, Michael P. and Dolezalek, Gero. "Paul Koschaker: Zum 125. Geburtstag am 19. April 2004," in *Jubiläen 2004. Personen-Ereignisse* (Leipzig: Universität Leipzig, 2004), pp. 31–34.
Strote, Noah. *Lions and Lambs: Conflict in Weimar and the Creation of Post-Nazi Germany* (Yale University Press, 2017).

Syme, Ronald. *The Roman Revolution* (Oxford: Oxford University Press, 1939).

Tamm, Ditlev. "The history of the Court of Justice of the European Union since its origin," in *The Court of Justice and the Construction of Europe: Analyses and Perspectives on Sixty Years of Case-Law – La Cour de Justice et la Construction de l'Europe: Analyses et Perspectives de Soixante Ans de Jurisprudence* (The Hague: Springer, 2013), pp. 9–35.

Tanguay, Daniel. *Leo Strauss: An Intellectual Biography* (New Haven, CT: Yale University Press, 2007).

Tompkins, Daniel P. "The making of Moses Finley," in Daniel Jew, Robin Osborne and Michael Scott (eds.), *M. I. Finley: An Ancient Historian and His Impact* (Cambridge: Cambridge University Press, 2016), pp. 13–30.

Träger, Marion. "Methode und Zivilrecht bei Franz Wieacker (1908–1994)," in Joachim Rückert and Ralf Seinecke (eds.), *Methodik des Zivilrechts – von Savigny bis Teubner* (Baden-Baden: Nomos, 2012), pp. 235–260.

Tuori, Kaius. *Ancient Roman Lawyers and Modern Legal Ideals: Studies on the Impact of Contemporary Concerns in the Interpretation of Ancient Roman Legal History* (Frankfurt am Main: Klostermann, 2007).

Tuori, Kaius. *The Emperor of Law: The Emergence of Roman Imperial Adjudication* (Oxford: Oxford University Press, 2016).

Tuori, Kaius. "Hadrian's cosmopolitanism and Nazi legal policy," *Classical Receptions Journal*, 9 (2017), 470–486.

Tuori, Kaius and Björklund, Heta (eds.). *Roman Law and the Idea of Europe* (London: Bloomsbury, 2019).

Tziovas, Dimitris (ed.). *Re-imagining the Past: Antiquity and Modern Greek Culture* (Oxford: Oxford University Press, 2014).

Valabrega, Paolo. *I dodici professori che non hanno giurato*. Speech on May 6, 2014, at Politecnico di Torino.

van Caenegem, Raoul C. *European Law in the Past and the Future: Unity and Diversity over Two Millennia* (Cambridge: Cambridge University Press, 2002).

van Caenegem, Raoul C. *An Historical Introduction to Private Law* (Cambridge: Cambridge University Press, 1992).

Vari, Massimo. "Diritto romano «ius commune» europeo?," *Index: quaderni camerti di studi romanistici = international survey of Roman law*, 30 (2002), 183–185.

Varvaro, Mario. "Circolazione e sviluppo di un modello metologico," in Martin Avenarius, Christian Baldus, Francesca Lamberti and Mario Varvaro (eds.), *Gradenwitz, Riccobono und die Entwicklung der Interpolationenkritik* (Tübingen: Mohr Siebeck, 2018), pp. 55–100.

Varvaro, Mario. "Gli 'studia humanitatis' ei 'fata iuris Romani' tra fascio e croce uncinate," *Index: quaderni camerti di studi romanistici = international survey of Roman law*, 42 (2014), 643–661.

Varvaro, Mario. "Riccobono, Salvatore sr.," in Italo Birocchi, Ennio Cortese, Antonello Mattone and Marco Nicola Miletti (eds.), *Dizionario biografico dei giuristi italiani (sec. XII–XX), II* (Bologna: Il Mulino, 2013), pp. 1685–1688.

Vermeiren, Jan. "Imperium Europaeum: Rudolf Pannwitz and the German Idea of Europe," in Mark Hewitson and Matthew D'Auria (eds.). *Europe in Crisis: Intellectuals and the European Idea, 1917–1957* (Oxford: Berghahn Books, 2012), pp. 135–154.

Vinogradoff, Paul. *Roman Law in Medieval Europe* (Oxford: Clarendon Press, 1968).

Volkmann, Hans. *Zur Rechtsprechung im Prinzipat des Augustus. Historische Beiträge* (Munich: C. H. Beck'sche Verlagsbuchhandlung, 1969 [1935]).

Vollnhals, Clemens. *Entnazifizierung. Politische Säuberung und Rehabilitierung in den vier Besatzungszonen 1945–1949* (Munich: Dtv, 1991).

Volpe, P. "Armonia e taxis nell'Encomio a Roma di Elio Aristide," in F. Giordano (ed.), *L'idea di Roma nella cultura antica, Atti del Convegno di Studi (Salerno 14–16 ottobre 1996)* (Naples: Edizioni scientifiche italiane, 2001), pp. 305–312.

Waddell, John. *Foundation Myths: the Beginnings of Irish Archaeology* (Wicklow: Bray, Co., 2005).

Waider, Herbert. "'Ars iuris' und 'suum in persona ipsa' bei Hugo Donellus," *Archiv für Geschichte der Philosophie*, 43 (1961), 60–62.

Waldinger, Fabian. "Peer effects in science: evidence from the dismissal of scientists in Nazi Germany," *The Review of Economic Studies*, 79 (2012), 838–861.

Wallace-Hadrill, Andrew. "Mutatio morum: the idea of a cultural revolution," in T. Habinek and A. Schiesaro (eds.), *The Roman Cultural Revolution* (Cambridge: Cambridge University Press, 1997), pp. 3–22.

Weber, Marianne. *Max Weber, ein Lebensbild* (Heidelberg: Verlag Lambert Schneider, 1950).

Weber, Max. *Wirtschaftsgeschichte* (Berlin: Duncker & Humblot, 1924).

Wege, Carl. *"Das Neue Europa" 1933–1945: German Thought Patterns about Europe* (Stuttgart: Edition Axel Menges, 2016).

Weinreich, Max. *Hitler's Professors: The Part of Scholarship in Germany's Crimes against the Jewish People* (New York: Yiddish Scientific Institute, 1946).

Weinreich, Max. *Hitler et les professeurs. Le rôle des universitaires allemands dans les crimes commis contre le peuple juif* (Paris: Les Belles Lettres, 2014).

Wenger, Leopold. *Der heutige Stand der römischen Rechtswissenschaft* (Munich: C. H. Beck'sche Verlagsbuchhandlung, 1927).

Wesener, Gunter. "Paul Koschaker," in Rafael Domingo (ed.), *Juristas universales, III. Juristas del siglo XIX. Da Savigny a Kelsen* (Madrid and Barcelona: Marcial Pons, 2004), pp. 971–974.

Wesener, Gunter. "Paul Koschaker (1879–1951), Begründer der altorientalischen Rechtsgeschichte und juristischen Keilschriftforschung," in Karl Acham (ed.), *Rechts-, Sozial- und Wirtschaftswissenschaftlichen aus Graz* (Vienna: Böhlau Verlag, 2011), pp. 273–285.

Wesener, Gunter. *Römisches Recht und Naturrecht* (Graz: Universität Graz, 1978).

Wheatland, Thomas. "Franz L. Neumann: negotiating political exile," *Bulletin of the German Historical Institute*, 54, suppl. 10 (2014), 111–138.

Whitman, James Q. *Hitler's American Model. The United States and the Making of Nazi Race Law* (Princeton, NJ: Princeton University Press, 2016).

Whitman, James Q. *The Legacy of Roman Law in the German Romantic Era* (Princeton, New Jersey: Princeton University Press, 1990).
Whitman, James Q. "On Nazi honor and the new European dignity," in Christian Joerges and Navraj Singh Ghaleigh (eds.), *Darker Legacies of Law in Europe* (Oxford and Portland, OR: Hart Publishing, 2003), pp. 243–266.
Whitmarsh, Tim. *Greek Literature and the Roman Empire: The Politics of Imitation* (Oxford: Oxford University Press, 2001).
Whitmarsh, Tim. *The Second Sophistic* (Oxford: Oxford University Press, 2005).
Wieacker, Franz. "Corpus Iuris," *Zeitschrift für die gesamte Staatswissenschaft*, 102 (1942), 444.
Wieacker, Franz. "Einflüsse des Humanismus auf die Rezeption. Eine Studie zu Johannes Apels Dialogus," *Zeitschrift für die gesamte Staatswissenschaft*, 100 (4) (1940), 423–456.
Wieacker, Franz. "Zur Erweckung des Naturrechts," *Süddeutsche Juristenzeitung* (1949), 295–301.
Wieacker, Franz. "Die Fortwirkung der antiken Rechtskulturen in der europäischen Welt," in *Vom Recht* (Hannover: Niedersächsische zentrale für Politische Bildung, 1963).
Wieacker, Franz. "Friedrich Carl von Savigny," in Hermann Heimpel (ed.), *Die grossen Deutschen III* (Berlin: Ullstein, 1956), pp. 39–51.
Wieacker, Franz. "Fritz Pringsheim 70 Jahre," *Juristenzeitung*, 7 (19) (1952), 605.
Wieacker, Franz. "Foundations of European Legal Culture," *The American Journal of Comparative Law*, 38 (1990), 1–29.
Wieacker, Franz. *Gesetz und Richterkunst. Zum Problem der außergesetzlichen Rechtsordnung* (Karlsruhe: Verlag C. F. Müller, 1958).
Wieacker, Franz. *Gründer und Bewahrer. Rechtslehrer der neueren deutschen Privatrechtsgeschichte* (Göttingen: Vandenhoeck & Ruprecht, 1959).
Wieacker, Franz. *A History of Private Law in Europe: With Particular Reference to Germany*. Translated by Tony Weir, foreword by Reinhard Zimmermann (Oxford: Clarendon Press, 1995).
Wieacker, Franz. "Das Kitzeberger Lager junger Rechtslehrer," in Christian Wollschläger (ed.), *Franz Wieacker. Zivilistische Schriften (1934–1942)* (Frankfurt: Vittorio Klostermann, 2000 [1935]), pp. 163–176.
Wieacker, Franz. *Privatrechtsgeschichte der Neuzeit, unter besonderer Berücksichtigung der deutschen Entwicklung* (Göttingen: Vandenhoeck & Ruprecht, 1952, 1st ed.; 1967, 2nd ed).
Wieacker, Franz. "Rezension Paul Koschaker: Europa und das römische Recht," *Gnomon*, 21 (1949), 190.
Wieacker, Franz. *Römische Rechtsgeschichte I* (Munich: C. H. Beck, 1988).
Wieacker, Franz. "Vom Römischen Juristen," *Zeitschrift für die gesamte Staatswissenschaft*, 99 (1939), 440–463.
Wieacker, Franz. *Vom römischen Recht. Wirklichkeit und Überlieferung* (Leipzig: Koehler & Ameland, 1944).
Wieacker, Franz. *Vom römischen Recht: zehn Versuche* (Leipzig: K. F. Koehler, 1961).

Wieacker, Franz. *Das römische Recht und das deutsche Rechtsbewußtsein* (Leipzig: Barth, 1944).
Wieacker, Franz. "Der Stand der Rechtserneuerung auf dem Gebiete des bürgerlichen Rechts," *Deutsche Rechtswissenschaft*, 2 (1937), 3–27.
Wieacker, Franz. "Studien zur Hadrianischen Justizpolitik," *Romanistische Studien: Freiburger Rechtsgeschichtliche Abhandlungen*, 5 (1935), 43–81.
Wieacker, Franz. "Über 'Aktualisierung' der Ausbildung im Römischen Recht," in *L'Europa e il diritto romano. Studi in memoria di Paolo Koschaker, I* (Milan: Giuffrè, 1954), pp. 515–541.
Wieacker, Franz. "Uber das Verhaltnis der romischen Fachjurisprudenz zur griechisch-hellenistischen Theorie," *Iura*, 20 (1969), 448–477.
Wieacker, Franz. "Ursprünge und Elemente des europäischen Rechtbewusstseins," in Martin Göhring (ed.), *Europa, Erbe und Aufgabe. Internationaler Gelehrtenkongress Mainz 1955* (Wiesbaden: Franz Steiner, 1956), pp. 105–119.
Wieacker, Franz. *Vulgarismus und Klassizismus im Recht der Spätantike* (Heidelberg: C. Winter, 1955).
Wieacker, Franz. "Wandlungen der Eigentumsverfassung," in Christian Wollschläger (ed.), *Franz Wieacker. Zivilistische Schriften (1934–1942)* (Frankfurt: Vittorio Klostermann, [1935] 2000).
Wiener, Christina. *Kieler Fakultät und "Kieler Schule" Die Rechtslehrer an der Rechts- und Staatswissenschaftlichen Fakultät zu Kiel in der Zeit des Nationalsozialismus und ihre Entnazifizierung* (Baden-Baden: Nomos Verlag, 2013).
Wijffels, Alain. "European private law: a new software-package for an outdated operating system?," in Mark van Hoecke and François Ost (eds.), *The Harmonisation of European Private Law* (Oxford: Hart, 2000), pp. 101–116.
Wijffels, Alain. "Le ius commune européen: Mythe ou référentiel indifférencié des discours sur la formation d'un droit européen?," in Boris Bernabé and Olivier Camy (eds.), *Les mythes de fondation et l'Europe* (Dijon: Editions Universitaires de Dijon, 2013), pp. 87–101.
von Wilamowitz-Möllendorf, Ulrich. "Der Rhetor Aristeides," *Sitzungsberichte der preussischen Akademie der Wissenschaften*, 28 (1925), 333–353.
Wildt, Michael. *An Uncompromising Generation: The Nazi Leadership of the Reich Security Main Office* (Wisconsin: University of Wisconsin Press, 2010).
Wilhelmsson, Thomas. "Introduction: Harmonization and National Cultures," in Thomas Wilhelmsson, Elina Paunio and Annika Pohjolainen (eds.), *Private Law and the Many Cultures of Europe* (Alphen aan den Rijn: Kluwer Law International, 2007), pp. 3–20.
Willoweit, Dietmar. "Deutsche Rechtsgeschichte und 'nationalsozialistische Weltanschauung'," in Michael Stolleis and Dieter Simon (eds.), *Rechtsgeschichte im Nationalsozialismus. Beiträge zur Geschichte einer Disziplin* (Tübingen: Mohr, 1989), pp. 25–42.
Winkel, Laurens. "The role of general principles in Roman law," *Fundamina*, 2 (1996), 103–120.

Winkler, Viktor. *Der Kampf gegen die Rechtswissenschaft. Franz Wieackers "Privatrechtsgeschichte der Neuzeit" und die deutsche Rechtswissenschaft des 20. Jahrhunderts* (Hamburg: Dr. Kovač, 2014).

Wittreck, Fabian. *Nationalsozialistische Rechtslehre und Naturrecht. Affinität und Aversion* (Tübingen: Mohr Siebeck, 2008).

Wolff, Hans Julius. *Roman Law: An Historical Introduction* (Norman, OK: University of Oklahoma Press, 1951).

Wolff, Hans Julius. *Written and Unwritten Marriages in Hellenistic and Postclassical Roman Law* (Haverford: American Philological Association, 1939).

Wolff, Joseph Georg. "Franz Wieacker (5. August 1908–17. Februar 1994)," in Stefan Grundmann (ed.), *Deutschsprachige Zivilrechtslehrer des 20. Jahrhunderts in Berichten ihrer Schüler. Eine Ideengeschichte in Einzeldarstellungen. Bd. 1.* (Berlin: De Gruyter, 2007), pp. 73–86.

Ziegler, Karl-Heinz. "Max Kaser," in Horst Schröder and Dieter Simon (eds.), *Rechsgeschichtswissenschaft in Deutschland 1945 bis 1952* (Frankfurt: Vittorio Klostermann, 2001), pp. 77–98.

Zimmermann, Reinhard. "'Double cross': comparing Scots and South African Law," in Reinhard Zimmermann, Daniel Visser and Kenneth Reid (eds.), *Mixed Legal Systems in Comparative Perspective* (Oxford: Oxford University Press, 2004), pp. 1–33.

Zimmermann, Reinhard. "Europa und das römische Recht," *Archiv für die civilistische Praxis*, 2 (2002), 243–316.

Zimmermann, Reinhard. "The present state of European private law," *American Journal of Comparative Law*, 57 (2009), 479–511.

Zimmermann, Reinhard. "Roman and comparative law: the European perspective (some remarks apropos a recent controversy)," *The Journal of Legal History*, 16(1) (1995), 21–33.

Zimmermann, Reinhard. "Roman law and the harmonization of private law in Europe," in Arthur S. Hartkamp, Martijn W. Hesselink, Ewoud Hondius, C. Mak and Edgar Du Perron (eds.), *Towards a European Civil Code* (Alphen aan den Rijn: Kluwer Law International, 2011), pp. 27–54.

Zimmermann, Reinhard. *Roman Law, Contemporary Law, European Law: The Civilian Tradition Today* (Oxford: Oxford University Press, 2001).

Zimmermann, Reinhard. "Savignys Vermächtnis," in Pio Caroni and Gerhard Dilcher (eds.), *Norm und Tradition. Welche Geschichtlichkeit für die Rechtsgeschichte?* (Köln, Weimar, Vienna: Böhlau Verlag, 1998), pp. 281–321.

Zimmermann, Reinhard. "'Was Heimat hieß, nun heißt es Hölle.' The emigration of lawyers from Hitler's Germany: political background, legal framework, and cultural context," in Jack Beatson and Reinhard Zimmermann (eds.), *Jurists Uprooted* (Oxford: Oxford University Press, 2004), pp. 1–72.

Zimmermann, Reinhard. "Winkler, Viktor: Der Kampf gegen die Rechtswissenschaft. Franz Wieackers 'Privatrechtsgeschichte der Neuzeit' und die deutsche Rechtswissenschaft des 20. Jahrhunderts," *Rabels Zeitschrift für ausländisches und internationales Privatrecht*, 79 (2015), 686–694.

# Index

Printed in the United Kingdom by TJ Clays Ltd.